合法ドラッグ

LEGAL DRUG

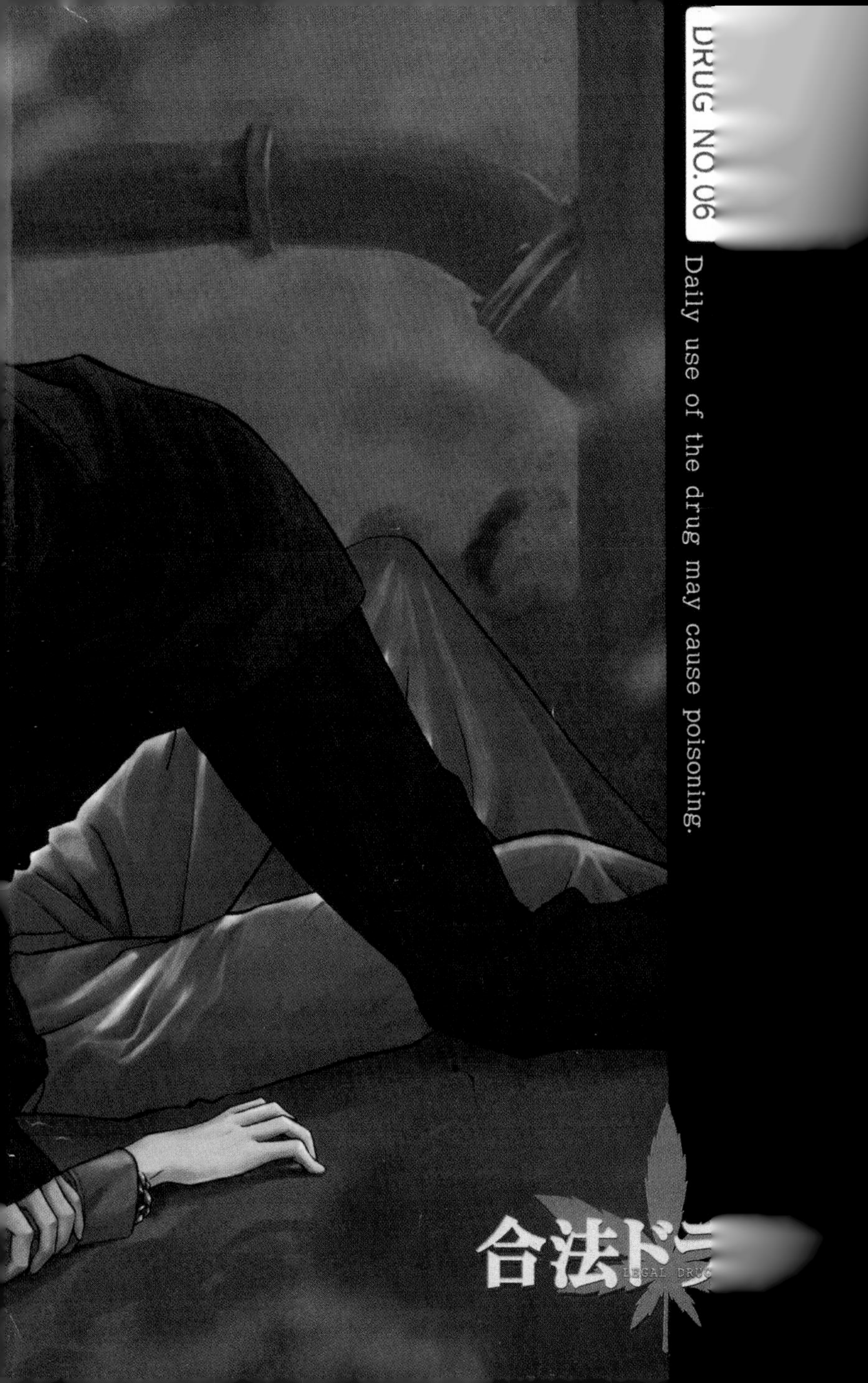

DRUG NO.06
Daily use of the drug may cause poisoning.
合法ドラ
LEGAL DRUG

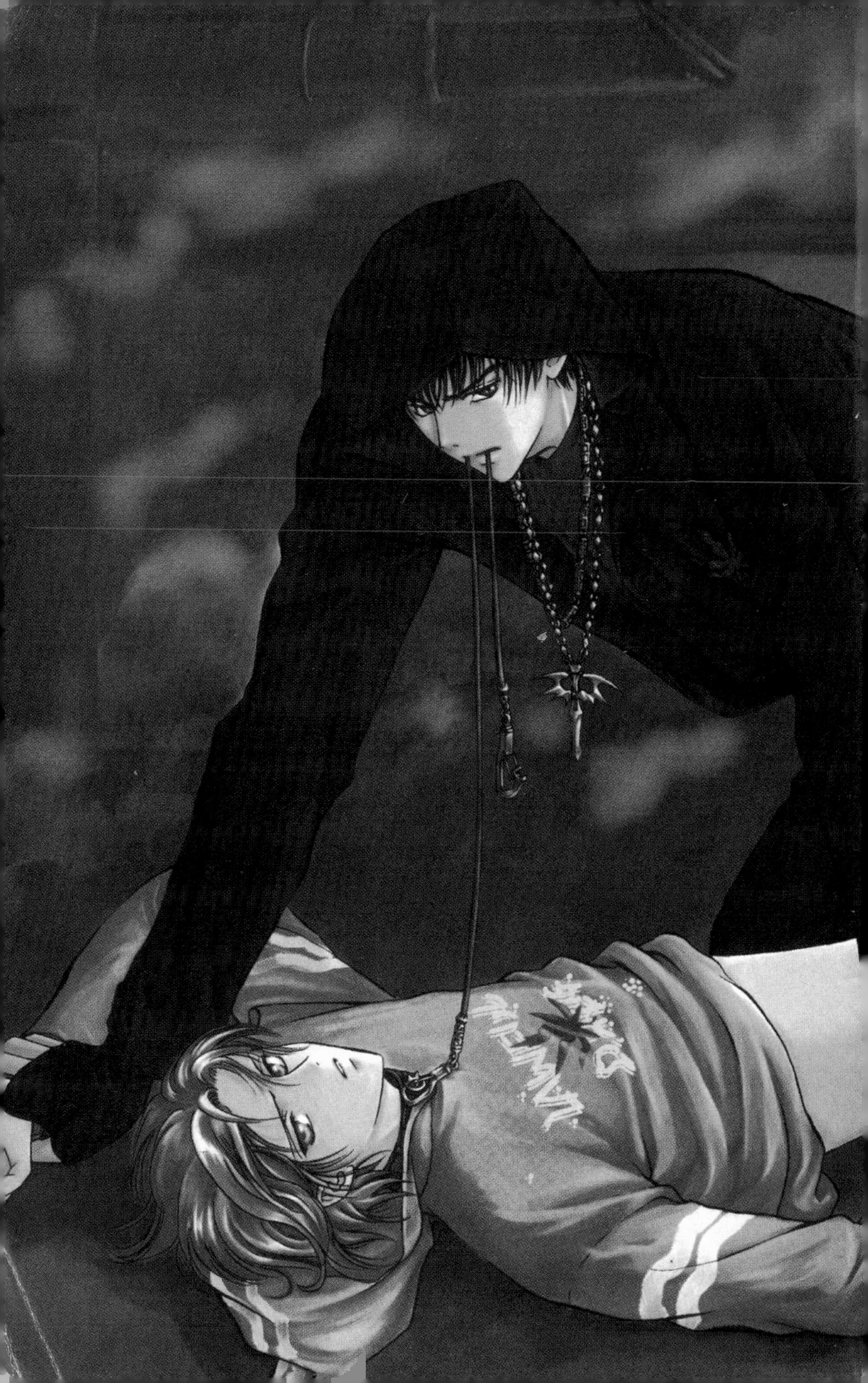

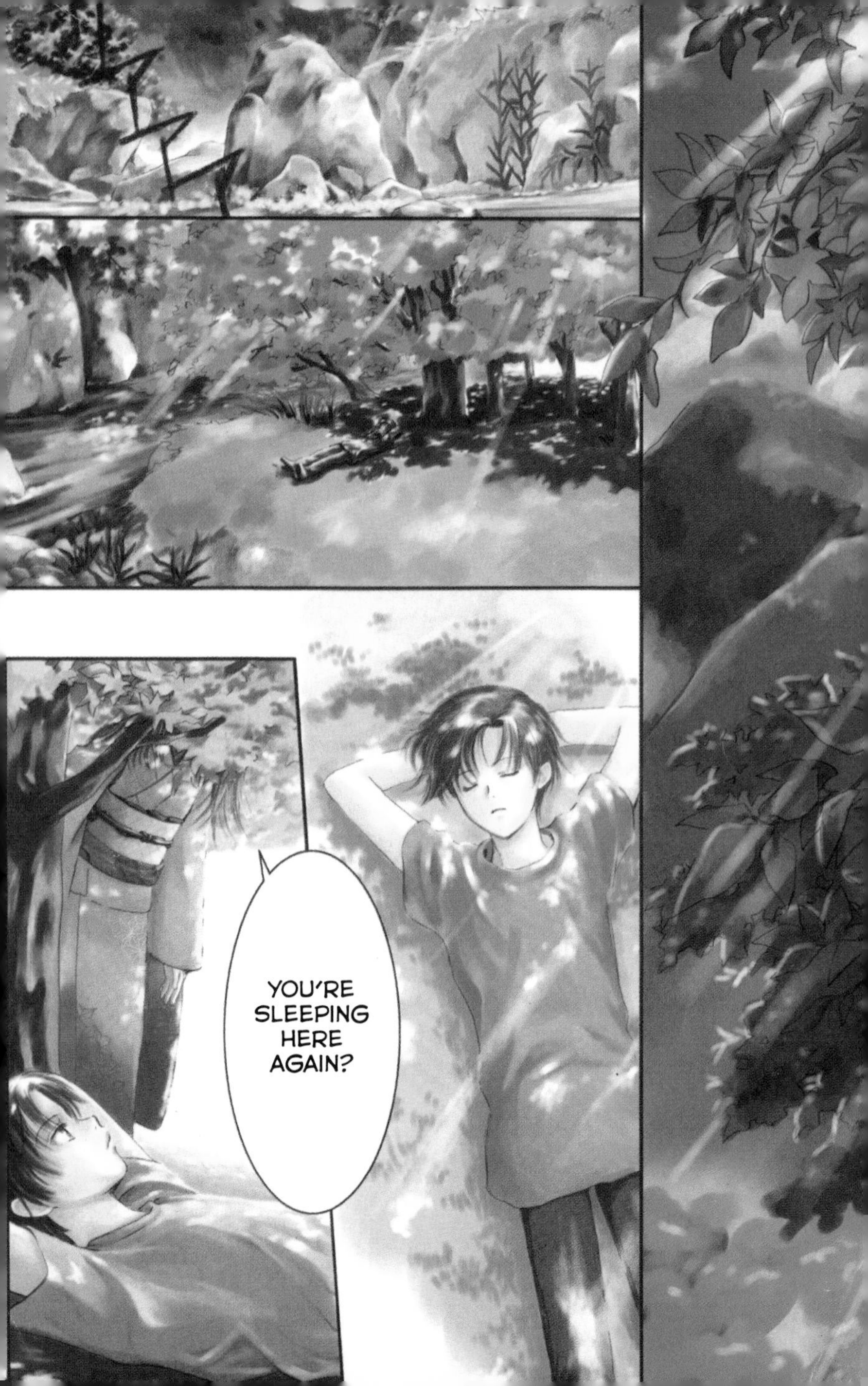
YOU'RE SLEEPING HERE AGAIN?

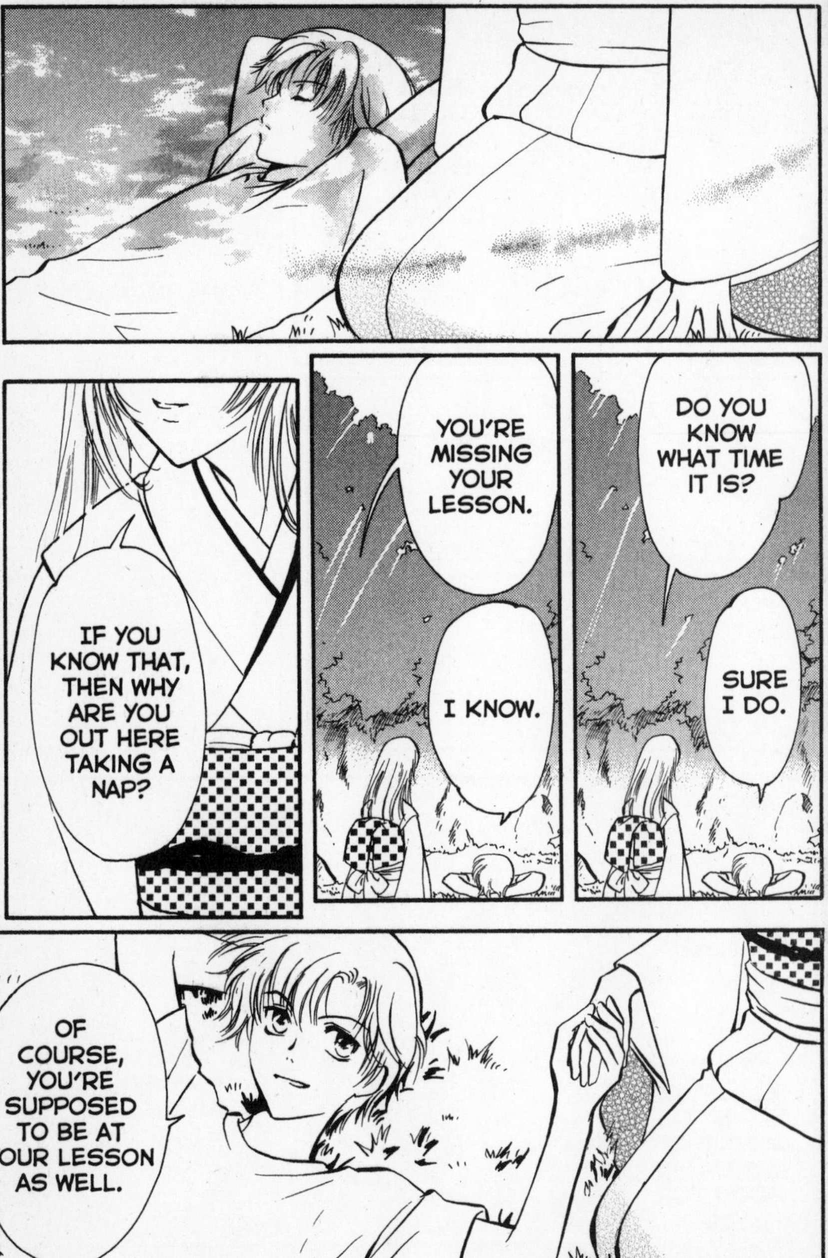
DO YOU KNOW WHAT TIME IT IS?
SURE I DO.
YOU'RE MISSING YOUR LESSON.
I KNOW.
IF YOU KNOW THAT, THEN WHY ARE YOU OUT HERE TAKING A NAP?
OF COURSE, YOU'RE SUPPOSED TO BE AT YOUR LESSON AS WELL.

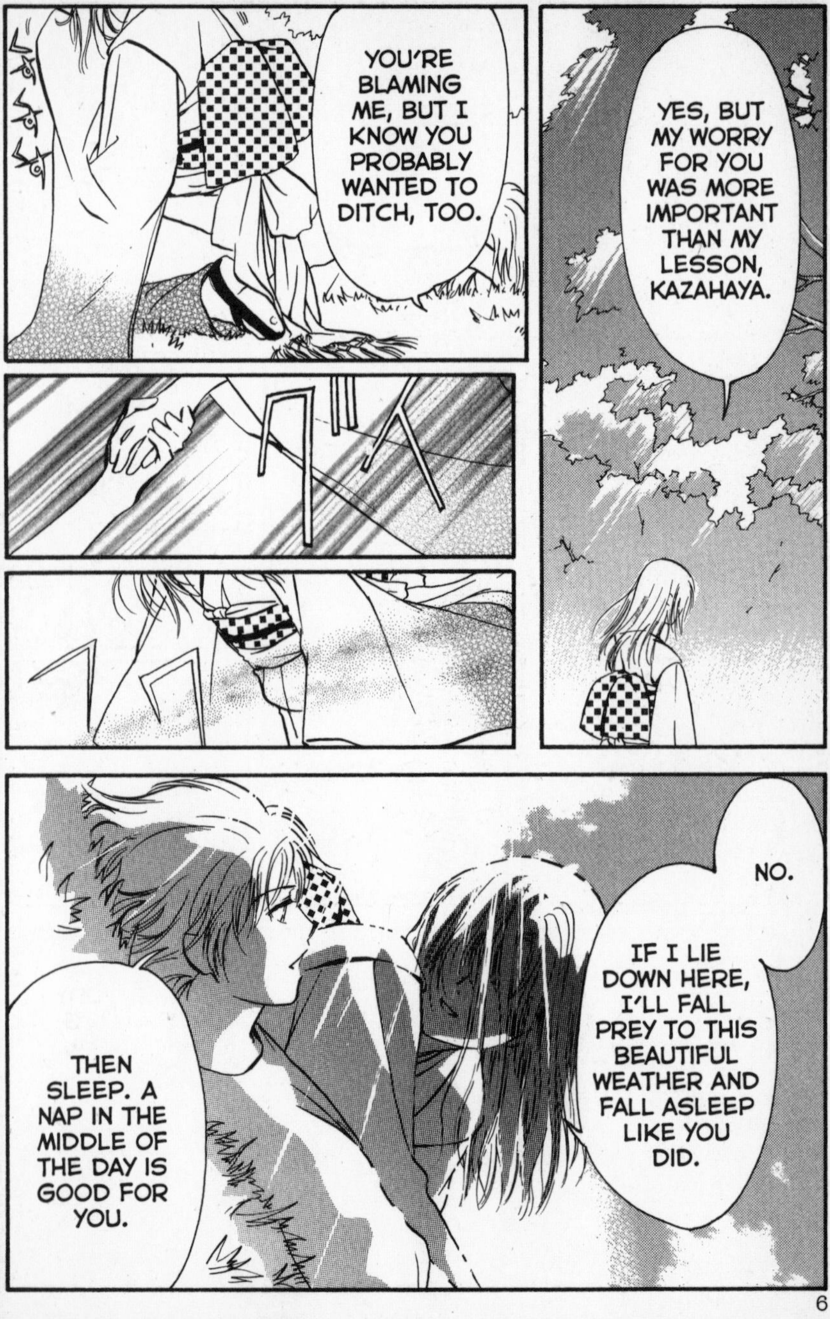
YES, BUT MY WORRY FOR YOU WAS MORE IMPORTANT THAN MY LESSON, KAZAHAYA.
YOU'RE BLAMING ME, BUT I KNOW YOU PROBABLY WANTED TO DITCH, TOO.
NO.
IF I LIE DOWN HERE, I'LL FALL PREY TO THIS BEAUTIFUL WEATHER AND FALL ASLEEP LIKE YOU DID.
THEN SLEEP. A NAP IN THE MIDDLE OF THE DAY IS GOOD FOR YOU.

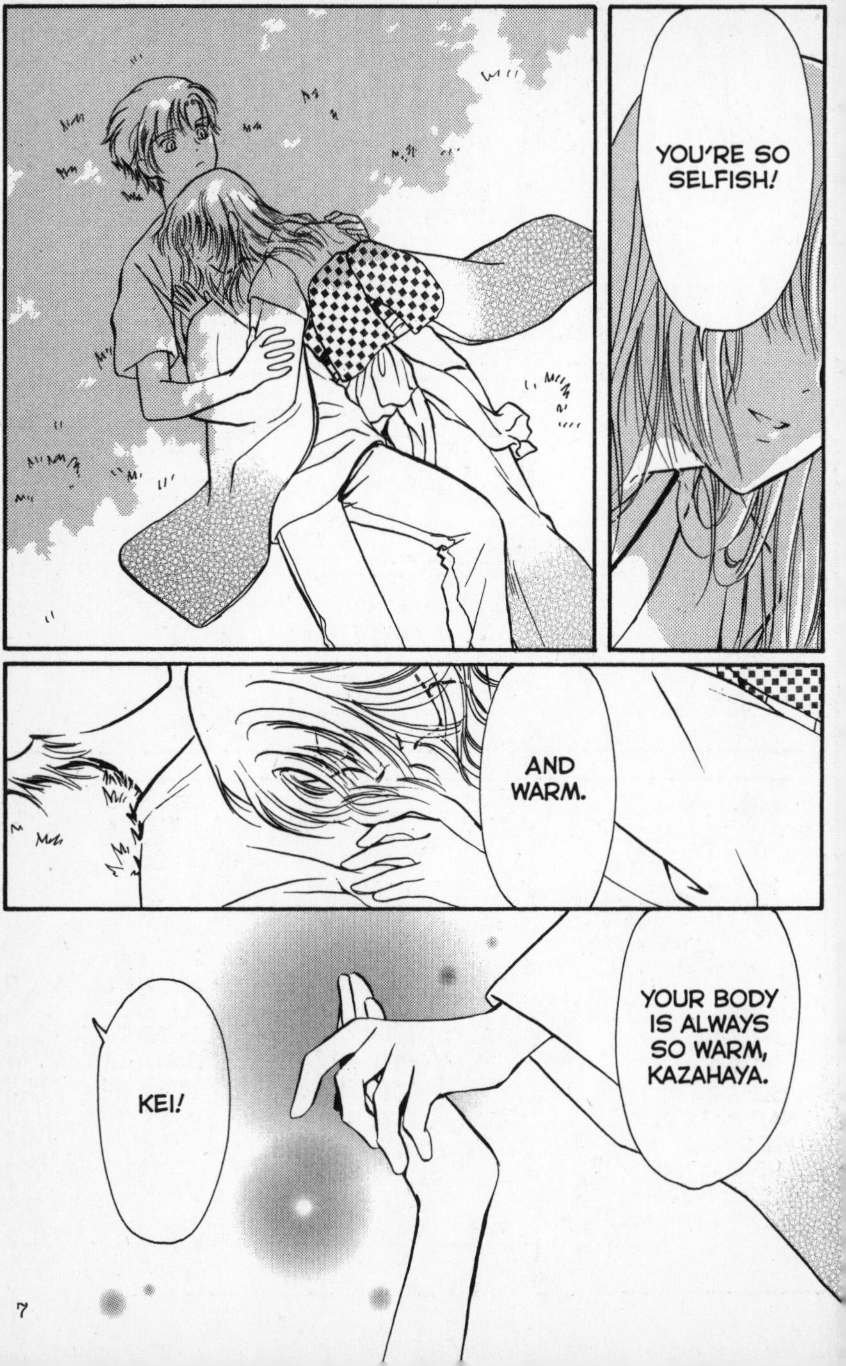
YOU'RE SO SELFISH!
AND WARM.
YOUR BODY IS ALWAYS SO WARM, KAZAHAYA.
KEI!

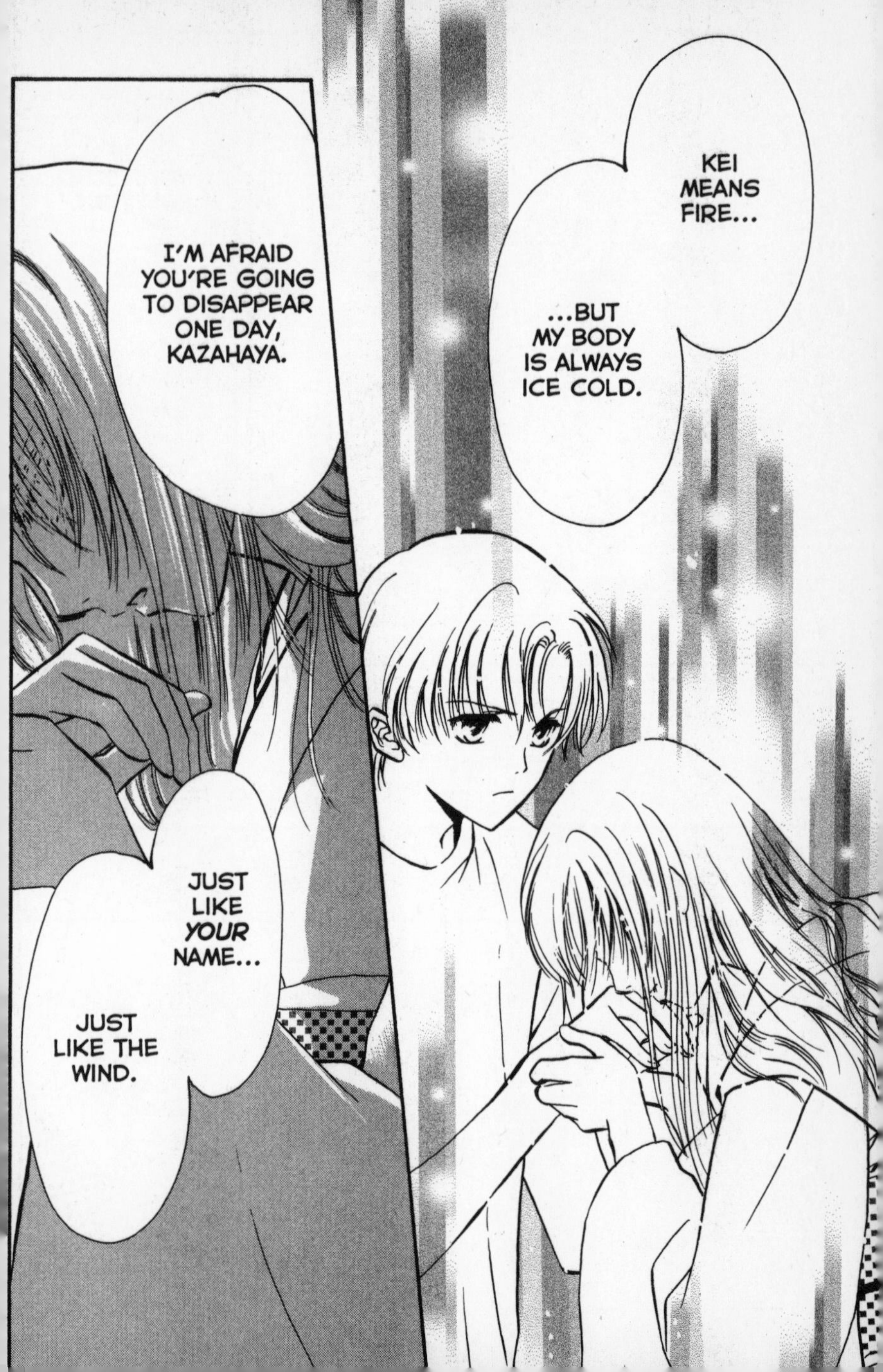
KEI MEANS FIRE...
...BUT MY BODY IS ALWAYS ICE COLD.
I'M AFRAID YOU'RE GOING TO DISAPPEAR ONE DAY, KAZAHAYA.
JUST LIKE *YOUR* NAME...
JUST LIKE THE WIND.

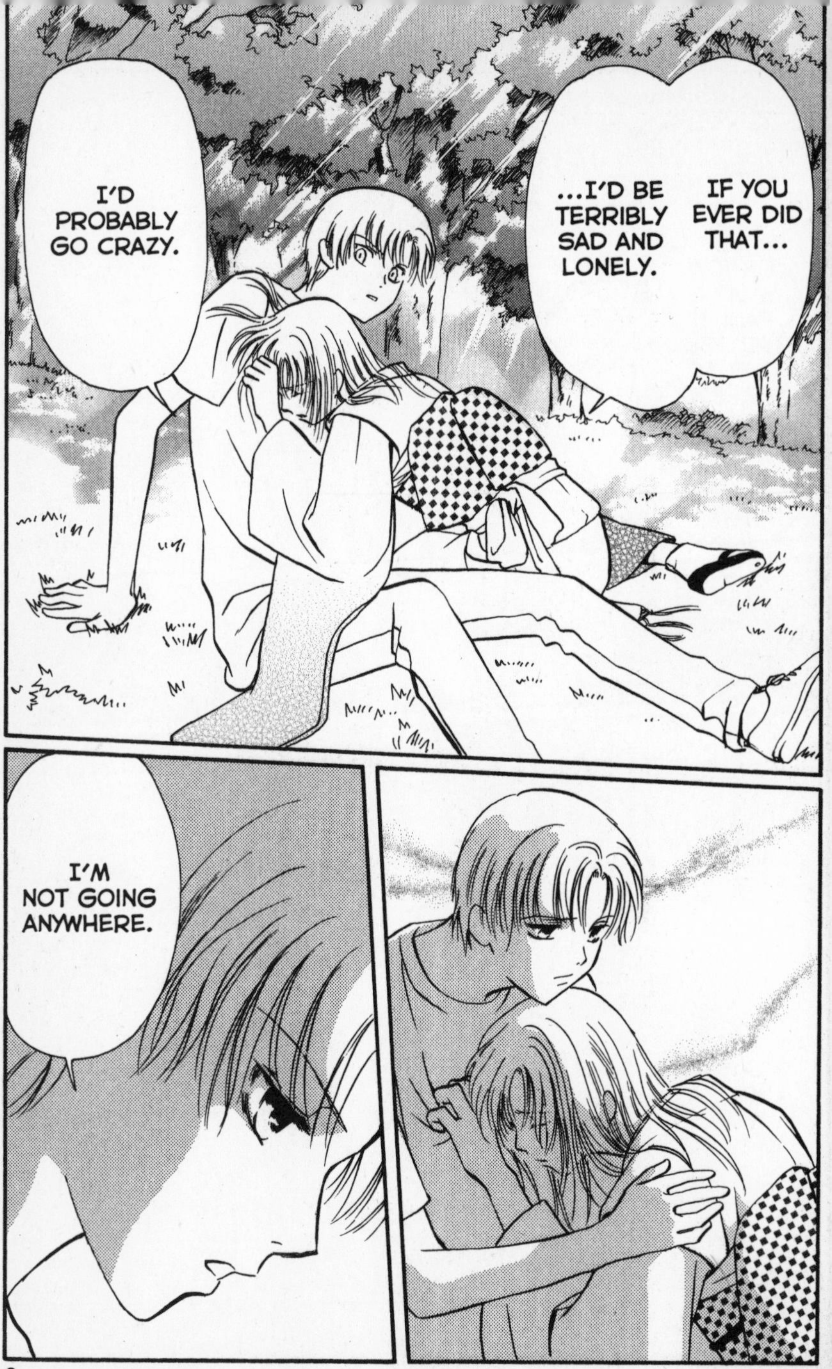
IF YOU EVER DID THAT...
...I'D BE TERRIBLY SAD AND LONELY.
I'D PROBABLY GO CRAZY.
I'M NOT GOING ANYWHERE.

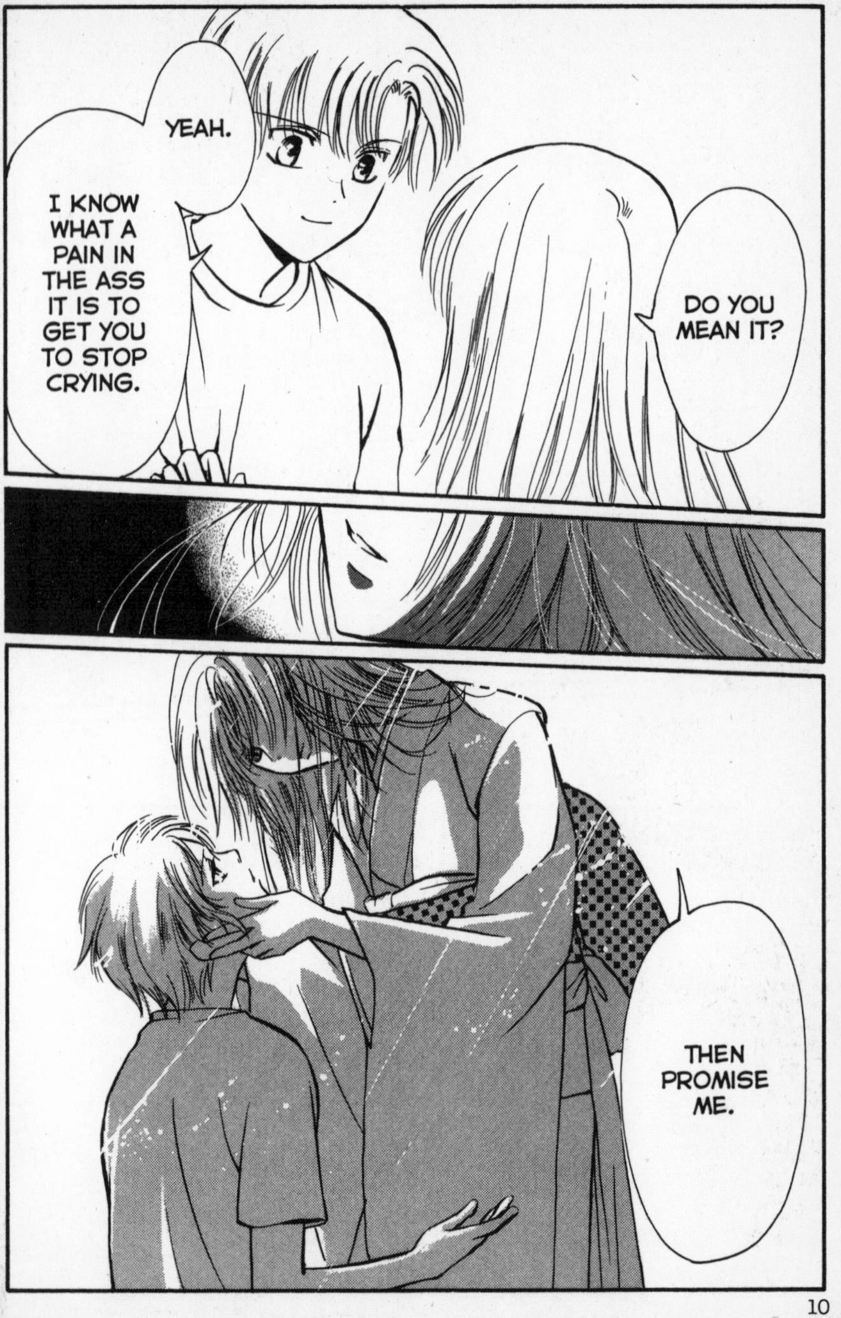
DO YOU MEAN IT?
YEAH.
I KNOW WHAT A PAIN IN THE ASS IT IS TO GET YOU TO STOP CRYING.
THEN PROMISE ME.

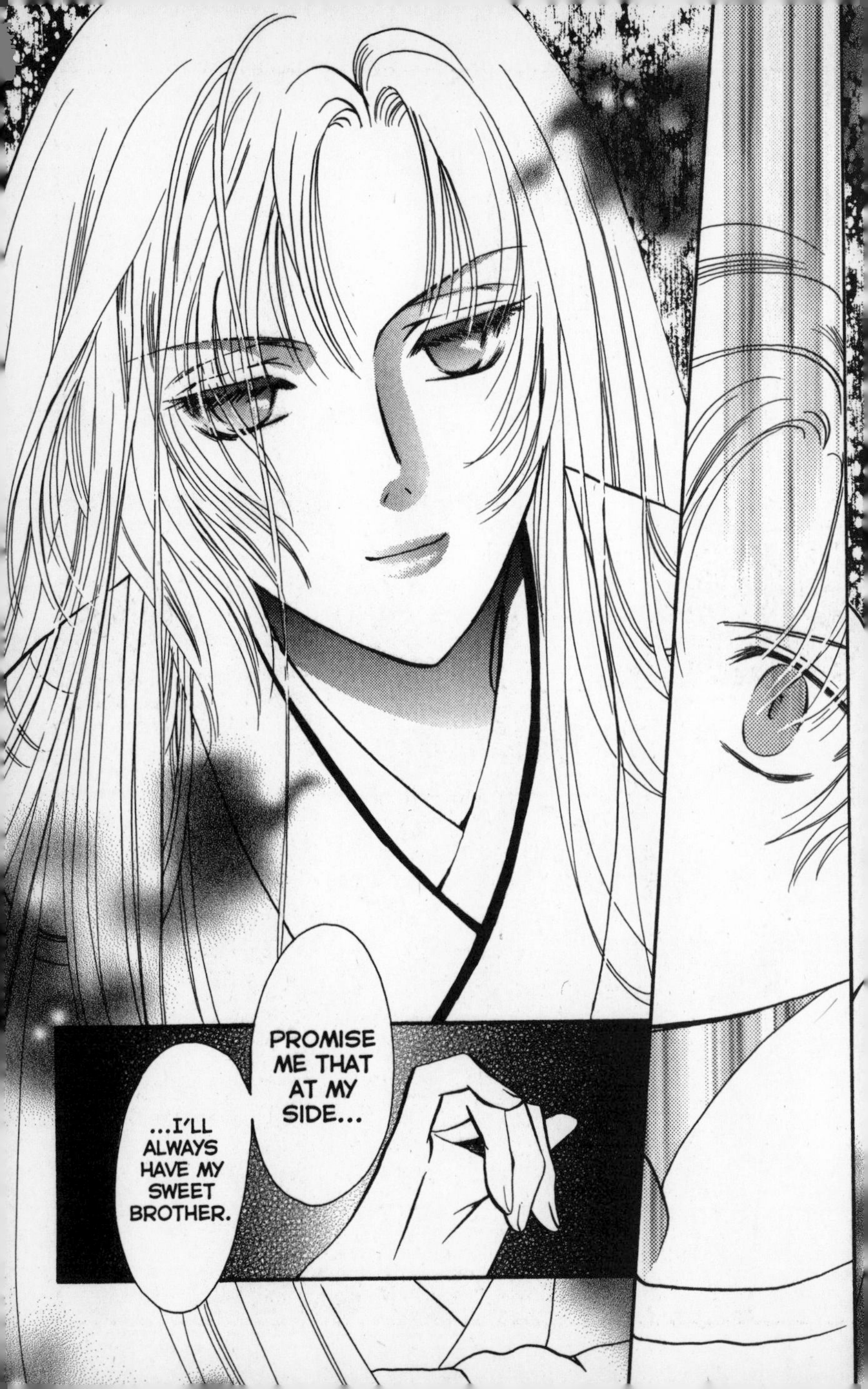
PROMISE ME THAT AT MY SIDE...
...I'LL ALWAYS HAVE MY SWEET BROTHER.

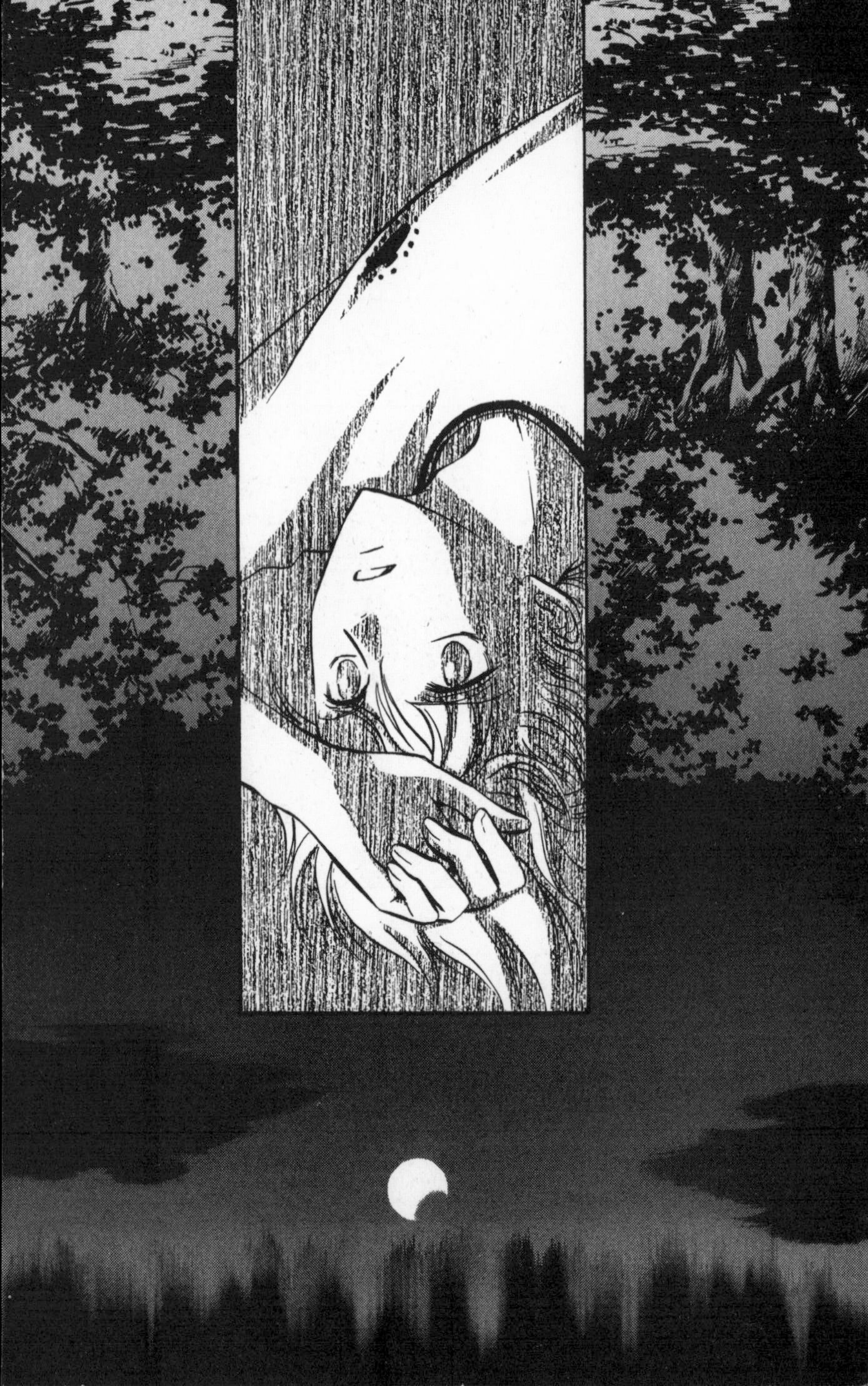

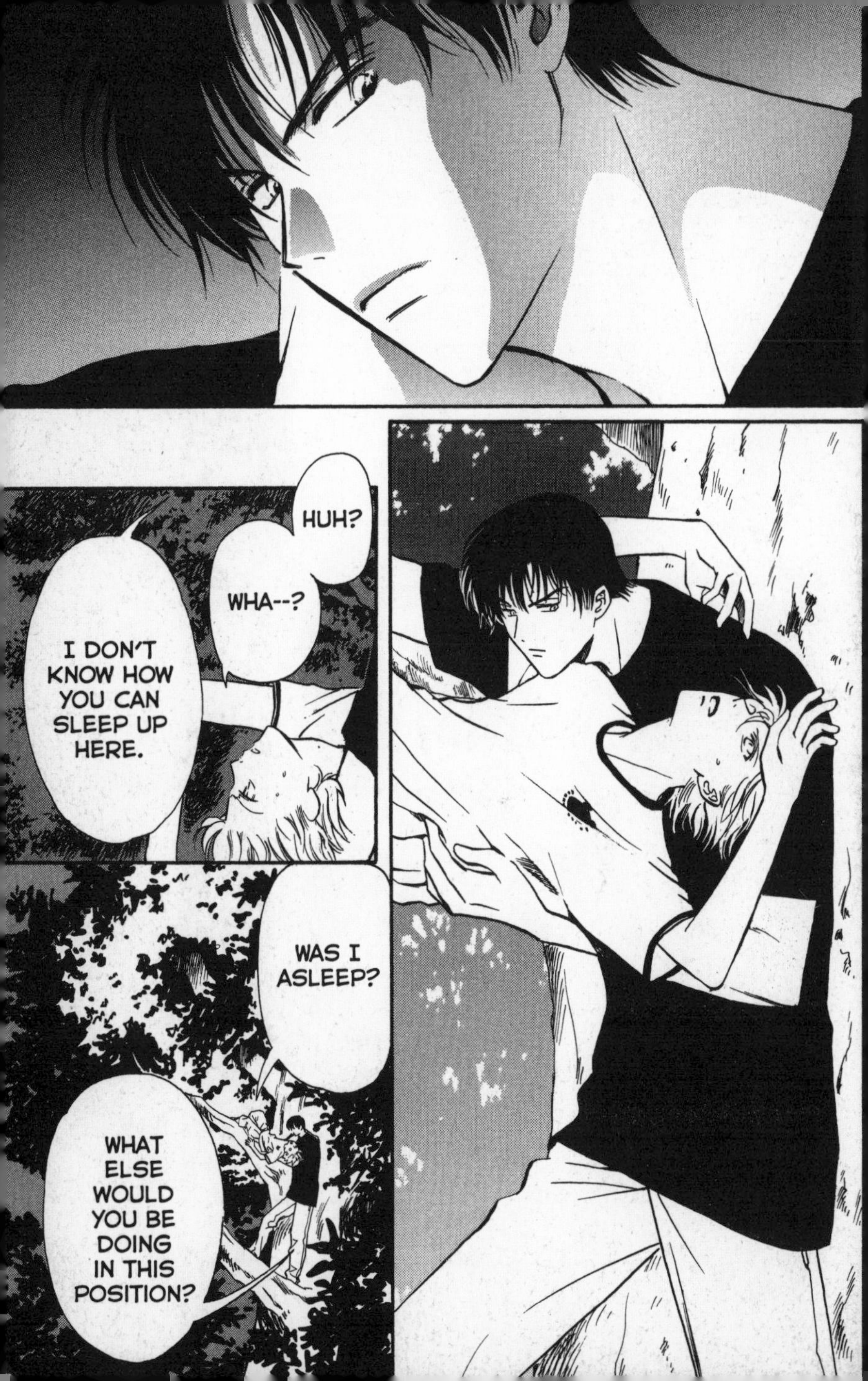
HUH?
WHA--?
I DON'T KNOW HOW YOU CAN SLEEP UP HERE.
WAS I ASLEEP?
WHAT ELSE WOULD YOU BE DOING IN THIS POSITION?

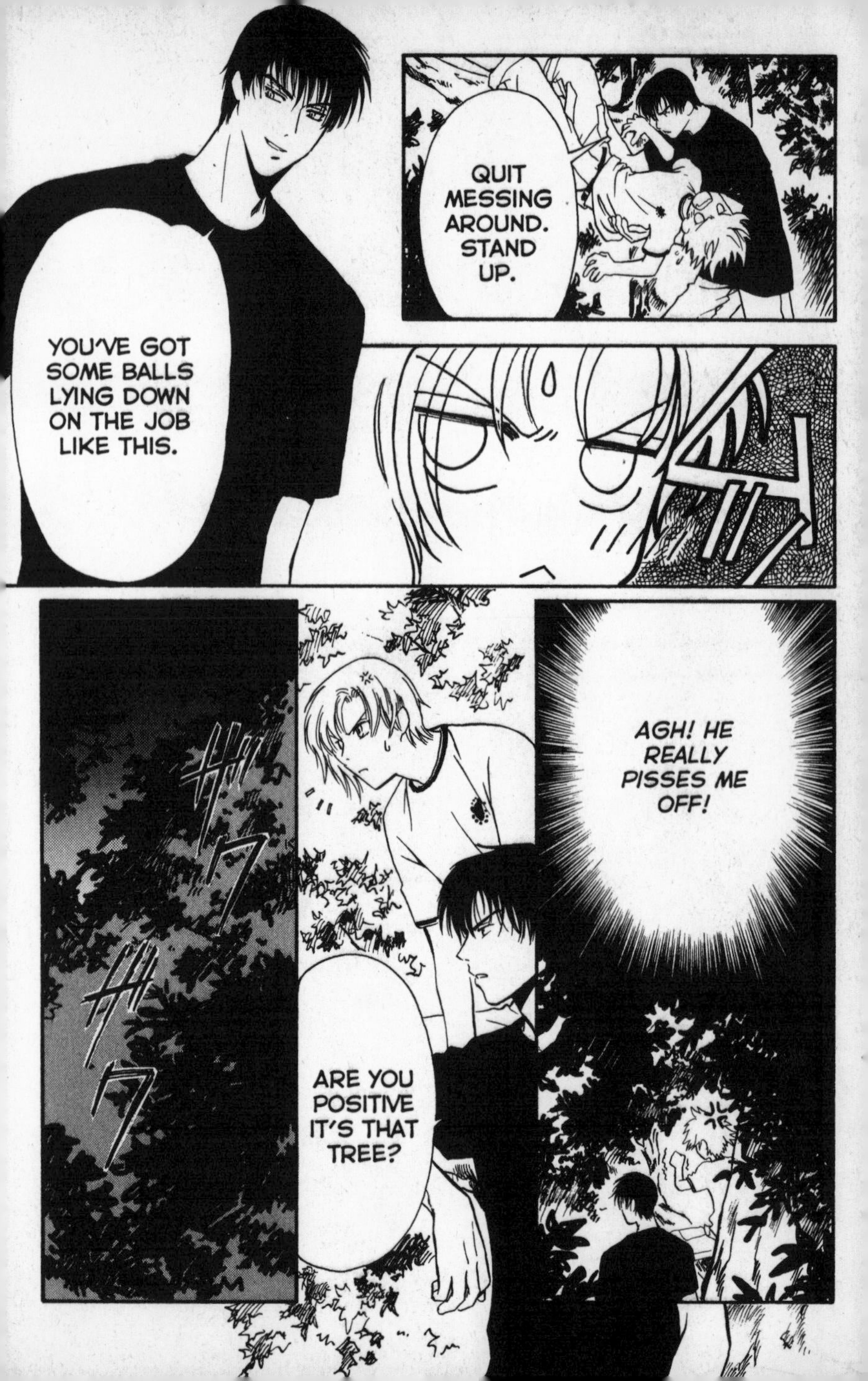
QUIT MESSING AROUND. STAND UP.
YOU'VE GOT SOME BALLS LYING DOWN ON THE JOB LIKE THIS.
AGH! HE REALLY PISSES ME OFF!
ARE YOU POSITIVE IT'S THAT TREE?

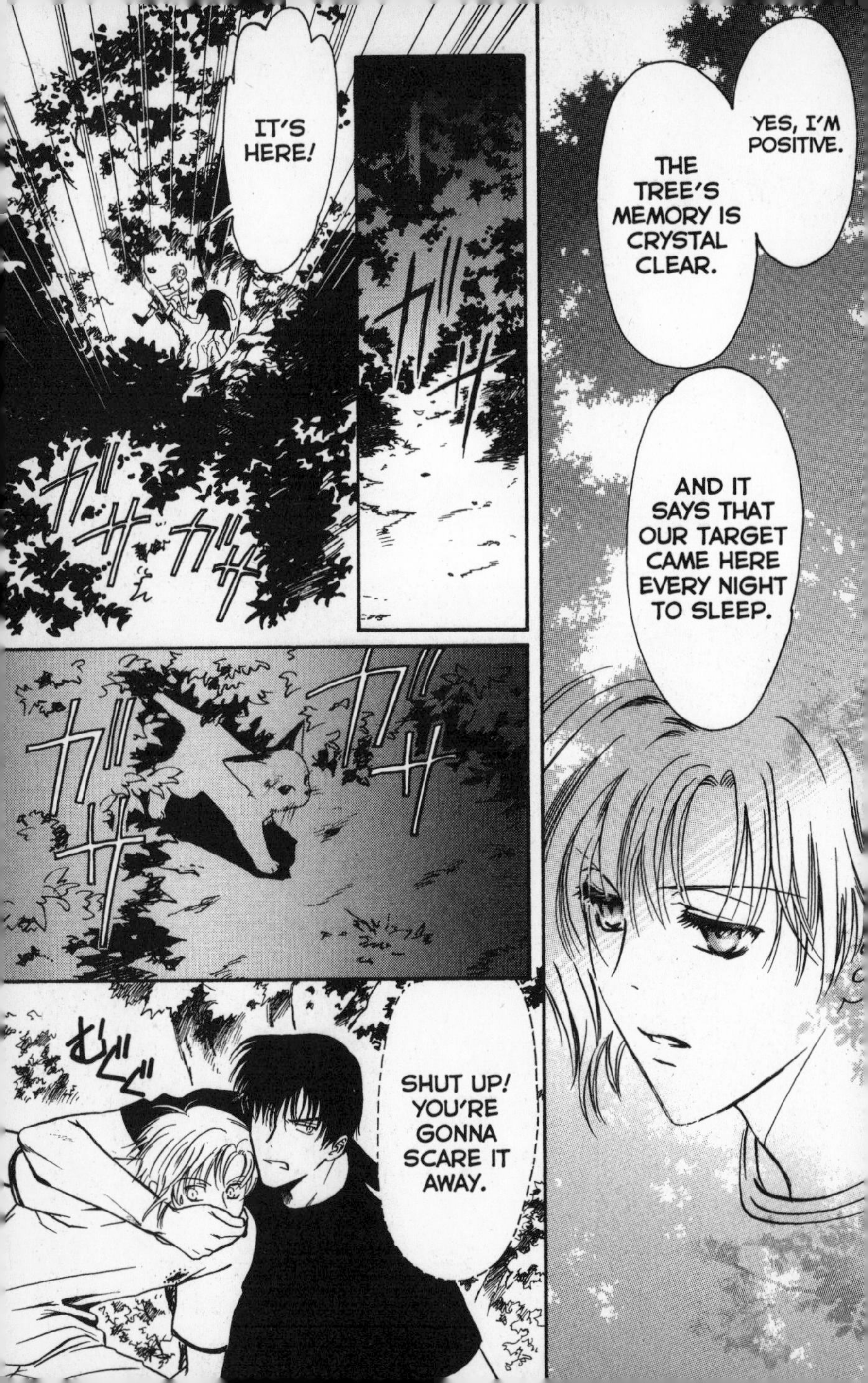
YES, I'M POSITIVE.
THE TREE'S MEMORY IS CRYSTAL CLEAR.
AND IT SAYS THAT OUR TARGET CAME HERE EVERY NIGHT TO SLEEP.
ガサ
IT'S HERE!
ガサ ガサ
ガサ ガサ
SHUT UP! YOU'RE GONNA SCARE IT AWAY.
むぐぐ

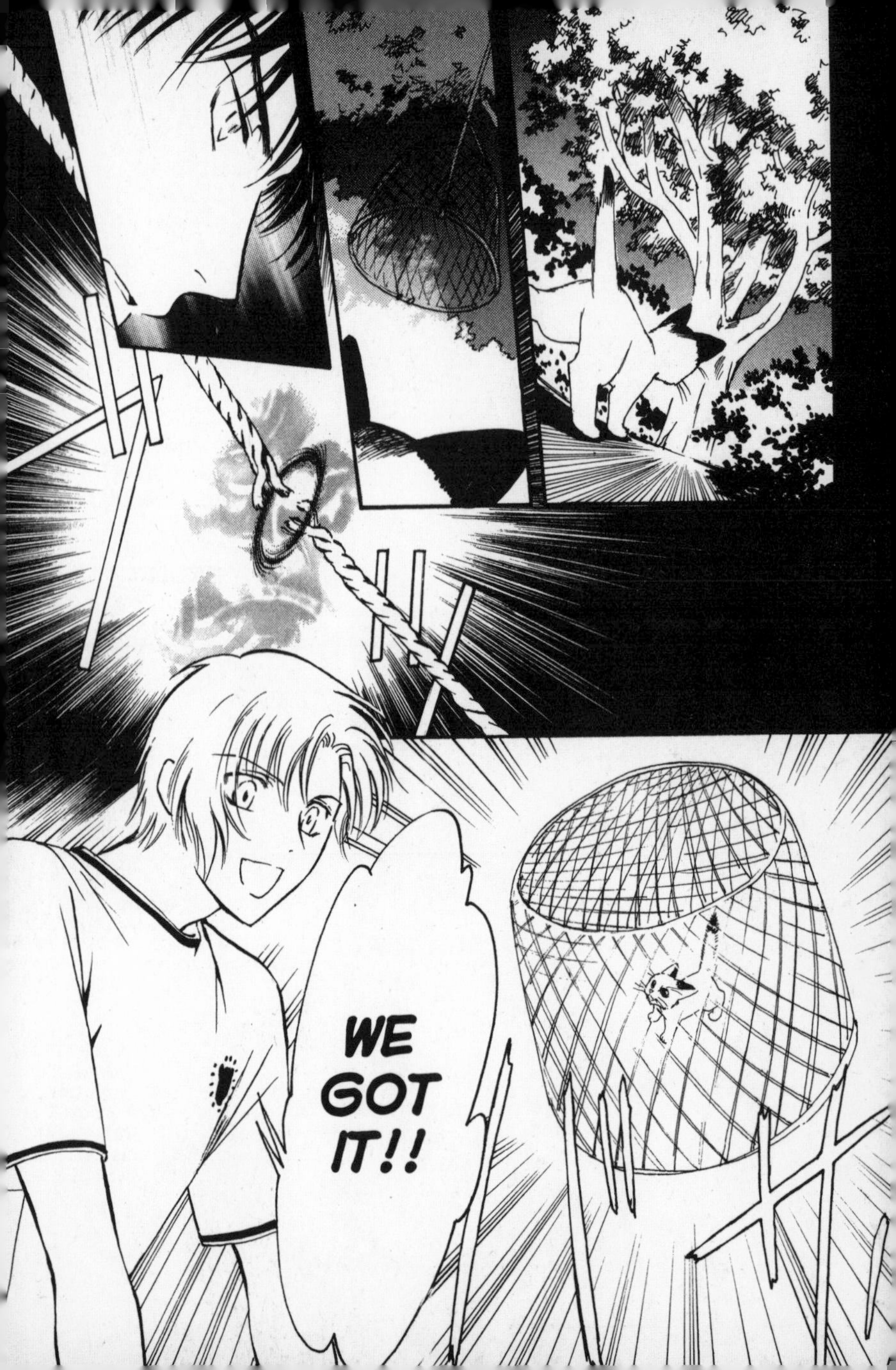
WE GOT IT!!

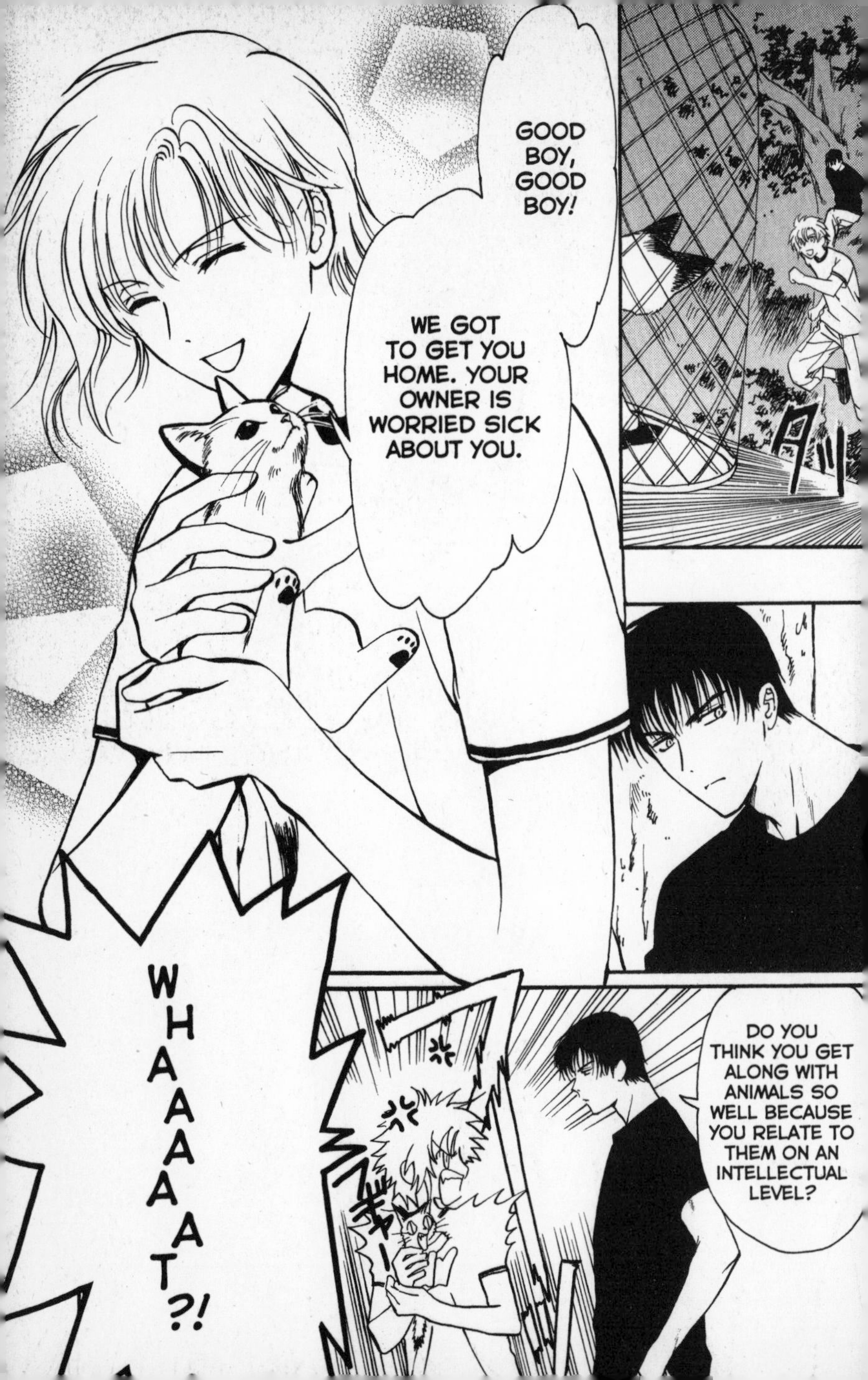
GOOD BOY, GOOD BOY!
WE GOT TO GET YOU HOME. YOUR OWNER IS WORRIED SICK ABOUT YOU.
DO YOU THINK YOU GET ALONG WITH ANIMALS SO WELL BECAUSE YOU RELATE TO THEM ON AN INTELLECTUAL LEVEL?
WHAAAAAT?!

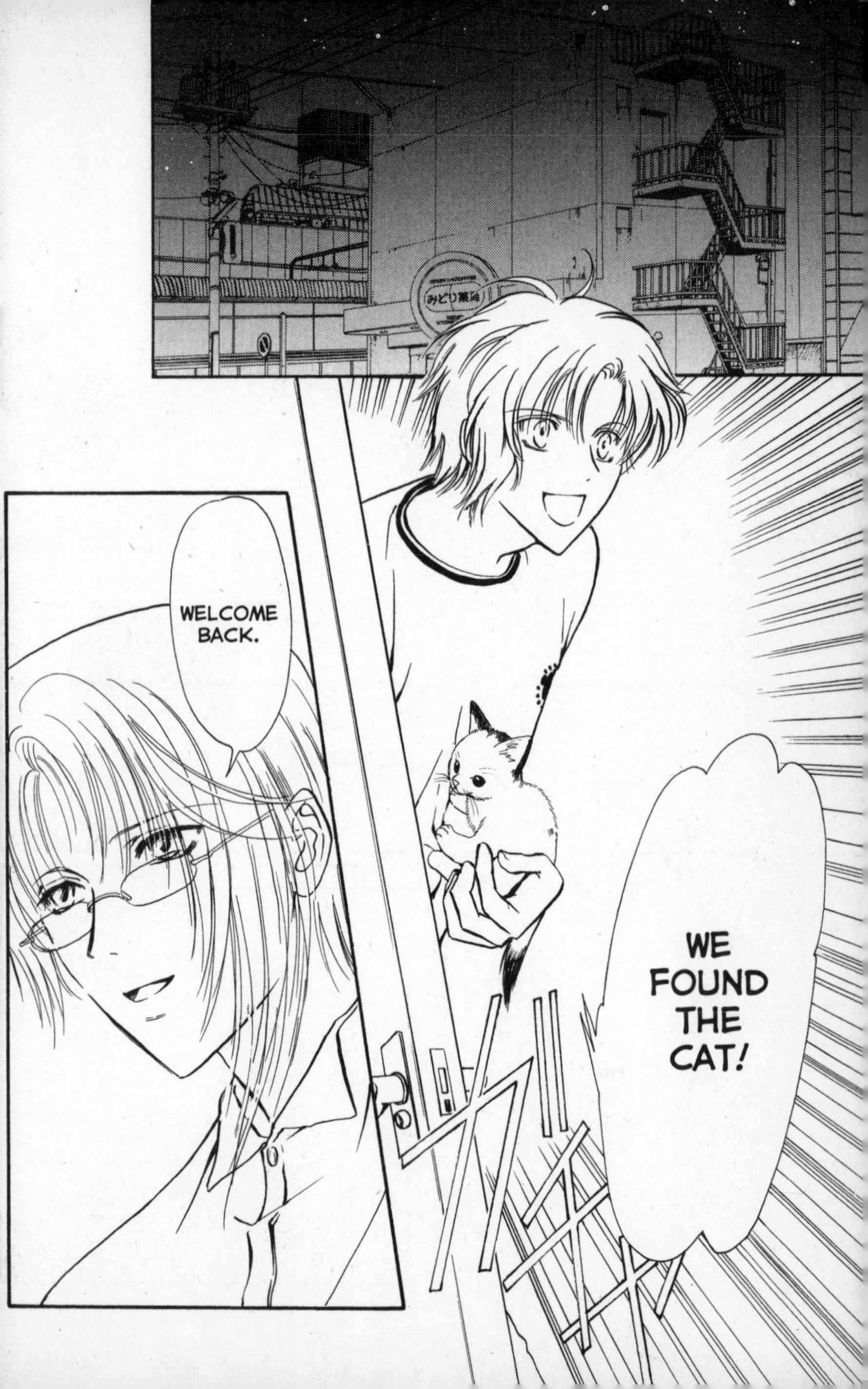
みどり薬局
WE FOUND THE CAT!
WELCOME BACK.

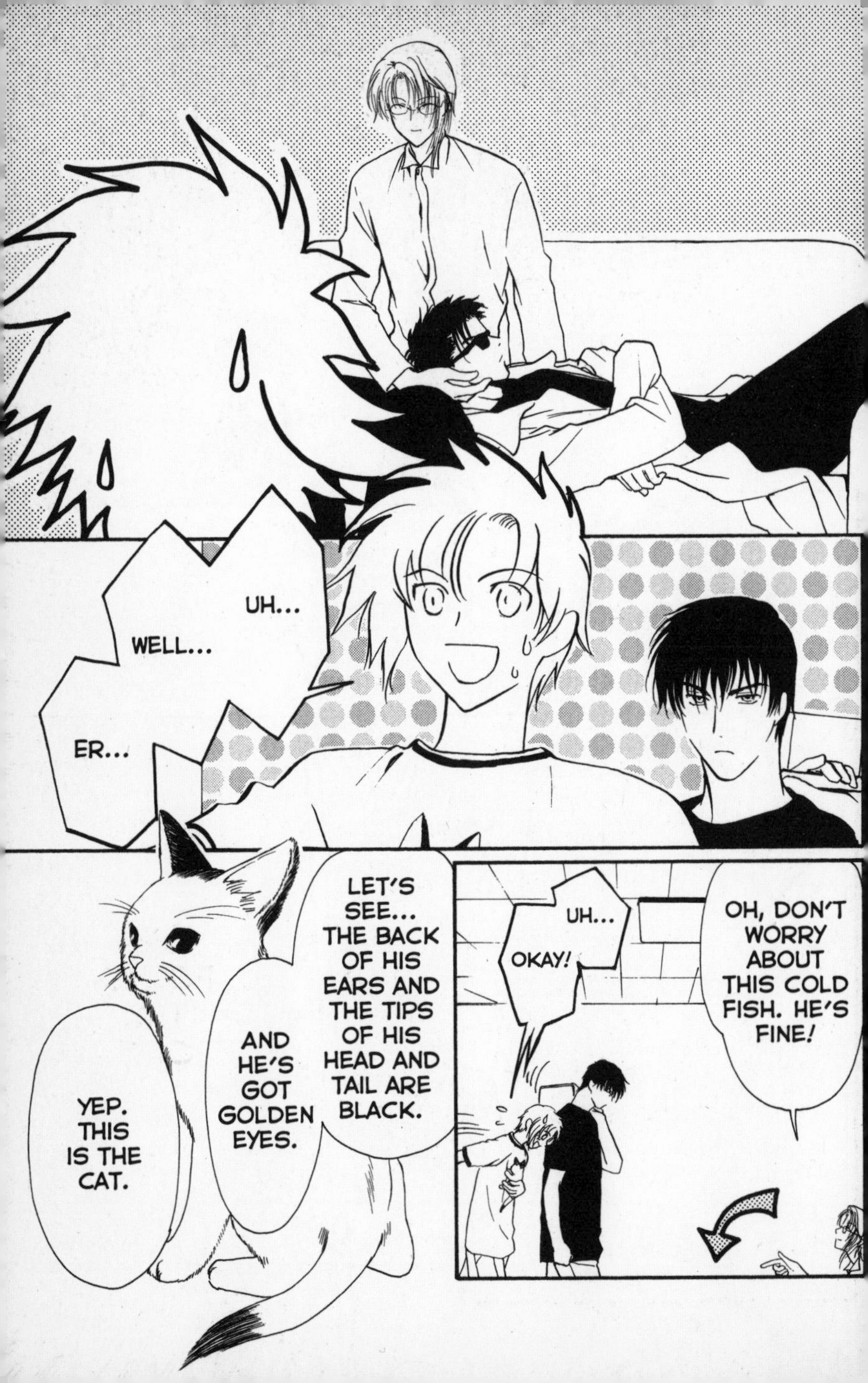
UH... WELL... ER...
OH, DON'T WORRY ABOUT THIS COLD FISH. HE'S FINE!
UH... OKAY!
LET'S SEE... THE BACK OF HIS EARS AND THE TIPS OF HIS HEAD AND TAIL ARE BLACK.
AND HE'S GOT GOLDEN EYES.
YEP. THIS IS THE CAT.

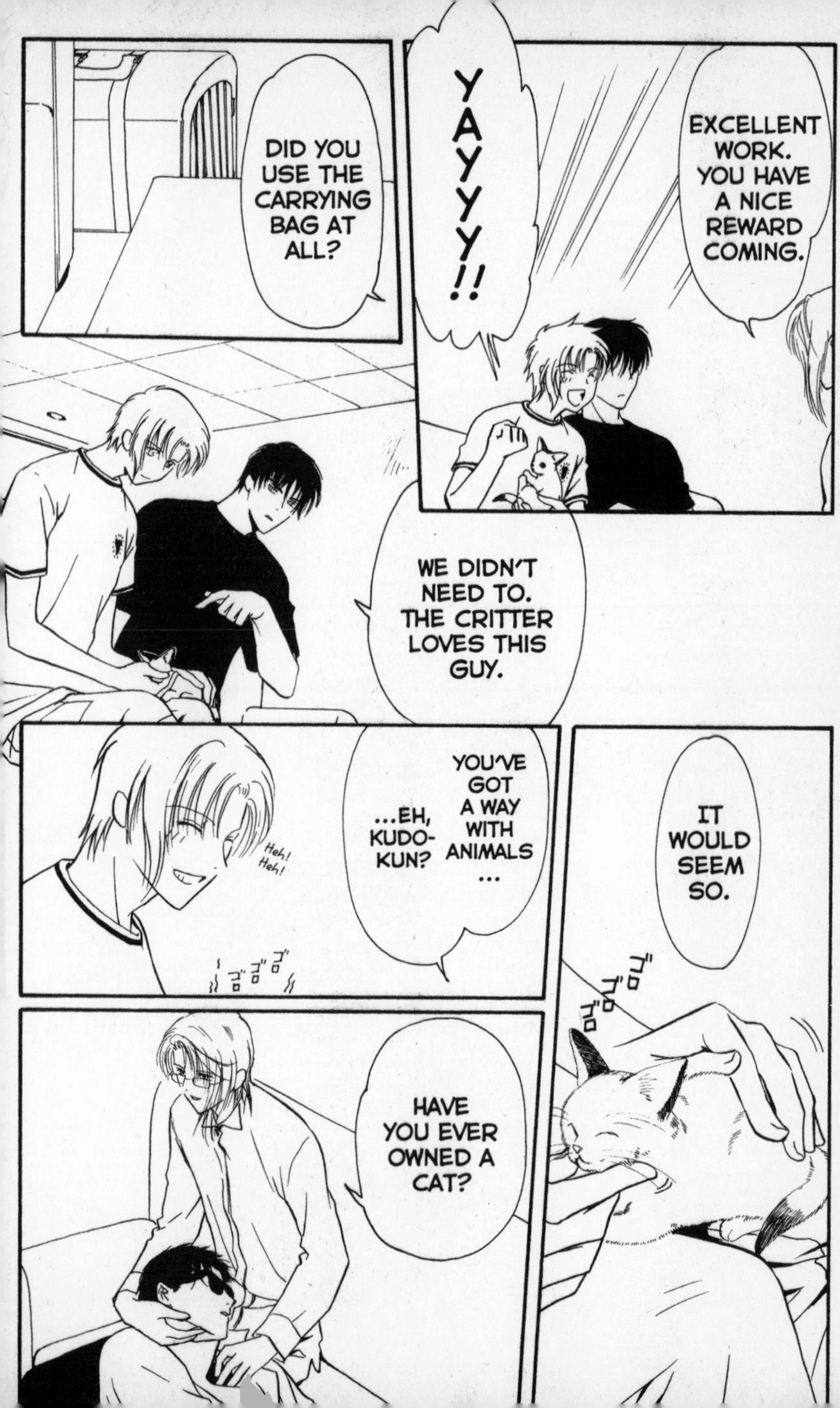
EXCELLENT WORK. YOU HAVE A NICE REWARD COMING.
YAYYY!!
DID YOU USE THE CARRYING BAG AT ALL?
WE DIDN'T NEED TO. THE CRITTER LOVES THIS GUY.
IT WOULD SEEM SO.
ゴロゴロゴロ
YOU'VE GOT A WAY WITH ANIMALS...
...EH, KUDO-KUN?
Heh! Heh!
ゴロゴロ
HAVE YOU EVER OWNED A CAT?

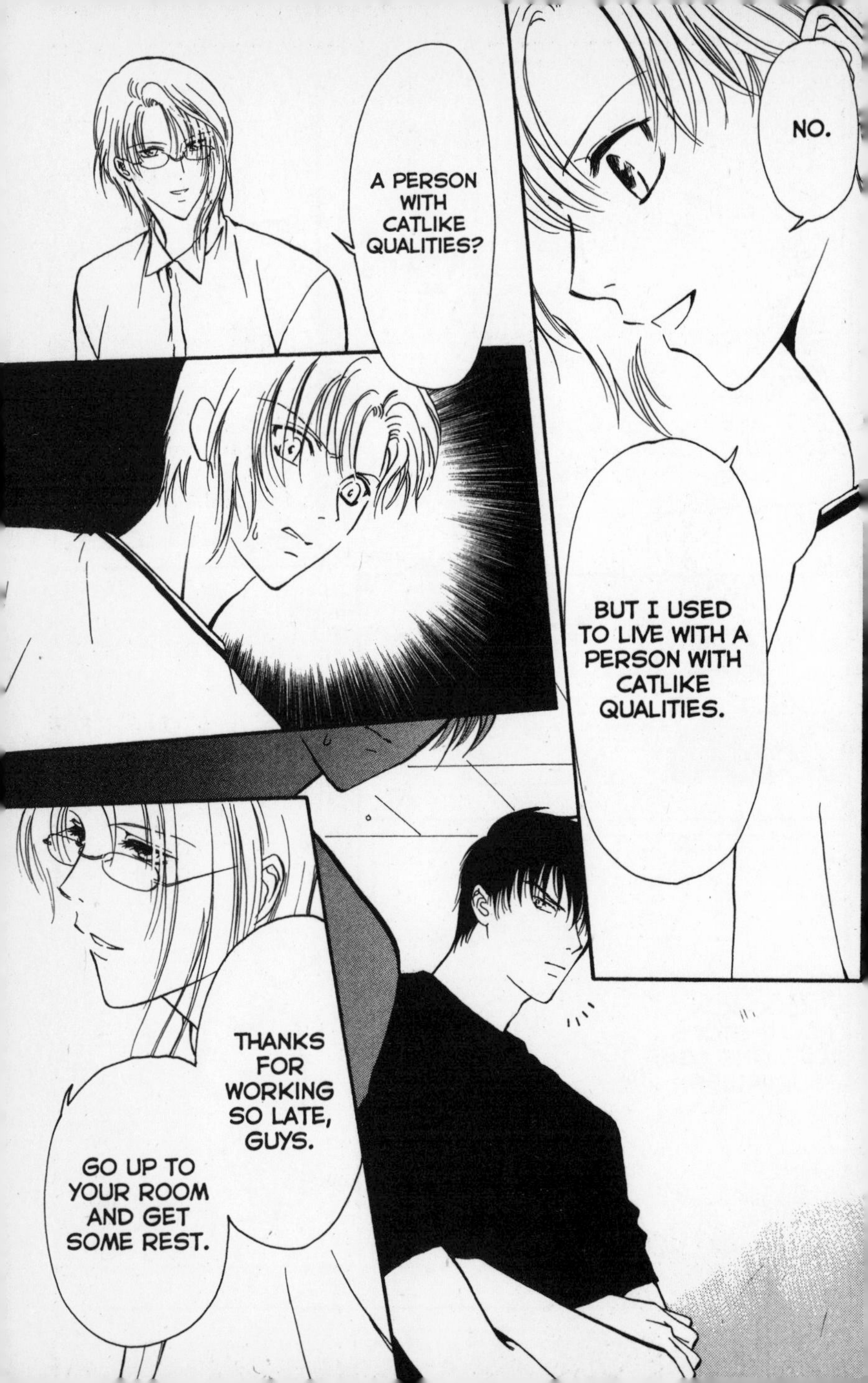
A PERSON WITH CATLIKE QUALITIES?
NO.
BUT I USED TO LIVE WITH A PERSON WITH CATLIKE QUALITIES.
THANKS FOR WORKING SO LATE, GUYS.
GO UP TO YOUR ROOM AND GET SOME REST.

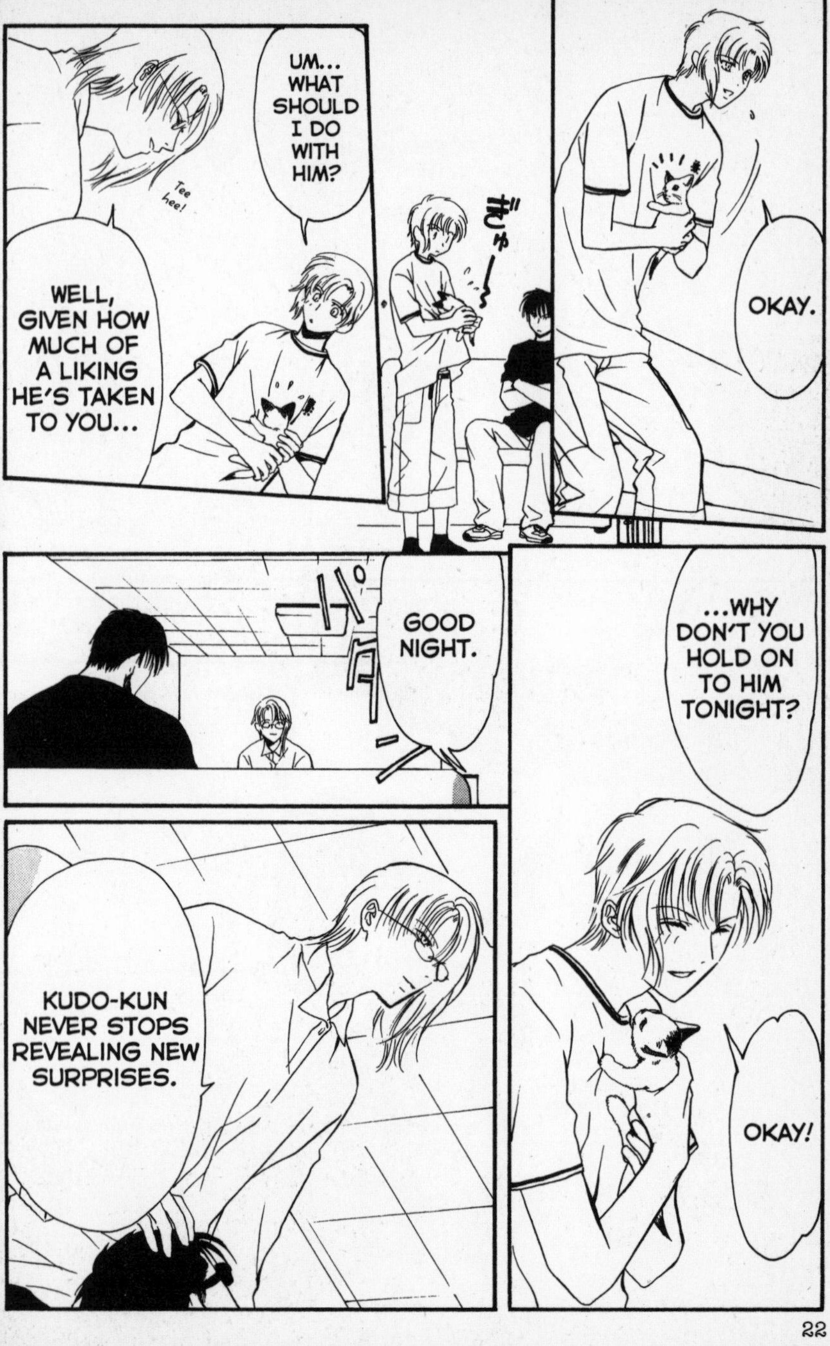
OKAY.
UM... WHAT SHOULD I DO WITH HIM?
Tee hee!
WELL, GIVEN HOW MUCH OF A LIKING HE'S TAKEN TO YOU...
ぎゅ～
...WHY DON'T YOU HOLD ON TO HIM TONIGHT?
OKAY!
パタン
GOOD NIGHT.
KUDO-KUN NEVER STOPS REVEALING NEW SURPRISES.

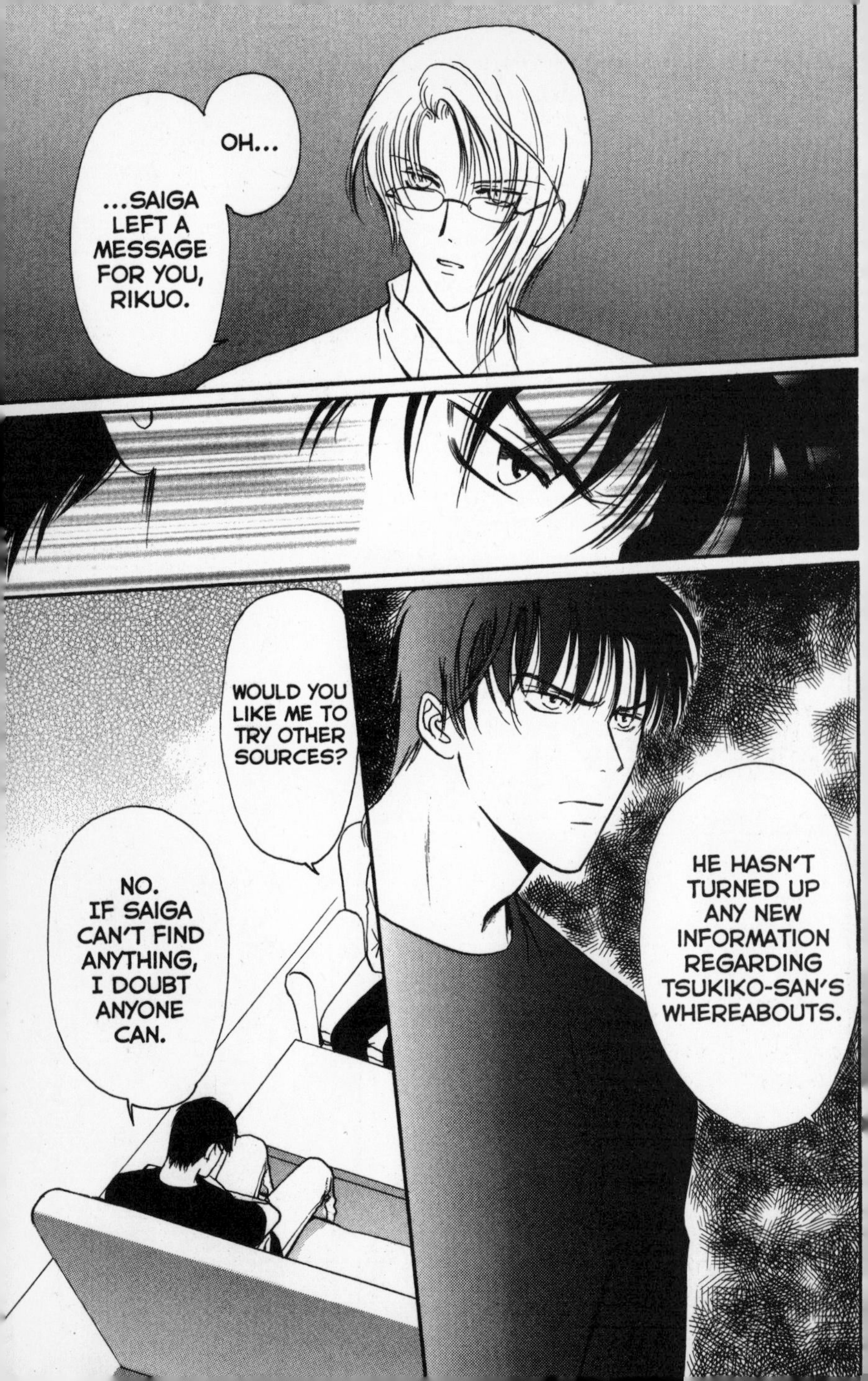
OH...
...SAIGA LEFT A MESSAGE FOR YOU, RIKUO.
HE HASN'T TURNED UP ANY NEW INFORMATION REGARDING TSUKIKO-SAN'S WHEREABOUTS.
WOULD YOU LIKE ME TO TRY OTHER SOURCES?
NO. IF SAIGA CAN'T FIND ANYTHING, I DOUBT ANYONE CAN.

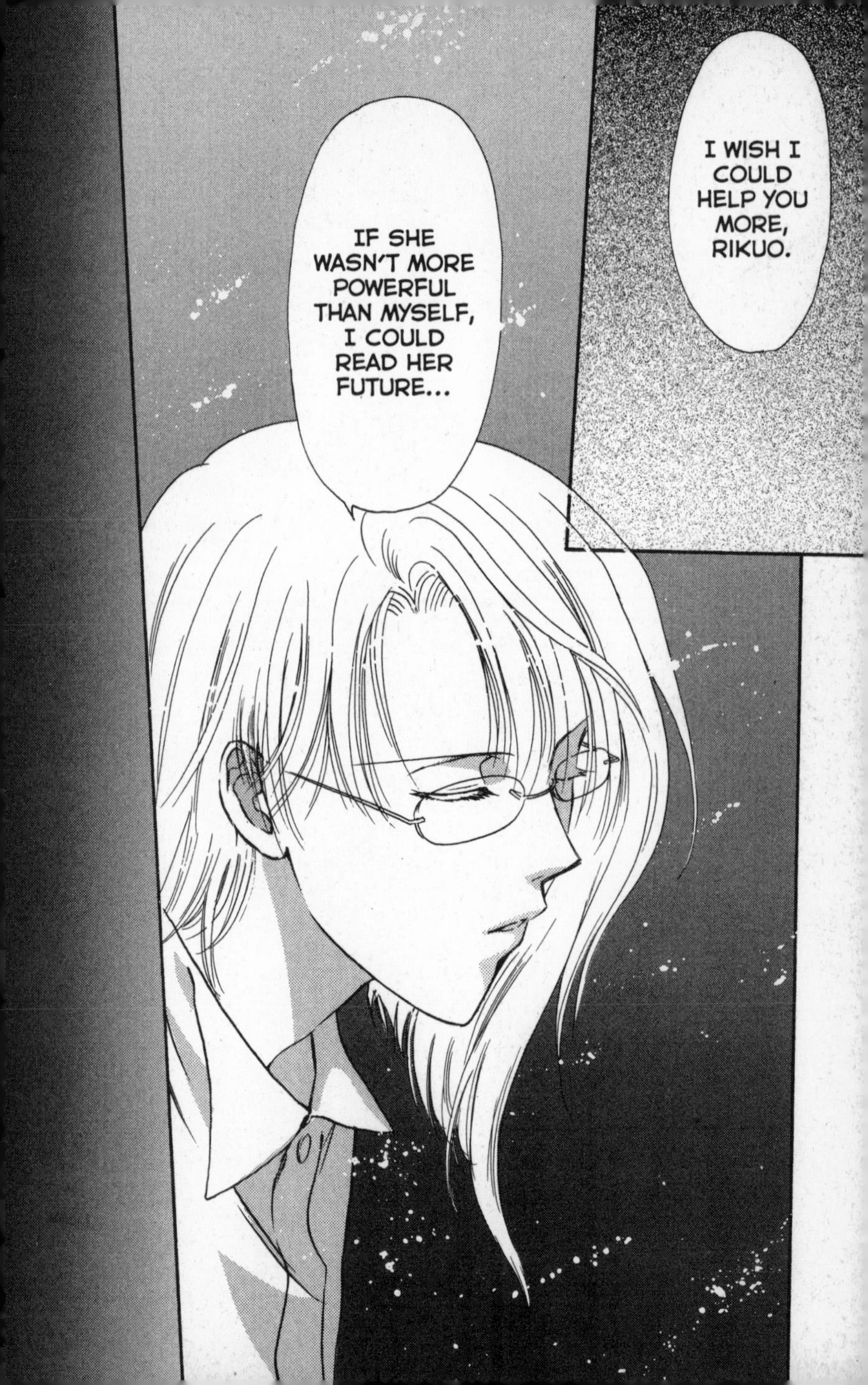
I WISH I COULD HELP YOU MORE, RIKUO.
IF SHE WASN'T MORE POWERFUL THAN MYSELF, I COULD READ HER FUTURE...

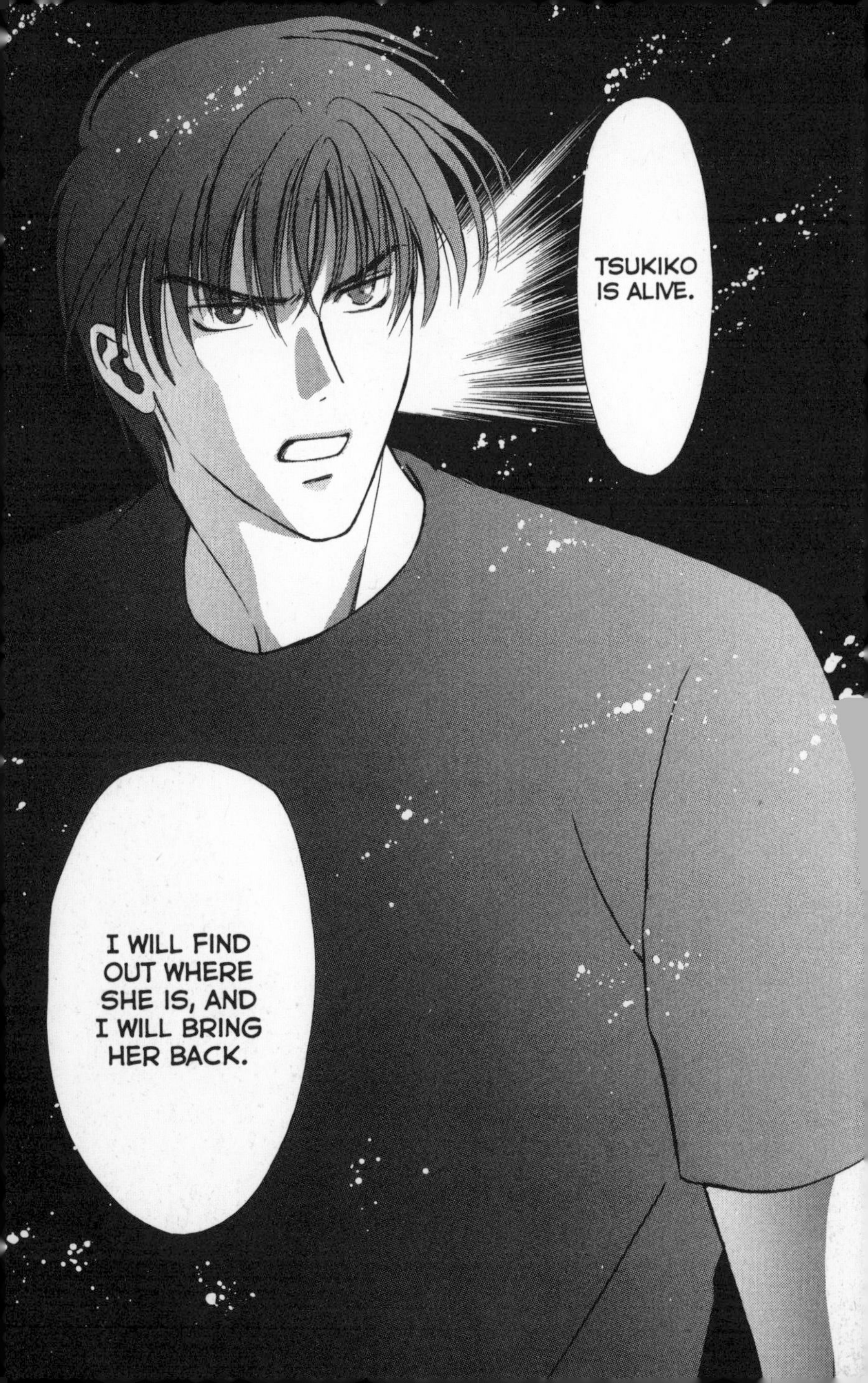
TSUKIKO IS ALIVE.
I WILL FIND OUT WHERE SHE IS, AND I WILL BRING HER BACK.

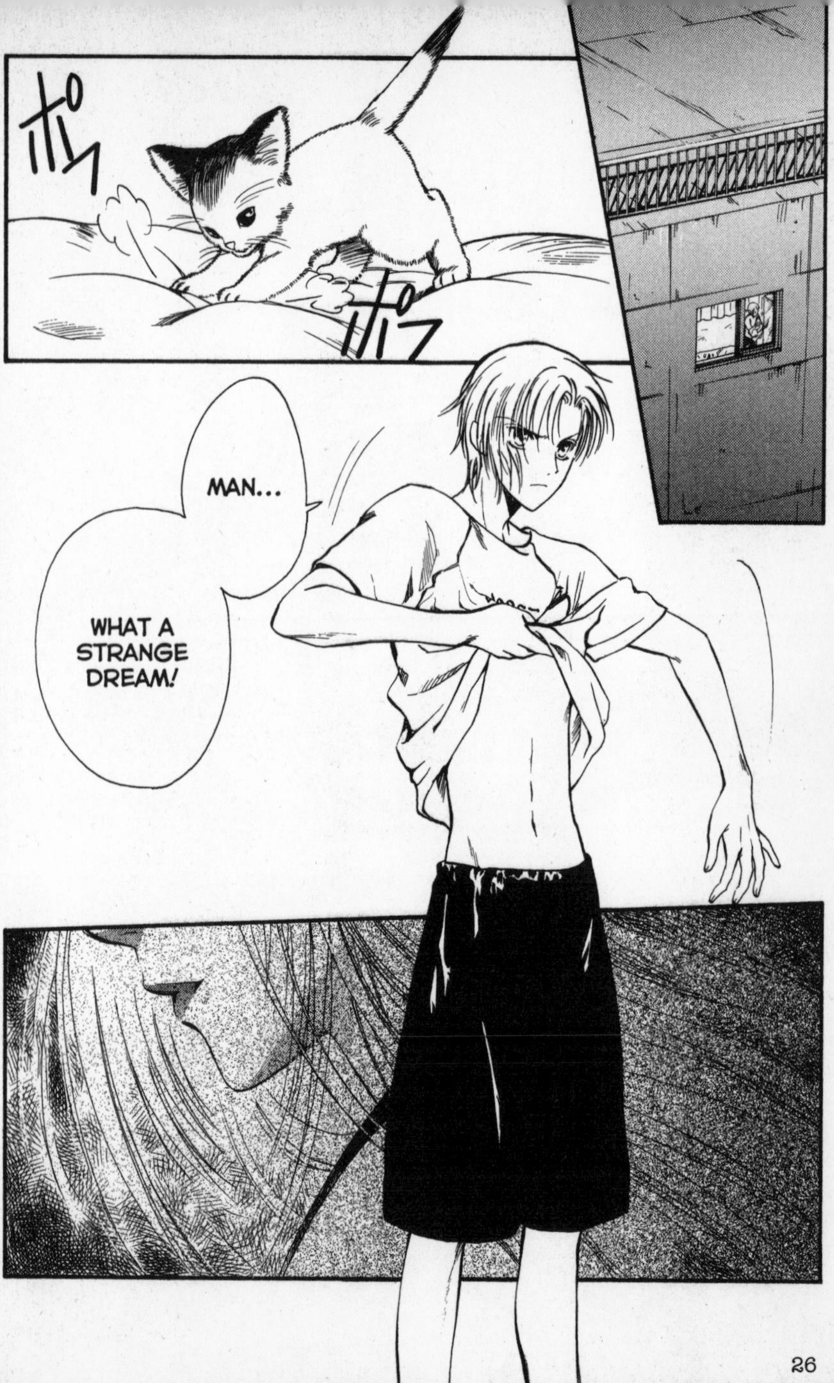
ポム
ポム
MAN...
WHAT A STRANGE DREAM!

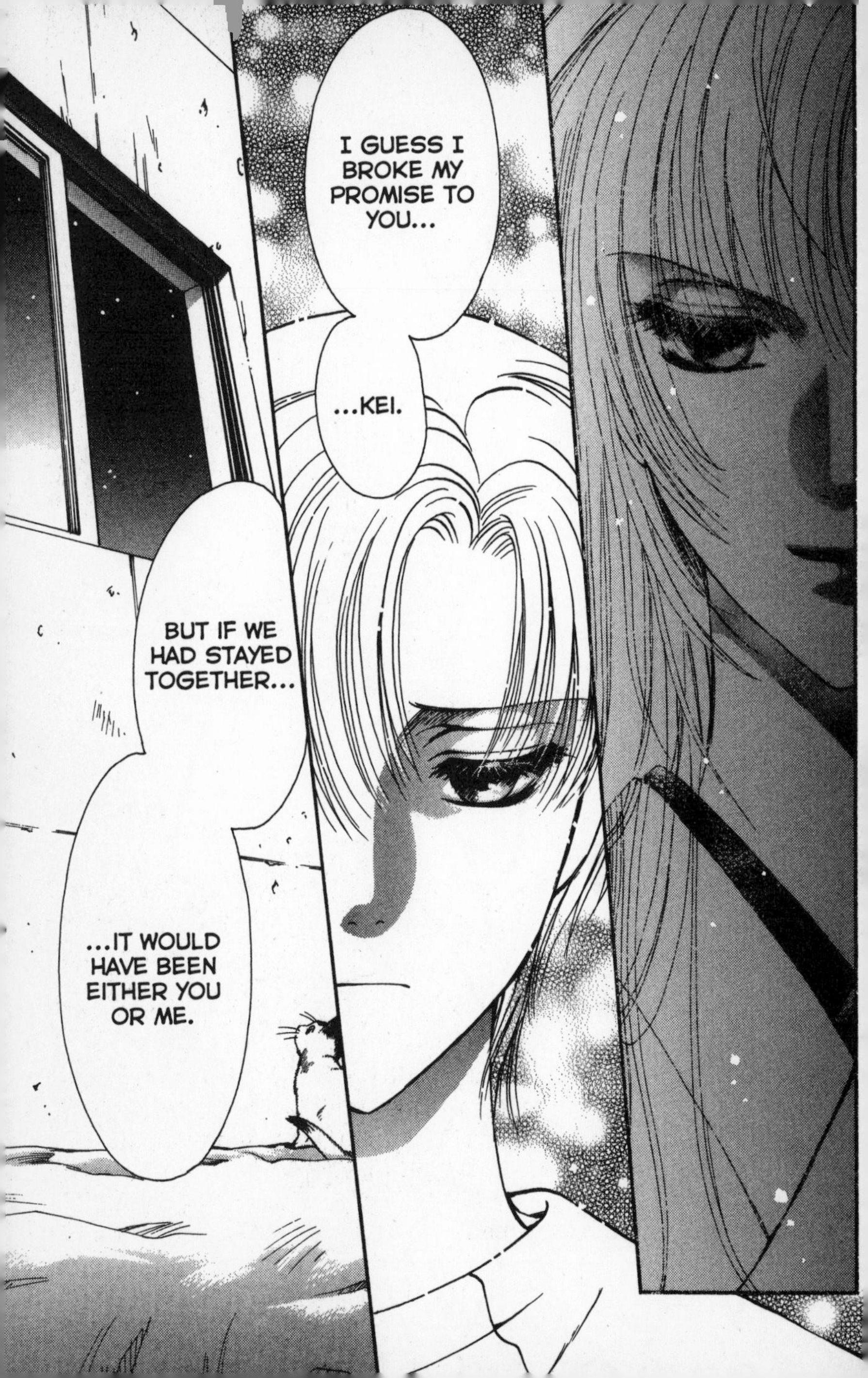
I GUESS I BROKE MY PROMISE TO YOU...
...KEI.
BUT IF WE HAD STAYED TOGETHER...
...IT WOULD HAVE BEEN EITHER YOU OR ME.

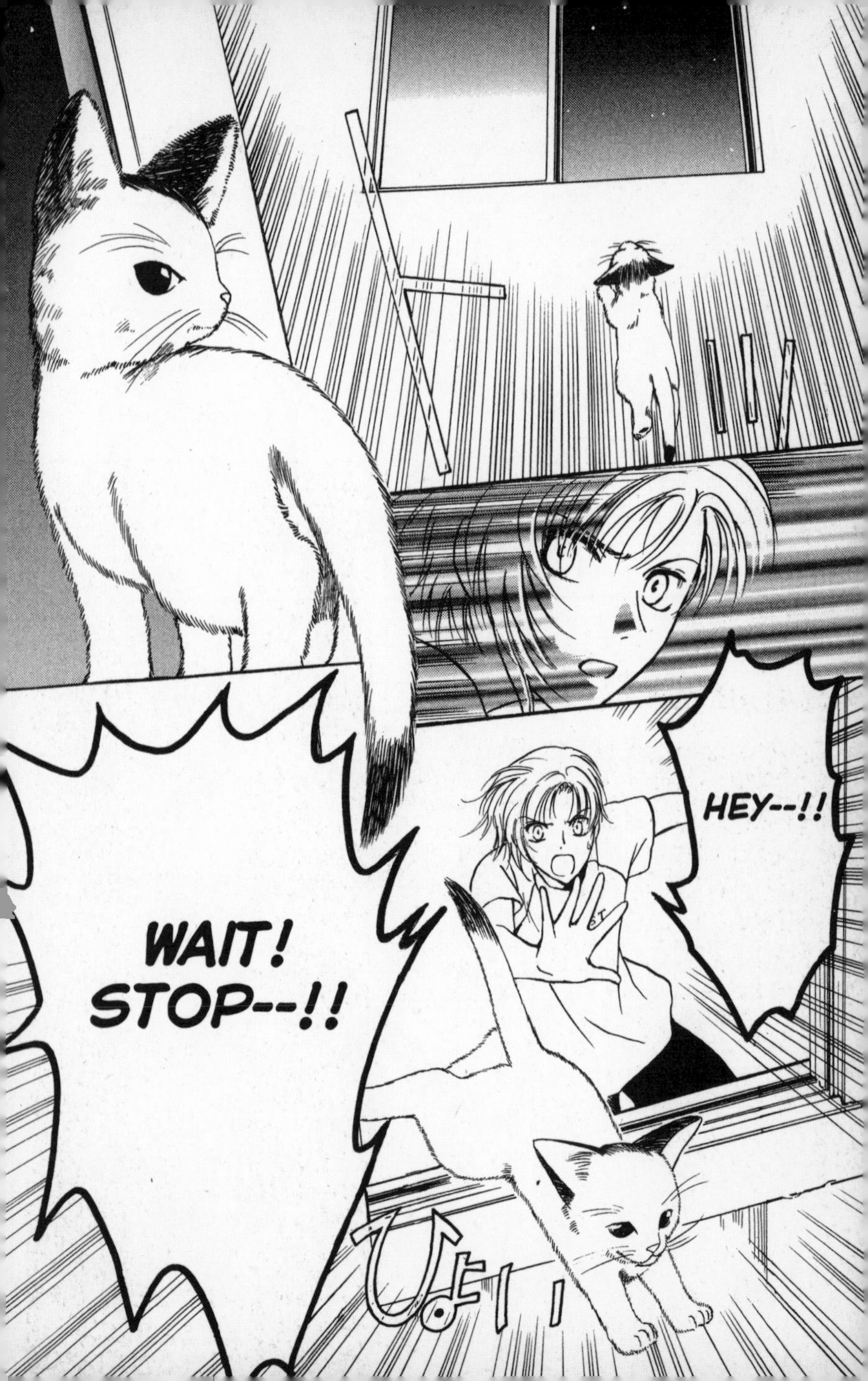
HEY--!!
WAIT! STOP--!!
ぴょ

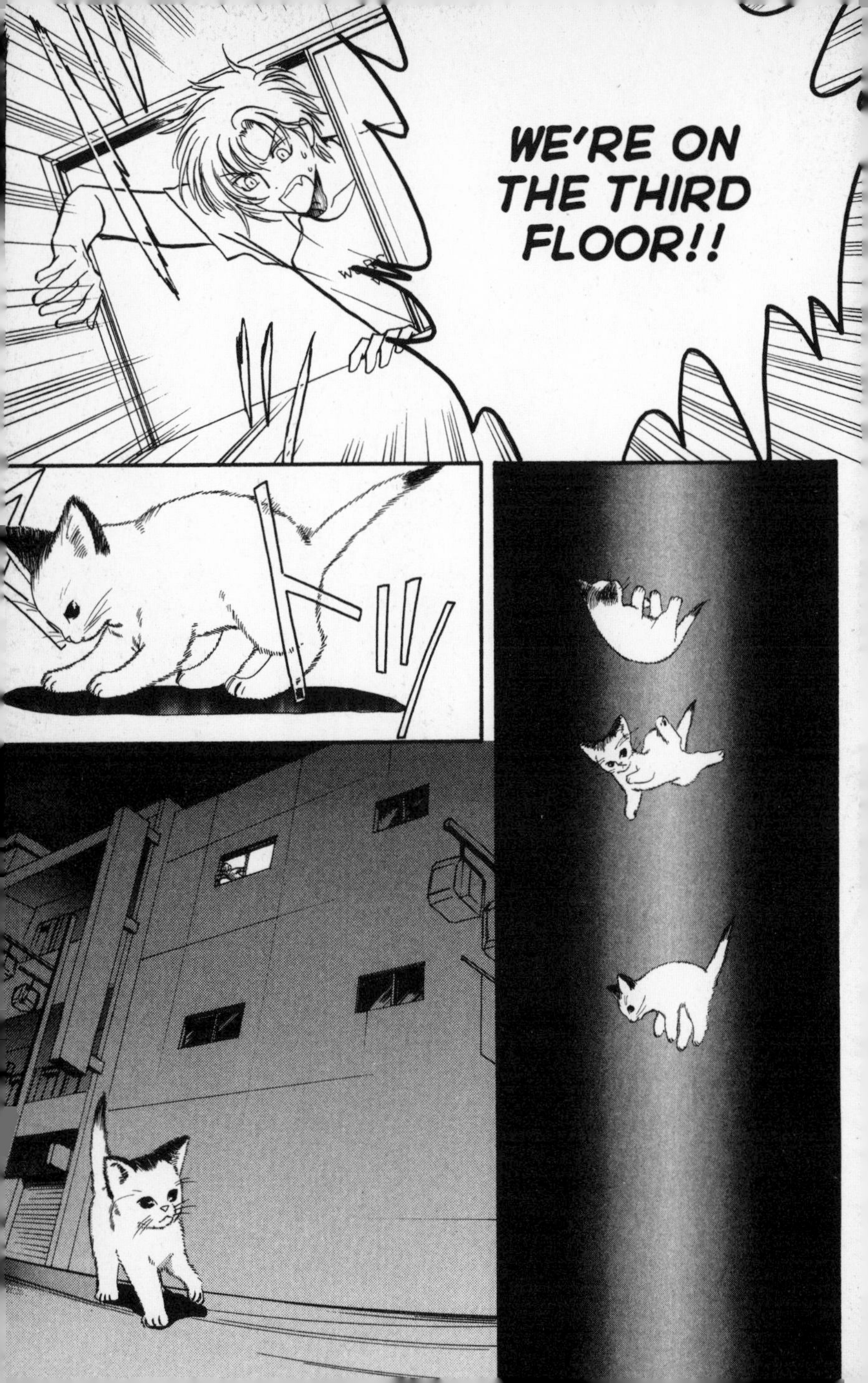
WE'RE ON THE THIRD FLOOR!!

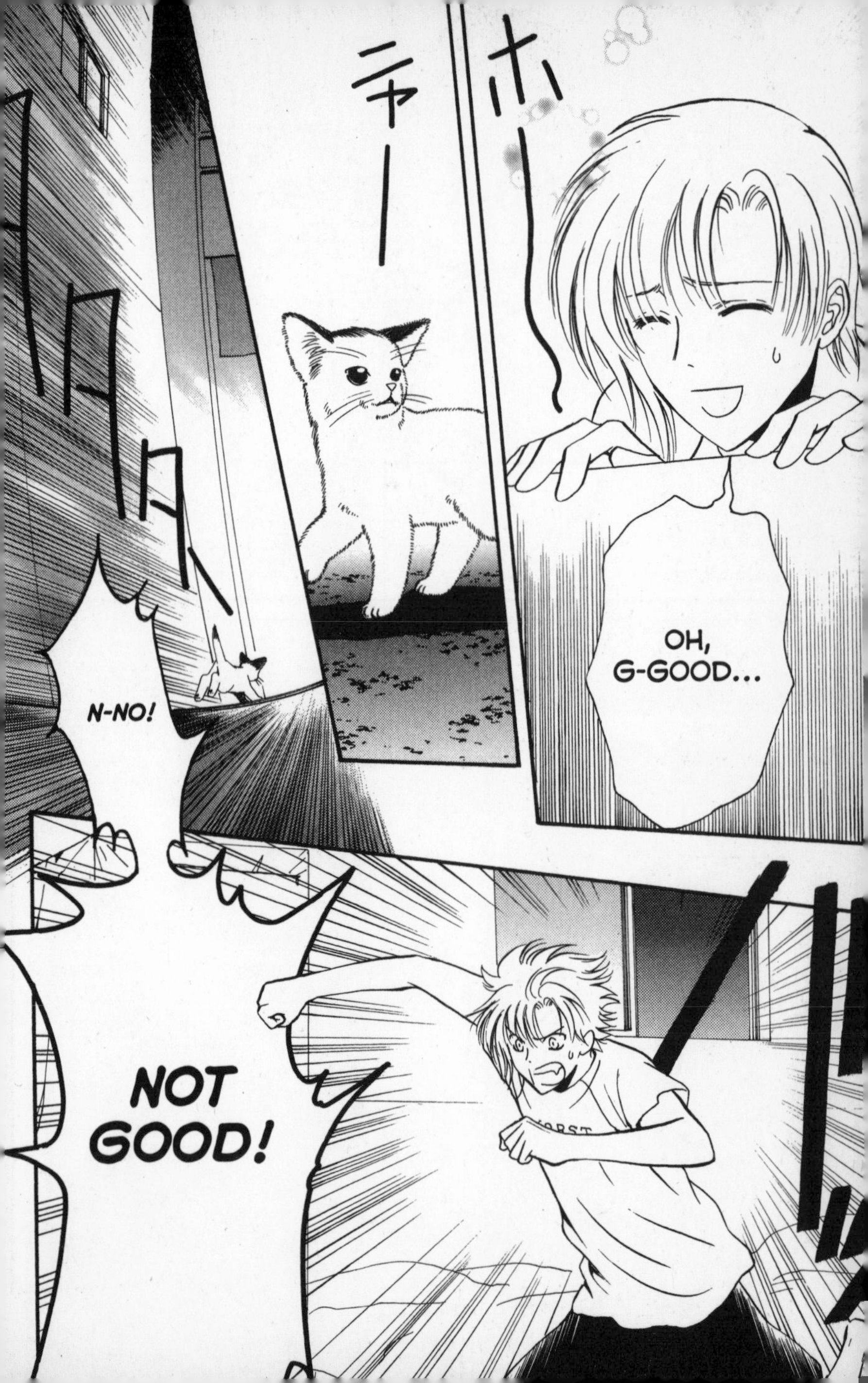
ホー
OH, G-GOOD...
ニャー
N-NO!
NOT GOOD!

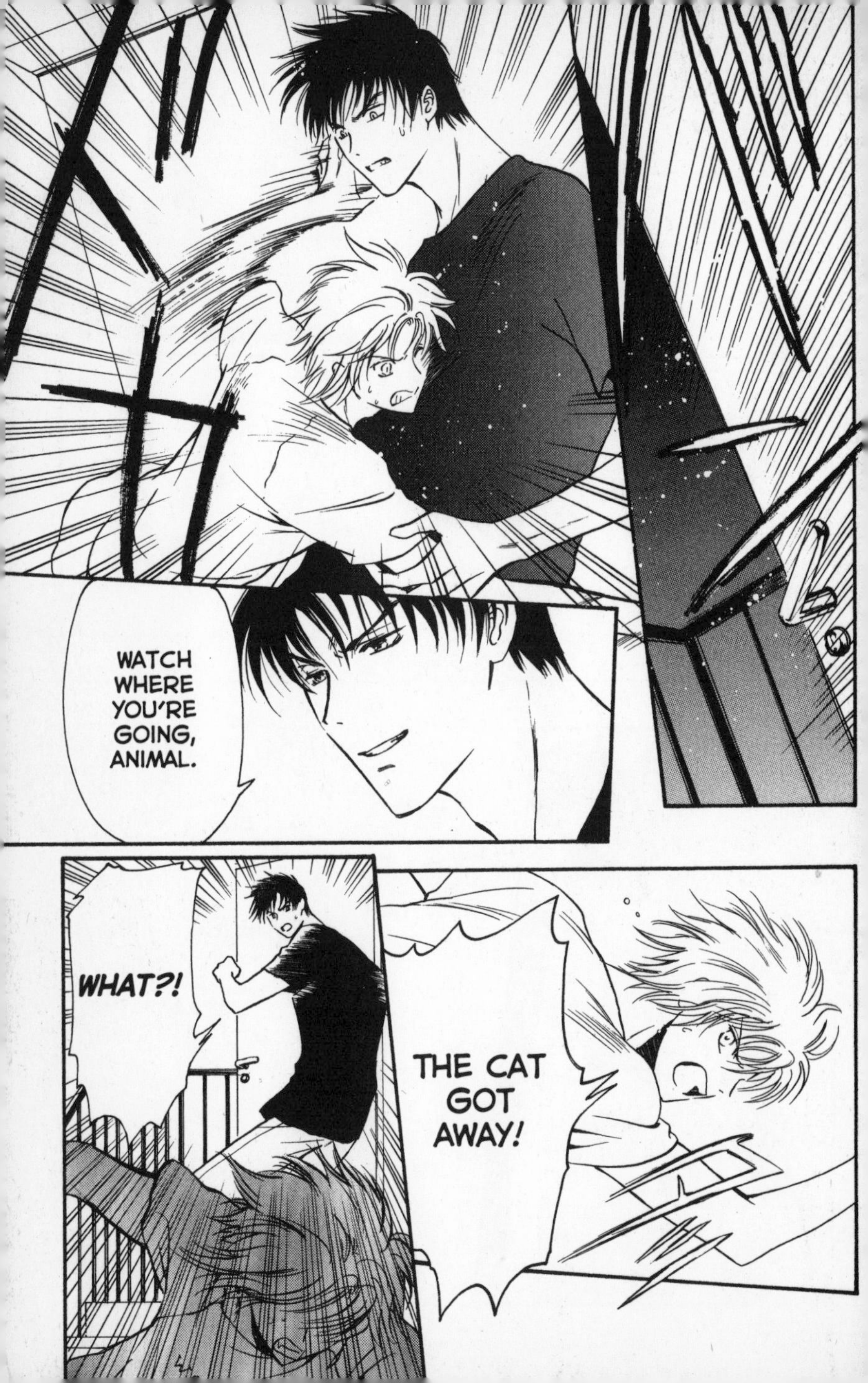
WATCH WHERE YOU'RE GOING, ANIMAL.
THE CAT GOT AWAY!
WHAT?!

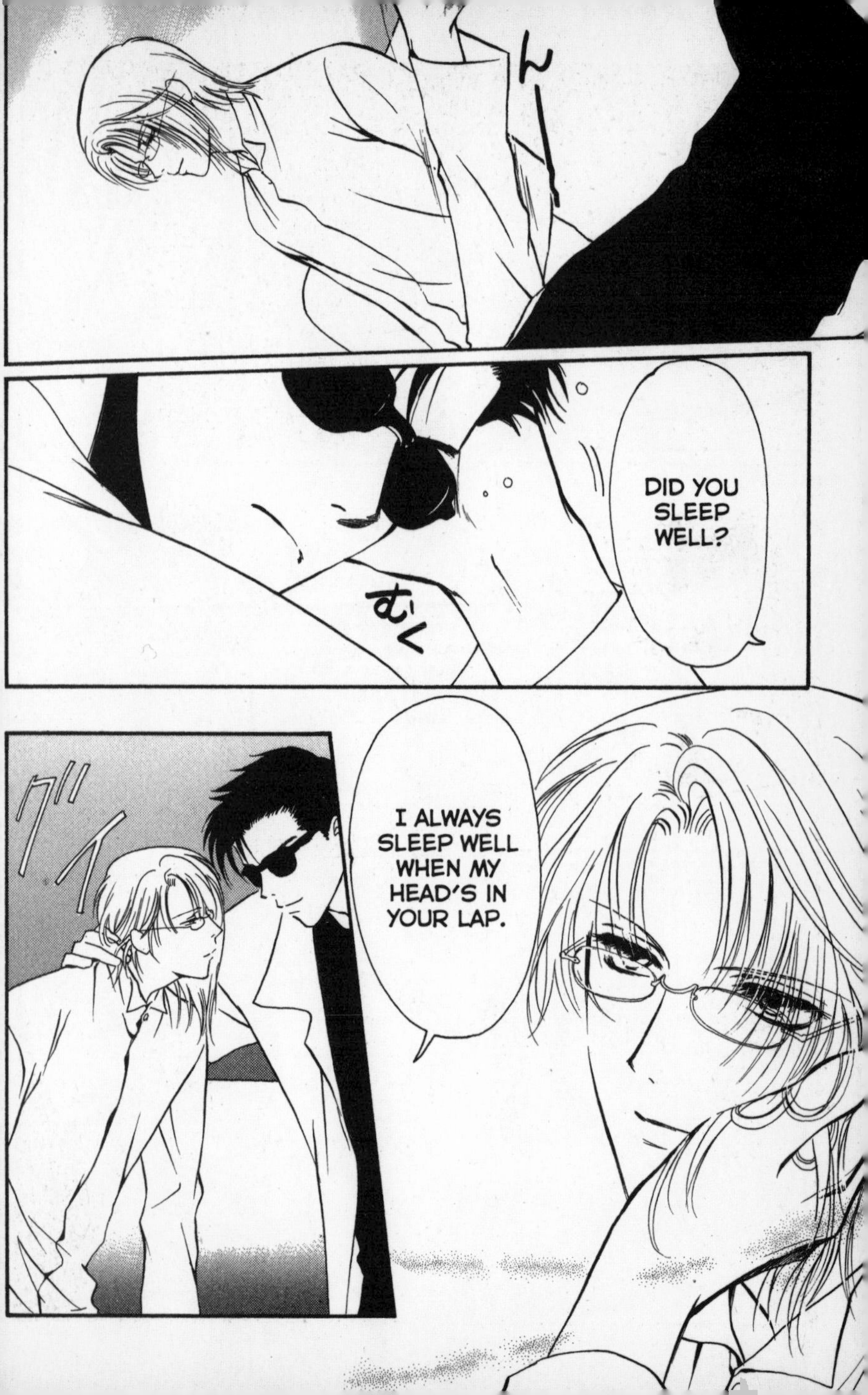
んー
DID YOU SLEEP WELL?
むく
I ALWAYS SLEEP WELL WHEN MY HEAD'S IN YOUR LAP.
グイ

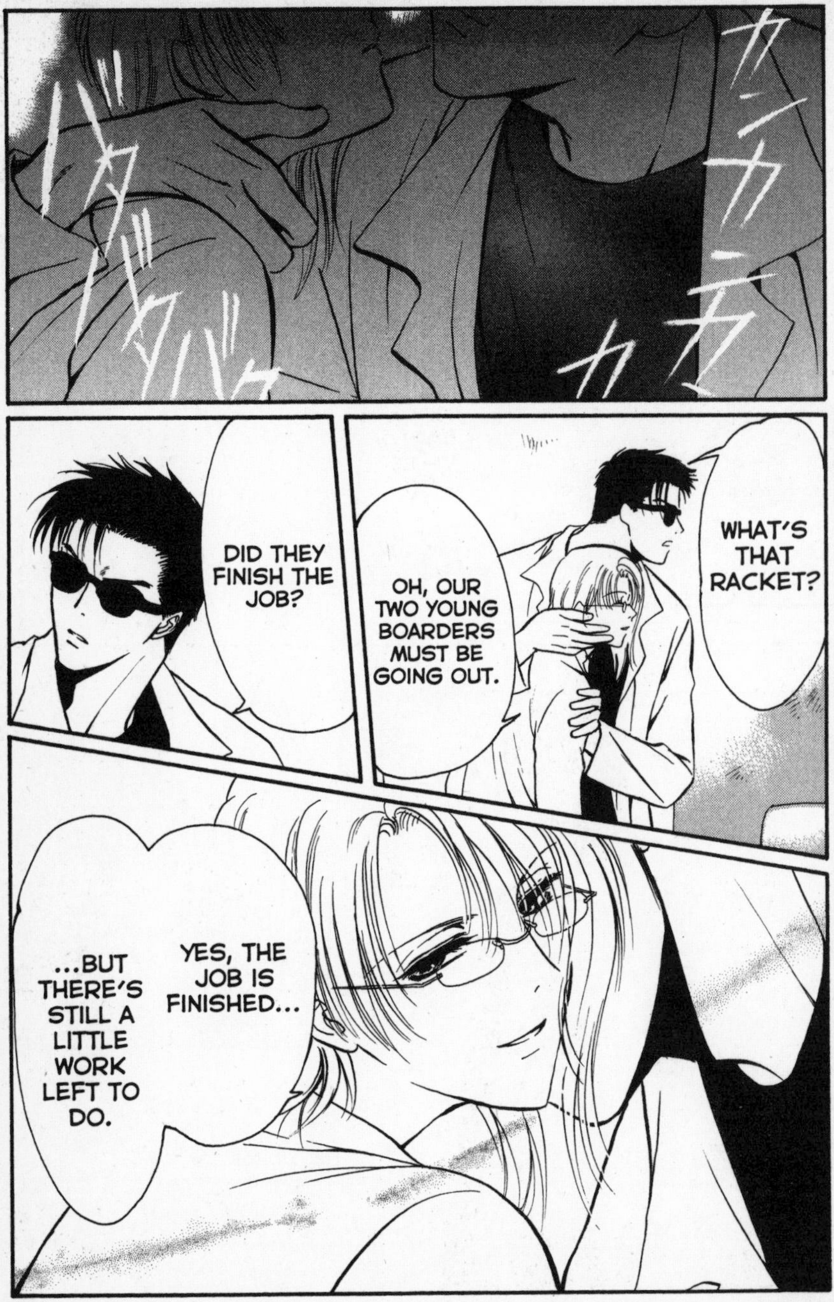
WHAT'S THAT RACKET?
OH, OUR TWO YOUNG BOARDERS MUST BE GOING OUT.
DID THEY FINISH THE JOB?
YES, THE JOB IS FINISHED...
...BUT THERE'S STILL A LITTLE WORK LEFT TO DO.

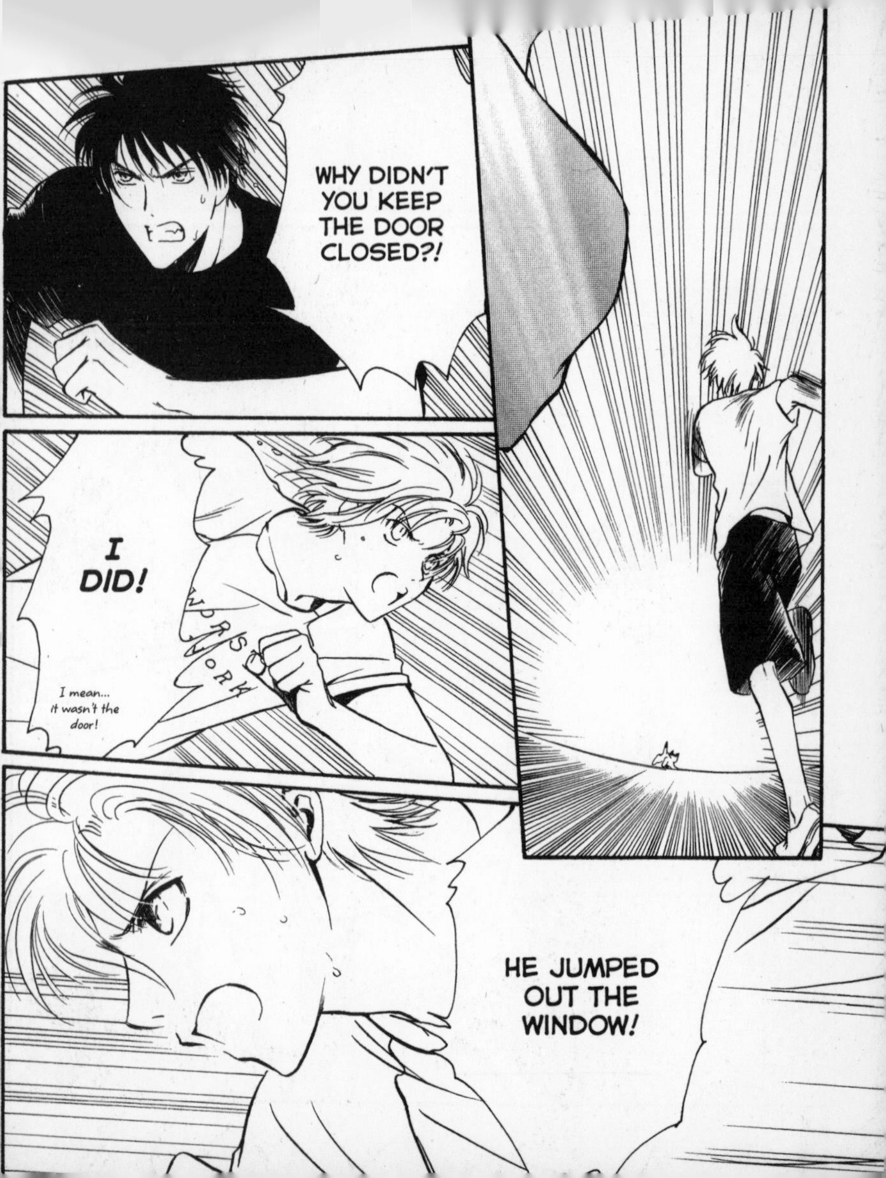
WHY DIDN'T YOU KEEP THE DOOR CLOSED?!
I DID!
I mean... it wasn't the door!
HE JUMPED OUT THE WINDOW!

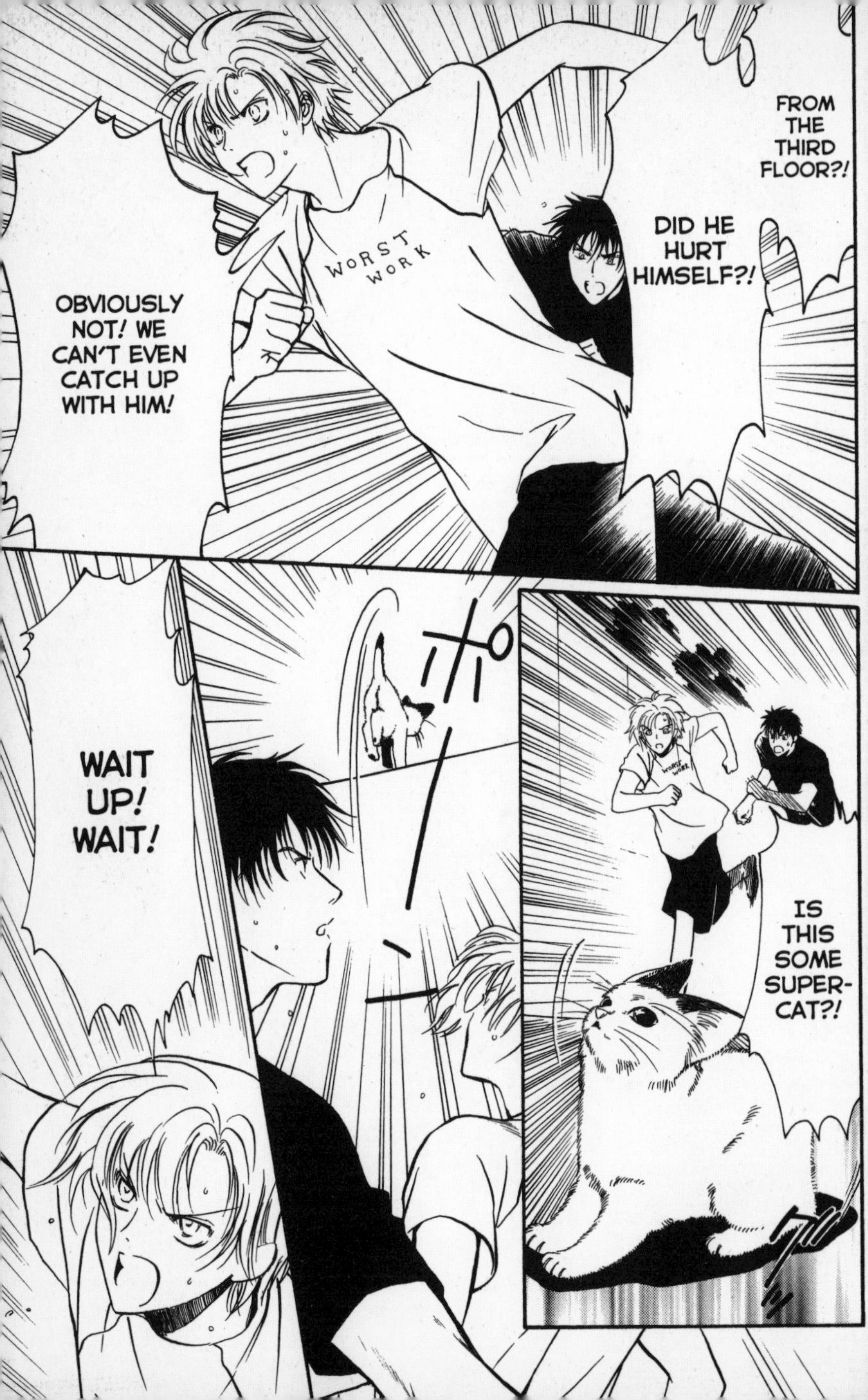
FROM THE THIRD FLOOR?!
DID HE HURT HIMSELF?!
WORST WORK
OBVIOUSLY NOT! WE CAN'T EVEN CATCH UP WITH HIM!
IS THIS SOME SUPER-CAT?!
WAIT UP! WAIT!

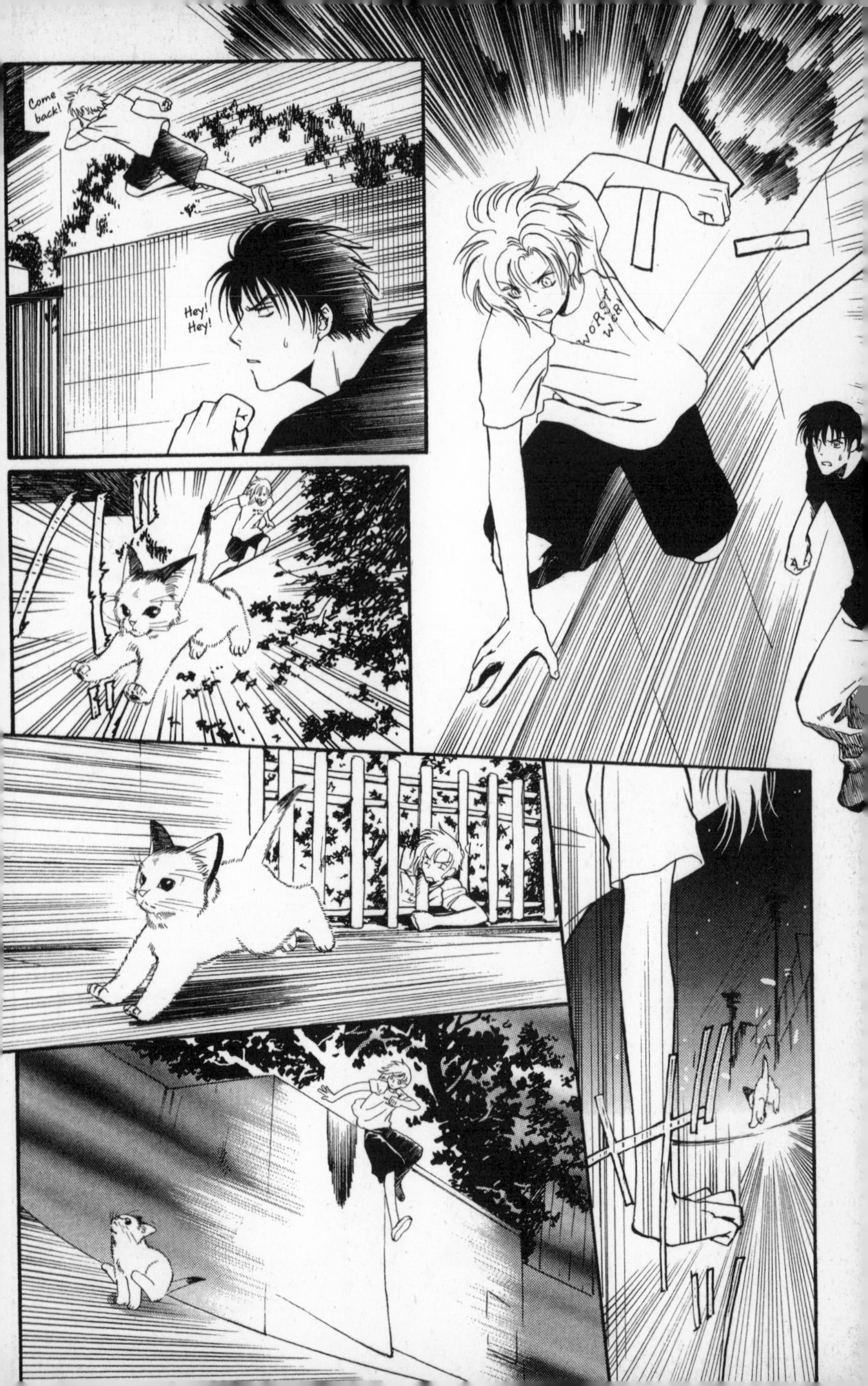
Come back!
Hey! Hey!

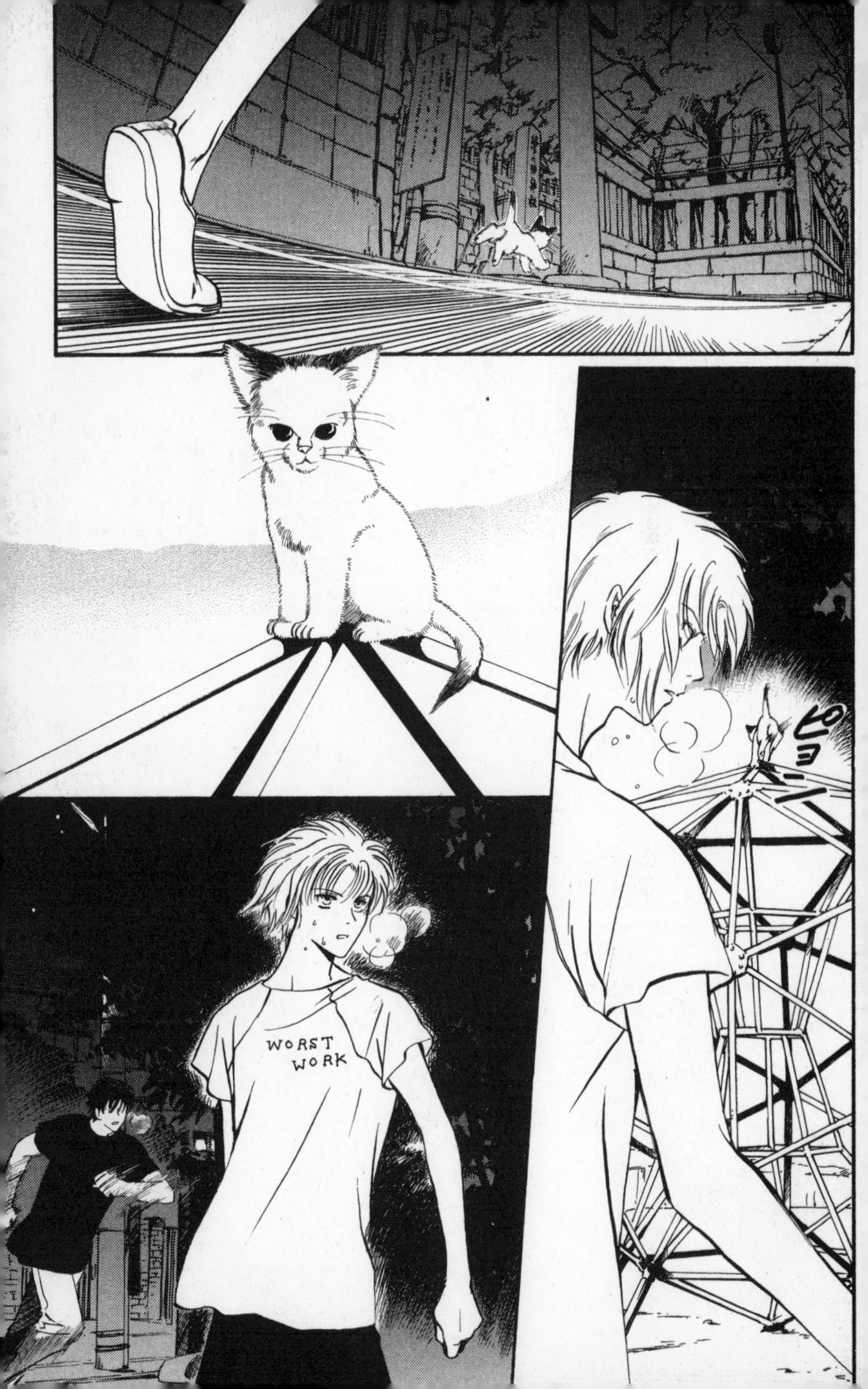
ピョーン
WORST WORK

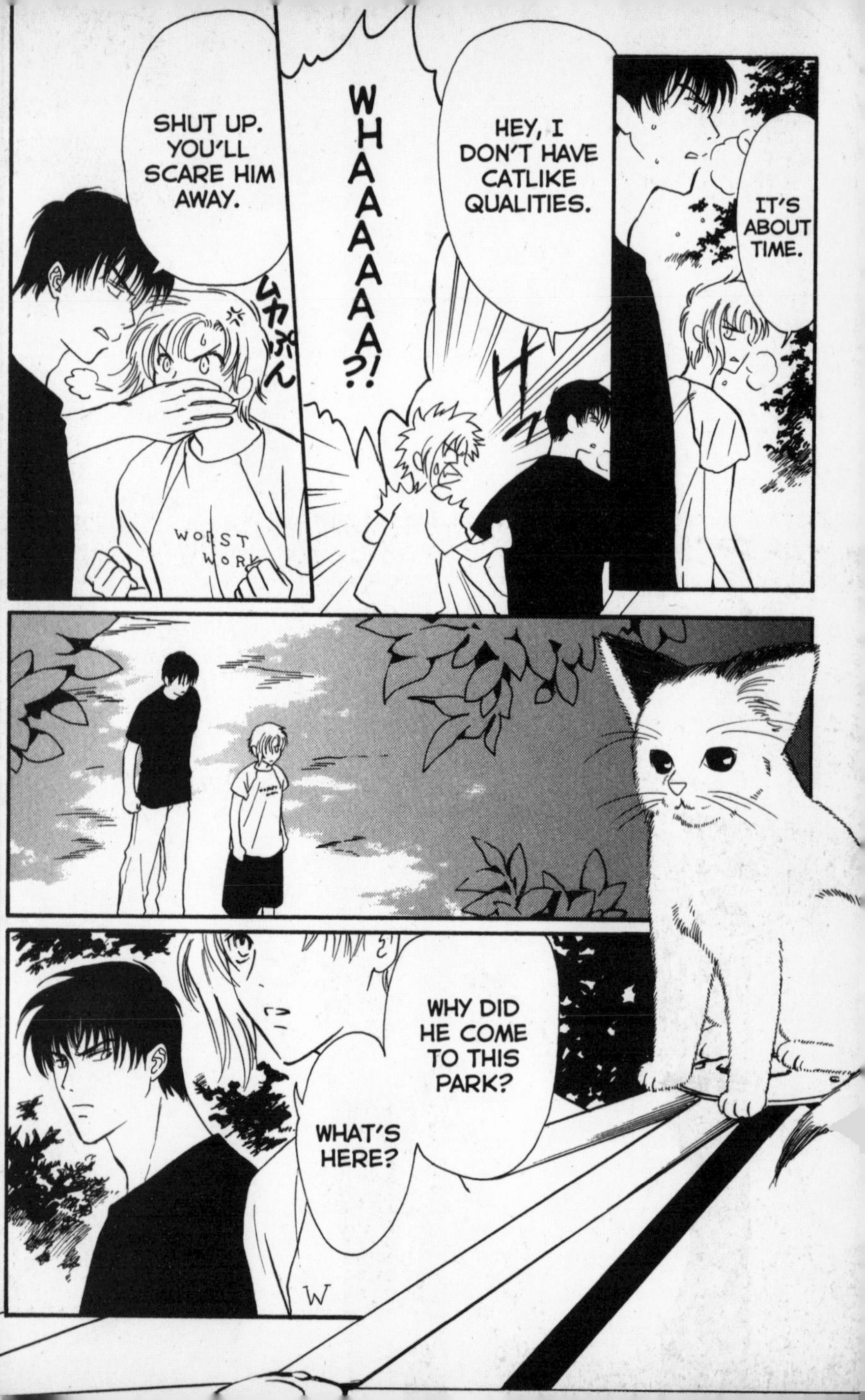
IT'S ABOUT TIME.
HEY, I DON'T HAVE CATLIKE QUALITIES.
けっ
WHAAAAAAA?!
SHUT UP. YOU'LL SCARE HIM AWAY.
ムカぷん
WORST WORK
WHY DID HE COME TO THIS PARK?
WHAT'S HERE?

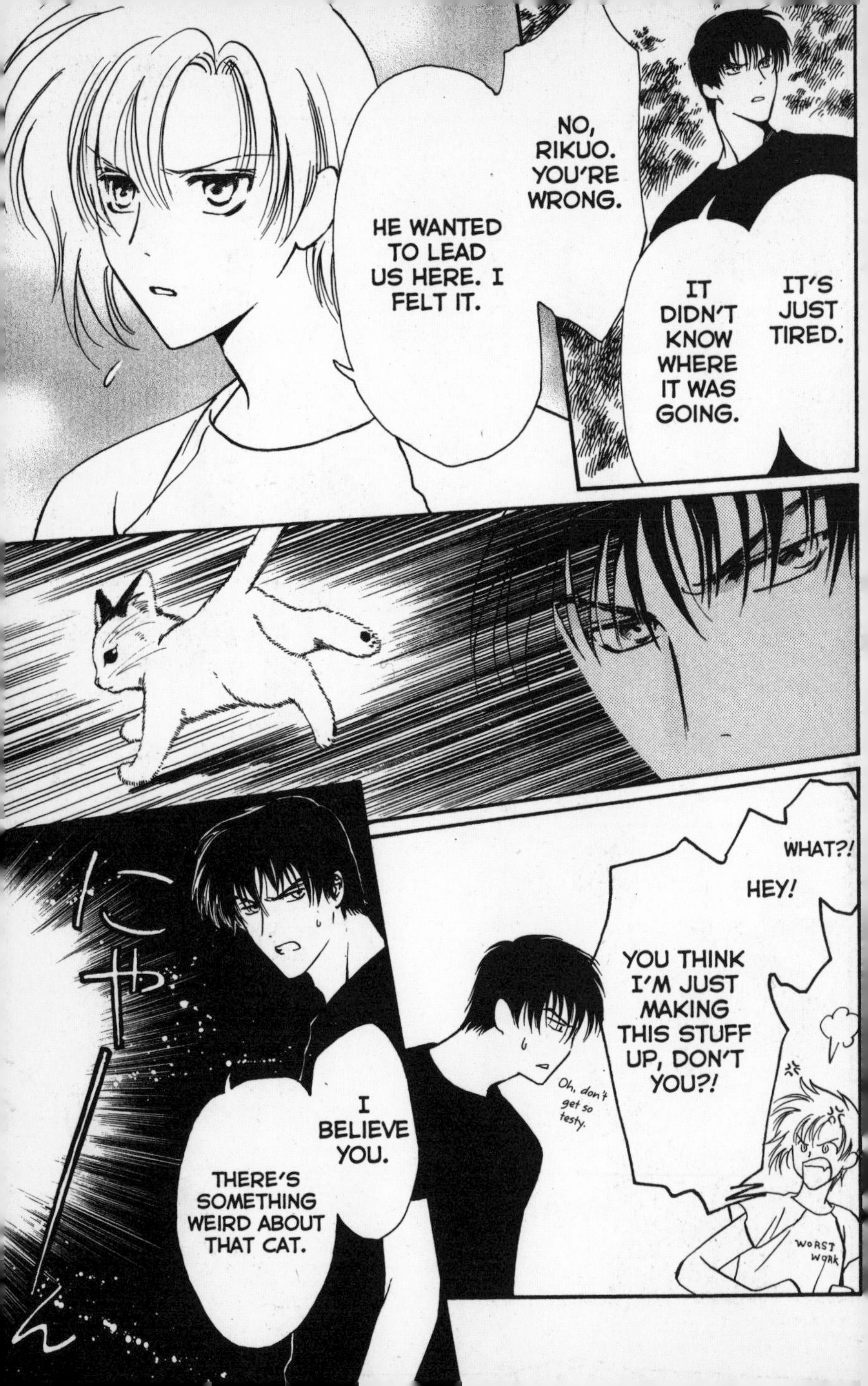
IT'S JUST TIRED.
IT DIDN'T KNOW WHERE IT WAS GOING.
NO, RIKUO. YOU'RE WRONG.
HE WANTED TO LEAD US HERE. I FELT IT.
WHAT?!
HEY!
YOU THINK I'M JUST MAKING THIS STUFF UP, DON'T YOU?!
Oh, don't get so testy.
WORST WORK
I BELIEVE YOU.
THERE'S SOMETHING WEIRD ABOUT THAT CAT.

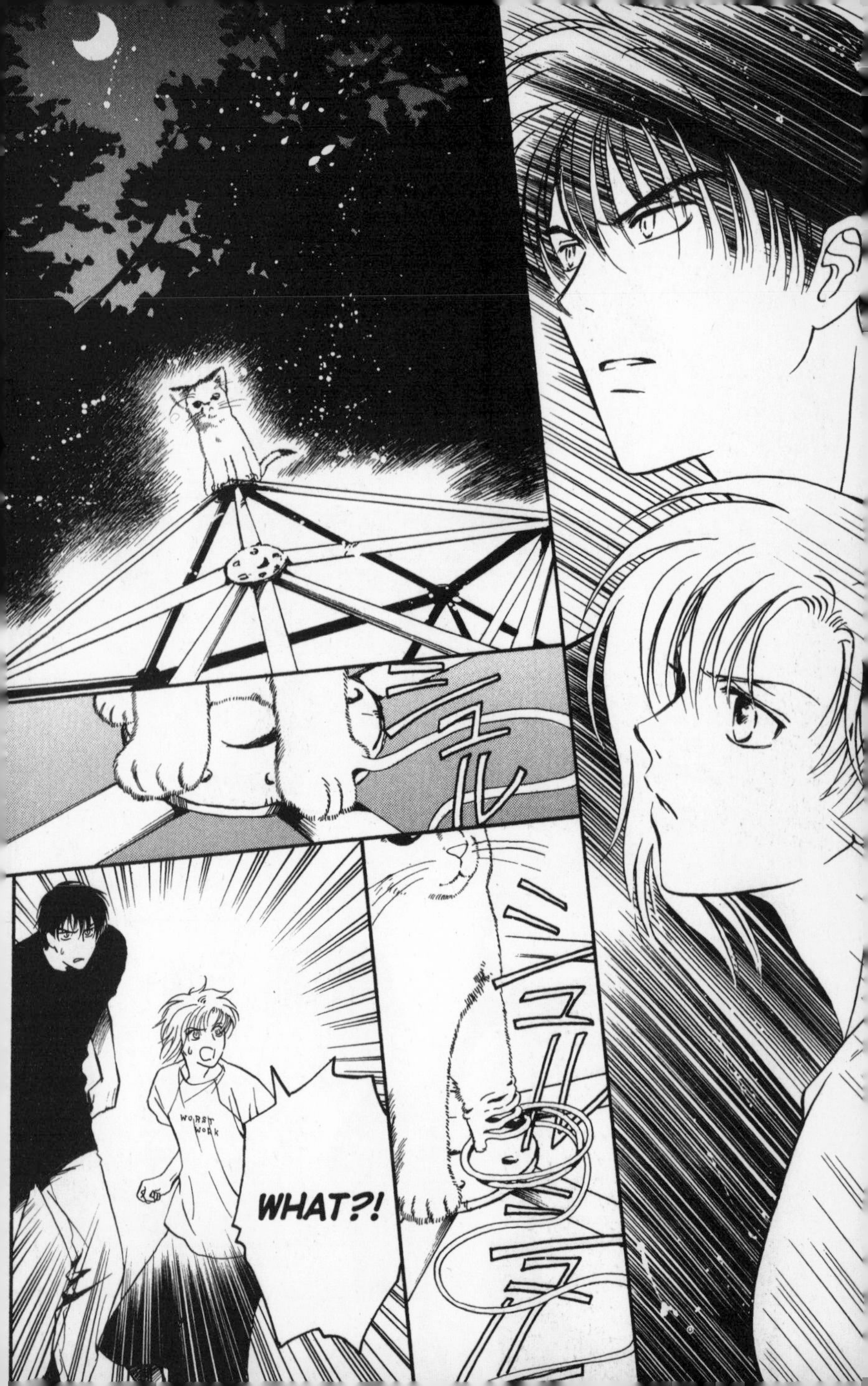
ニュル
ミュルルルル
WHAT?!

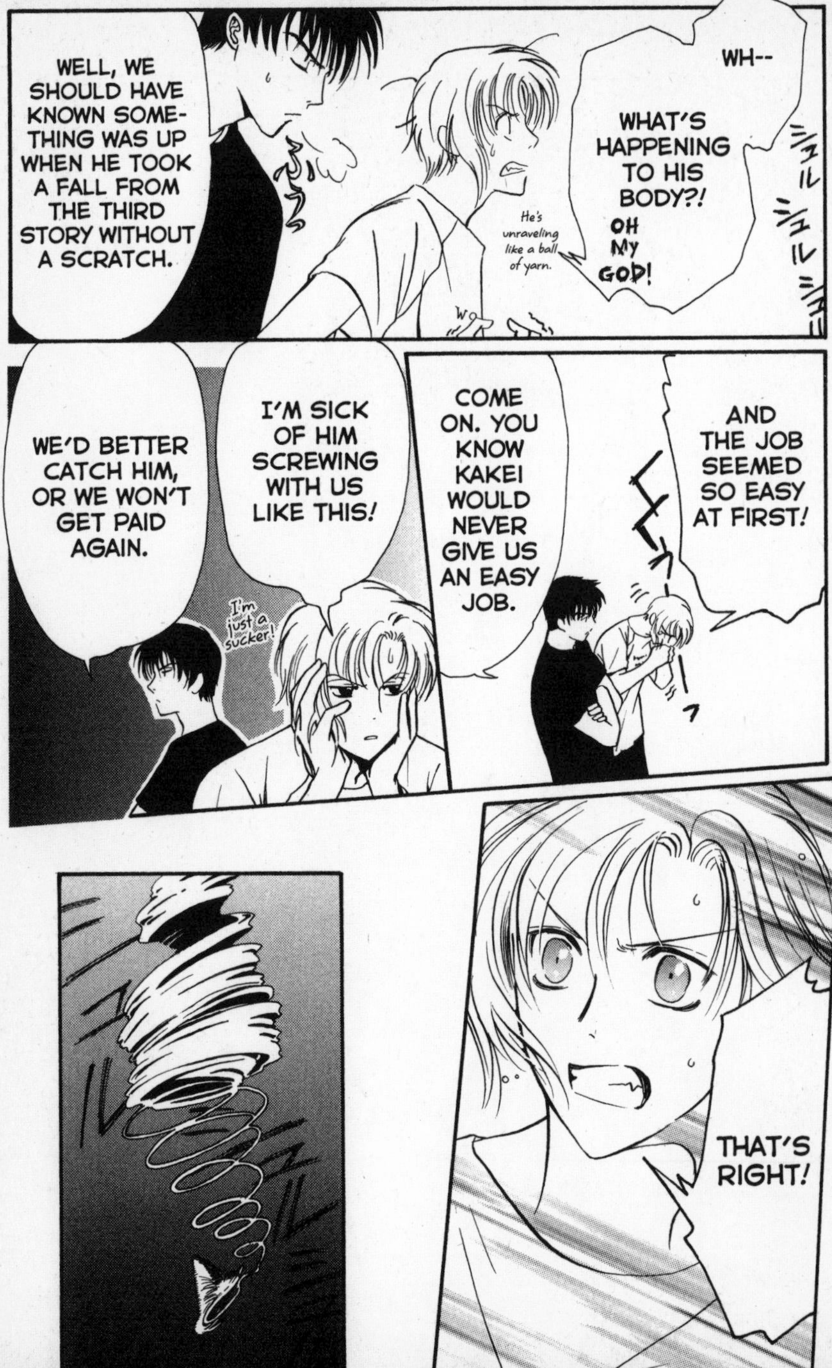
WH--
WHAT'S HAPPENING TO HIS BODY?!
OH MY GOD!
He's unraveling like a ball of yarn.
WELL, WE SHOULD HAVE KNOWN SOME-THING WAS UP WHEN HE TOOK A FALL FROM THE THIRD STORY WITHOUT A SCRATCH.
AND THE JOB SEEMED SO EASY AT FIRST!
COME ON. YOU KNOW KAKEI WOULD NEVER GIVE US AN EASY JOB.
I'M SICK OF HIM SCREWING WITH US LIKE THIS!
I'm just a sucker!
WE'D BETTER CATCH HIM, OR WE WON'T GET PAID AGAIN.
THAT'S RIGHT!

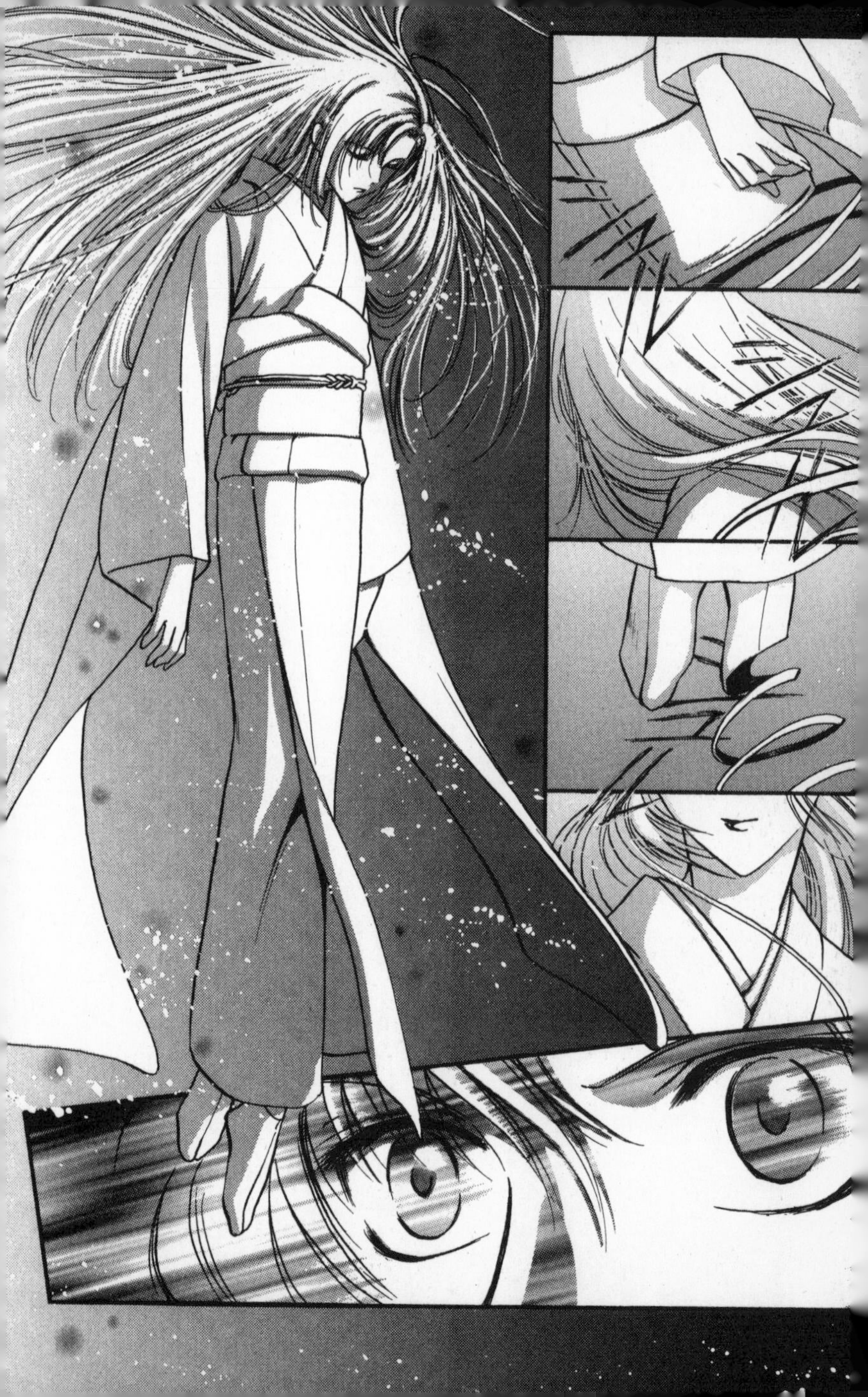

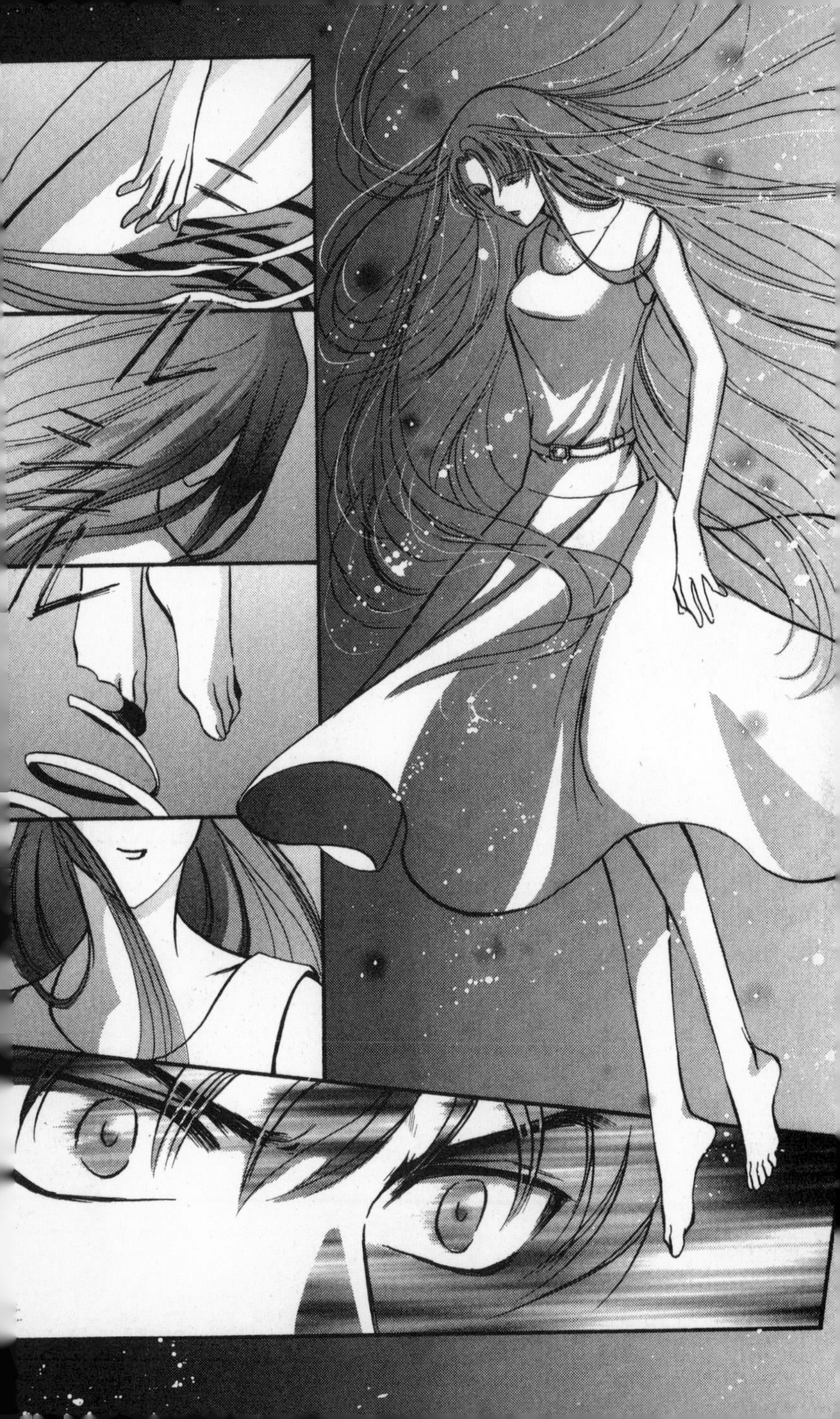

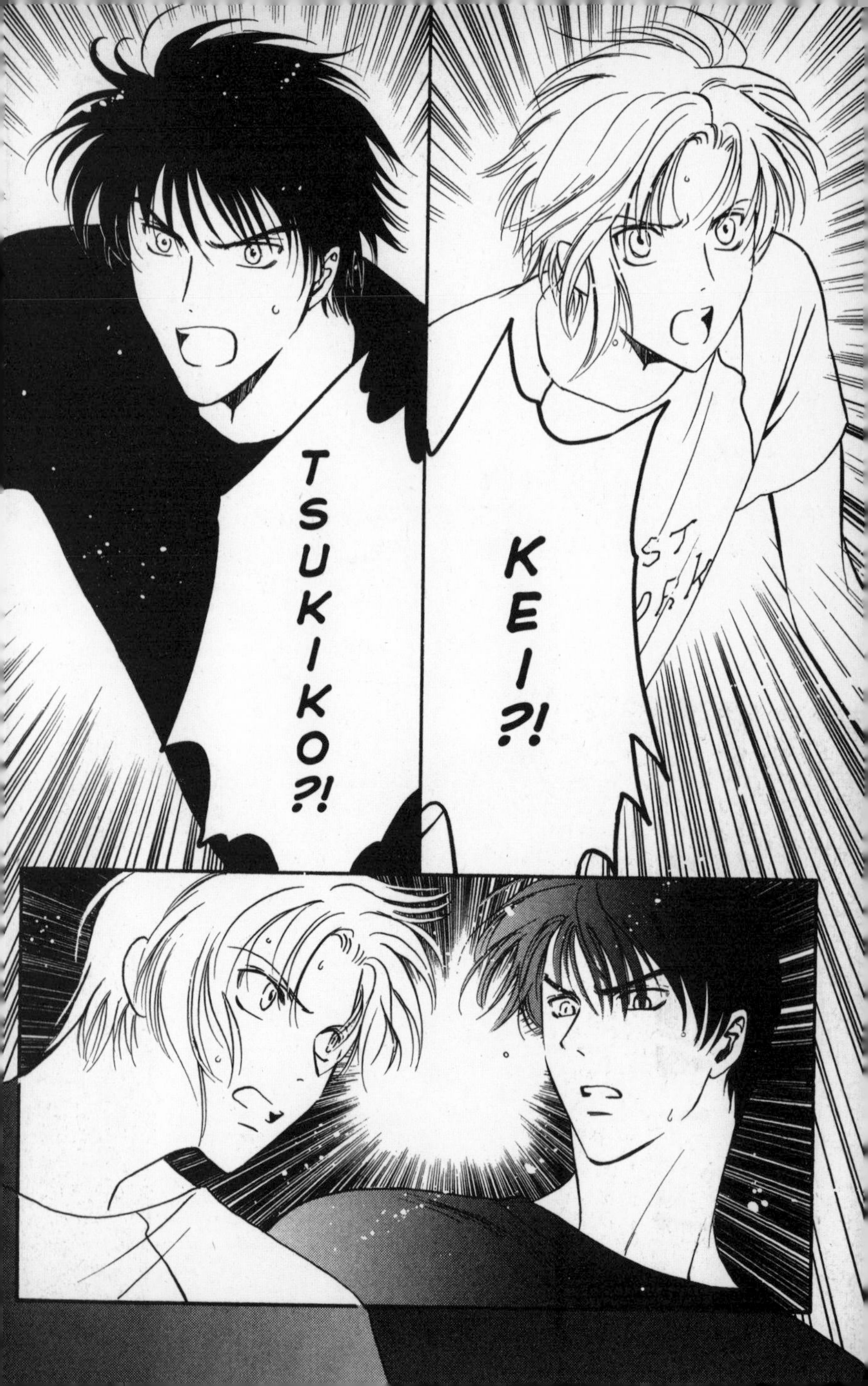
KEI?!
TSUKIKO?!

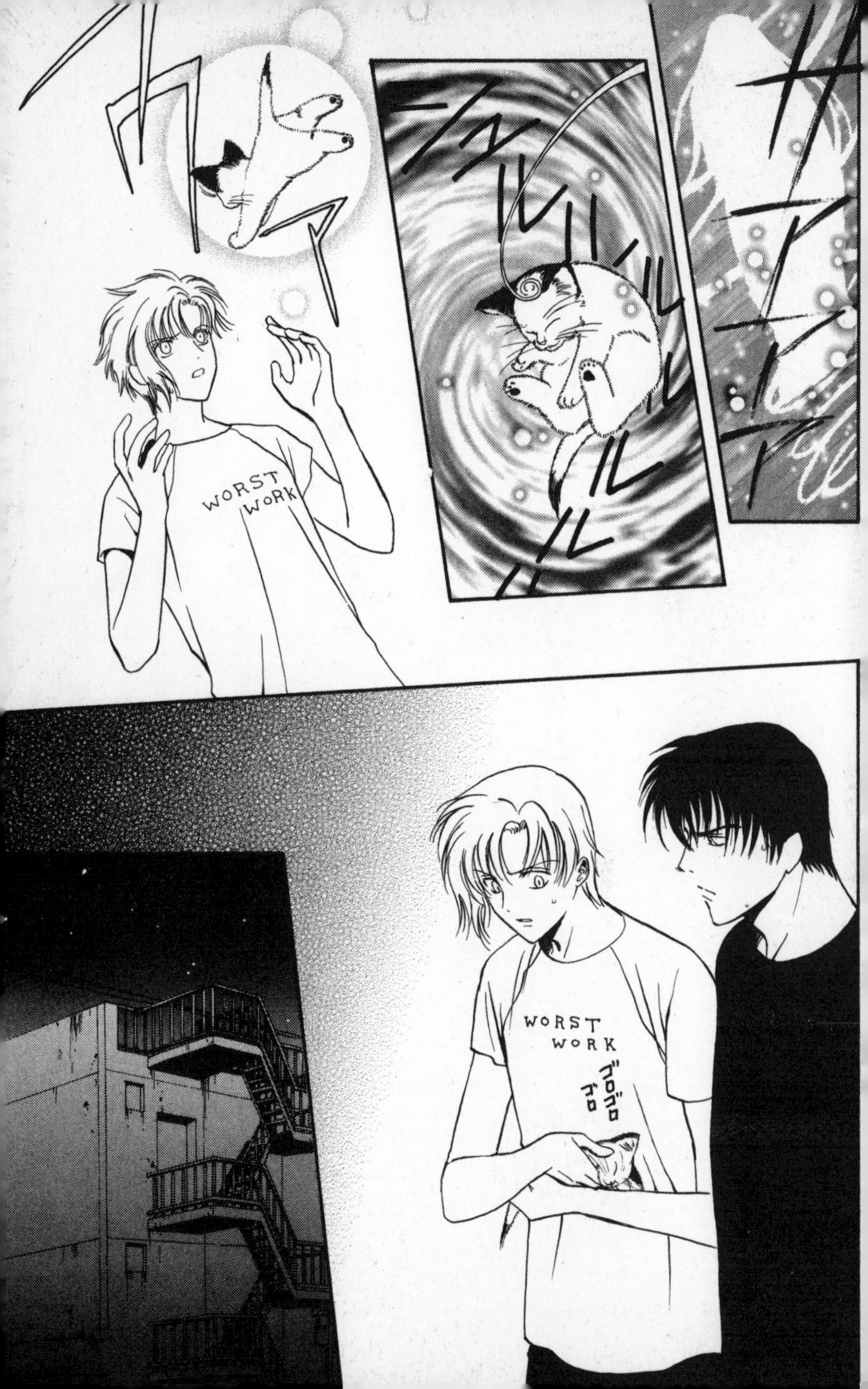
サァァァァ
フォルルルルル
カァ
WORST WORK
WORST WORK
ゴロゴロ ゴロ

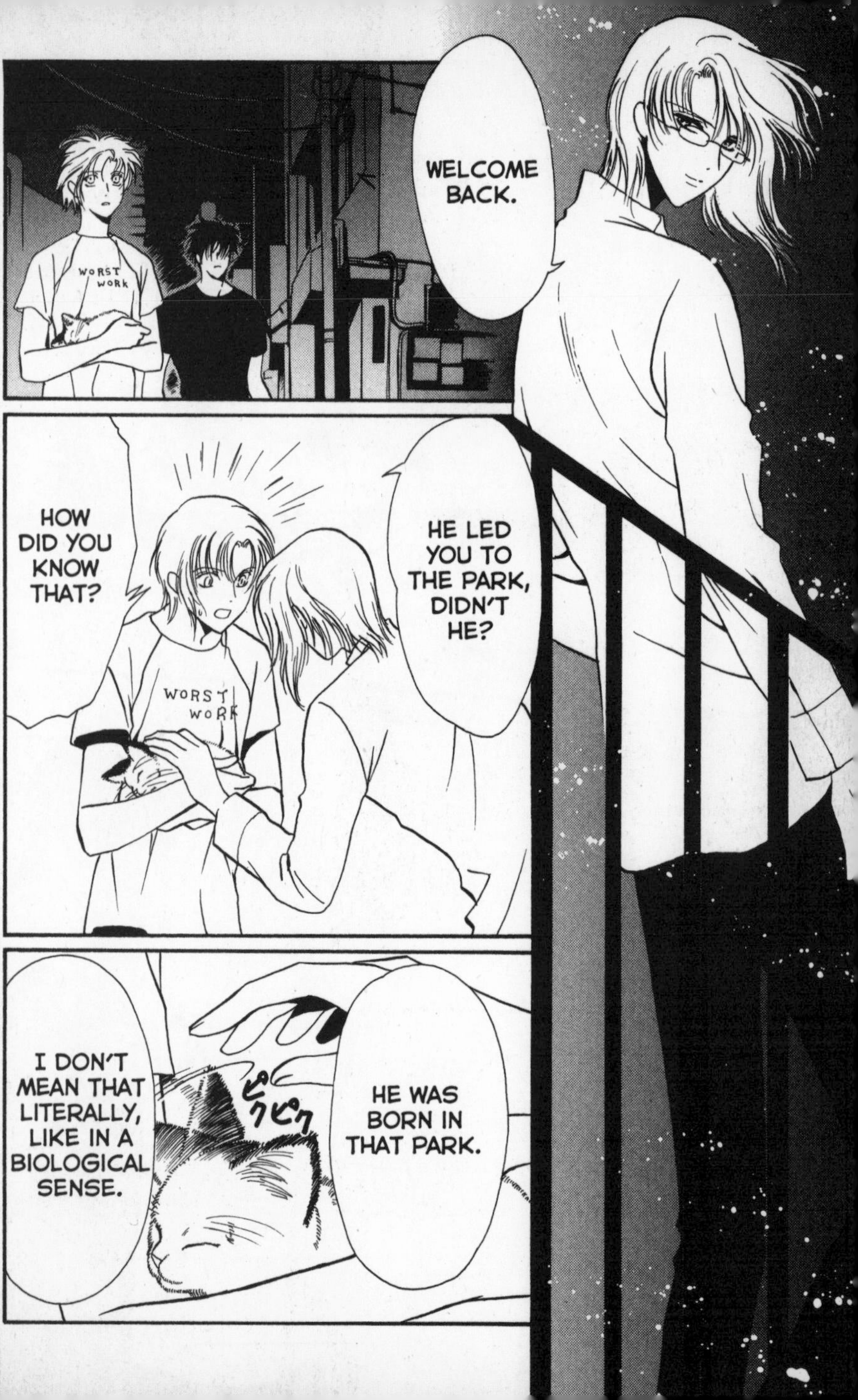
WELCOME BACK.
HE LED YOU TO THE PARK, DIDN'T HE?
HOW DID YOU KNOW THAT?
HE WAS BORN IN THAT PARK.
ピクピク
I DON'T MEAN THAT LITERALLY, LIKE IN A BIOLOGICAL SENSE.

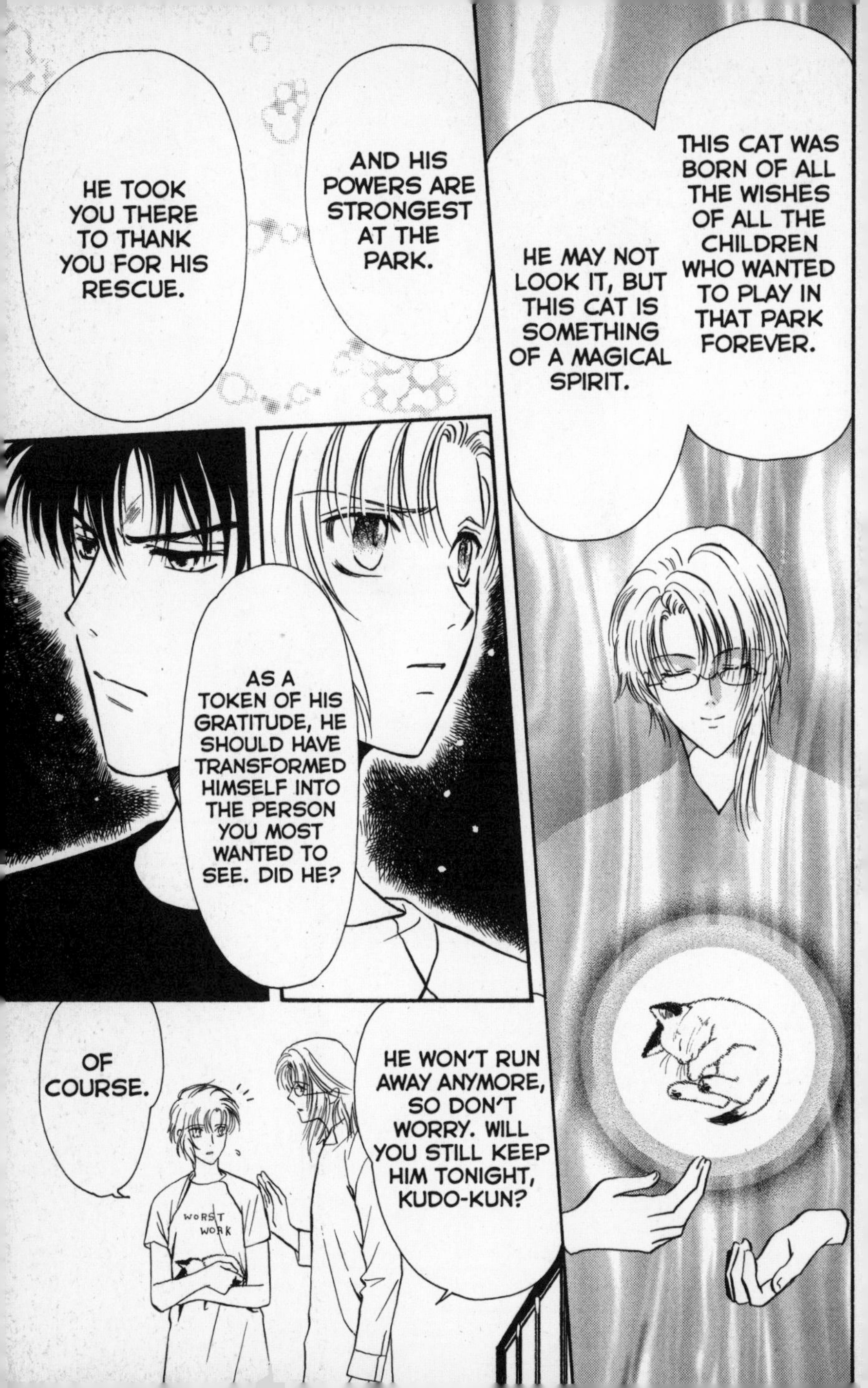
THIS CAT WAS BORN OF ALL THE WISHES OF ALL THE CHILDREN WHO WANTED TO PLAY IN THAT PARK FOREVER.
HE MAY NOT LOOK IT, BUT THIS CAT IS SOMETHING OF A MAGICAL SPIRIT.
AND HIS POWERS ARE STRONGEST AT THE PARK.
HE TOOK YOU THERE TO THANK YOU FOR HIS RESCUE.
AS A TOKEN OF HIS GRATITUDE, HE SHOULD HAVE TRANSFORMED HIMSELF INTO THE PERSON YOU MOST WANTED TO SEE. DID HE?
HE WON'T RUN AWAY ANYMORE, SO DON'T WORRY. WILL YOU STILL KEEP HIM TONIGHT, KUDO-KUN?
OF COURSE.
WORST WORK

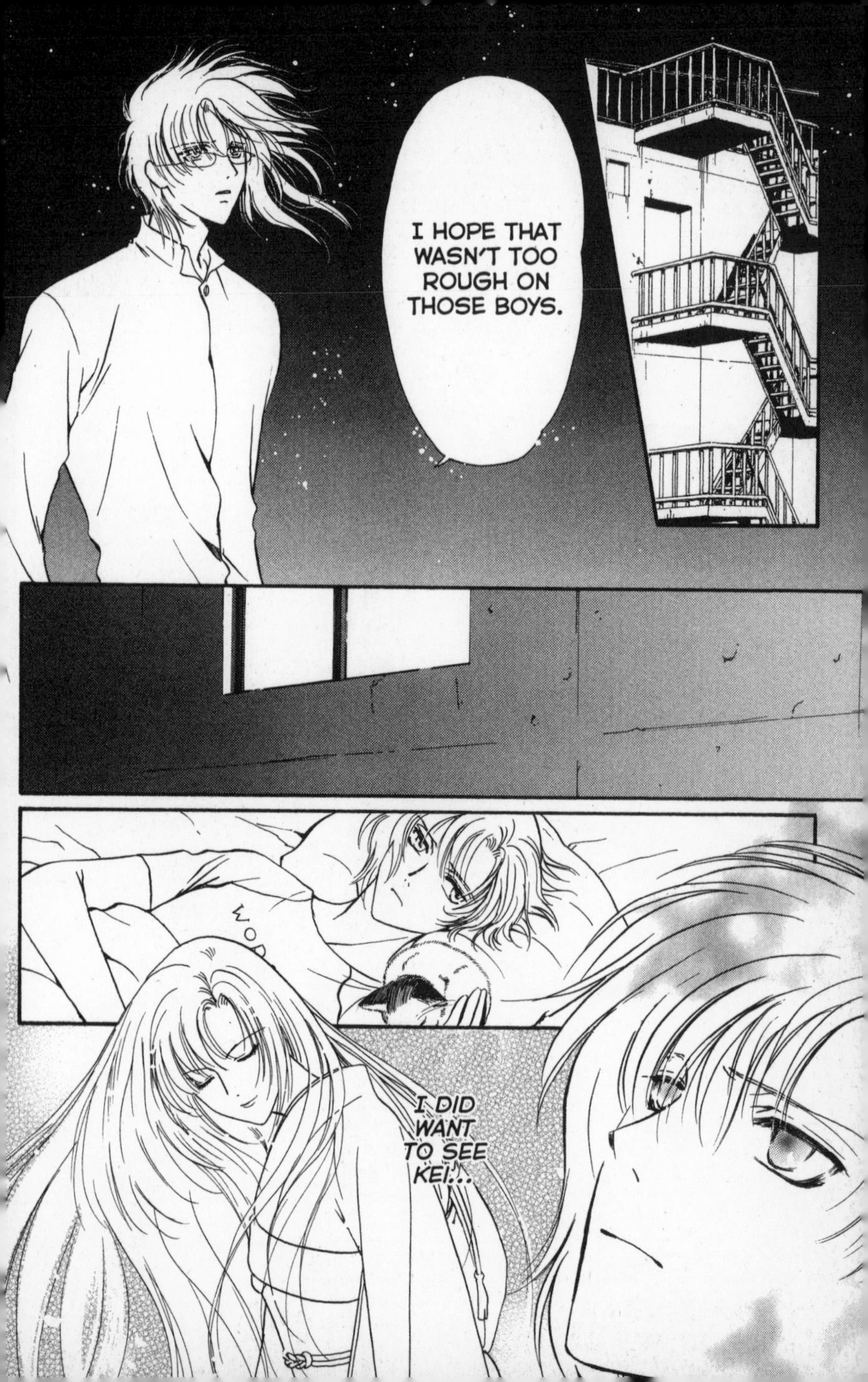
I HOPE THAT WASN'T TOO ROUGH ON THOSE BOYS.
I DID WANT TO SEE KEI...

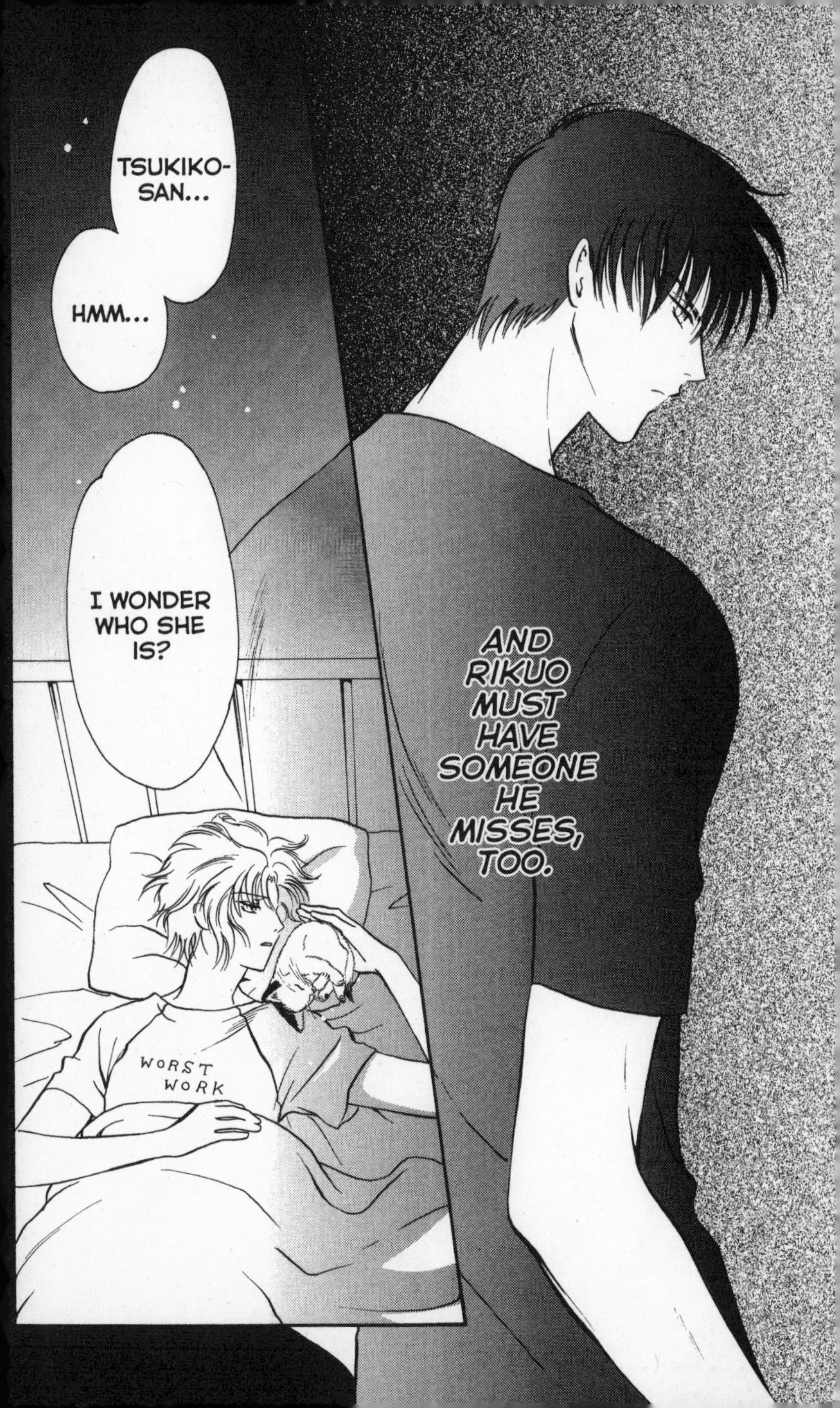
TSUKIKO-SAN...
HMM...
I WONDER WHO SHE IS?
AND RIKUO MUST HAVE SOMEONE HE MISSES, TOO.
WORST WORK

DRUG NO.07

Daily use of the drug may be hazardous.

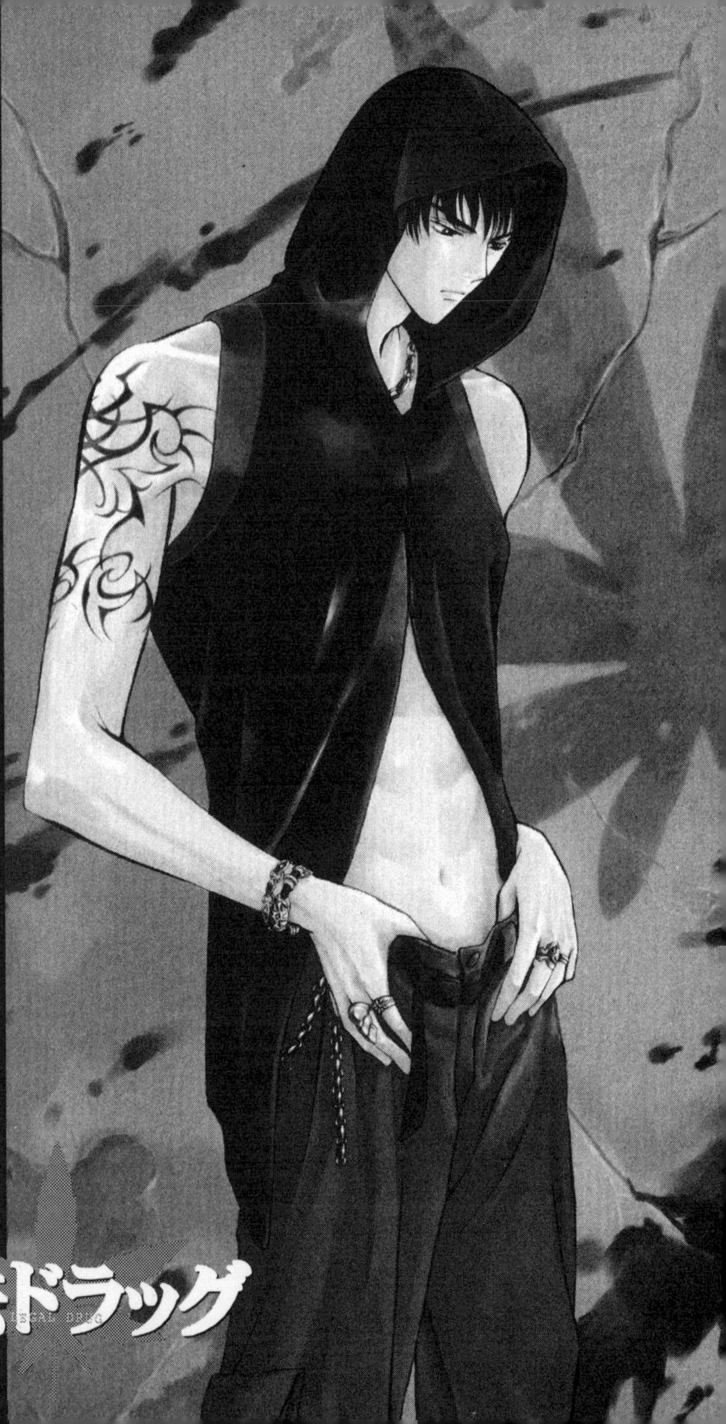
合法ドラッグ
LEGAL DRUG

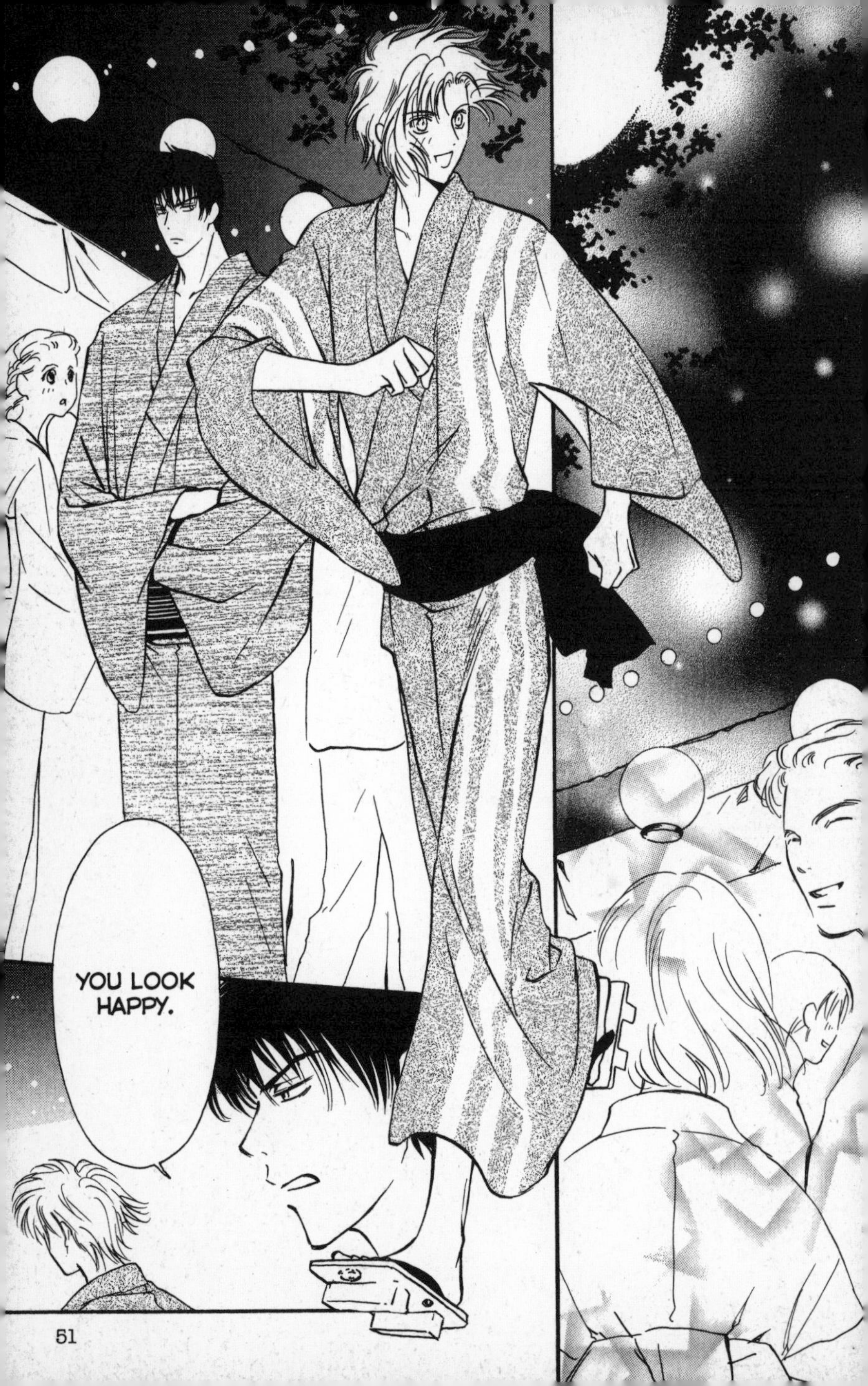
YOU LOOK HAPPY.

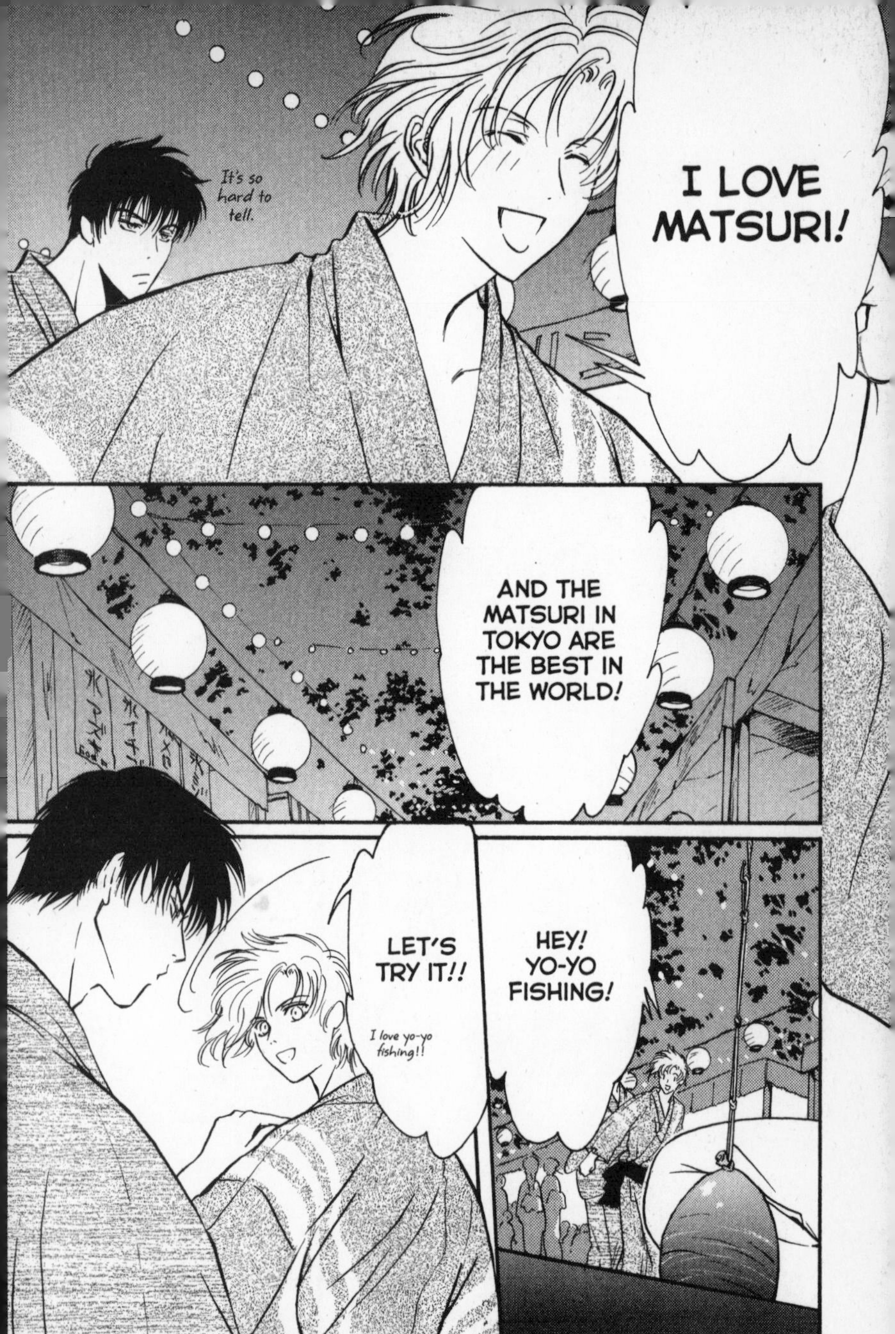
I LOVE MATSURI!
It's so hard to tell.
AND THE MATSURI IN TOKYO ARE THE BEST IN THE WORLD!
HEY! YO-YO FISHING!
LET'S TRY IT!!
I love yo-yo fishing!!

Matsuri – Japanese street festivals

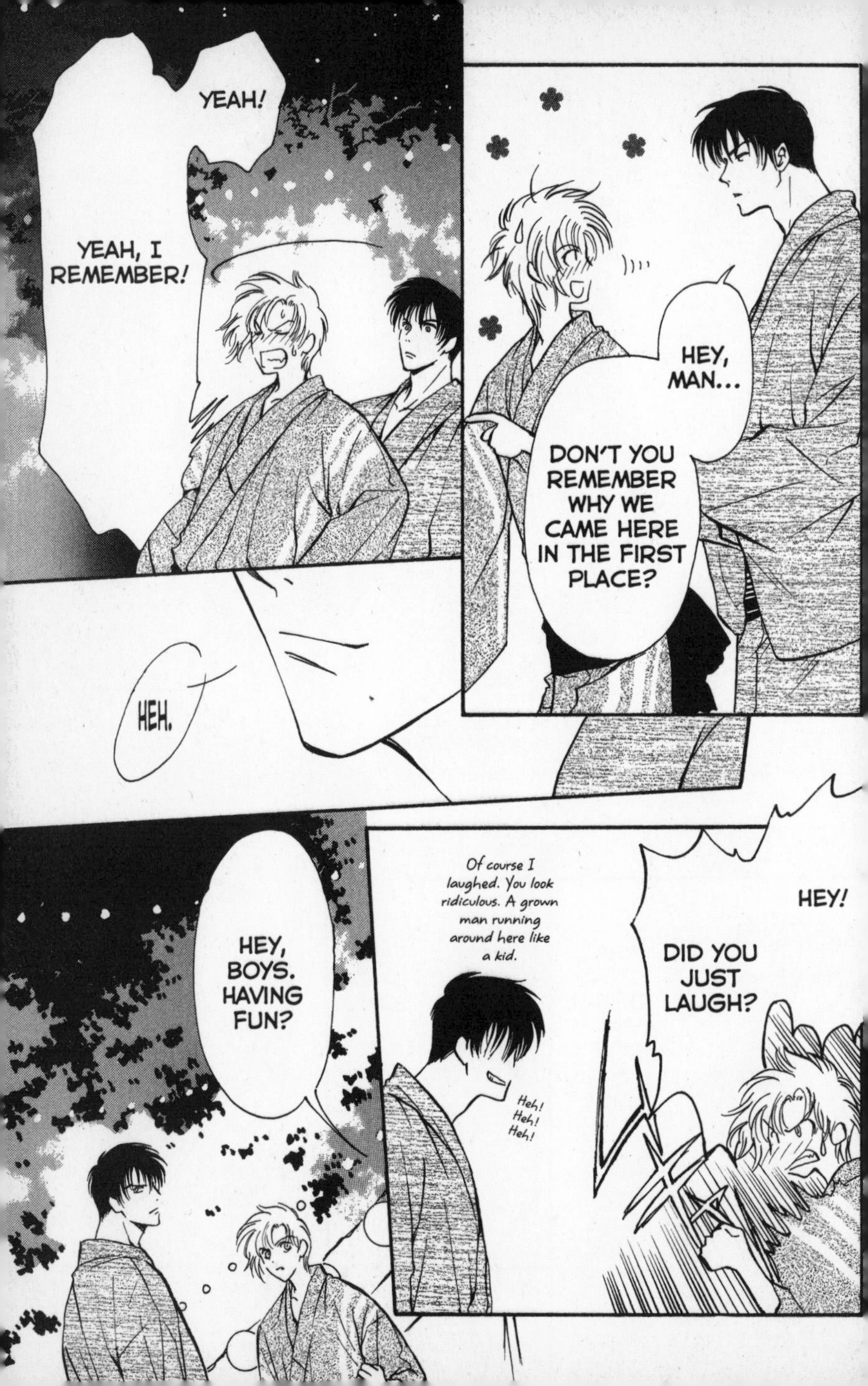
HEY, MAN...
DON'T YOU REMEMBER WHY WE CAME HERE IN THE FIRST PLACE?
YEAH!
YEAH, I REMEMBER!
HEH.
HEY!
DID YOU JUST LAUGH?
Of course I laughed. You look ridiculous. A grown man running around here like a kid.
Heh! Heh! Heh!
HEY, BOYS. HAVING FUN?

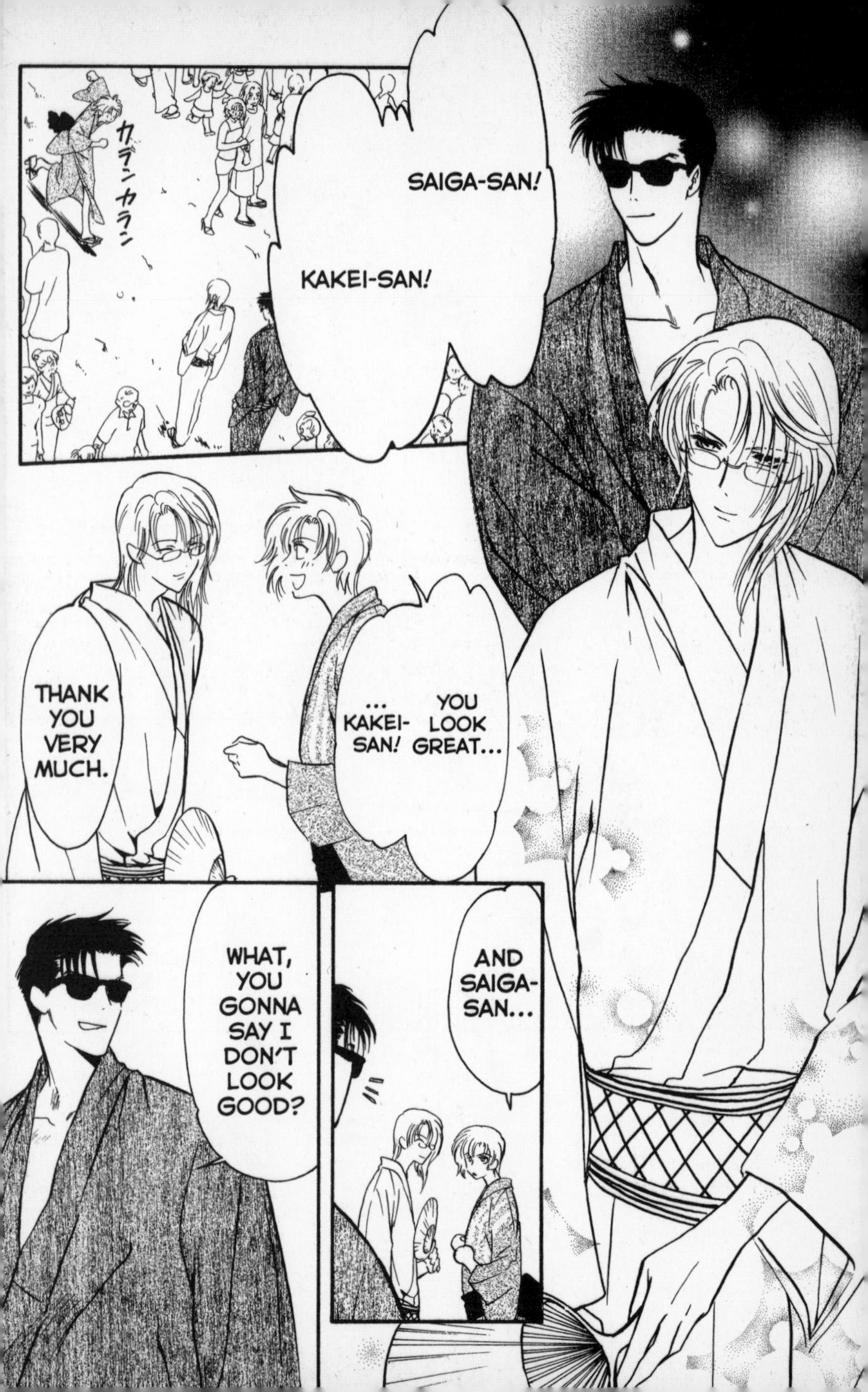

SAIGA-SAN!
KAKEI-SAN!
カランカラン
... KAKEI-SAN! YOU LOOK GREAT...
THANK YOU VERY MUCH.
AND SAIGA-SAN...
WHAT, YOU GONNA SAY I DON'T LOOK GOOD?

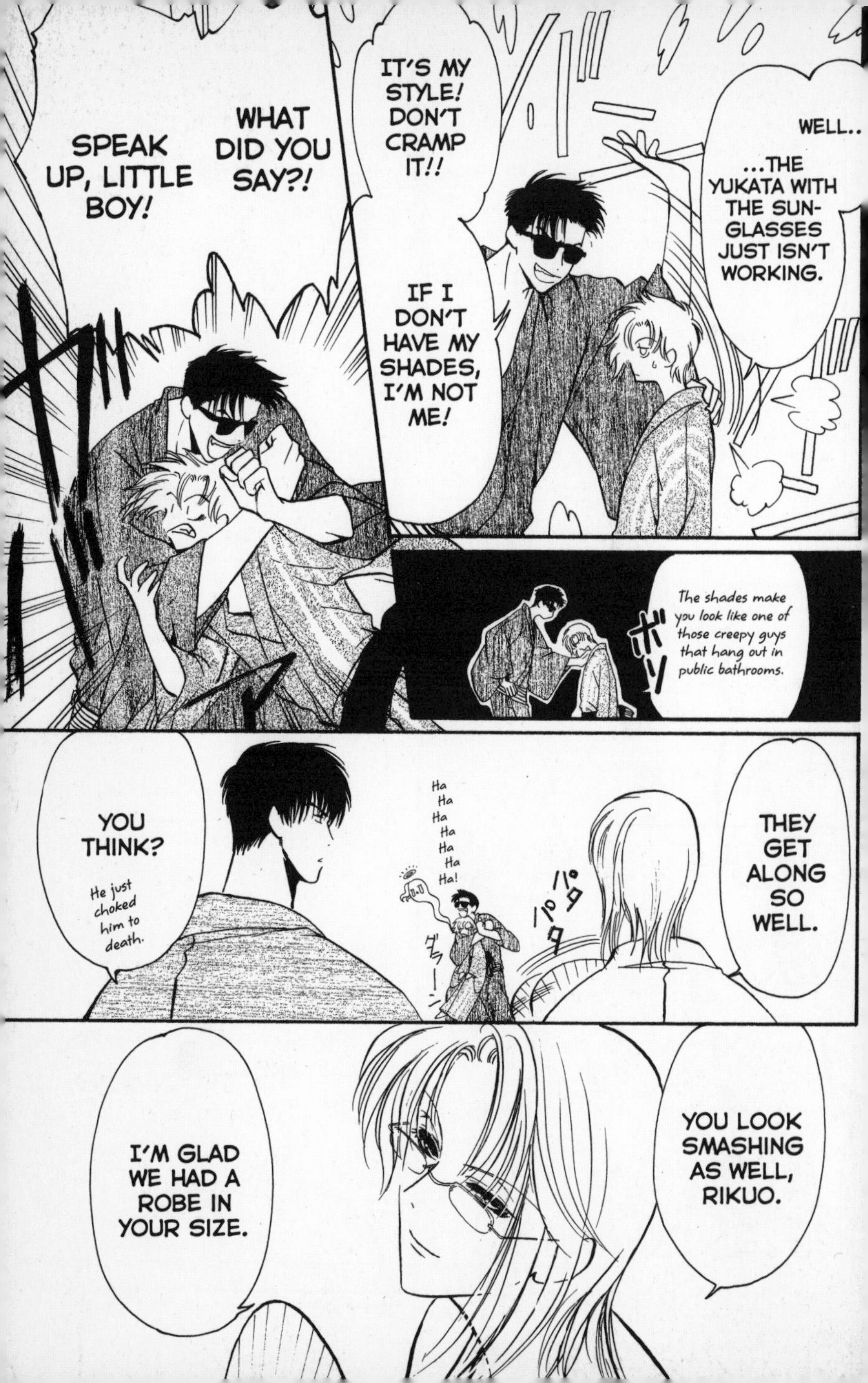
WELL..
...THE YUKATA WITH THE SUN-GLASSES JUST ISN'T WORKING.
IT'S MY STYLE! DON'T CRAMP IT!!
IF I DON'T HAVE MY SHADES, I'M NOT ME!
The shades make you look like one of those creepy guys that hang out in public bathrooms.
WHAT DID YOU SAY?!
SPEAK UP, LITTLE BOY!
THEY GET ALONG SO WELL.
パタパタ
Ha Ha Ha Ha Ha Ha Ha!
YOU THINK?
He just choked him to death.
YOU LOOK SMASHING AS WELL, RIKUO.
I'M GLAD WE HAD A ROBE IN YOUR SIZE.

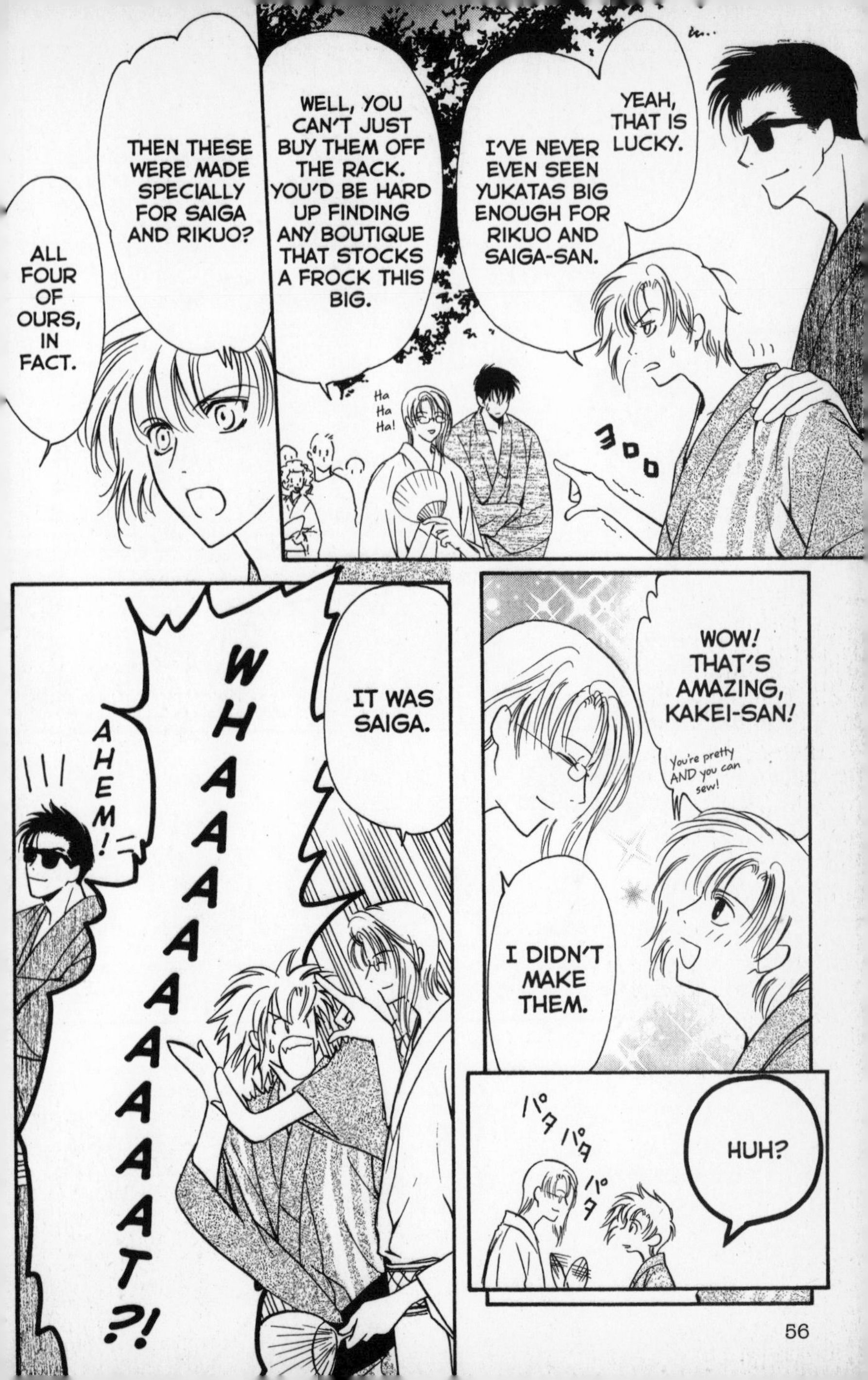
YEAH, THAT IS LUCKY.
I'VE NEVER EVEN SEEN YUKATAS BIG ENOUGH FOR RIKUO AND SAIGA-SAN.
WELL, YOU CAN'T JUST BUY THEM OFF THE RACK. YOU'D BE HARD UP FINDING ANY BOUTIQUE THAT STOCKS A FROCK THIS BIG.
Ha Ha Ha!
ヨロ
THEN THESE WERE MADE SPECIALLY FOR SAIGA AND RIKUO?
ALL FOUR OF OURS, IN FACT.
WOW! THAT'S AMAZING, KAKEI-SAN!
You're pretty AND you can sew!
I DIDN'T MAKE THEM.
HUH?
パタパタパタ
IT WAS SAIGA.
WHAAAAAAAAAT?!
AHEM!

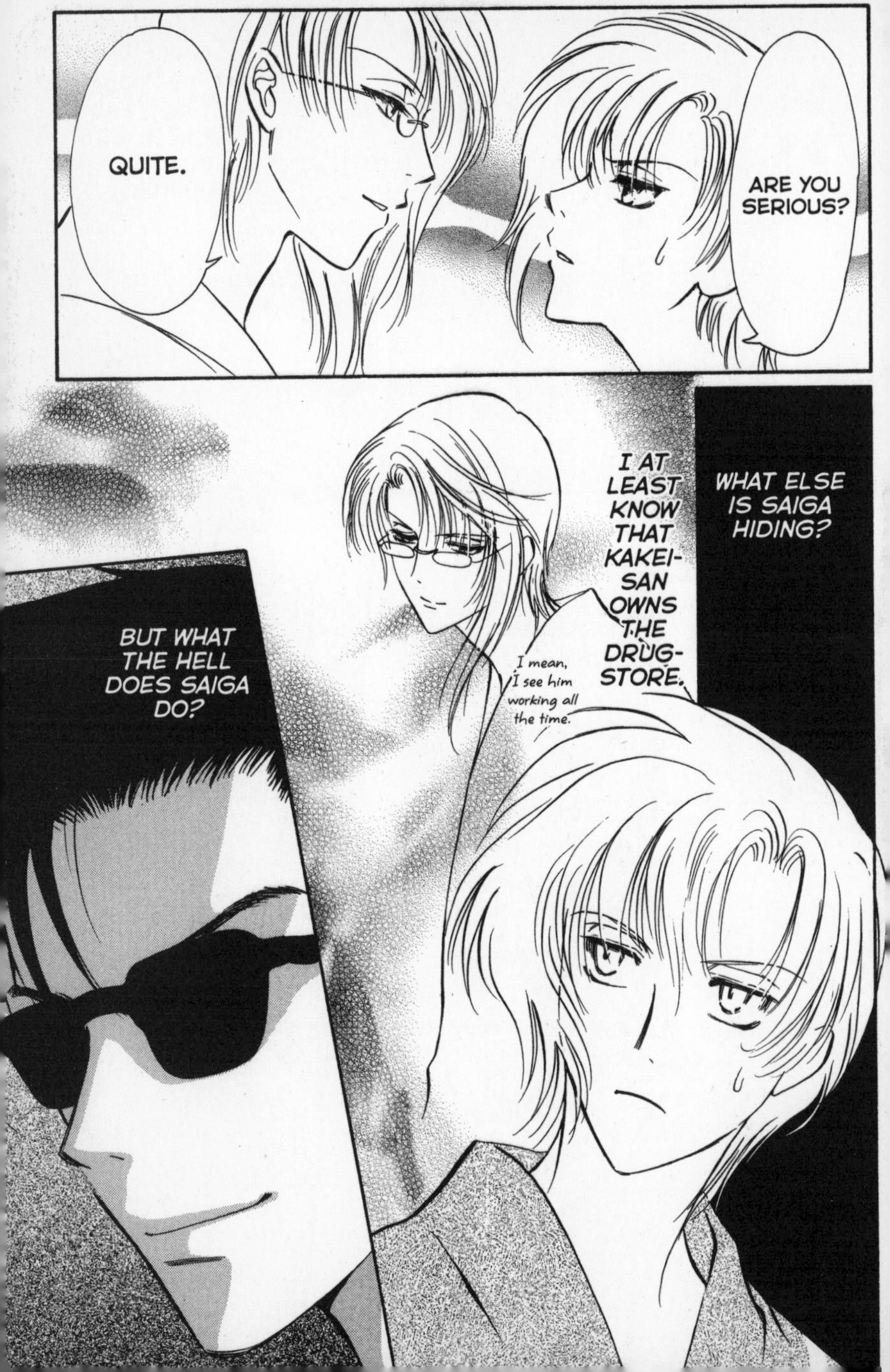
ARE YOU SERIOUS?
QUITE.
WHAT ELSE IS SAIGA HIDING?
I AT LEAST KNOW THAT KAKEI-SAN OWNS THE DRUG-STORE.
I mean, I see him working all the time.
BUT WHAT THE HELL DOES SAIGA DO?

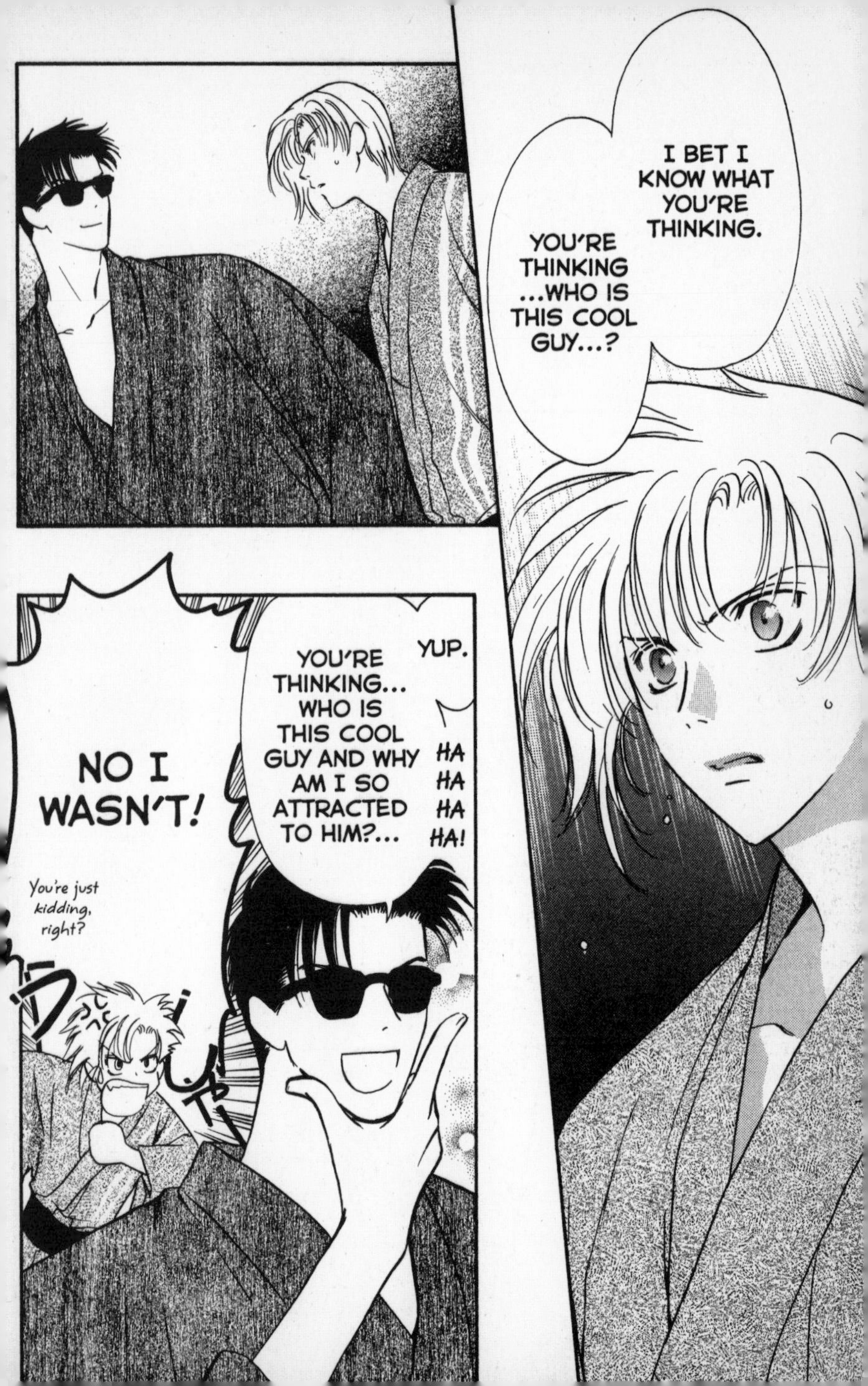
I BET I KNOW WHAT YOU'RE THINKING.
YOU'RE THINKING ...WHO IS THIS COOL GUY...?
YOU'RE THINKING... WHO IS THIS COOL GUY AND WHY AM I SO ATTRACTED TO HIM?...
YUP.
HA HA HA HA!
NO I WASN'T!
You're just kidding, right?

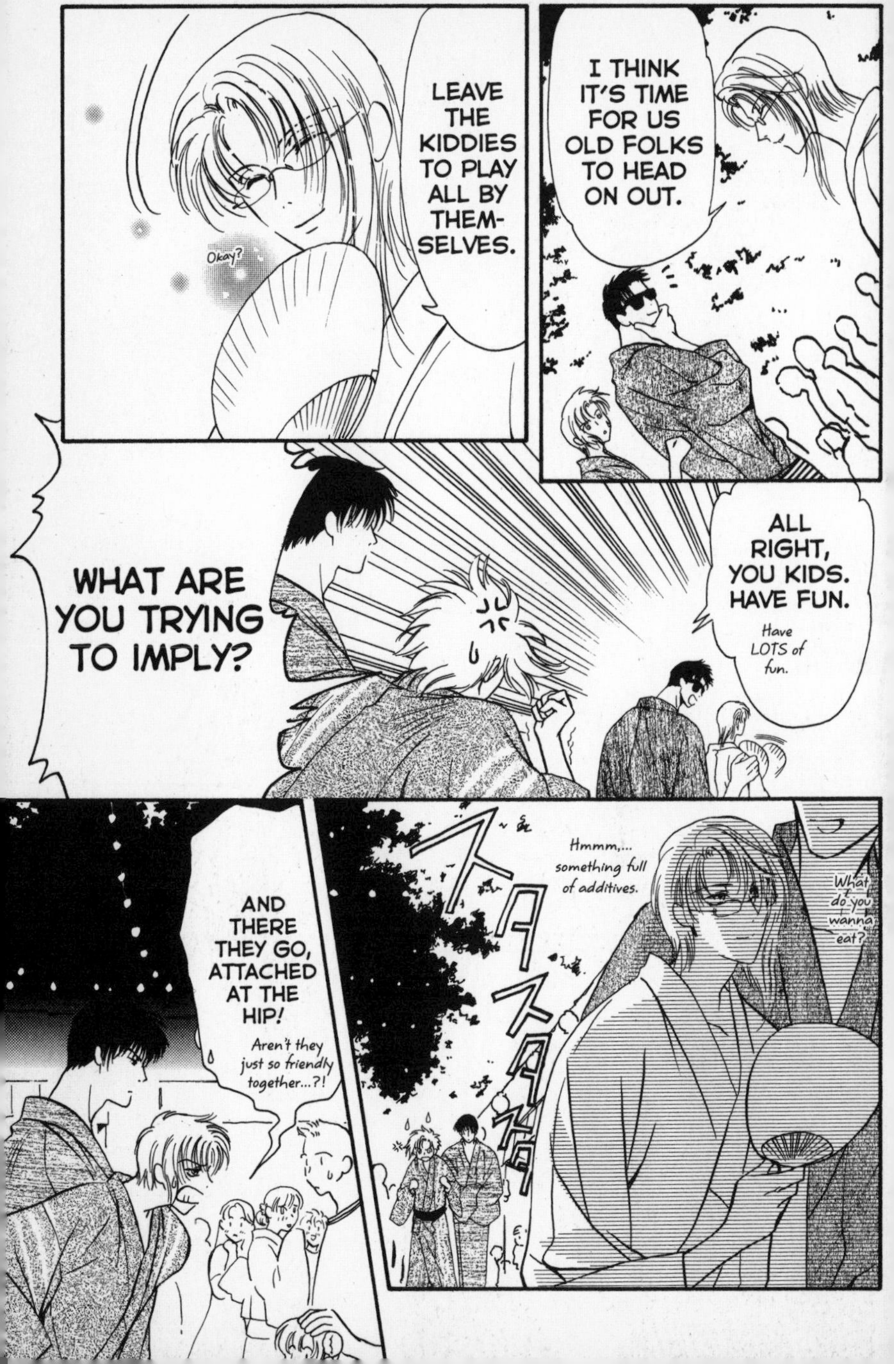
I THINK IT'S TIME FOR US OLD FOLKS TO HEAD ON OUT.
LEAVE THE KIDDIES TO PLAY ALL BY THEM-SELVES.
Okay?
ALL RIGHT, YOU KIDS. HAVE FUN.
Have LOTS of fun.
WHAT ARE YOU TRYING TO IMPLY?
What do you wanna eat?
Hmmm,... something full of additives.
AND THERE THEY GO, ATTACHED AT THE HIP!
Aren't they just so friendly together...?!

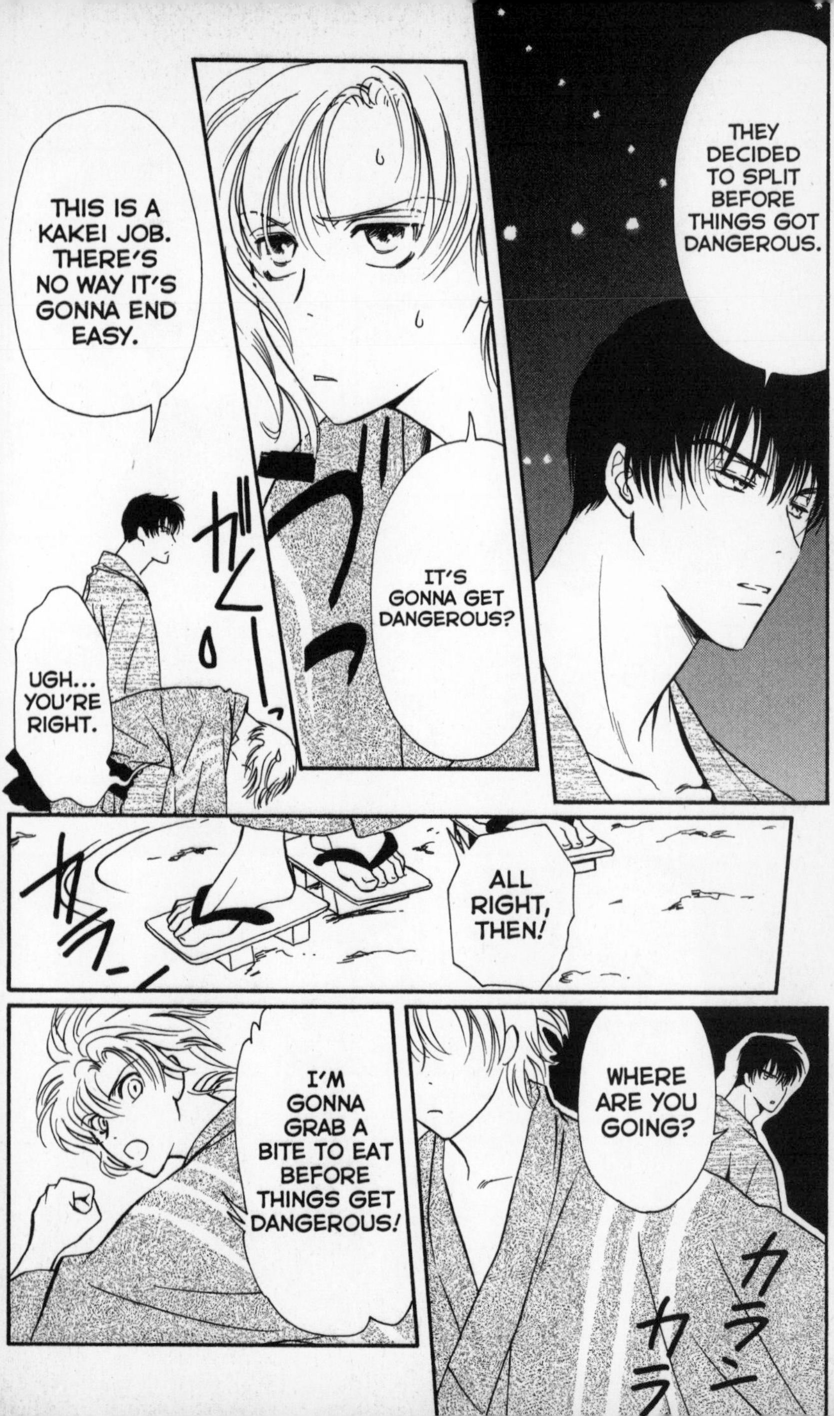
THEY DECIDED TO SPLIT BEFORE THINGS GOT DANGEROUS.
IT'S GONNA GET DANGEROUS?
THIS IS A KAKEI JOB. THERE'S NO WAY IT'S GONNA END EASY.
UGH... YOU'RE RIGHT.
ALL RIGHT, THEN!
WHERE ARE YOU GOING?
カラン
カラ
I'M GONNA GRAB A BITE TO EAT BEFORE THINGS GET DANGEROUS!

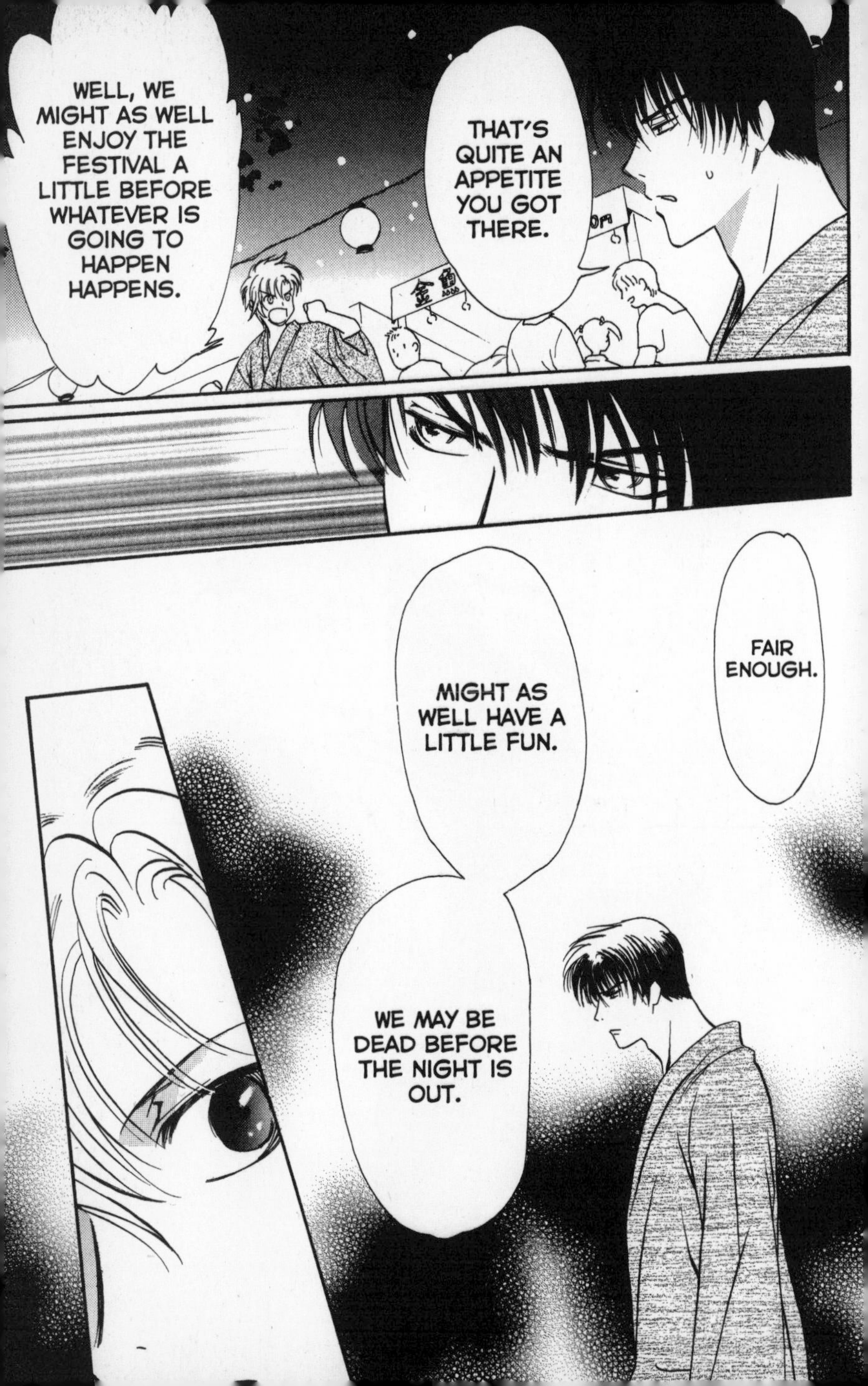
THAT'S QUITE AN APPETITE YOU GOT THERE.
WELL, WE MIGHT AS WELL ENJOY THE FESTIVAL A LITTLE BEFORE WHATEVER IS GOING TO HAPPEN HAPPENS.
FAIR ENOUGH.
MIGHT AS WELL HAVE A LITTLE FUN.
WE MAY BE DEAD BEFORE THE NIGHT IS OUT.

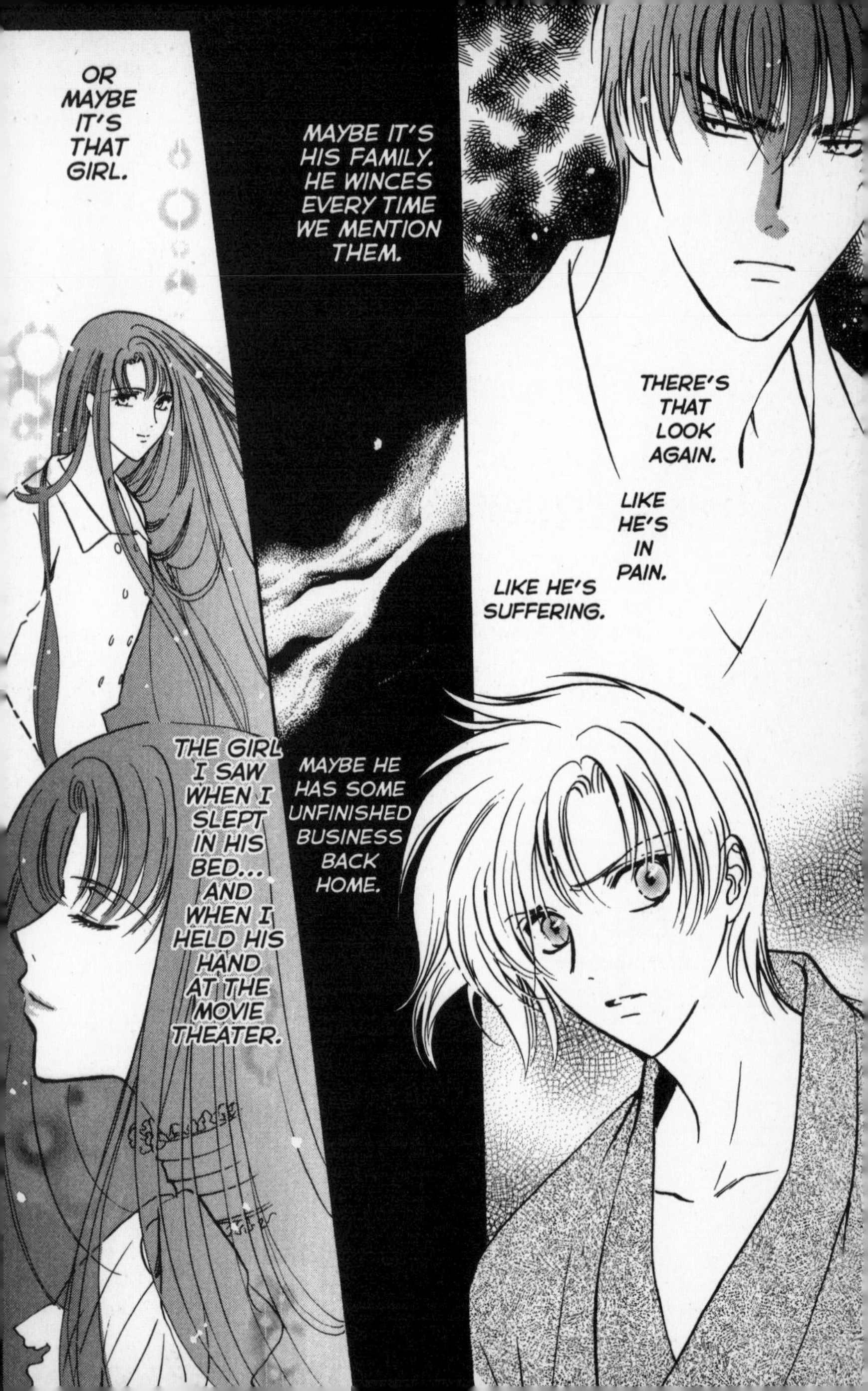
THERE'S THAT LOOK AGAIN.
LIKE HE'S IN PAIN.
LIKE HE'S SUFFERING.
MAYBE IT'S HIS FAMILY. HE WINCES EVERY TIME WE MENTION THEM.
OR MAYBE IT'S THAT GIRL.
MAYBE HE HAS SOME UNFINISHED BUSINESS BACK HOME.
THE GIRL I SAW WHEN I SLEPT IN HIS BED... AND WHEN I HELD HIS HAND AT THE MOVIE THEATER.

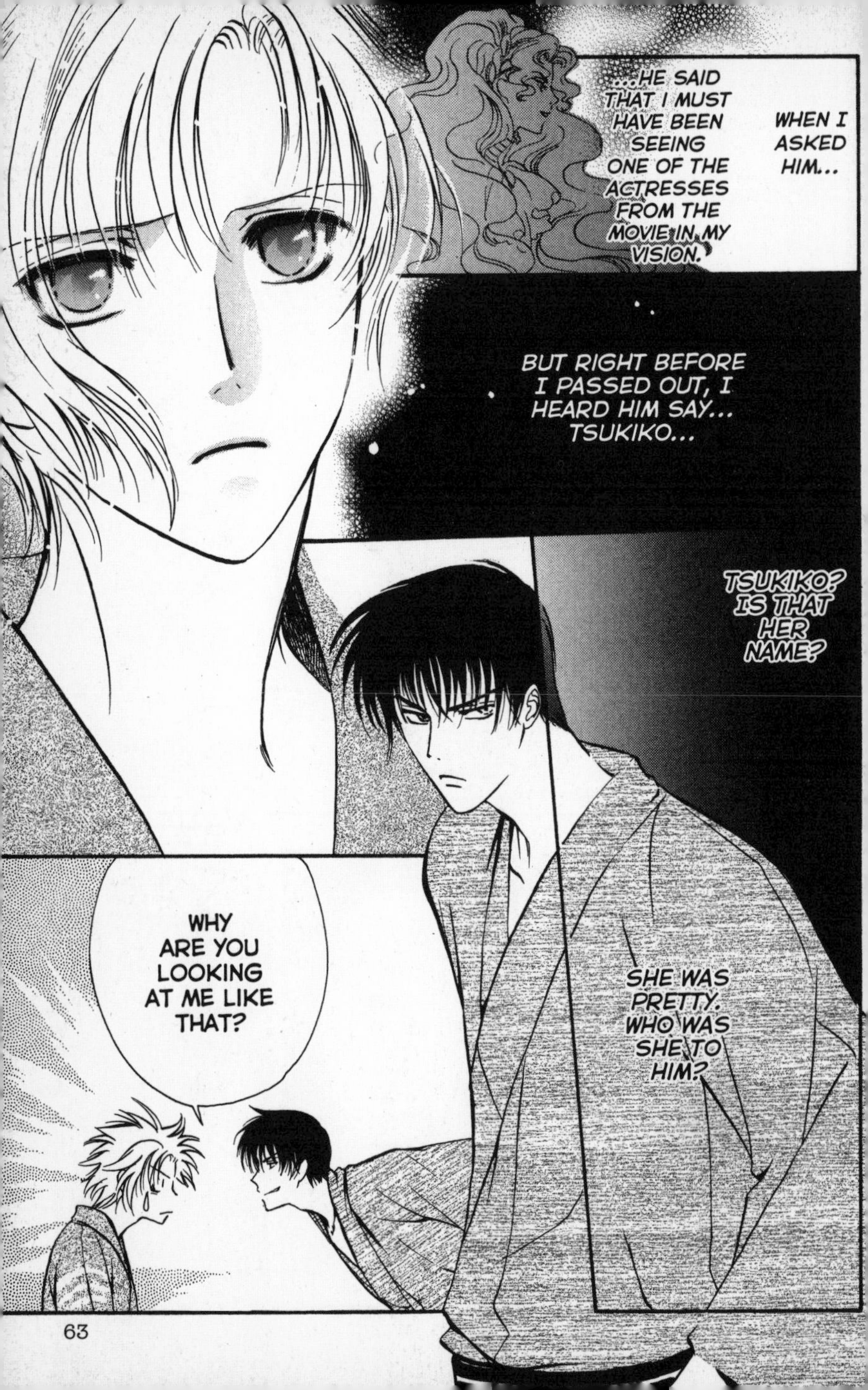
WHEN I ASKED HIM...
...HE SAID THAT I MUST HAVE BEEN SEEING ONE OF THE ACTRESSES FROM THE MOVIE IN MY VISION.
BUT RIGHT BEFORE I PASSED OUT, I HEARD HIM SAY... TSUKIKO...
TSUKIKO? IS THAT HER NAME?
SHE WAS PRETTY. WHO WAS SHE TO HIM?
WHY ARE YOU LOOKING AT ME LIKE THAT?

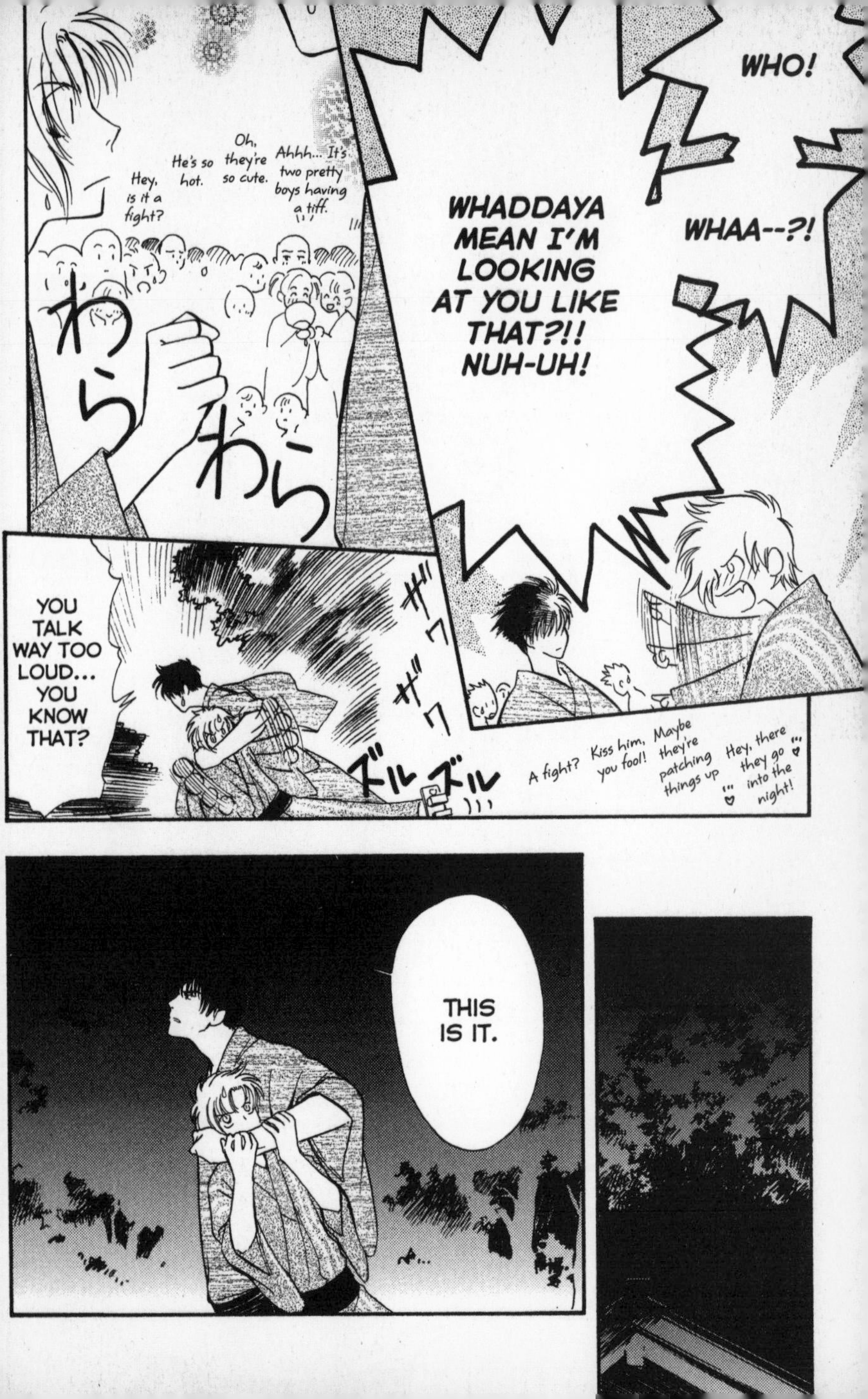
WHO!
WHAA--?!
WHADDAYA MEAN I'M LOOKING AT YOU LIKE THAT?!! NUH-UH!
Ahhh... It's two pretty boys having a tiff.
Oh, they're so cute.
He's so hot.
Hey, is it a fight?
わら
わら
Hey, there they go into the night!
Maybe they're patching things up
Kiss him, you fool!
A fight?
ザワ
ザワ
ズル
ズル
YOU TALK WAY TOO LOUD... YOU KNOW THAT?
THIS IS IT.

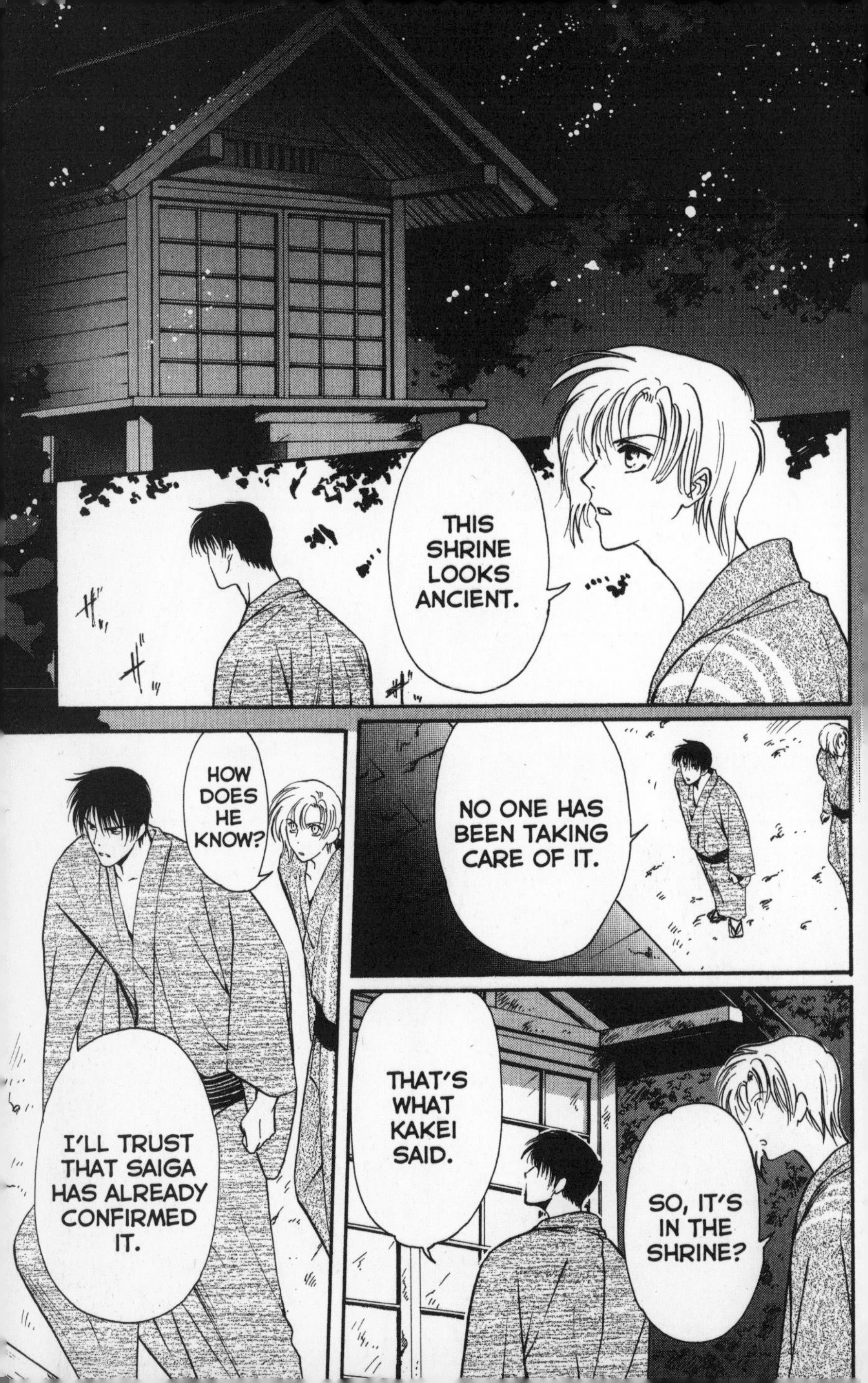
THIS SHRINE LOOKS ANCIENT.
NO ONE HAS BEEN TAKING CARE OF IT.
SO, IT'S IN THE SHRINE?
THAT'S WHAT KAKEI SAID.
HOW DOES HE KNOW?
I'LL TRUST THAT SAIGA HAS ALREADY CONFIRMED IT.

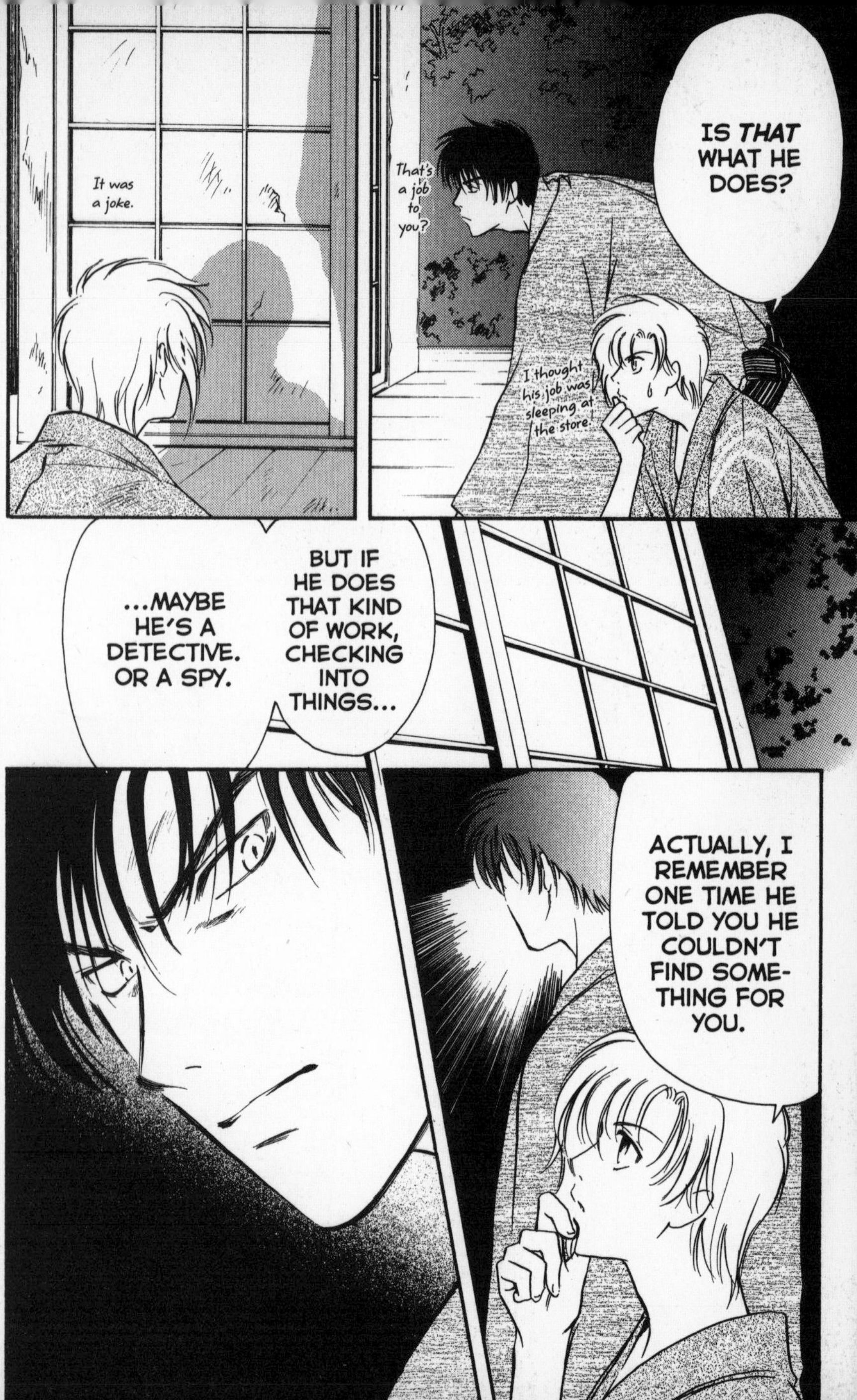
IS *THAT* WHAT HE DOES?
That's a job to you?
I thought his job was sleeping at the store.
It was a joke.
BUT IF HE DOES THAT KIND OF WORK, CHECKING INTO THINGS...
...MAYBE HE'S A DETECTIVE. OR A SPY.
ACTUALLY, I REMEMBER ONE TIME HE TOLD YOU HE COULDN'T FIND SOMETHING FOR YOU.

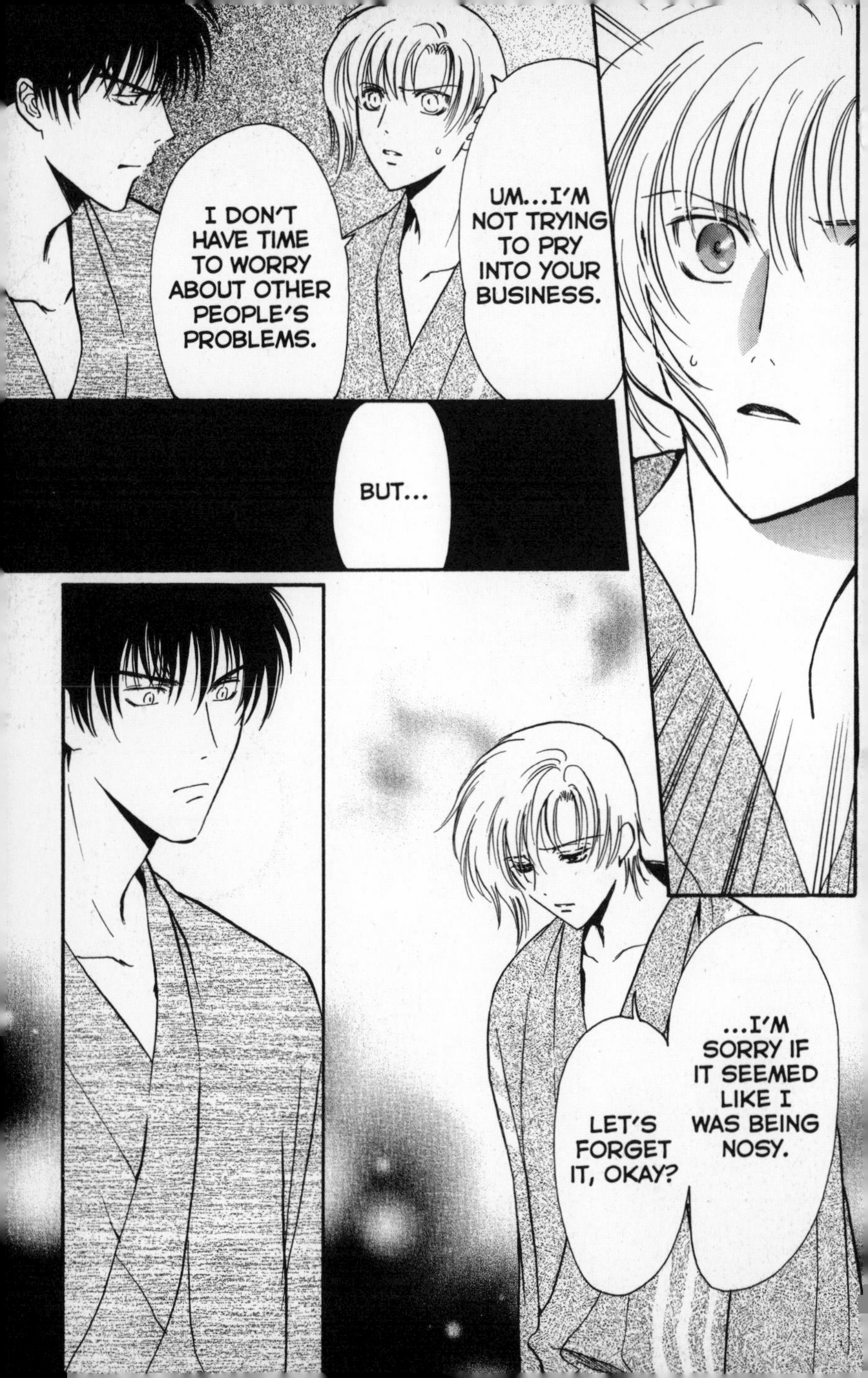
UM...I'M NOT TRYING TO PRY INTO YOUR BUSINESS.
I DON'T HAVE TIME TO WORRY ABOUT OTHER PEOPLE'S PROBLEMS.
BUT...
...I'M SORRY IF IT SEEMED LIKE I WAS BEING NOSY.
LET'S FORGET IT, OKAY?

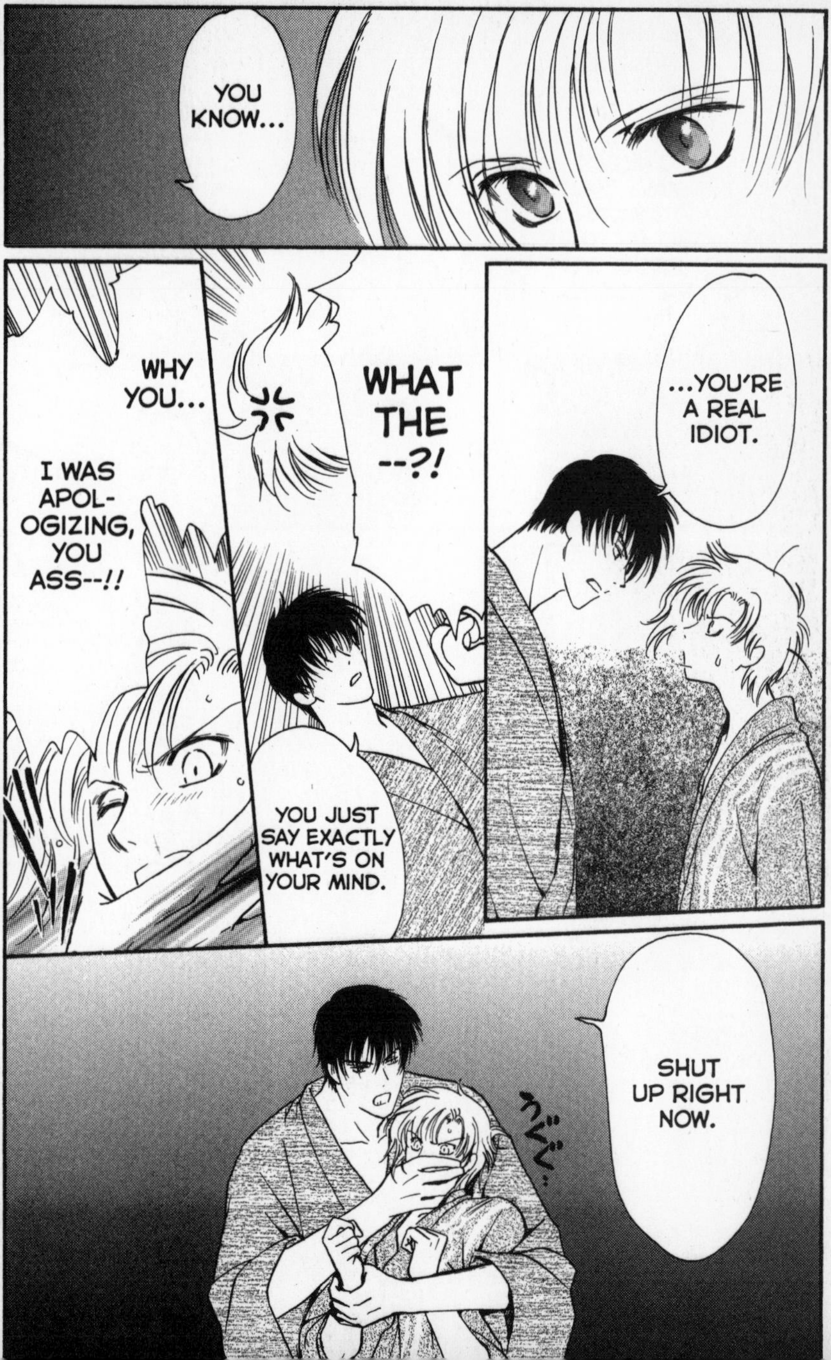
YOU KNOW...
...YOU'RE A REAL IDIOT.
WHAT THE --?!
YOU JUST SAY EXACTLY WHAT'S ON YOUR MIND.
WHY YOU...
I WAS APOLOGIZING, YOU ASS--!!
SHUT UP RIGHT NOW.
うぐぐ…

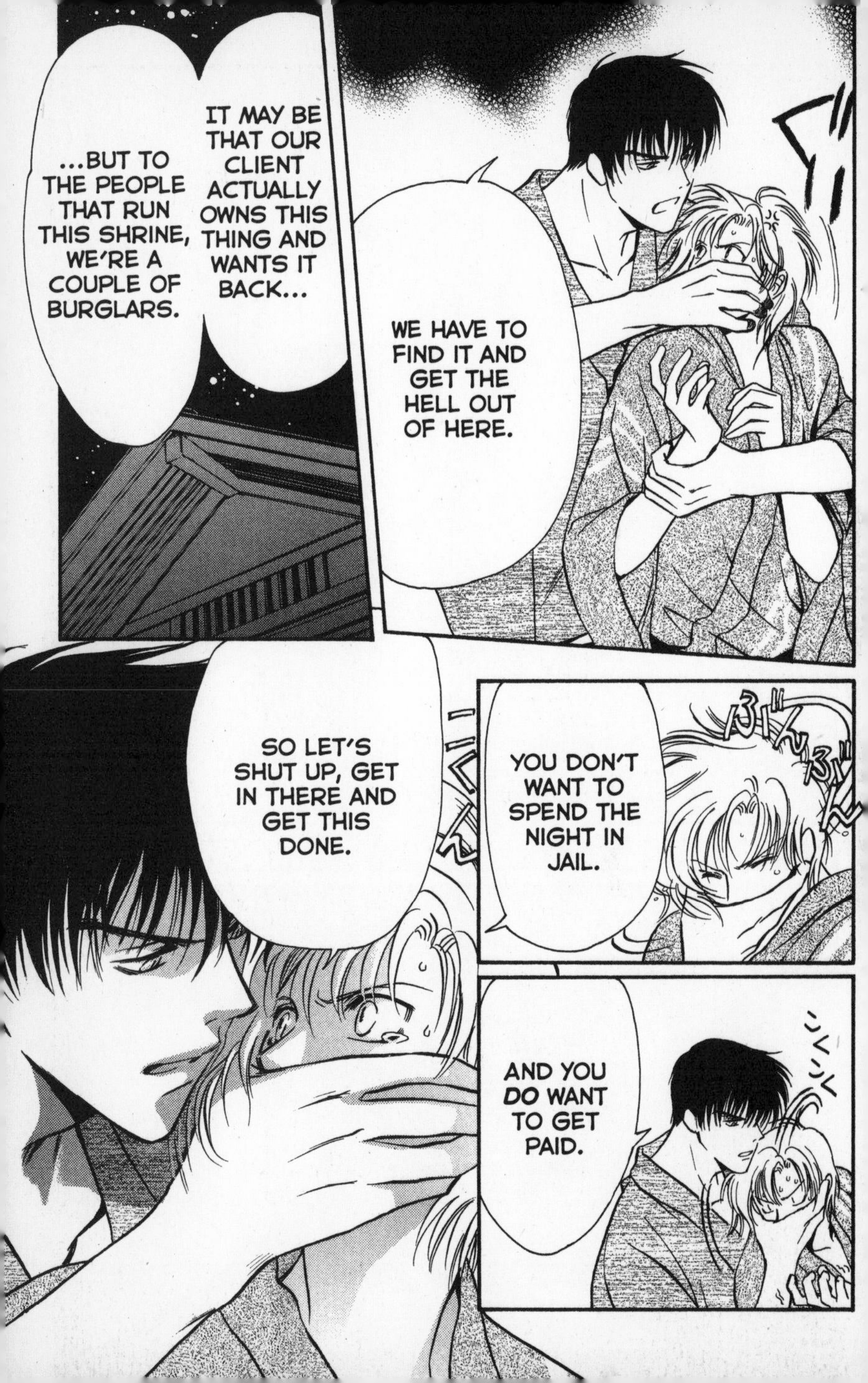
WE HAVE TO FIND IT AND GET THE HELL OUT OF HERE.
IT MAY BE THAT OUR CLIENT ACTUALLY OWNS THIS THING AND WANTS IT BACK...
...BUT TO THE PEOPLE THAT RUN THIS SHRINE, WE'RE A COUPLE OF BURGLARS.
YOU DON'T WANT TO SPEND THE NIGHT IN JAIL.
AND YOU *DO* WANT TO GET PAID.
SO LET'S SHUT UP, GET IN THERE AND GET THIS DONE.

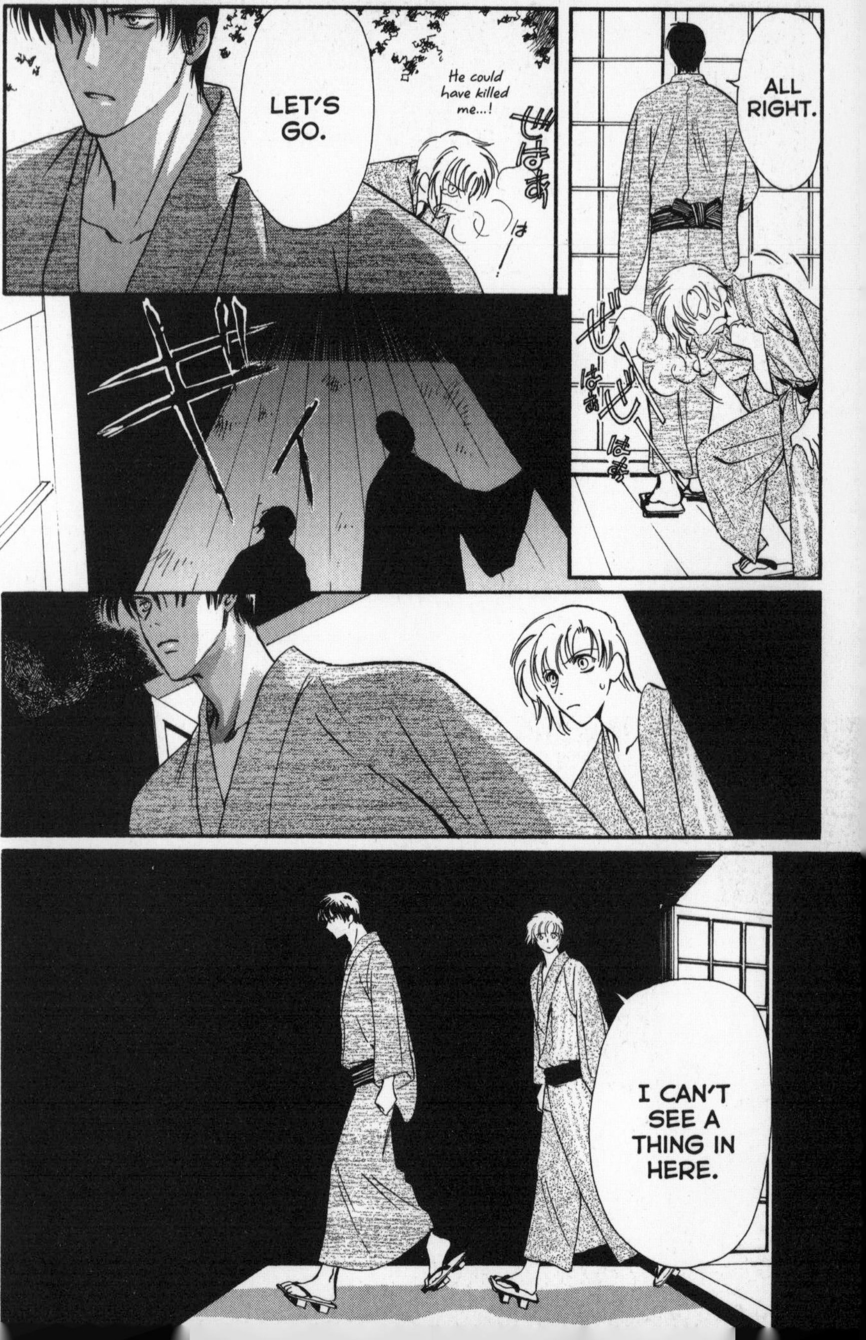
ALL RIGHT.
He could have killed me...!
LET'S GO.
ギイ
I CAN'T SEE A THING IN HERE.

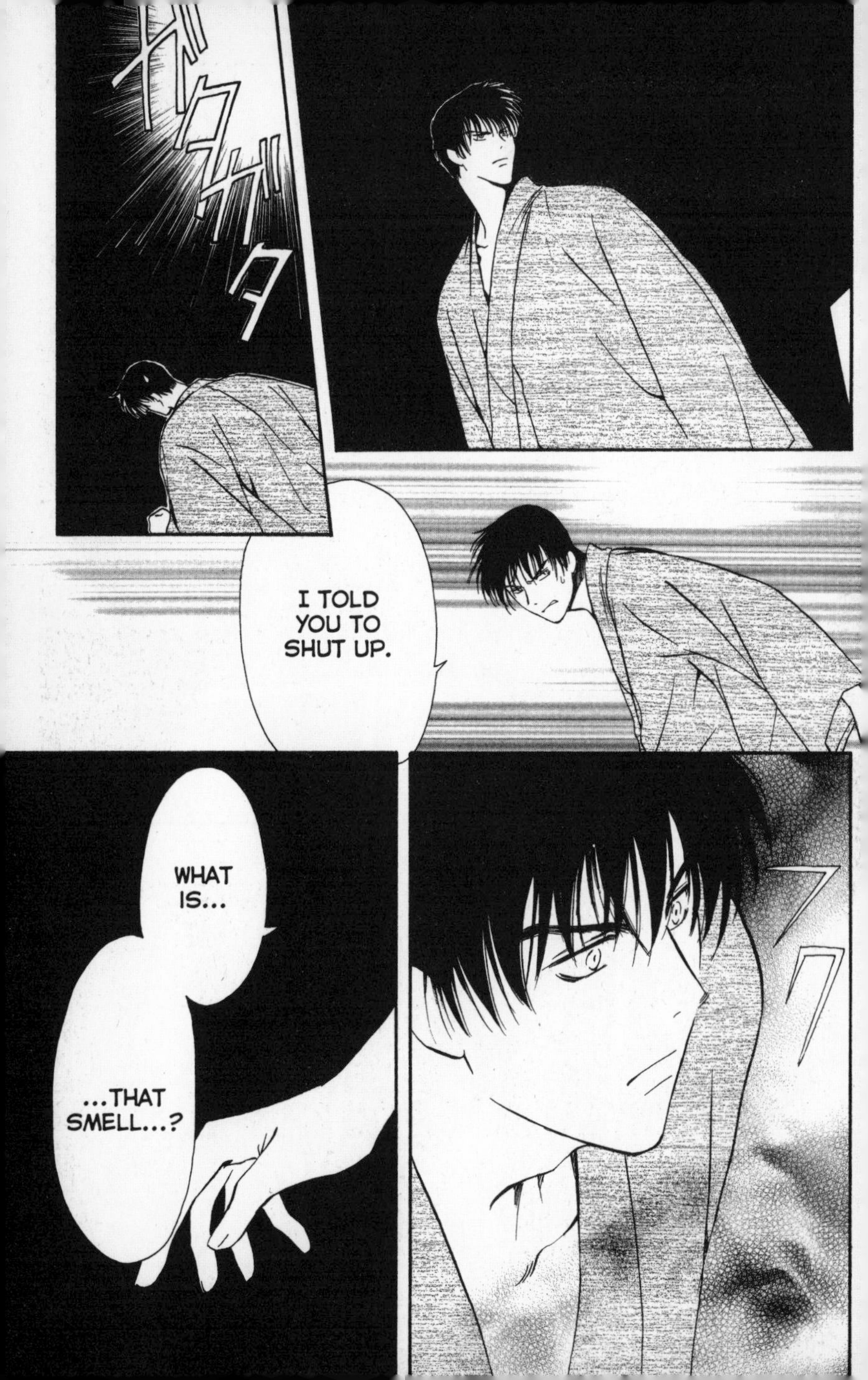
I TOLD YOU TO SHUT UP.
WHAT IS...
...THAT SMELL...?

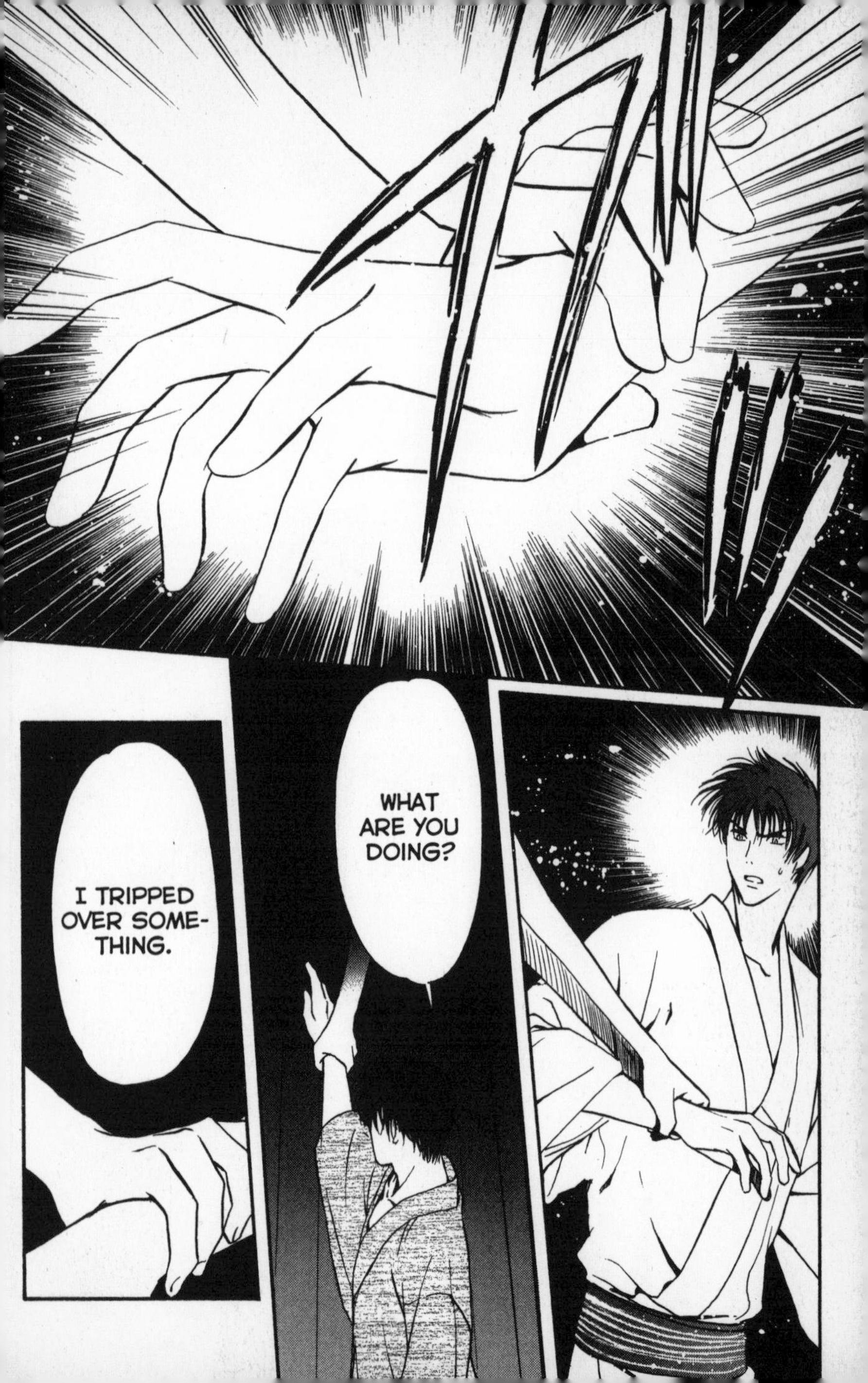
WHAT ARE YOU DOING?
I TRIPPED OVER SOME-THING.

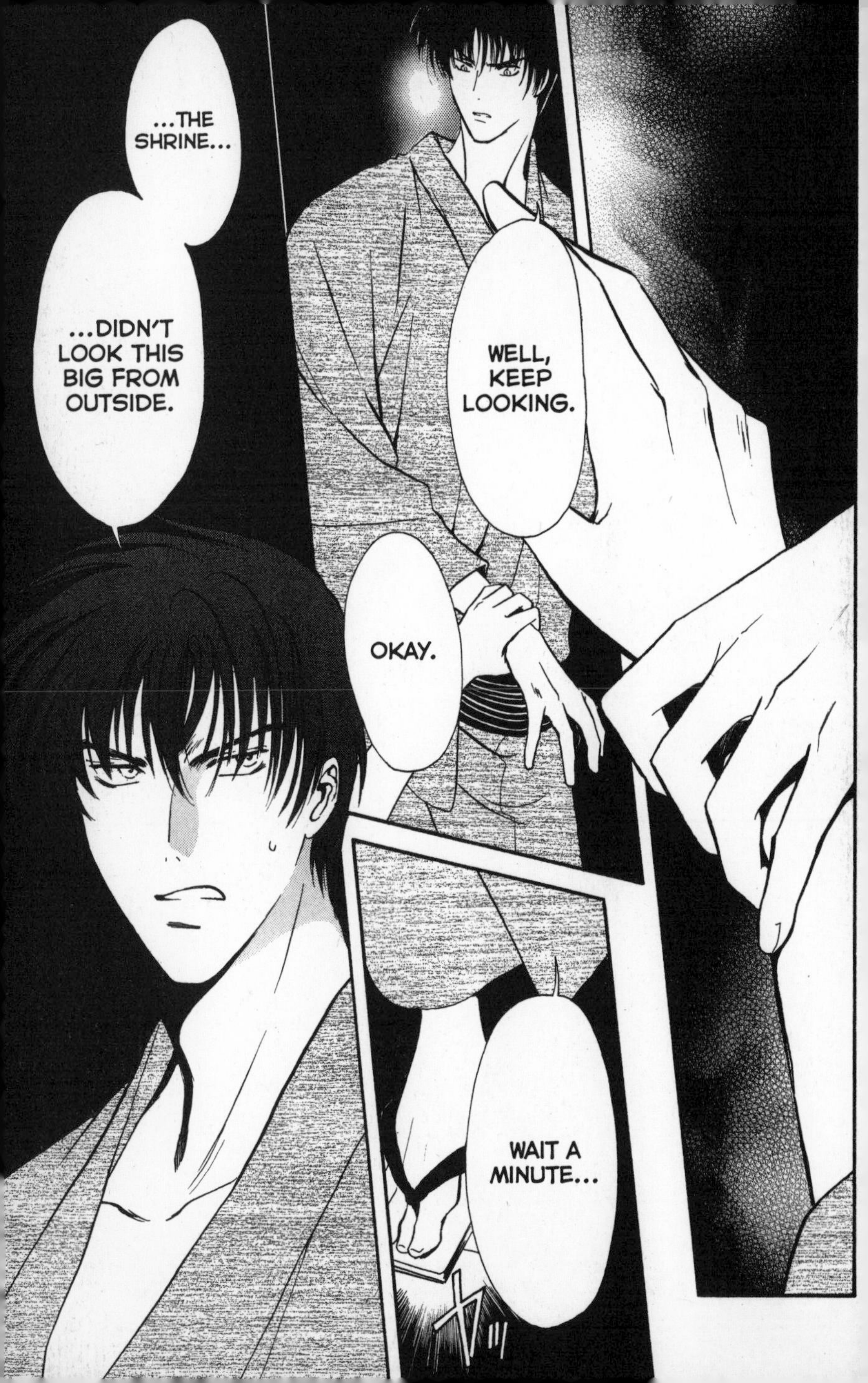
...THE SHRINE...
...DIDN'T LOOK THIS BIG FROM OUTSIDE.
WELL, KEEP LOOKING.
OKAY.
WAIT A MINUTE...

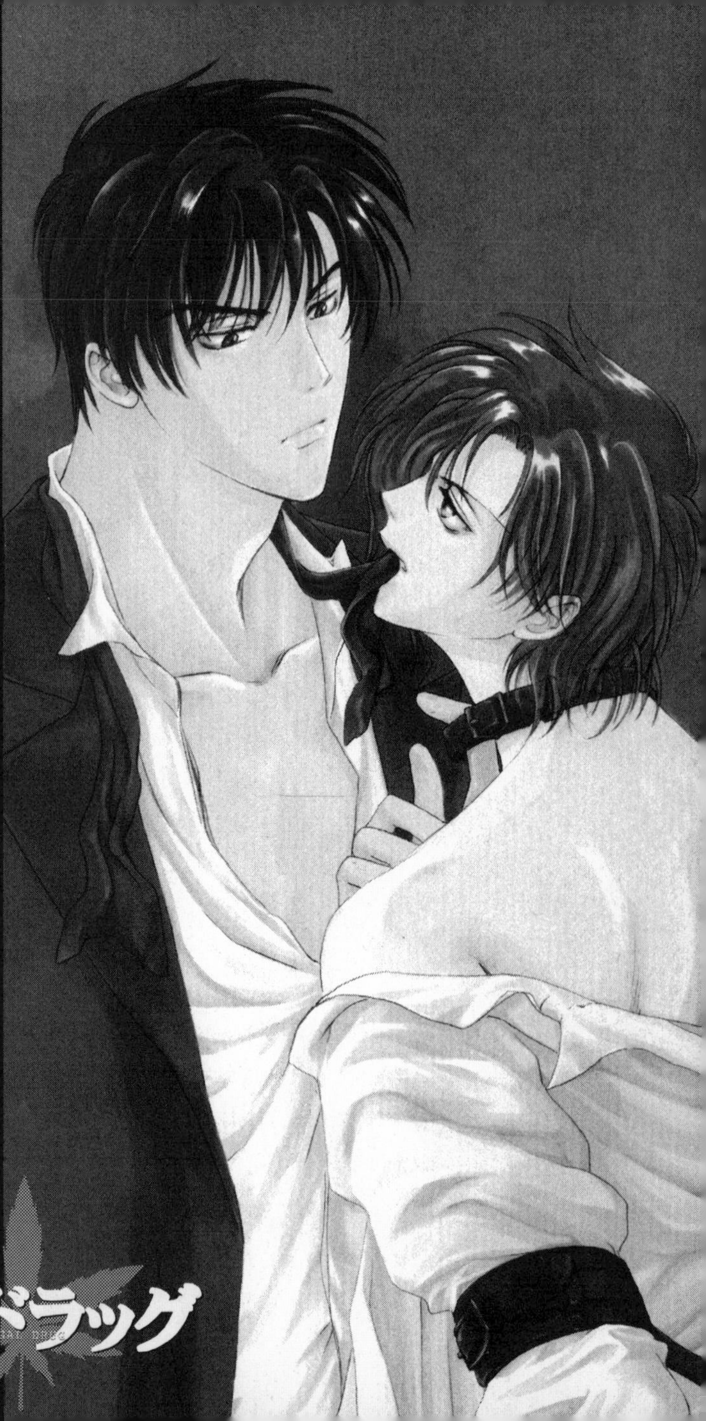
合法ドラッグ

DRUG NO.08

Daily use of the drug may be hazardous.

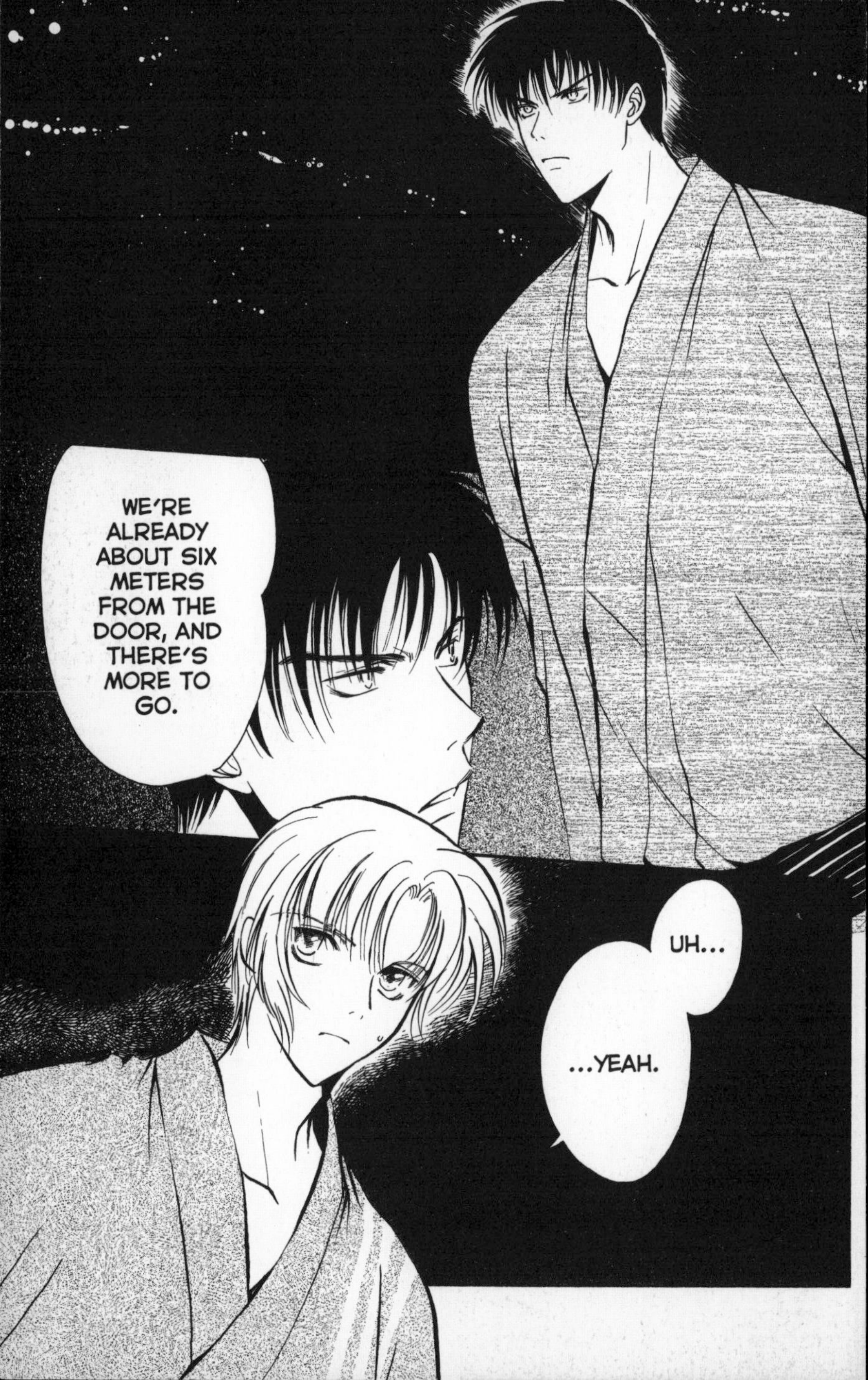
WE'RE ALREADY ABOUT SIX METERS FROM THE DOOR, AND THERE'S MORE TO GO.
UH...
...YEAH.

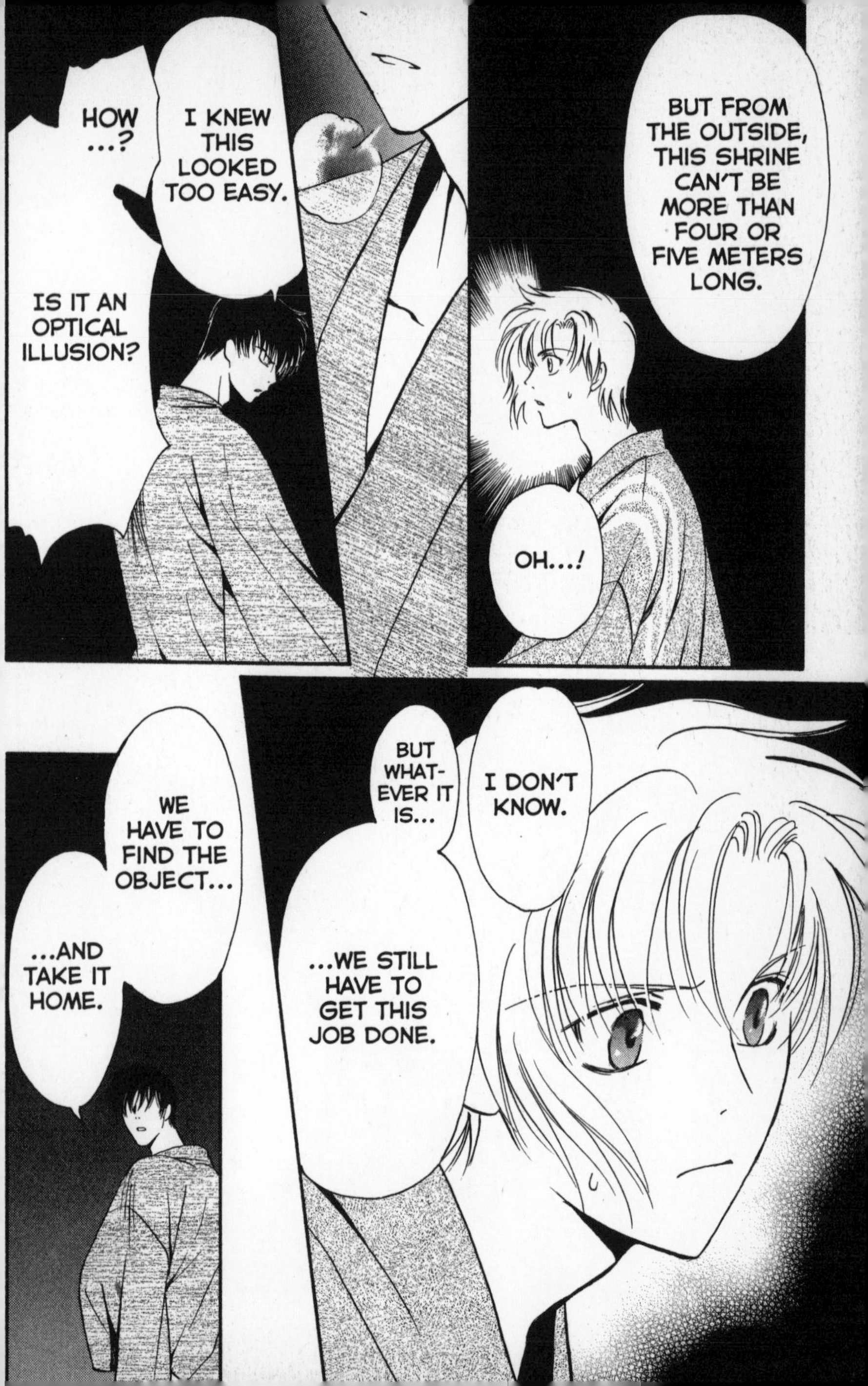
BUT FROM THE OUTSIDE, THIS SHRINE CAN'T BE MORE THAN FOUR OR FIVE METERS LONG.
OH...!
I KNEW THIS LOOKED TOO EASY.
HOW...?
IS IT AN OPTICAL ILLUSION?
I DON'T KNOW.
BUT WHATEVER IT IS...
...WE STILL HAVE TO GET THIS JOB DONE.
WE HAVE TO FIND THE OBJECT...
...AND TAKE IT HOME.

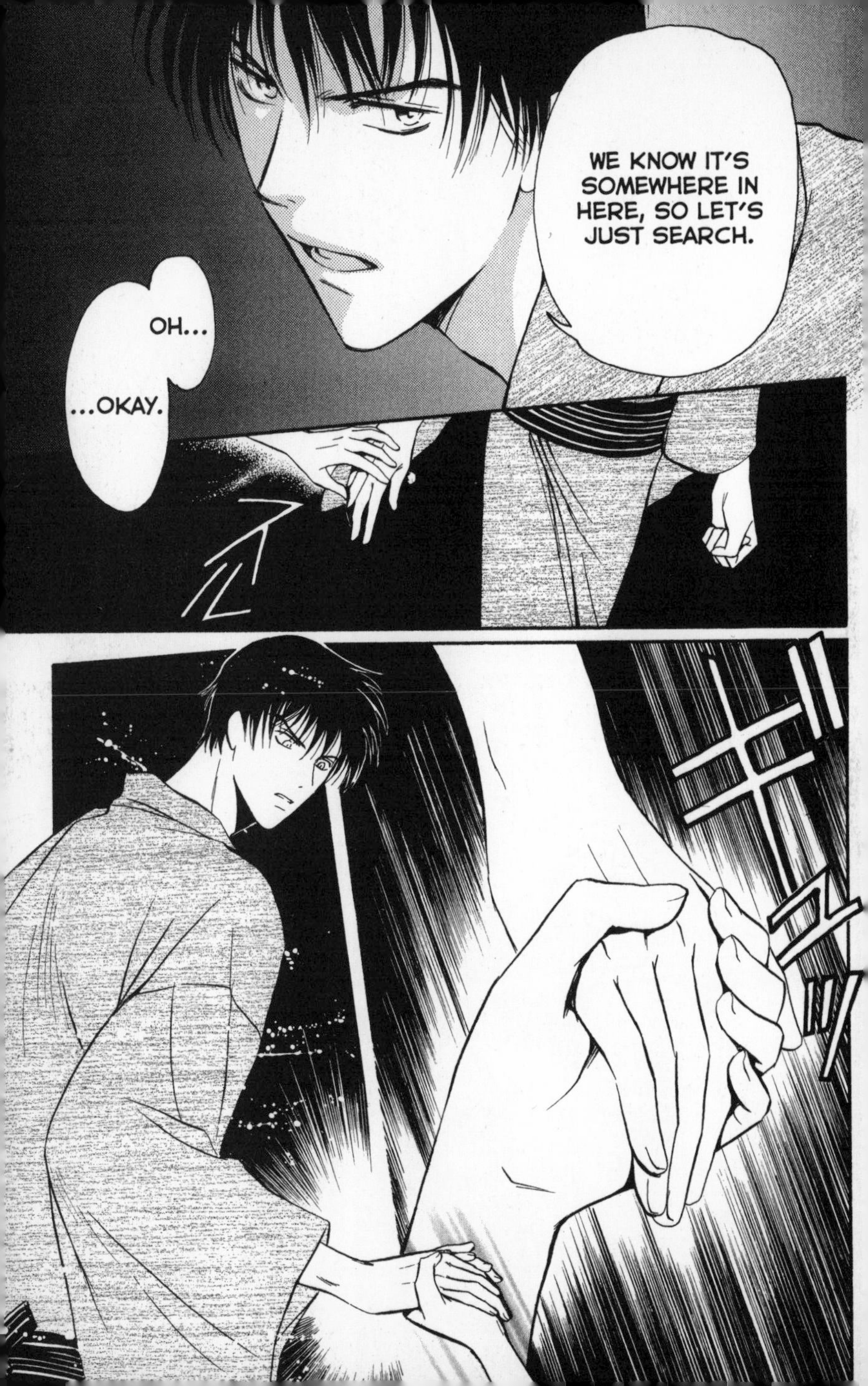
WE KNOW IT'S SOMEWHERE IN HERE, SO LET'S JUST SEARCH.
OH...
...OKAY.

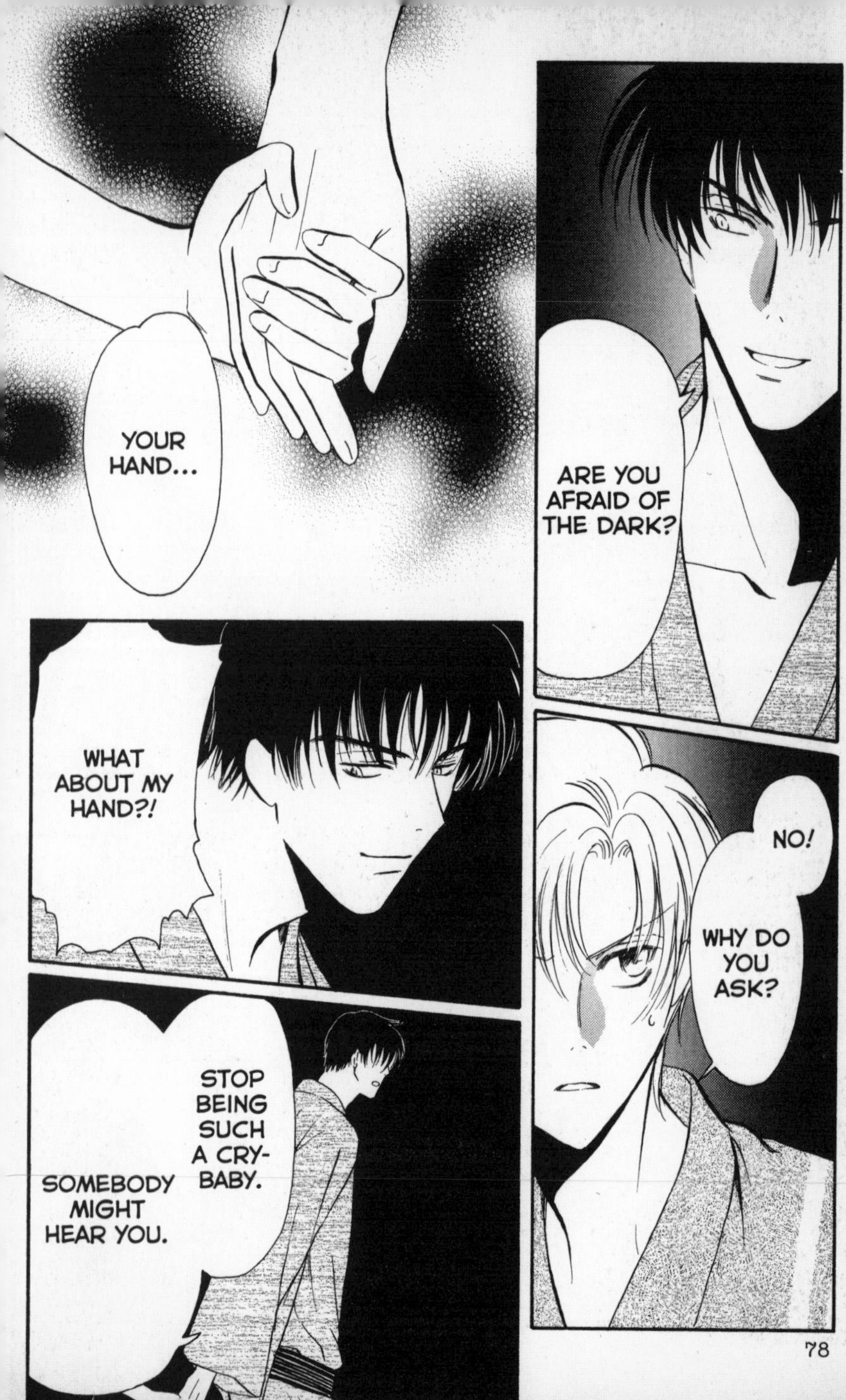
ARE YOU AFRAID OF THE DARK?
YOUR HAND...
NO!
WHY DO YOU ASK?
WHAT ABOUT MY HAND?!
STOP BEING SUCH A CRY-BABY.
SOMEBODY MIGHT HEAR YOU.

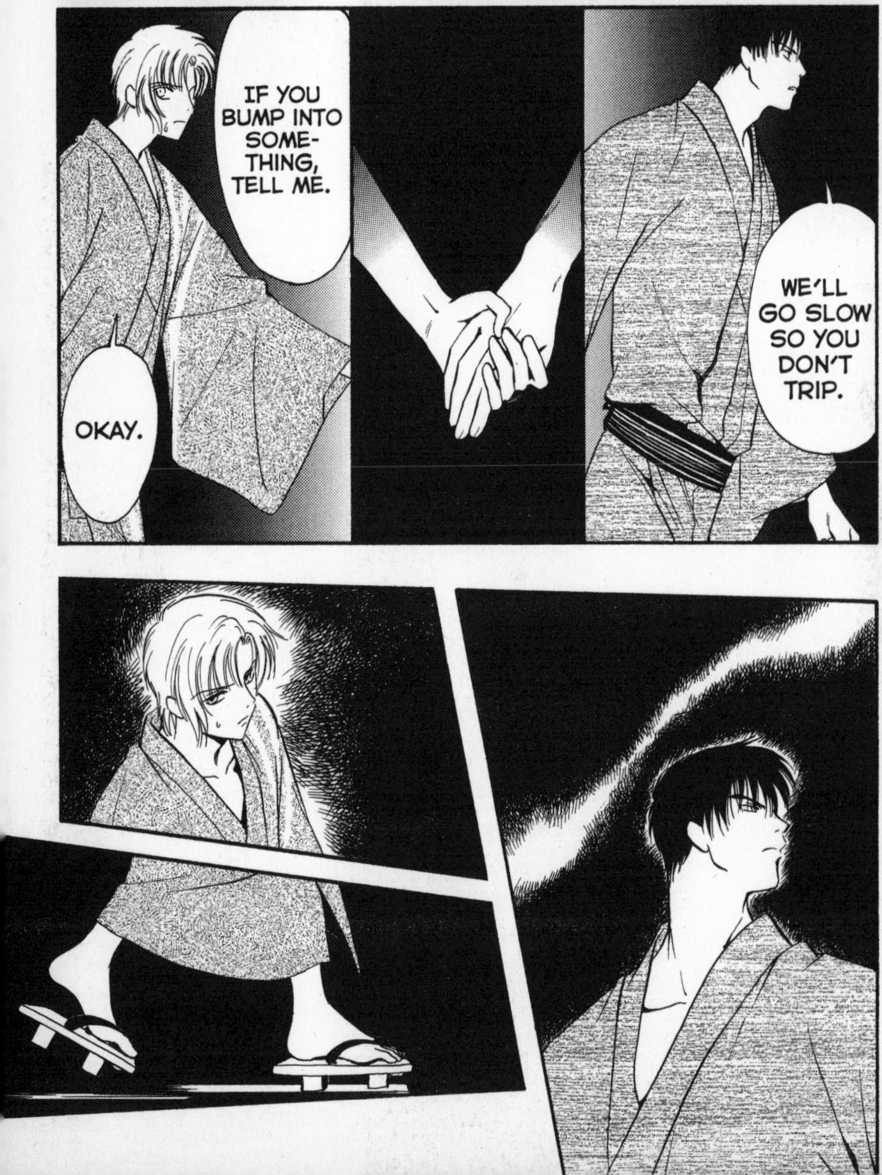
WE'LL GO SLOW SO YOU DON'T TRIP.
IF YOU BUMP INTO SOME-THING, TELL ME.
OKAY.

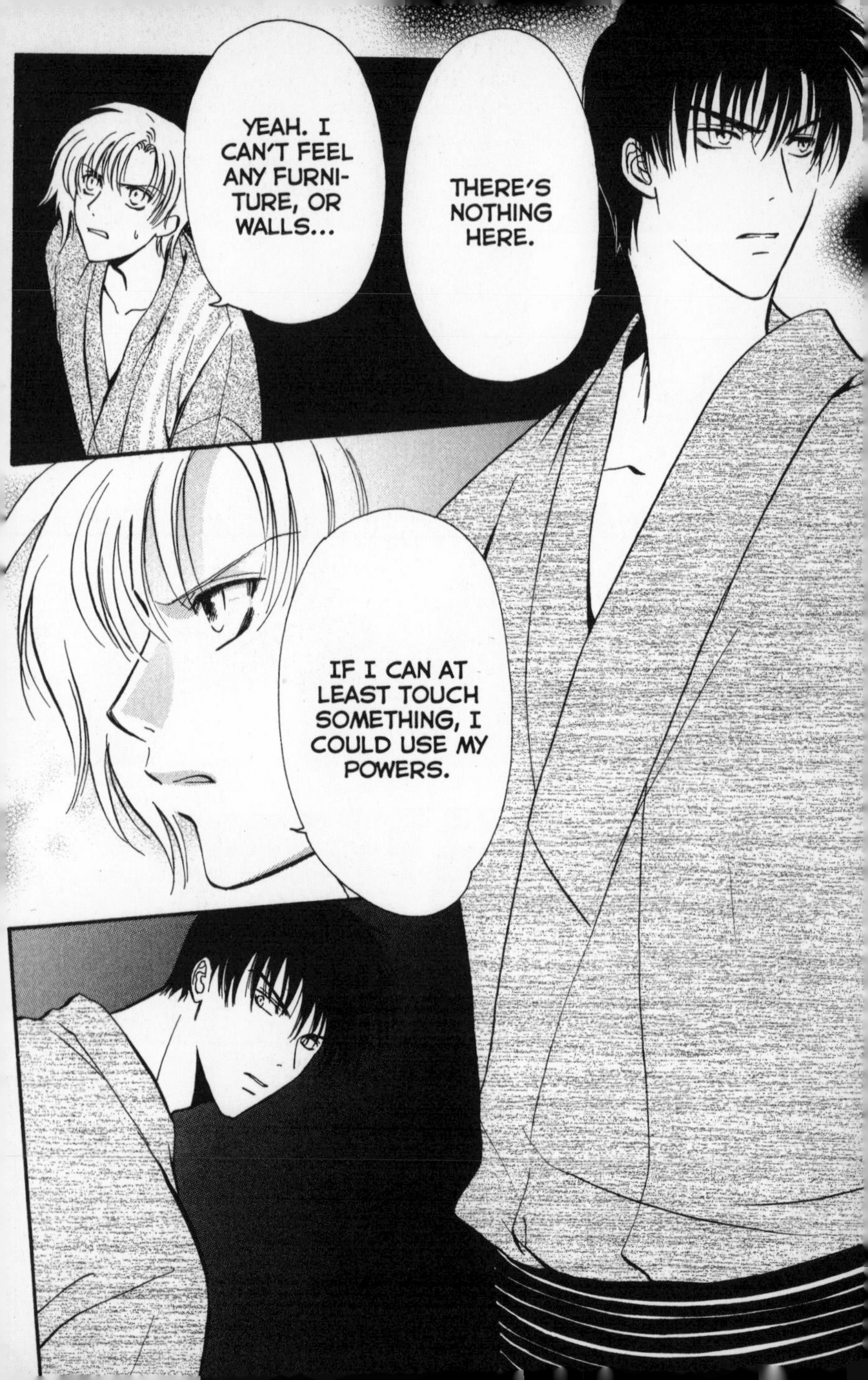
THERE'S NOTHING HERE.
YEAH. I CAN'T FEEL ANY FURNI-TURE, OR WALLS...
IF I CAN AT LEAST TOUCH SOMETHING, I COULD USE MY POWERS.

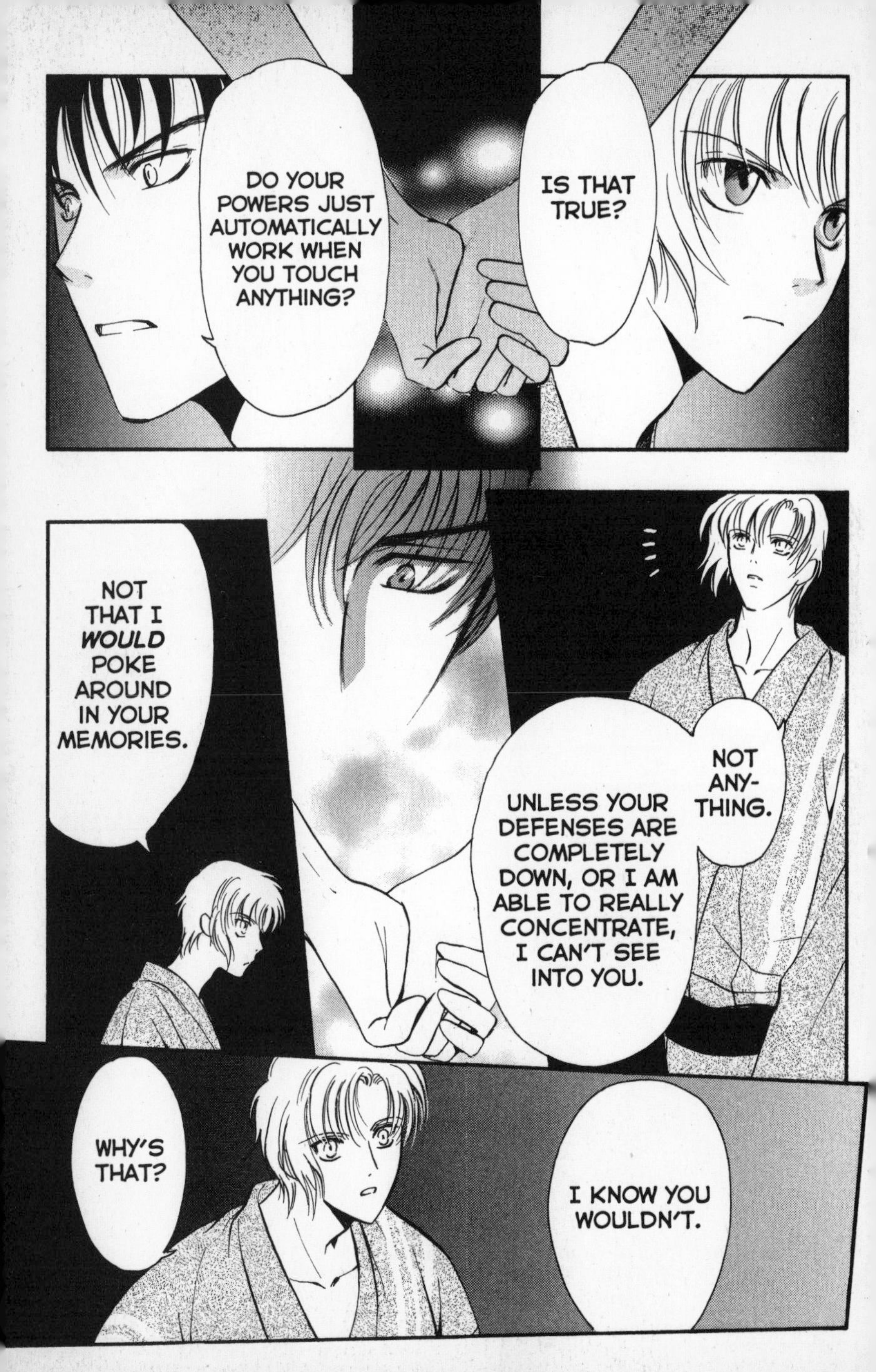
IS THAT TRUE?
DO YOUR POWERS JUST AUTOMATICALLY WORK WHEN YOU TOUCH ANYTHING?
NOT ANY-THING.
UNLESS YOUR DEFENSES ARE COMPLETELY DOWN, OR I AM ABLE TO REALLY CONCENTRATE, I CAN'T SEE INTO YOU.
NOT THAT I *WOULD* POKE AROUND IN YOUR MEMORIES.
I KNOW YOU WOULDN'T.
WHY'S THAT?

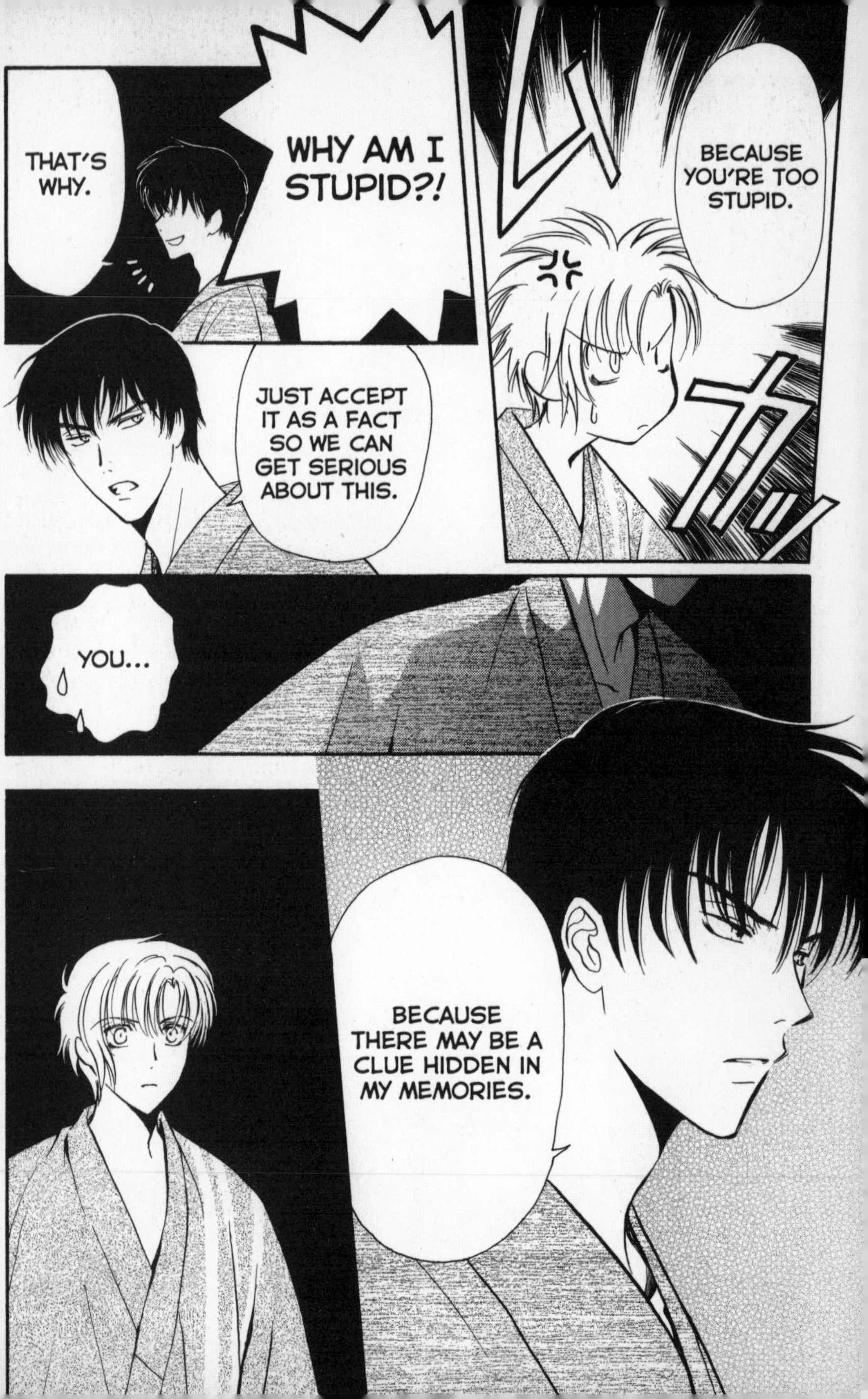
BECAUSE YOU'RE TOO STUPID.
WHY AM I STUPID?!
THAT'S WHY.
JUST ACCEPT IT AS A FACT SO WE CAN GET SERIOUS ABOUT THIS.
YOU...
BECAUSE THERE MAY BE A CLUE HIDDEN IN MY MEMORIES.

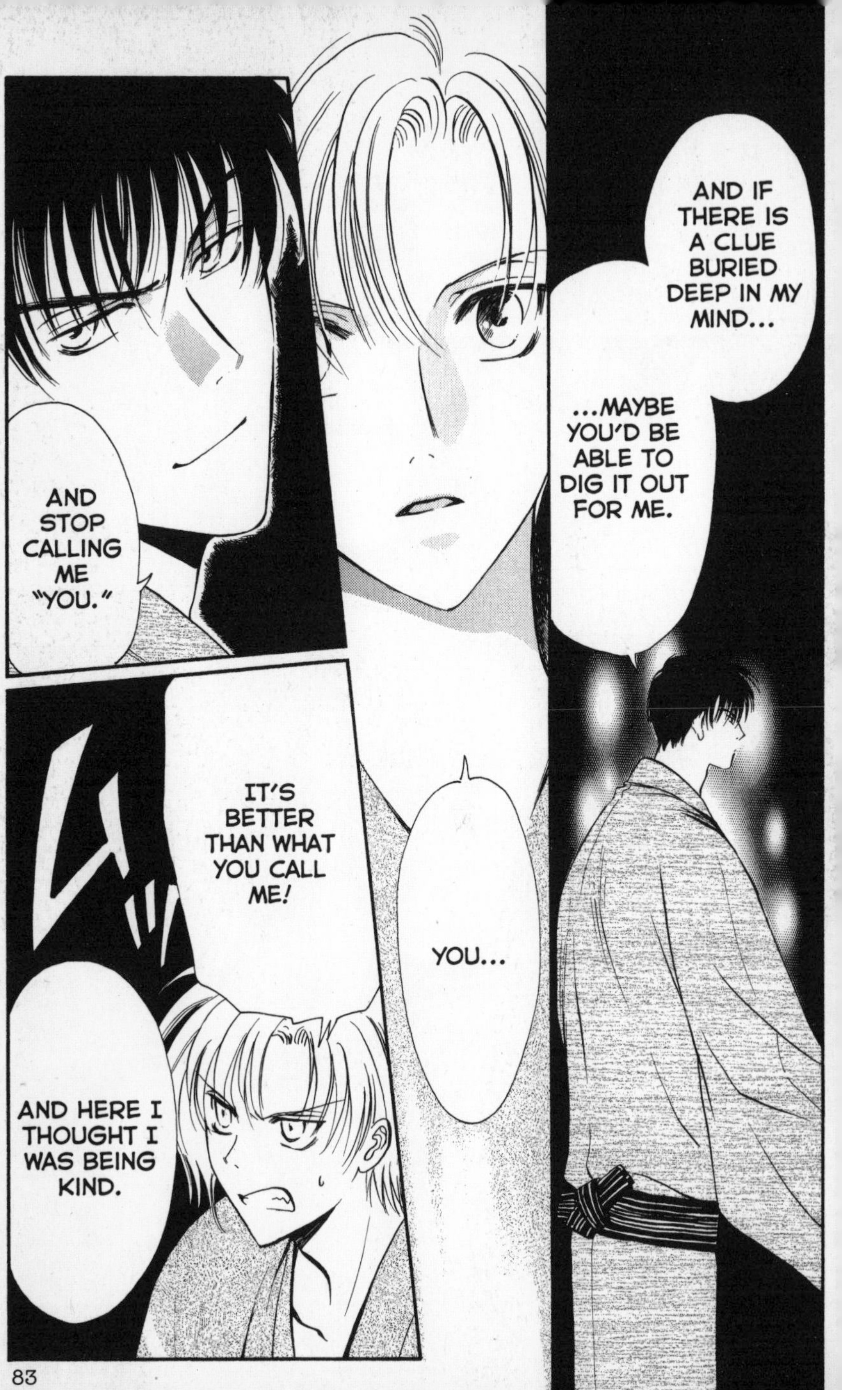
AND IF THERE IS A CLUE BURIED DEEP IN MY MIND...
...MAYBE YOU'D BE ABLE TO DIG IT OUT FOR ME.
YOU...
AND STOP CALLING ME "YOU."
IT'S BETTER THAN WHAT YOU CALL ME!
AND HERE I THOUGHT I WAS BEING KIND.

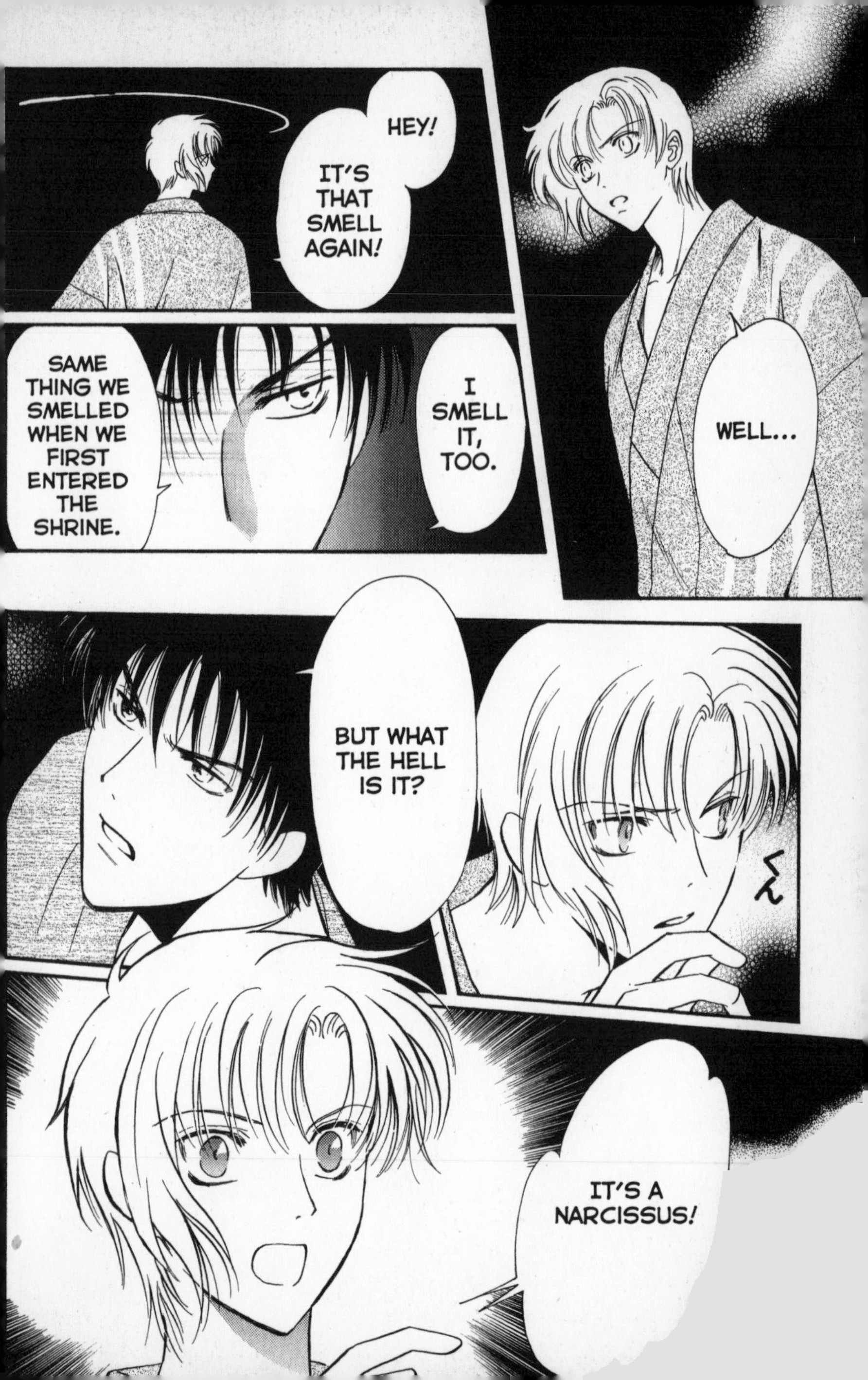
WELL...
HEY!
IT'S THAT SMELL AGAIN!
I SMELL IT, TOO.
SAME THING WE SMELLED WHEN WE FIRST ENTERED THE SHRINE.
BUT WHAT THE HELL IS IT?
くん
IT'S A NARCISSUS!

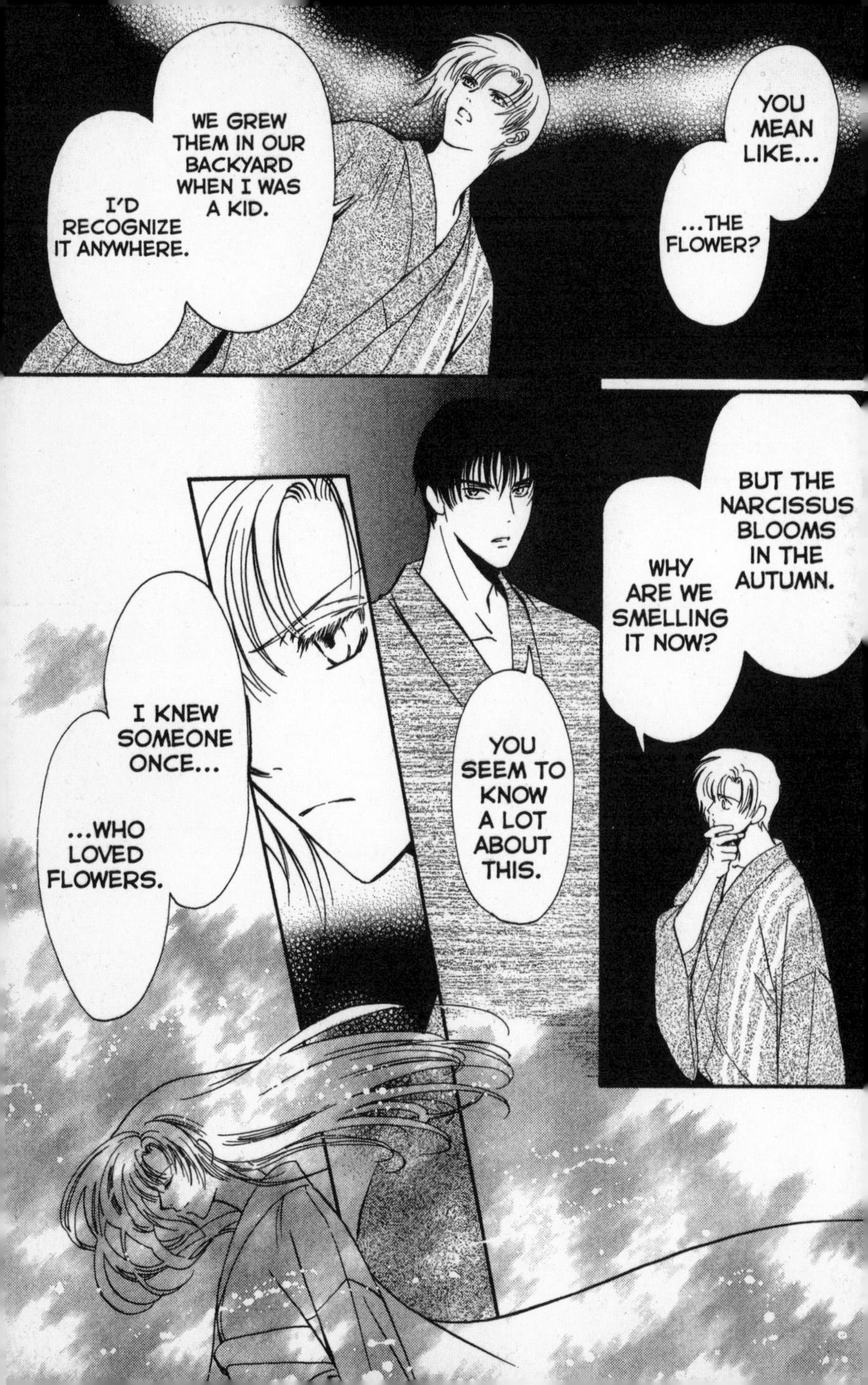
YOU MEAN LIKE...
...THE FLOWER?
WE GREW THEM IN OUR BACKYARD WHEN I WAS A KID.
I'D RECOGNIZE IT ANYWHERE.
BUT THE NARCISSUS BLOOMS IN THE AUTUMN.
WHY ARE WE SMELLING IT NOW?
YOU SEEM TO KNOW A LOT ABOUT THIS.
I KNEW SOMEONE ONCE...
...WHO LOVED FLOWERS.

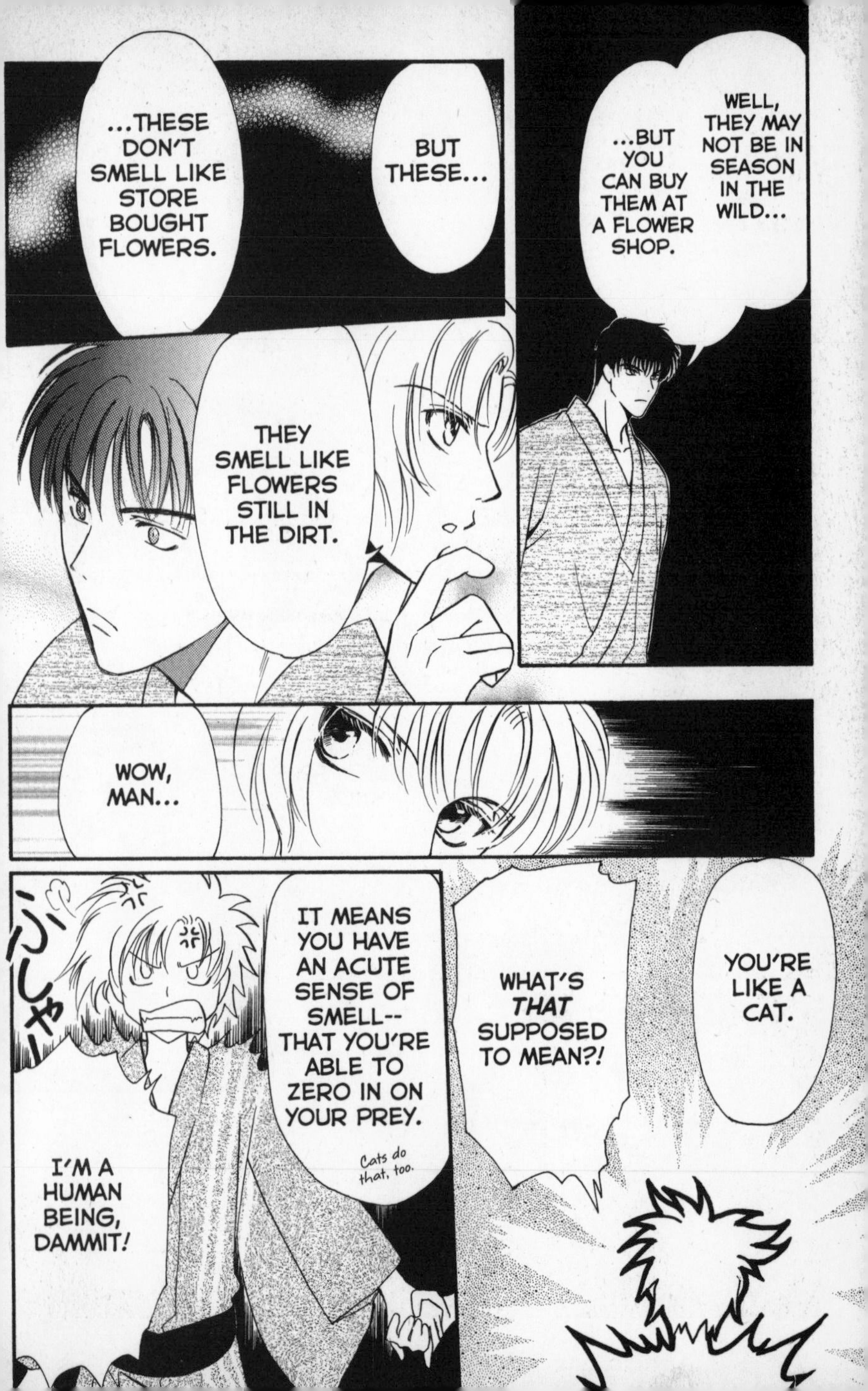
WELL, THEY MAY NOT BE IN SEASON IN THE WILD...
...BUT YOU CAN BUY THEM AT A FLOWER SHOP.
BUT THESE...
...THESE DON'T SMELL LIKE STORE BOUGHT FLOWERS.
THEY SMELL LIKE FLOWERS STILL IN THE DIRT.
WOW, MAN...
YOU'RE LIKE A CAT.
WHAT'S *THAT* SUPPOSED TO MEAN?!
IT MEANS YOU HAVE AN ACUTE SENSE OF SMELL--THAT YOU'RE ABLE TO ZERO IN ON YOUR PREY.
Cats do that, too.
ふしゃー
I'M A HUMAN BEING, DAMMIT!

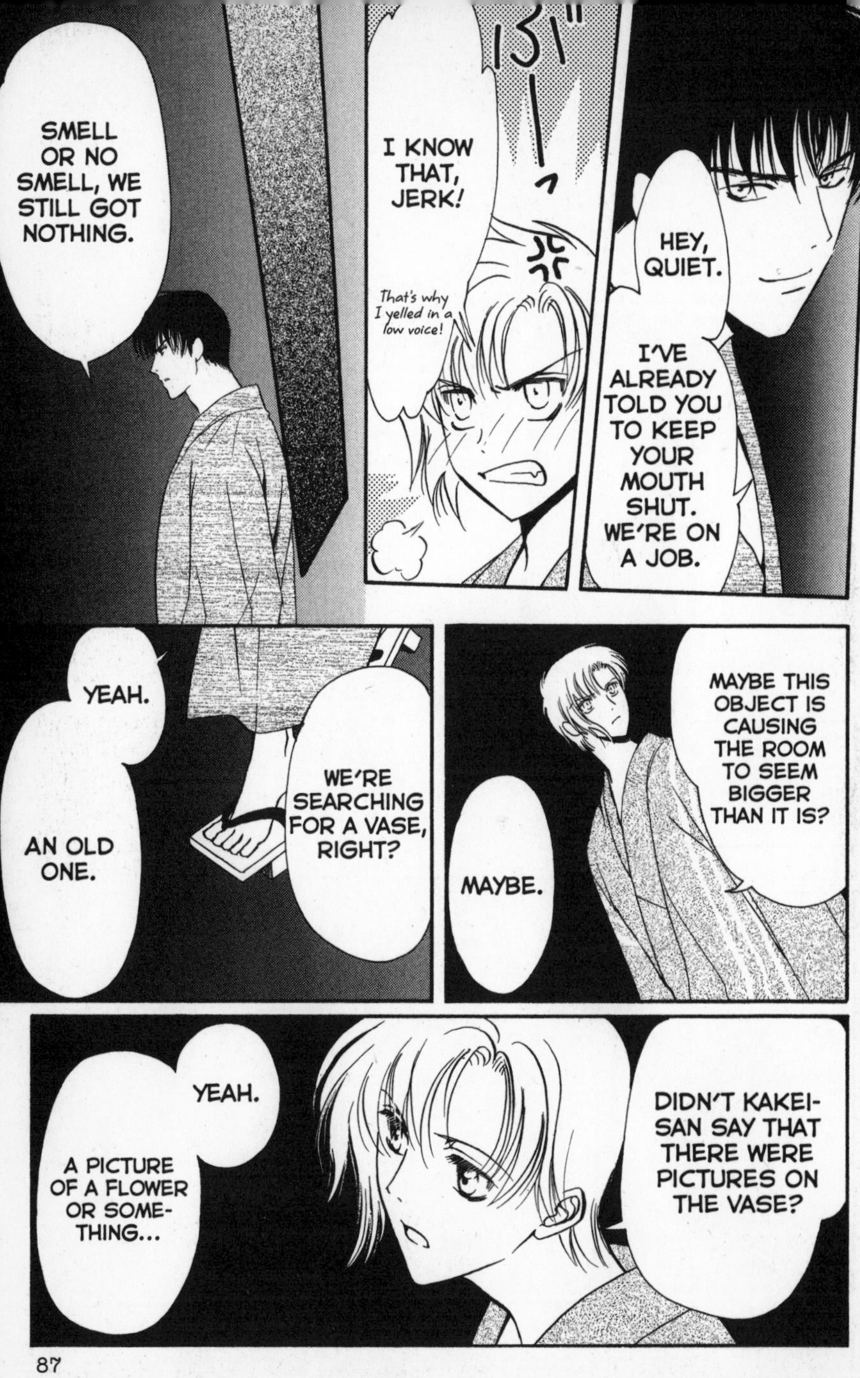
HEY, QUIET.
I'VE ALREADY TOLD YOU TO KEEP YOUR MOUTH SHUT. WE'RE ON A JOB.
I KNOW THAT, JERK!
That's why I yelled in a low voice!
SMELL OR NO SMELL, WE STILL GOT NOTHING.
MAYBE THIS OBJECT IS CAUSING THE ROOM TO SEEM BIGGER THAN IT IS?
MAYBE.
WE'RE SEARCHING FOR A VASE, RIGHT?
YEAH.
AN OLD ONE.
DIDN'T KAKEI-SAN SAY THAT THERE WERE PICTURES ON THE VASE?
YEAH.
A PICTURE OF A FLOWER OR SOMETHING...

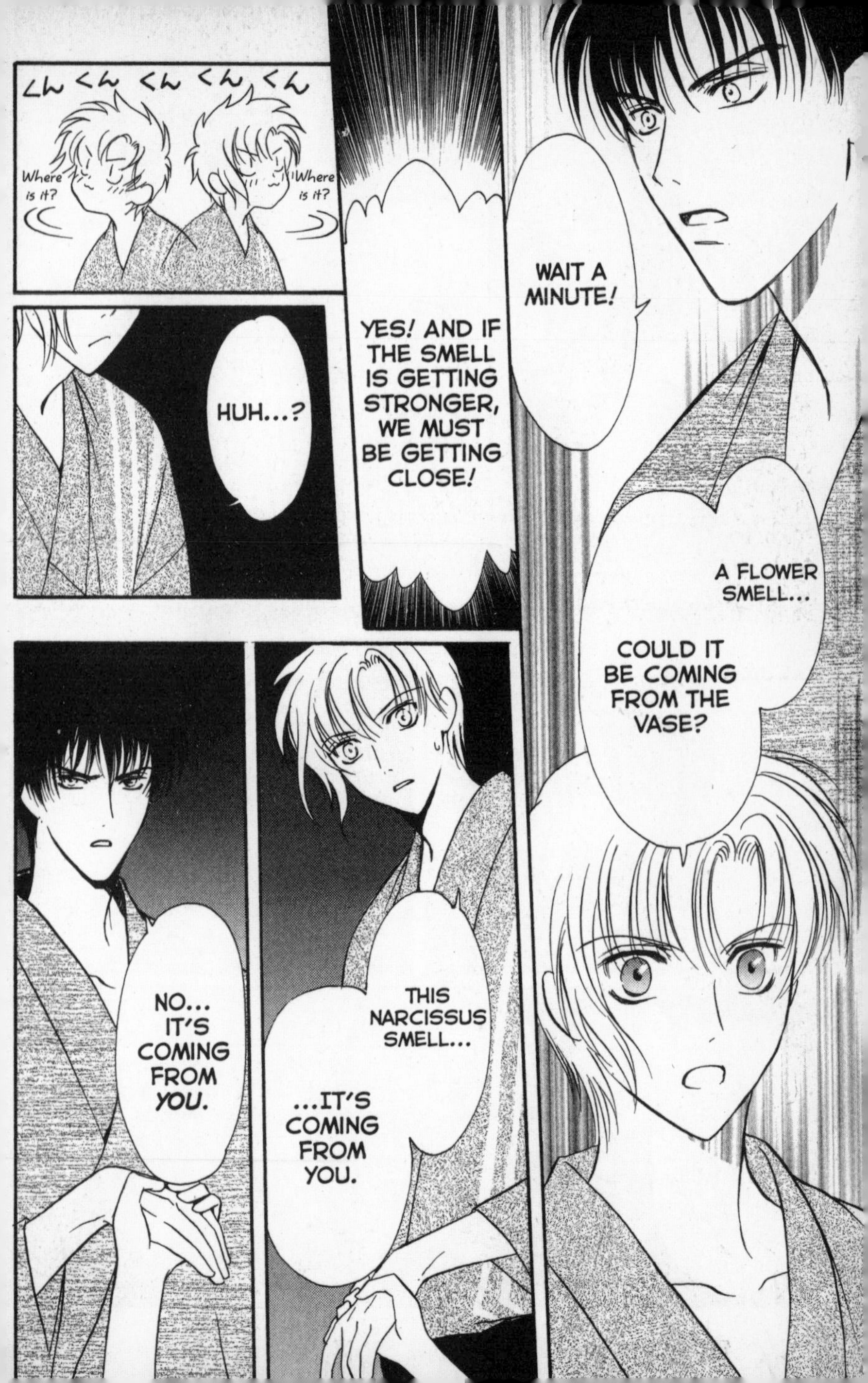
WAIT A MINUTE!
A FLOWER SMELL...
COULD IT BE COMING FROM THE VASE?
YES! AND IF THE SMELL IS GETTING STRONGER, WE MUST BE GETTING CLOSE!
くん くん くん くん くん
Where is it?
Where is it?
HUH...?
THIS NARCISSUS SMELL...
...IT'S COMING FROM YOU.
NO... IT'S COMING FROM *YOU*.

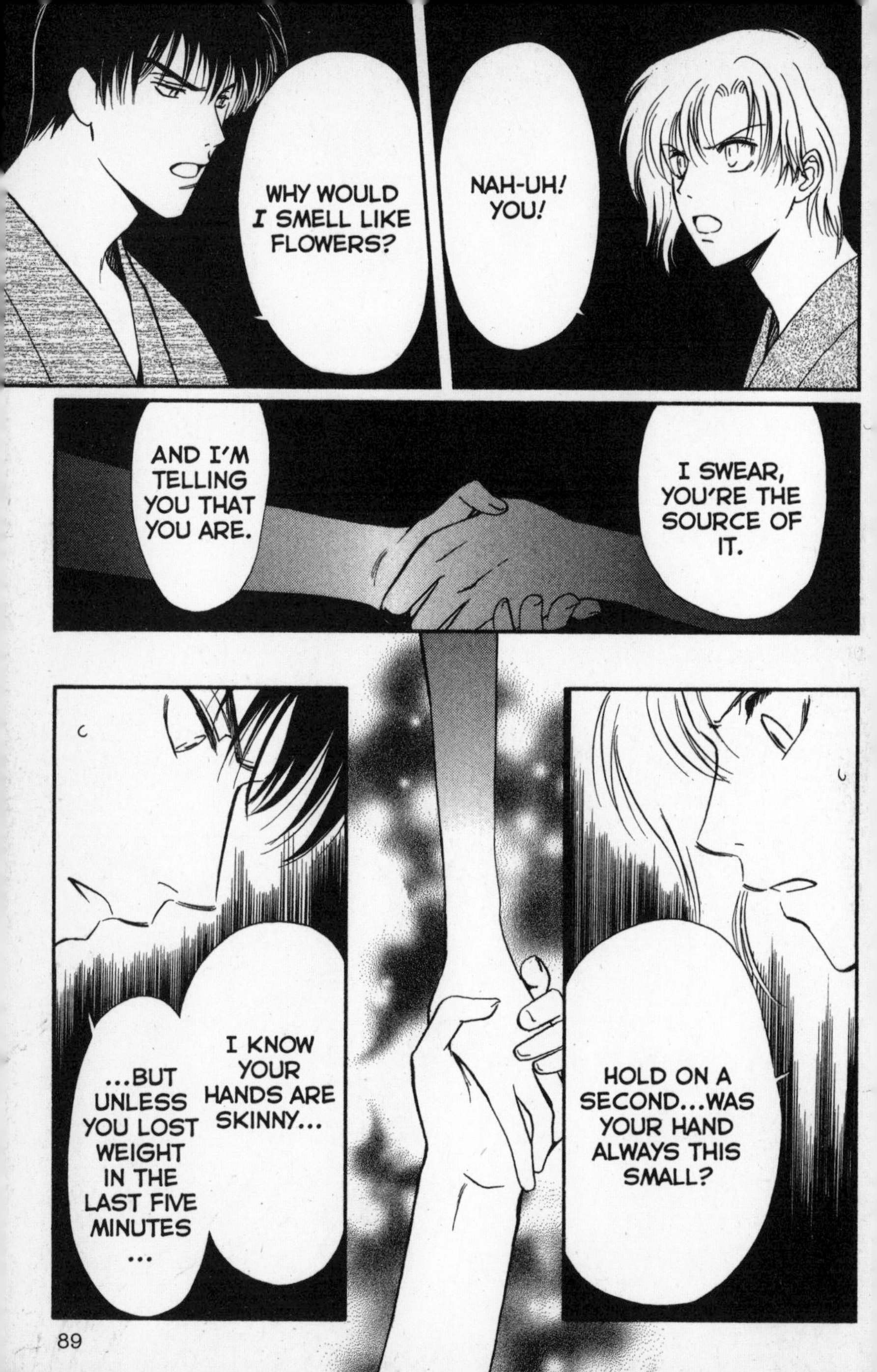
NAH-UH! YOU!
WHY WOULD I SMELL LIKE FLOWERS?
I SWEAR, YOU'RE THE SOURCE OF IT.
AND I'M TELLING YOU THAT YOU ARE.
HOLD ON A SECOND...WAS YOUR HAND ALWAYS THIS SMALL?
I KNOW YOUR HANDS ARE SKINNY...
...BUT UNLESS YOU LOST WEIGHT IN THE LAST FIVE MINUTES ...

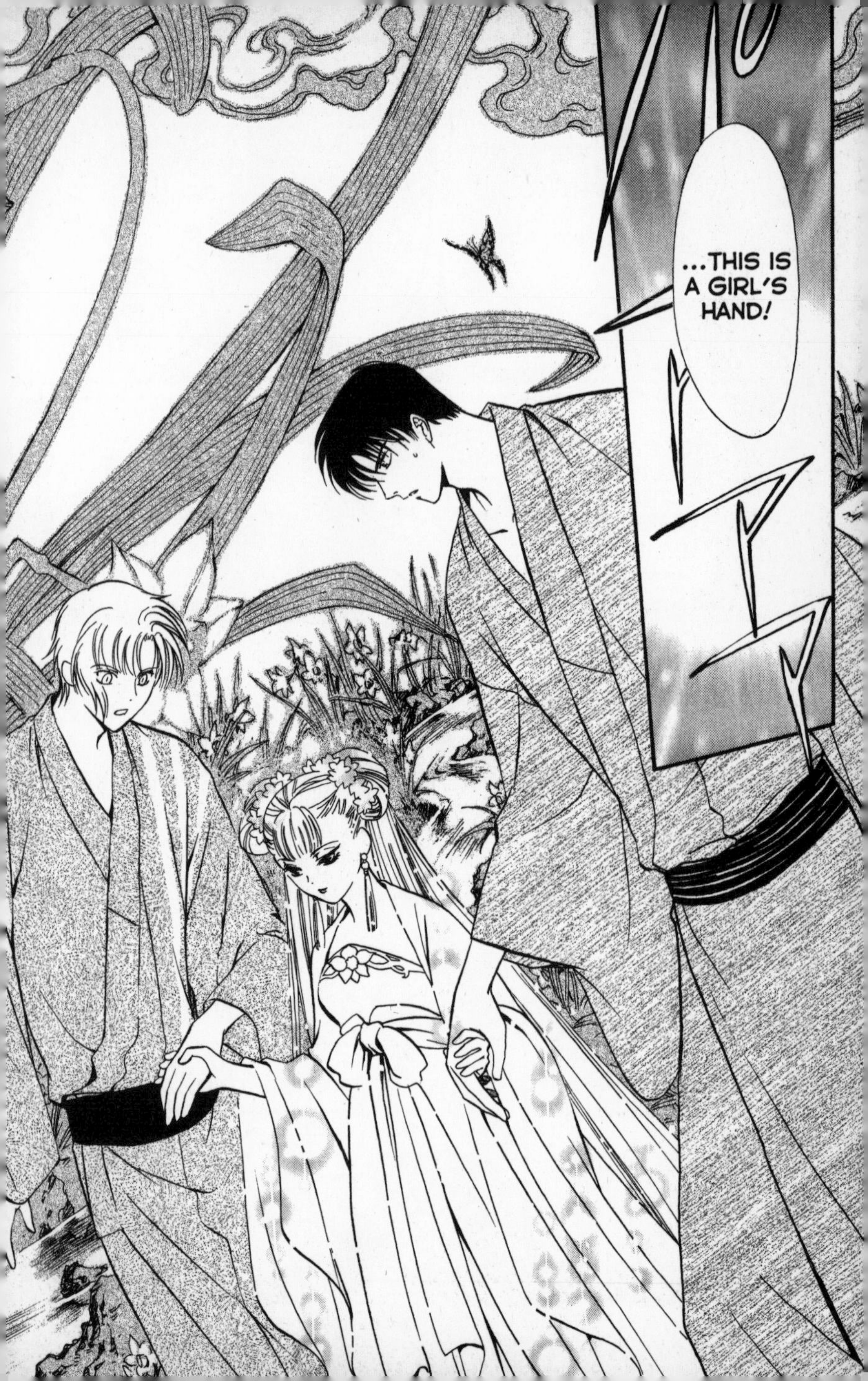
...THIS IS A GIRL'S HAND!

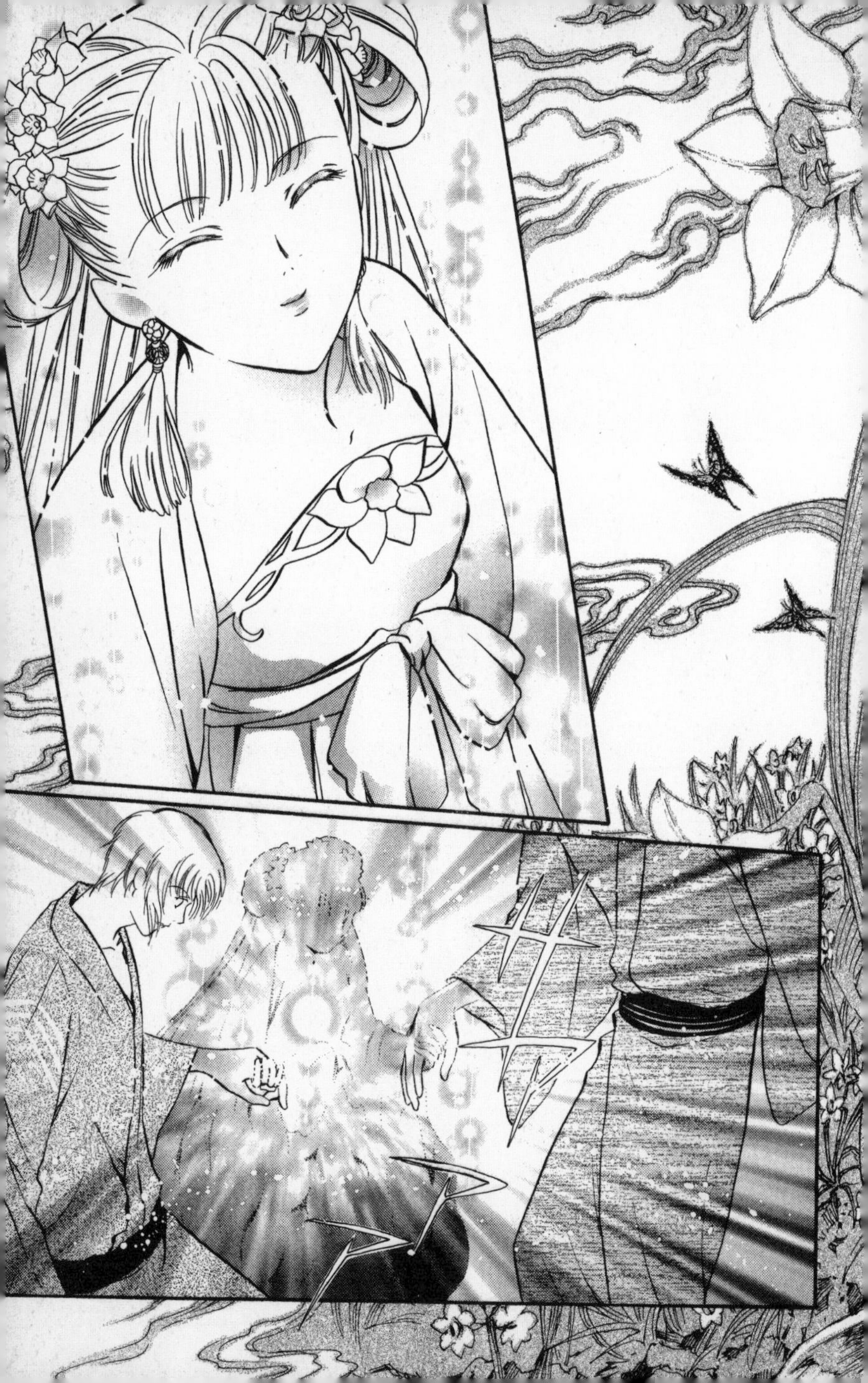

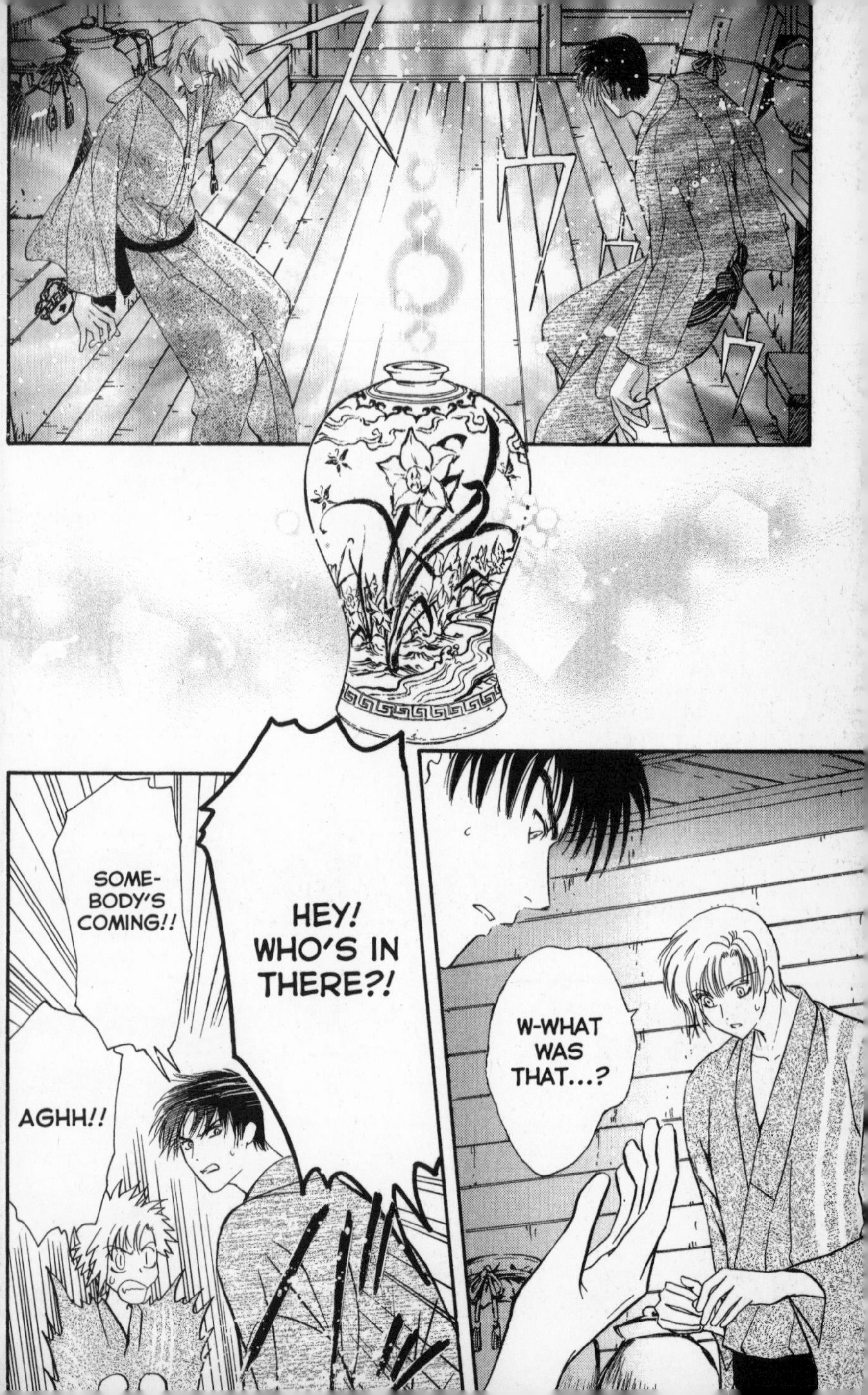
W-WHAT WAS THAT...?
HEY! WHO'S IN THERE?!
SOME-BODY'S COMING!!
AGHH!!

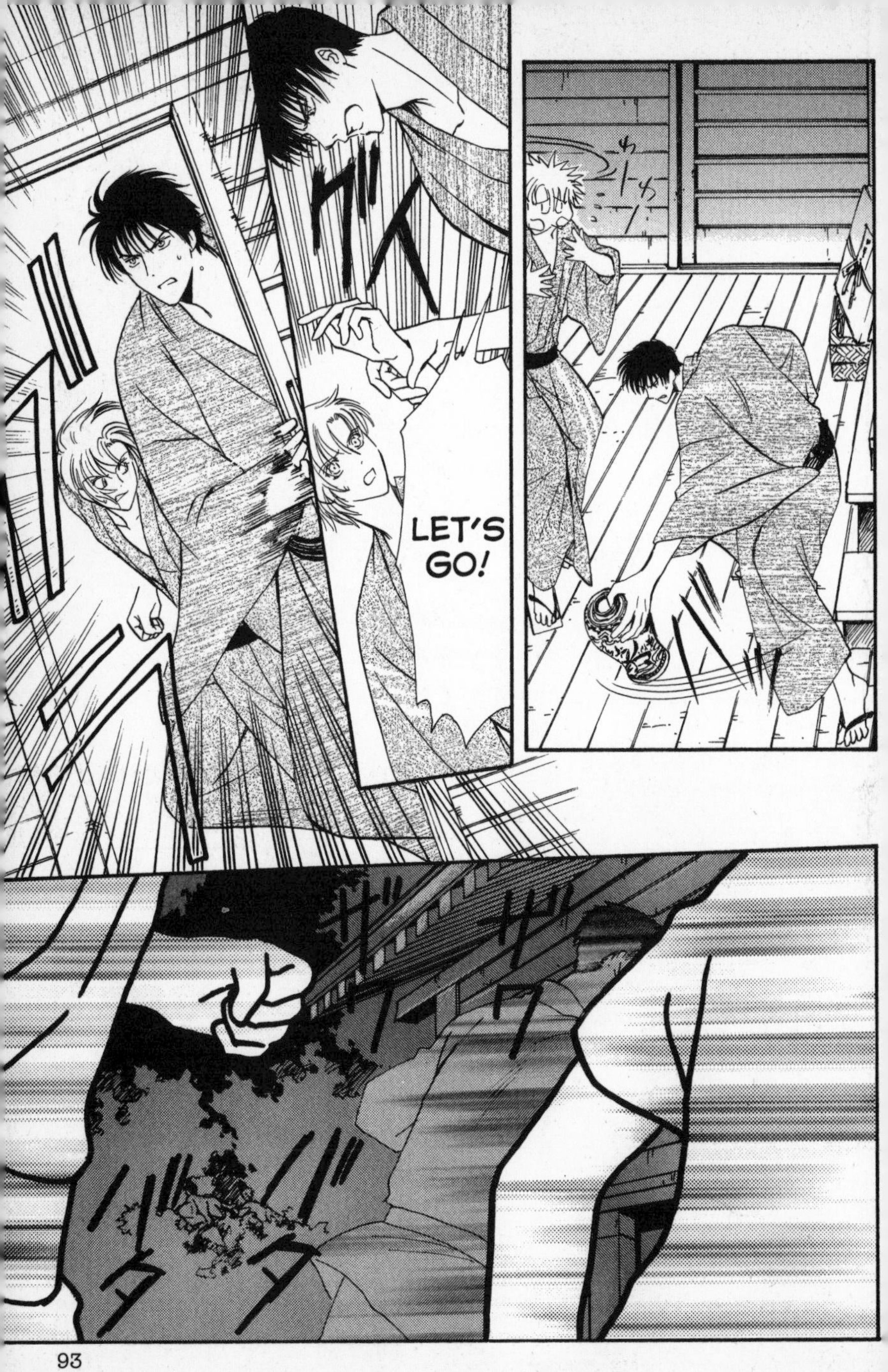
LET'S GO!

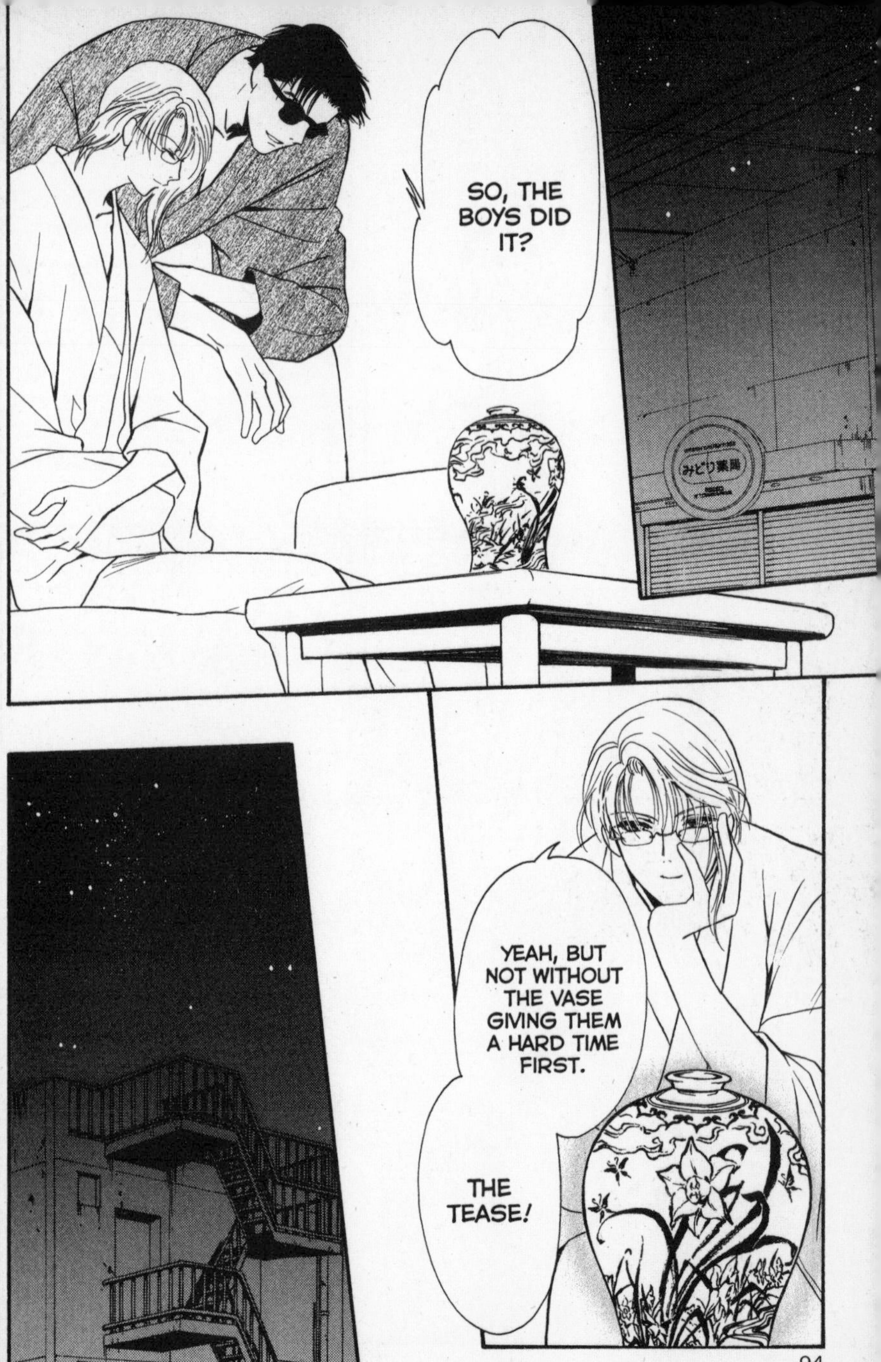
SO, THE BOYS DID IT?
みどり薬局
YEAH, BUT NOT WITHOUT THE VASE GIVING THEM A HARD TIME FIRST.
THE TEASE!

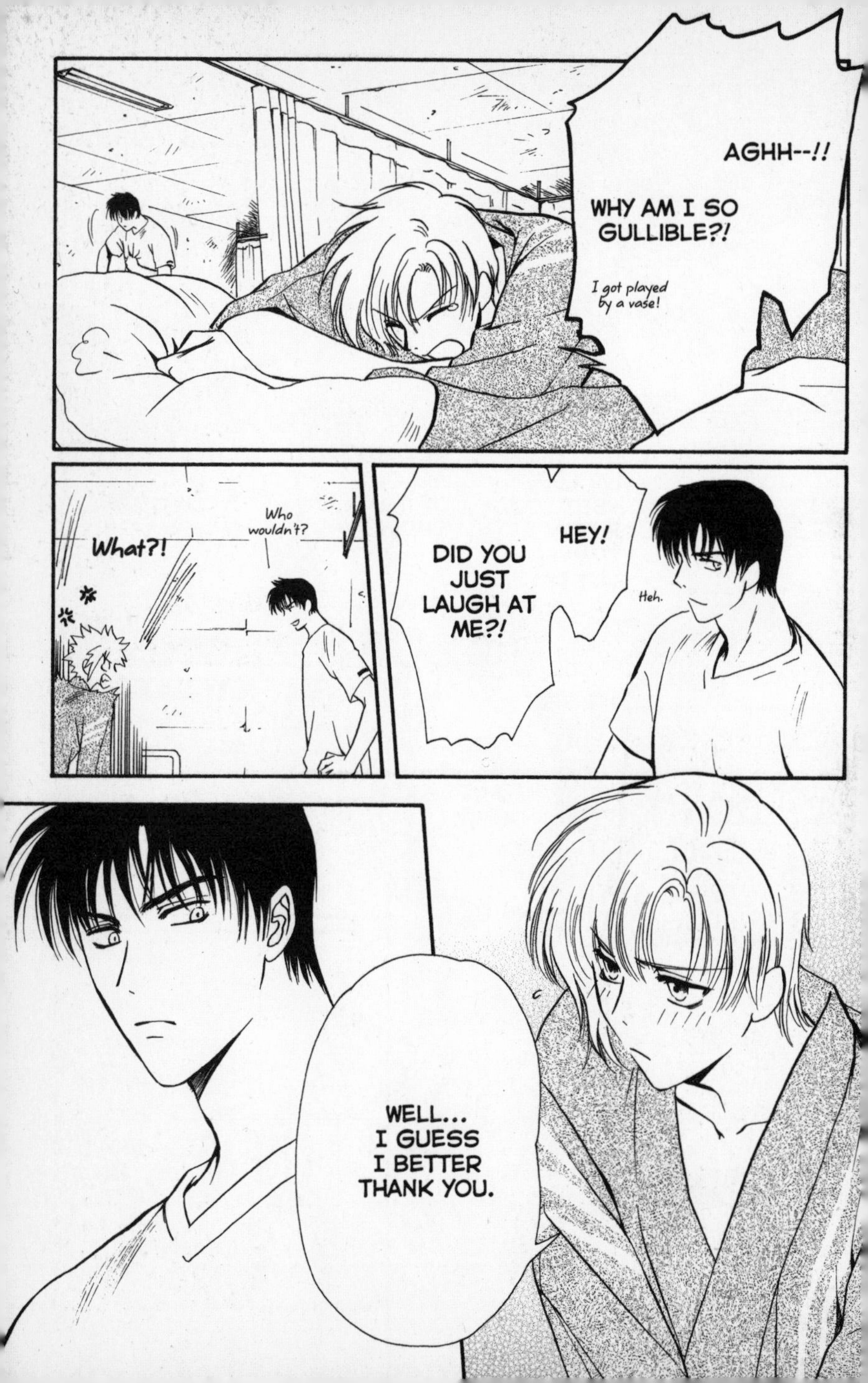
AGHH--!!
WHY AM I SO GULLIBLE?!
I got played by a vase!
Heh.
HEY! DID YOU JUST LAUGH AT ME?!
Who wouldn't?
What?!
WELL... I GUESS I BETTER THANK YOU.

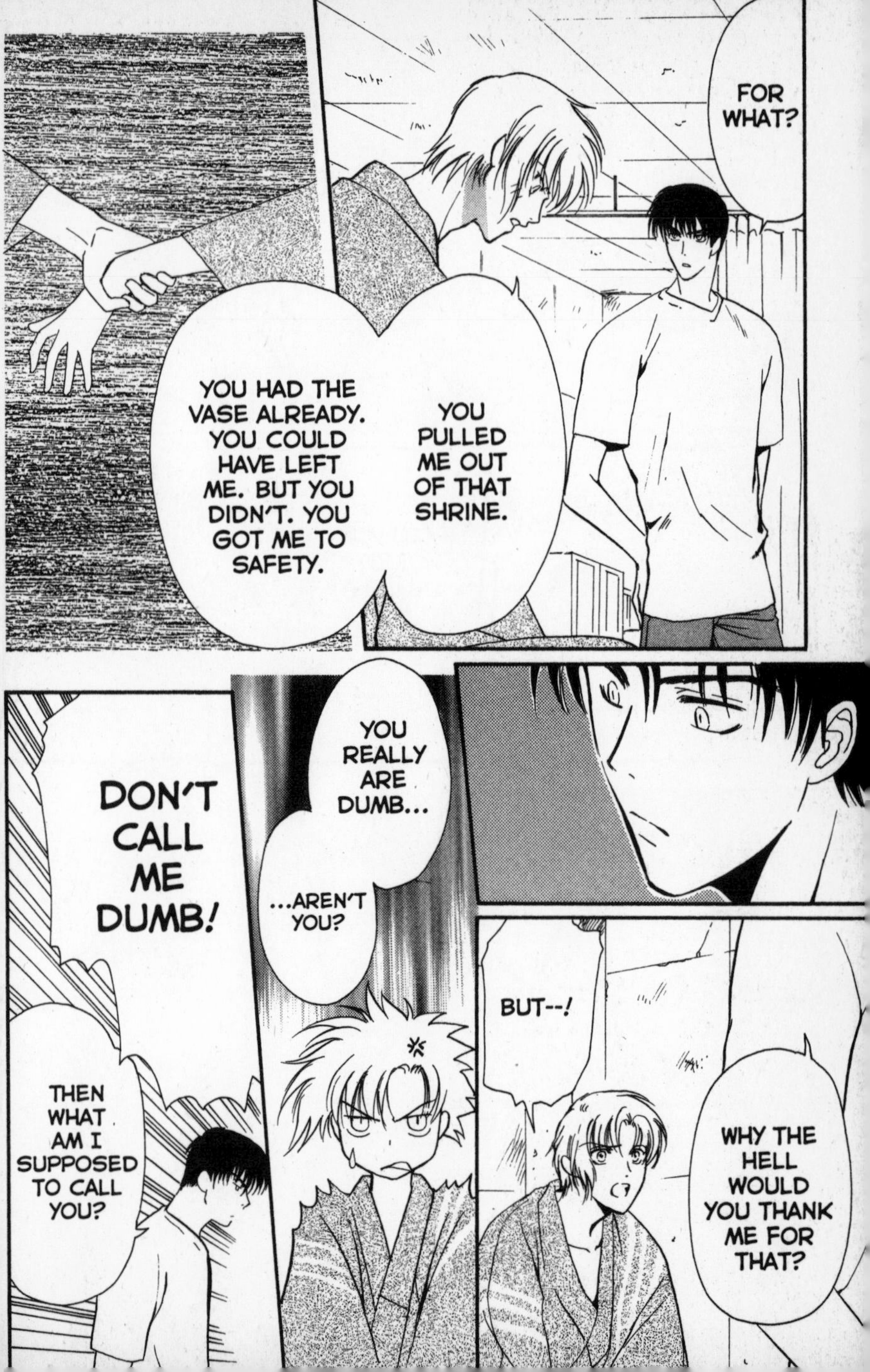
FOR WHAT?
YOU PULLED ME OUT OF THAT SHRINE.
YOU HAD THE VASE ALREADY. YOU COULD HAVE LEFT ME. BUT YOU DIDN'T. YOU GOT ME TO SAFETY.
WHY THE HELL WOULD YOU THANK ME FOR THAT?
BUT--!
YOU REALLY ARE DUMB...
...AREN'T YOU?
DON'T CALL ME DUMB!
THEN WHAT AM I SUPPOSED TO CALL YOU?

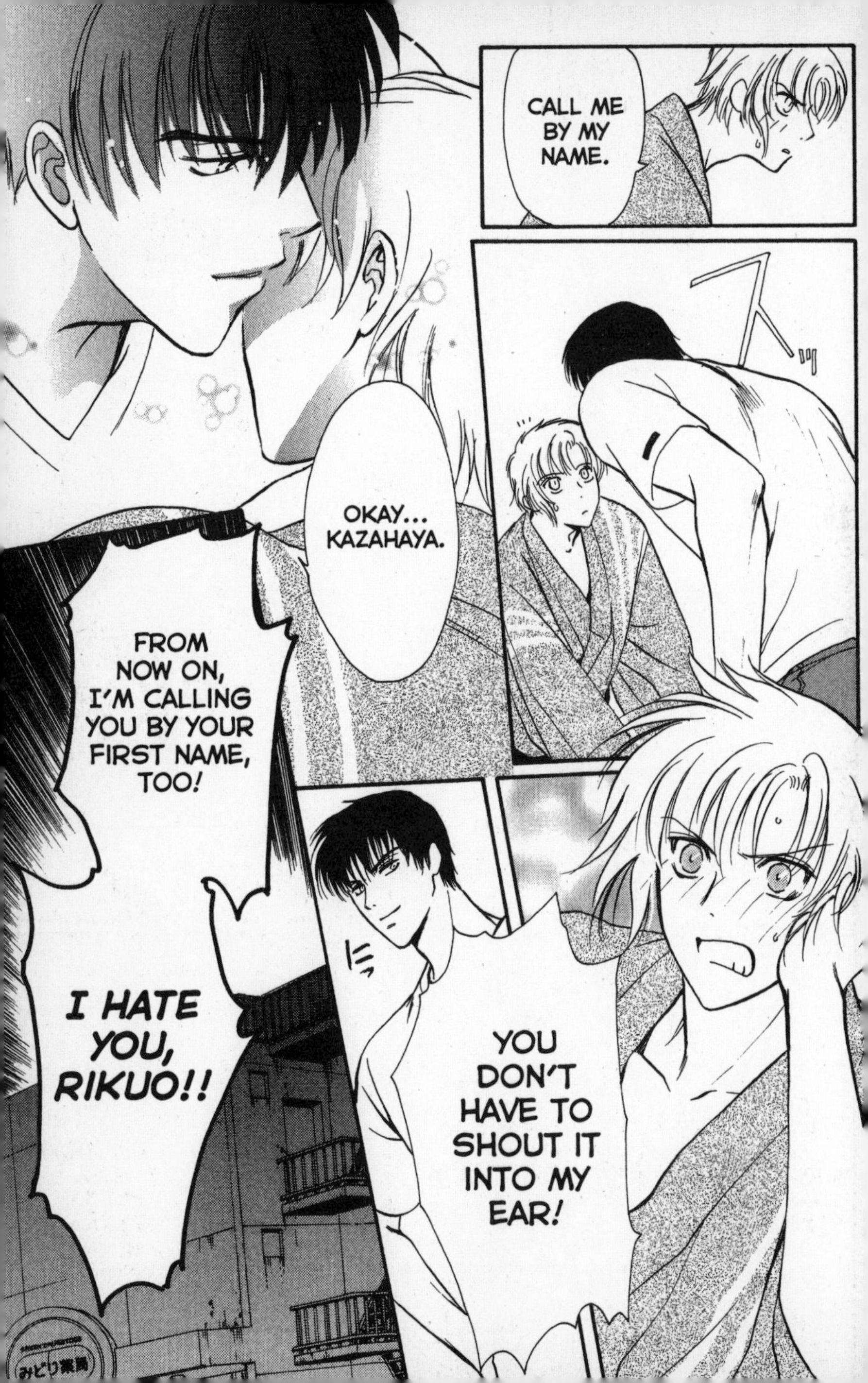
CALL ME BY MY NAME.
OKAY... KAZAHAYA.
FROM NOW ON, I'M CALLING YOU BY YOUR FIRST NAME, TOO!
I HATE YOU, RIKUO!!
YOU DON'T HAVE TO SHOUT IT INTO MY EAR!
みどり薬局

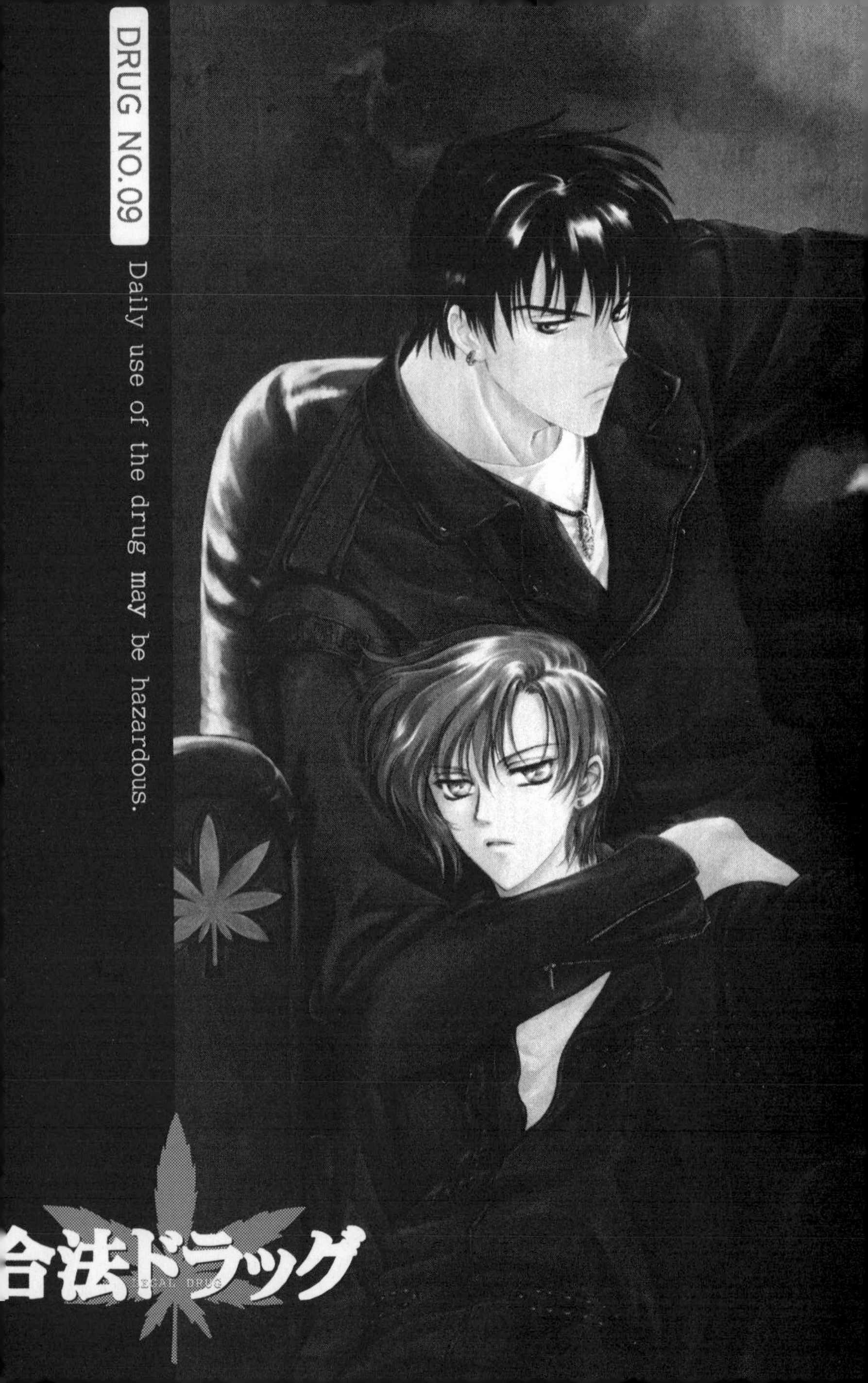
DRUG NO.09
Daily use of the drug may be hazardous.
合法ドラッグ
LEGAL DRUG

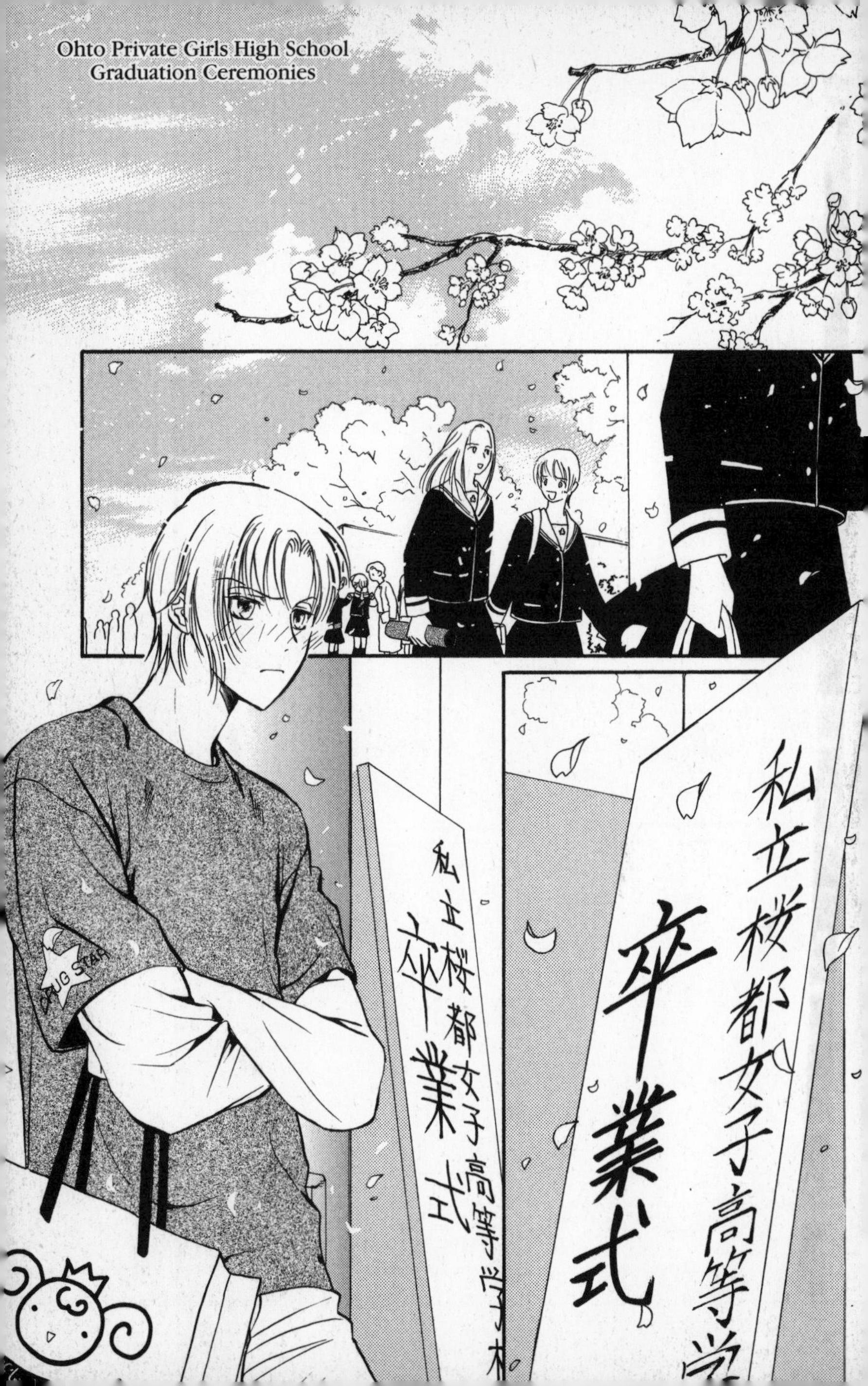
Ohto Private Girls High School
Graduation Ceremonies
私立桜都女子高等学
卒業式
私立桜都女子高等学
卒業式

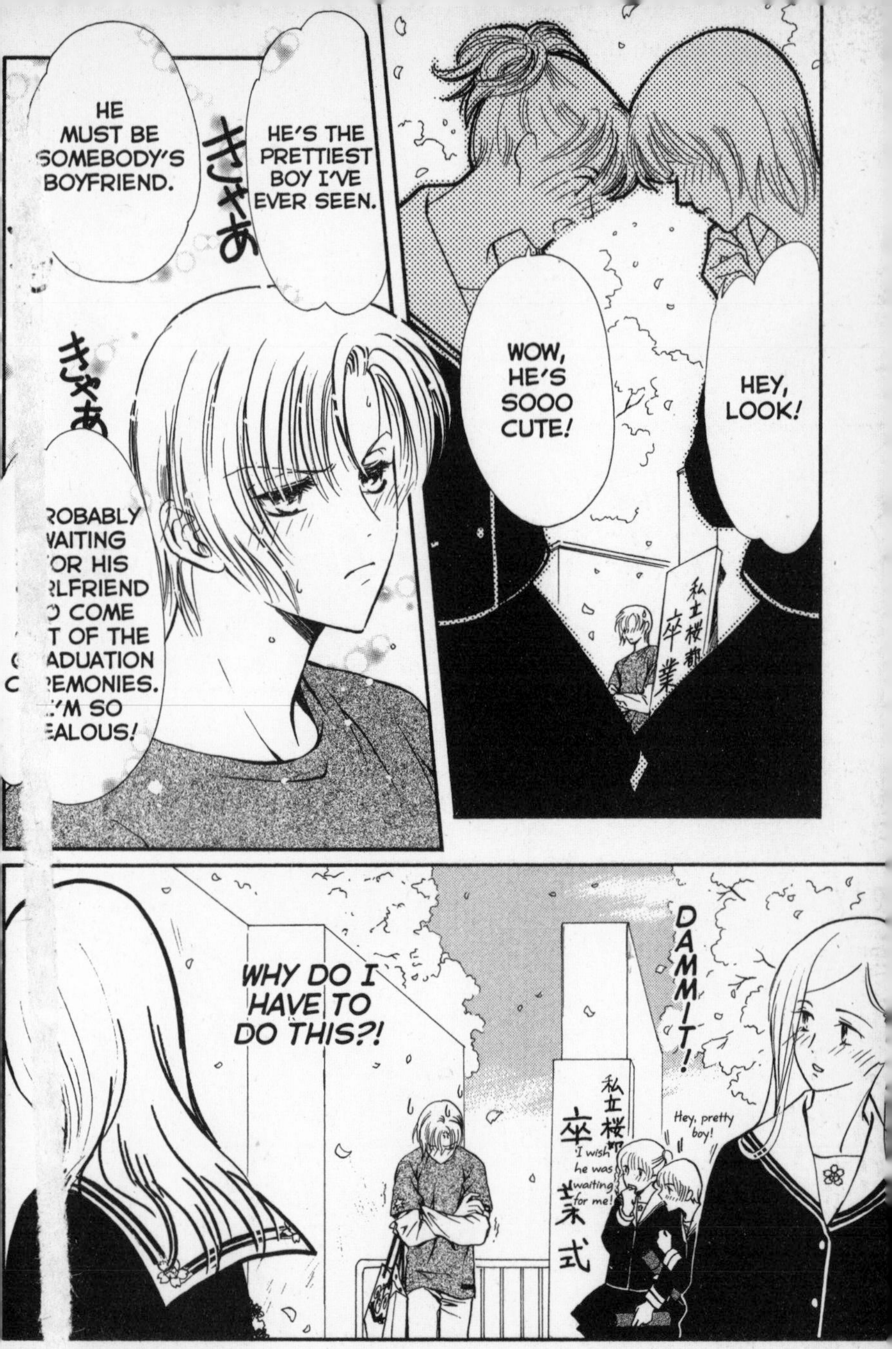
HEY, LOOK!
WOW, HE'S SOOO CUTE!
HE'S THE PRETTIEST BOY I'VE EVER SEEN.
きゃあ
HE MUST BE SOMEBODY'S BOYFRIEND.
きゃあ
ROBABLY AITING OR HIS RLFRIEND O COME T OF THE ADUATION REMONIES. 'M SO EALOUS!
DAMMIT!
WHY DO I HAVE TO DO THIS?!
Hey, pretty boy!
I wish he was waiting for me!

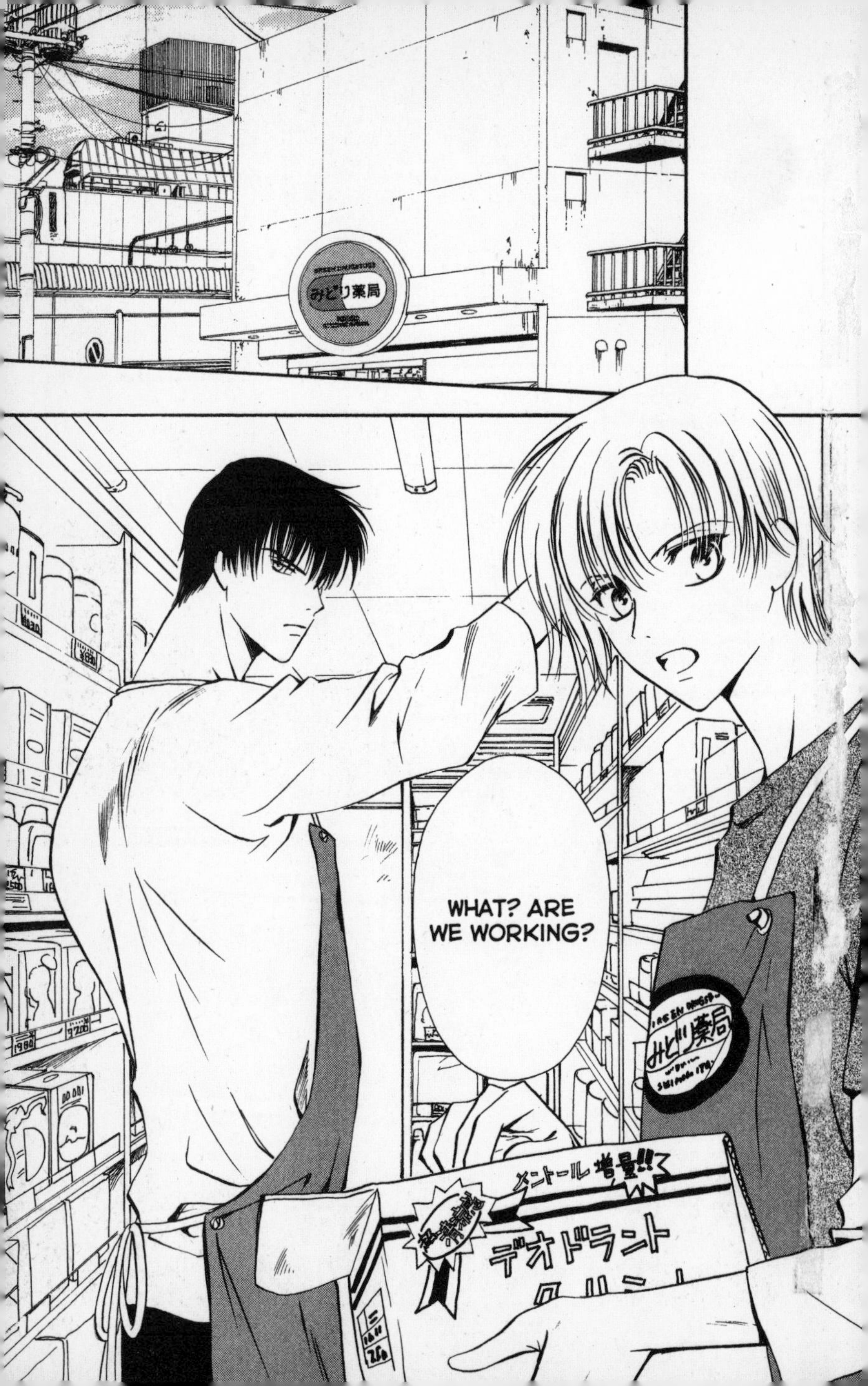
みどり薬局
WHAT? ARE WE WORKING?
みどり薬局
メントール 増量!!
デオドラント

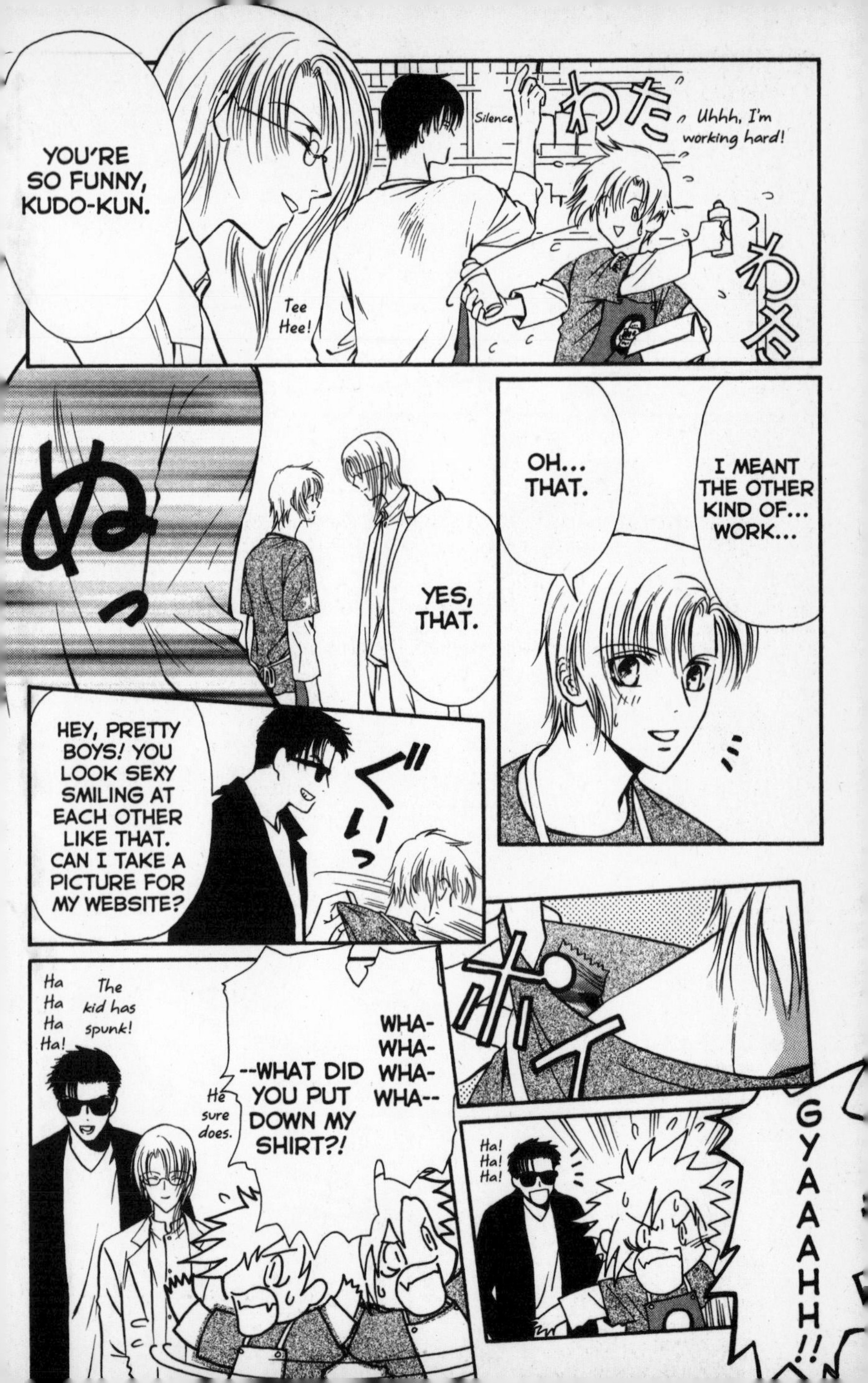
わた
Uhhh, I'm working hard!
Silence
YOU'RE SO FUNNY, KUDO-KUN.
Tee Hee!
I MEANT THE OTHER KIND OF... WORK...
OH... THAT.
YES, THAT.
ぬっ
HEY, PRETTY BOYS! YOU LOOK SEXY SMILING AT EACH OTHER LIKE THAT. CAN I TAKE A PICTURE FOR MY WEBSITE?
ぐいっ
ポイ
GYAAAHH!!
Ha! Ha! Ha!
WHA-WHA-WHA-WHA--
--WHAT DID YOU PUT DOWN MY SHIRT?!
The kid has spunk!
Ha Ha Ha Ha!
He sure does.

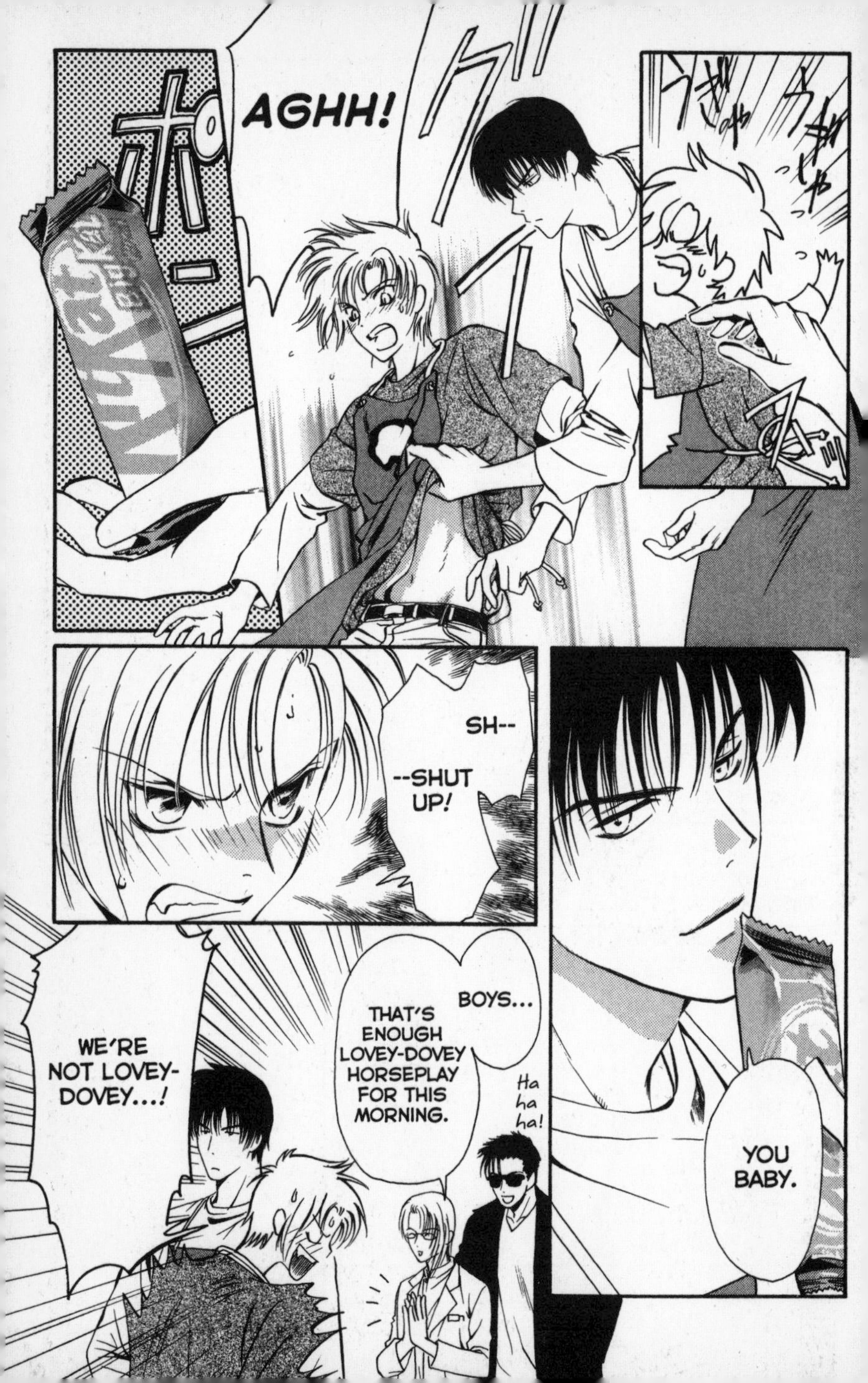
AGHH!
YOU BABY.
SH--
--SHUT UP!
BOYS...
THAT'S ENOUGH LOVEY-DOVEY HORSEPLAY FOR THIS MORNING.
Ha ha ha!
WE'RE NOT LOVEY-DOVEY...!

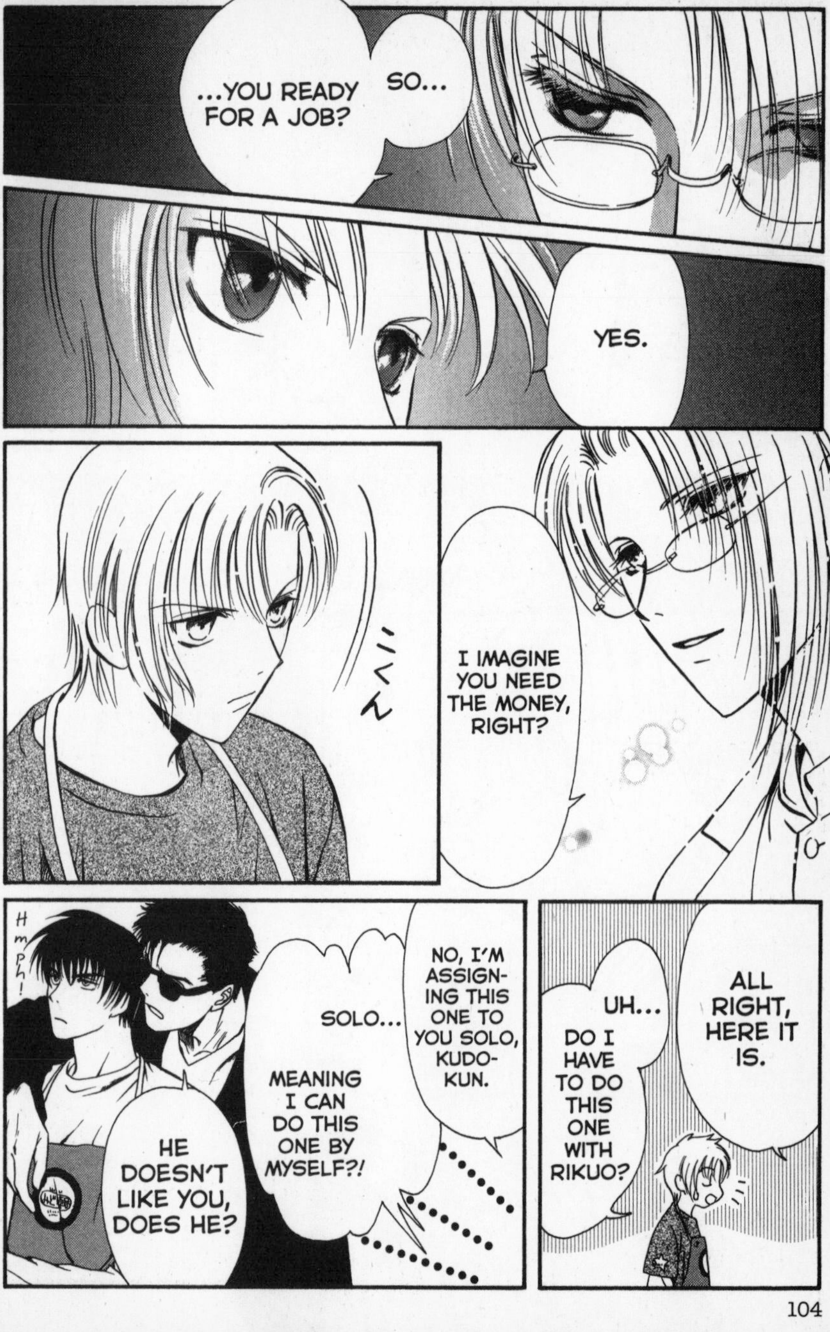
SO...
...YOU READY FOR A JOB?
YES.
I IMAGINE YOU NEED THE MONEY, RIGHT?
ALL RIGHT, HERE IT IS.
UH...
DO I HAVE TO DO THIS ONE WITH RIKUO?
NO, I'M ASSIGNING THIS ONE TO YOU SOLO, KUDO-KUN.
SOLO...
MEANING I CAN DO THIS ONE BY MYSELF?!
......
HE DOESN'T LIKE YOU, DOES HE?
Hmph!

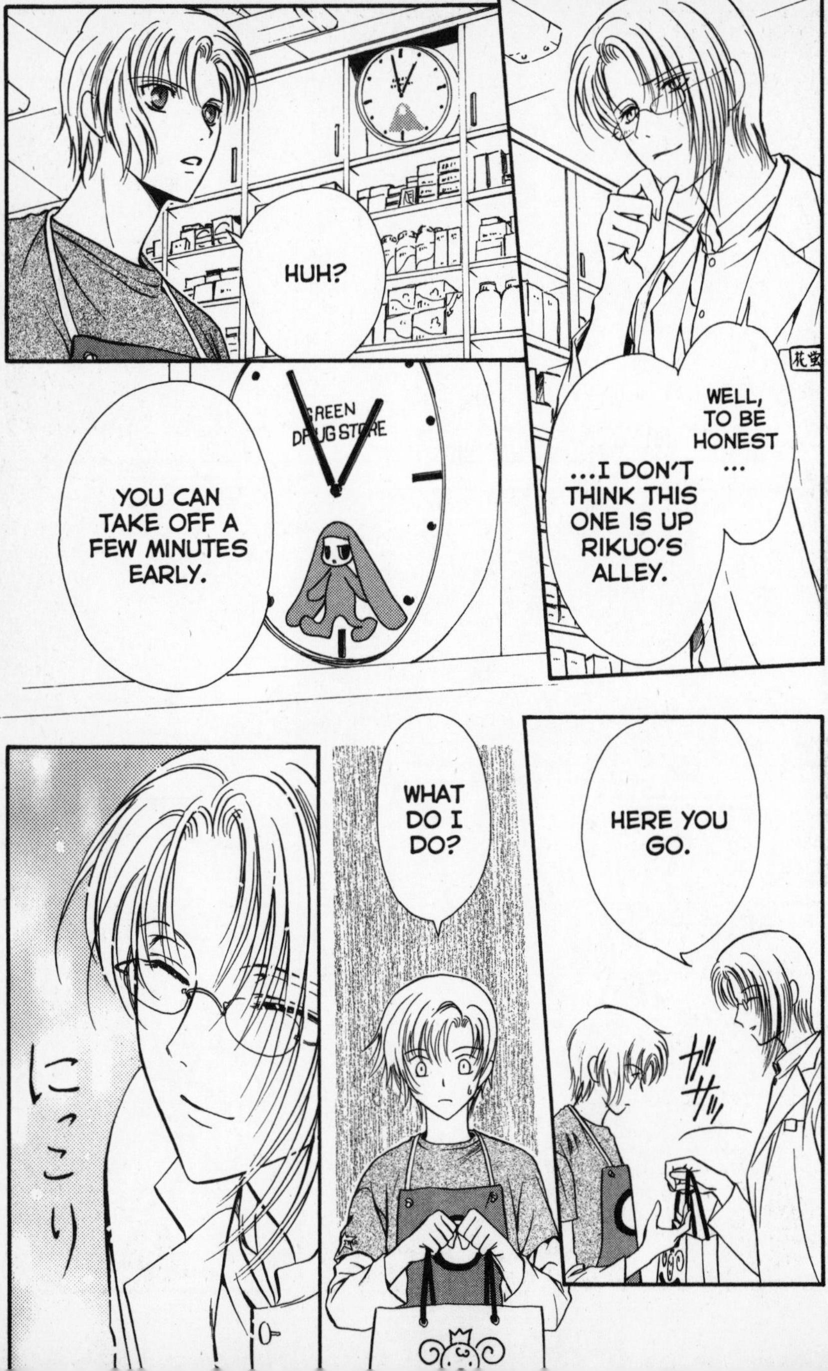
WELL, TO BE HONEST ...
...I DON'T THINK THIS ONE IS UP RIKUO'S ALLEY.
HUH?
GREEN DRUG STORE
YOU CAN TAKE OFF A FEW MINUTES EARLY.
HERE YOU GO.
ガサッ
WHAT DO I DO?
にっこり

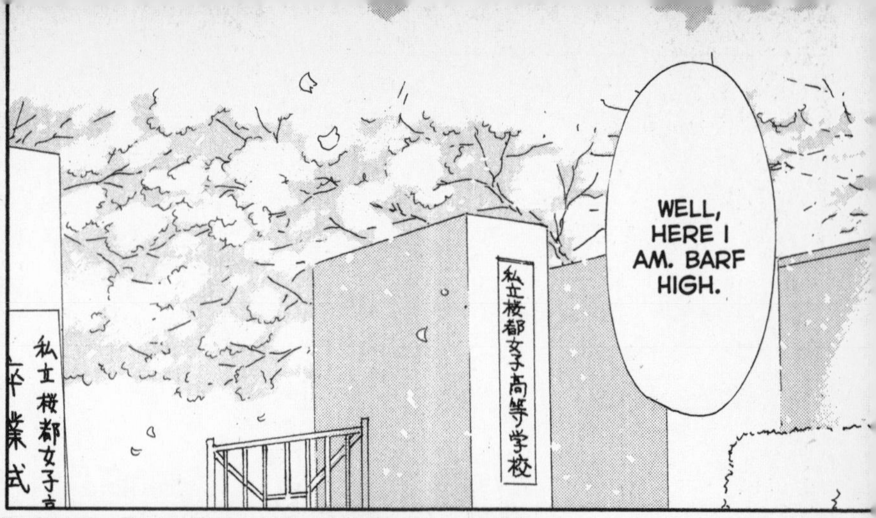
WELL, HERE I AM. BARF HIGH.
私立桜都女子高等学校
私立桜都女子高
卒業式

Translator's Note: The word Ohto can also be written with kanji that mean barf.

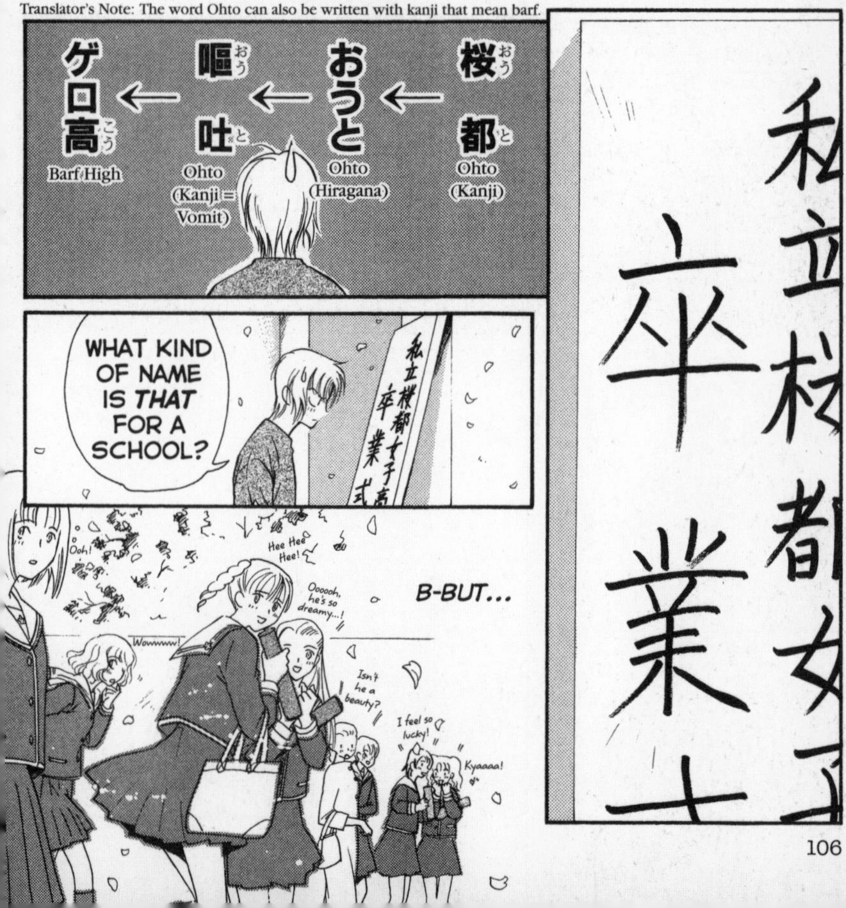
私立桜都女
卒業
桜都
Ohto (Kanji)
おうと
Ohto (Hiragana)
嘔吐
Ohto (Kanji = Vomit)
ゲロ高
Barf High
WHAT KIND OF NAME IS *THAT* FOR A SCHOOL?
私立桜都女子高
卒業式
B-BUT...
Hee Hee Hee!
Ooh!
Oooooh, he's so dreamy...!
Wowwww!
Isn't he a beauty?
I feel so lucky!
Kyaaaa!

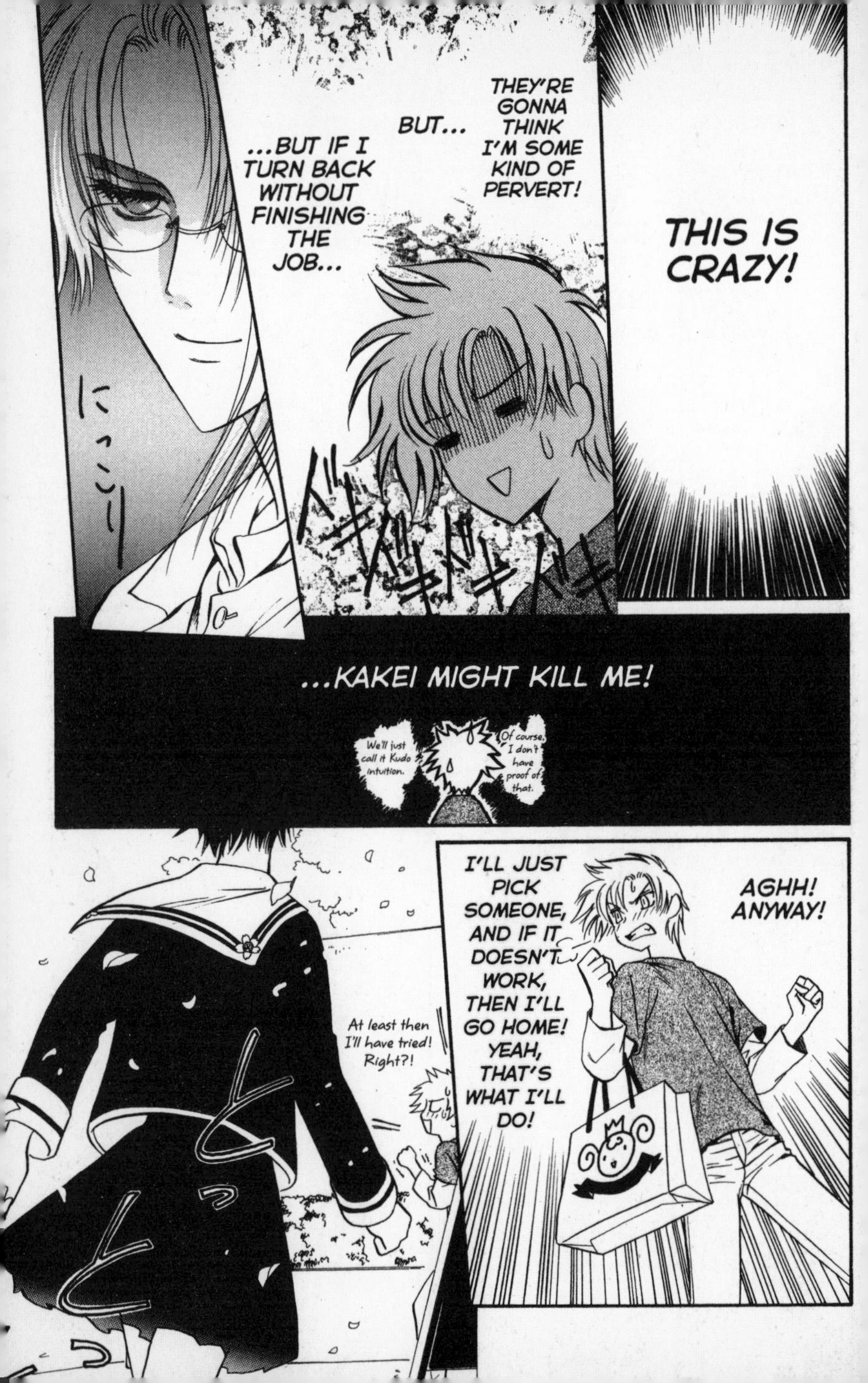
THIS IS CRAZY!
THEY'RE GONNA THINK I'M SOME KIND OF PERVERT!
BUT...
...BUT IF I TURN BACK WITHOUT FINISHING THE JOB...
にっこり
...KAKEI MIGHT KILL ME!
Of course, I don't have proof of that.
We'll just call it Kudo intuition.
AGHH! ANYWAY!
I'LL JUST PICK SOMEONE, AND IF IT DOESN'T WORK, THEN I'LL GO HOME! YEAH, THAT'S WHAT I'LL DO!
At least then I'll have tried! Right?!

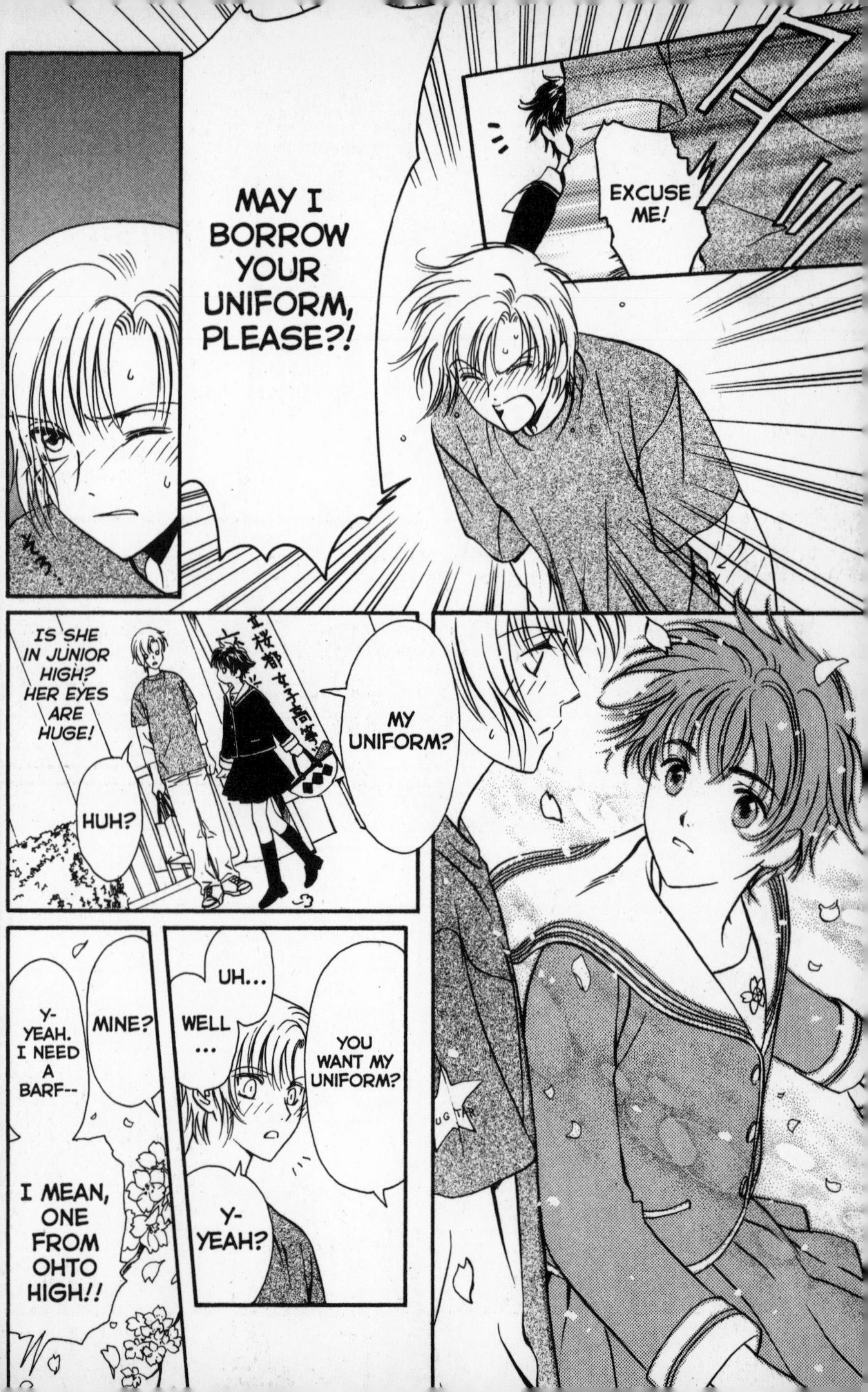
EXCUSE ME!
MAY I BORROW YOUR UNIFORM, PLEASE?!
MY UNIFORM?
IS SHE IN JUNIOR HIGH? HER EYES ARE HUGE!
HUH?
YOU WANT MY UNIFORM?
UH...
WELL ...
Y-YEAH?
MINE?
Y-YEAH. I NEED A BARF--
I MEAN, ONE FROM OHTO HIGH!!

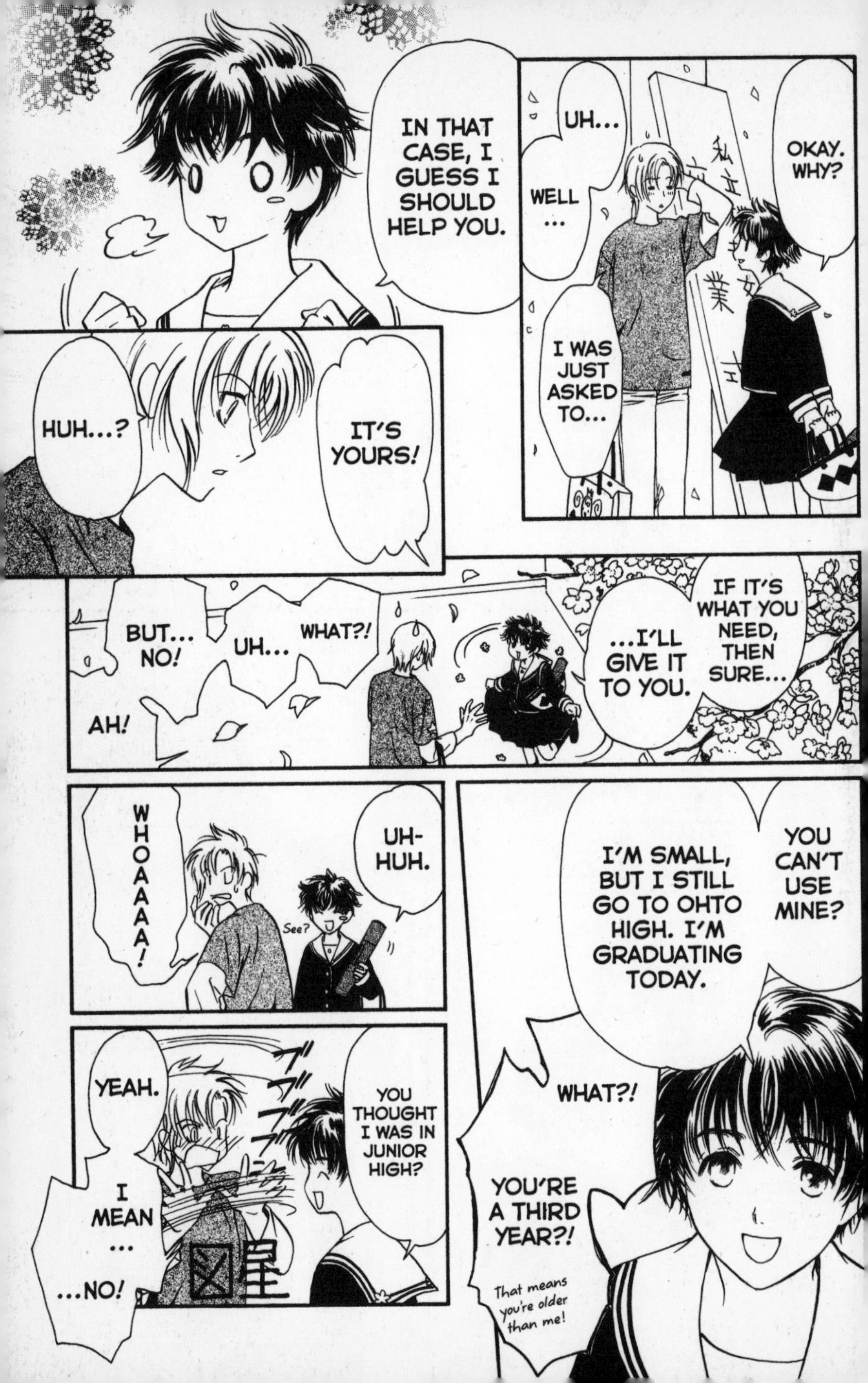
OKAY. WHY?
UH...
WELL ...
I WAS JUST ASKED TO...
IN THAT CASE, I GUESS I SHOULD HELP YOU.
IT'S YOURS!
HUH...?
IF IT'S WHAT YOU NEED, THEN SURE...
...I'LL GIVE IT TO YOU.
WHAT?!
UH...
BUT... NO!
AH!
YOU CAN'T USE MINE?
I'M SMALL, BUT I STILL GO TO OHTO HIGH. I'M GRADUATING TODAY.
WHAT?!
YOU'RE A THIRD YEAR?!
That means you're older than me!
UH-HUH.
See?
WHOAAAAA!
YOU THOUGHT I WAS IN JUNIOR HIGH?
YEAH.
I MEAN ...
...NO!

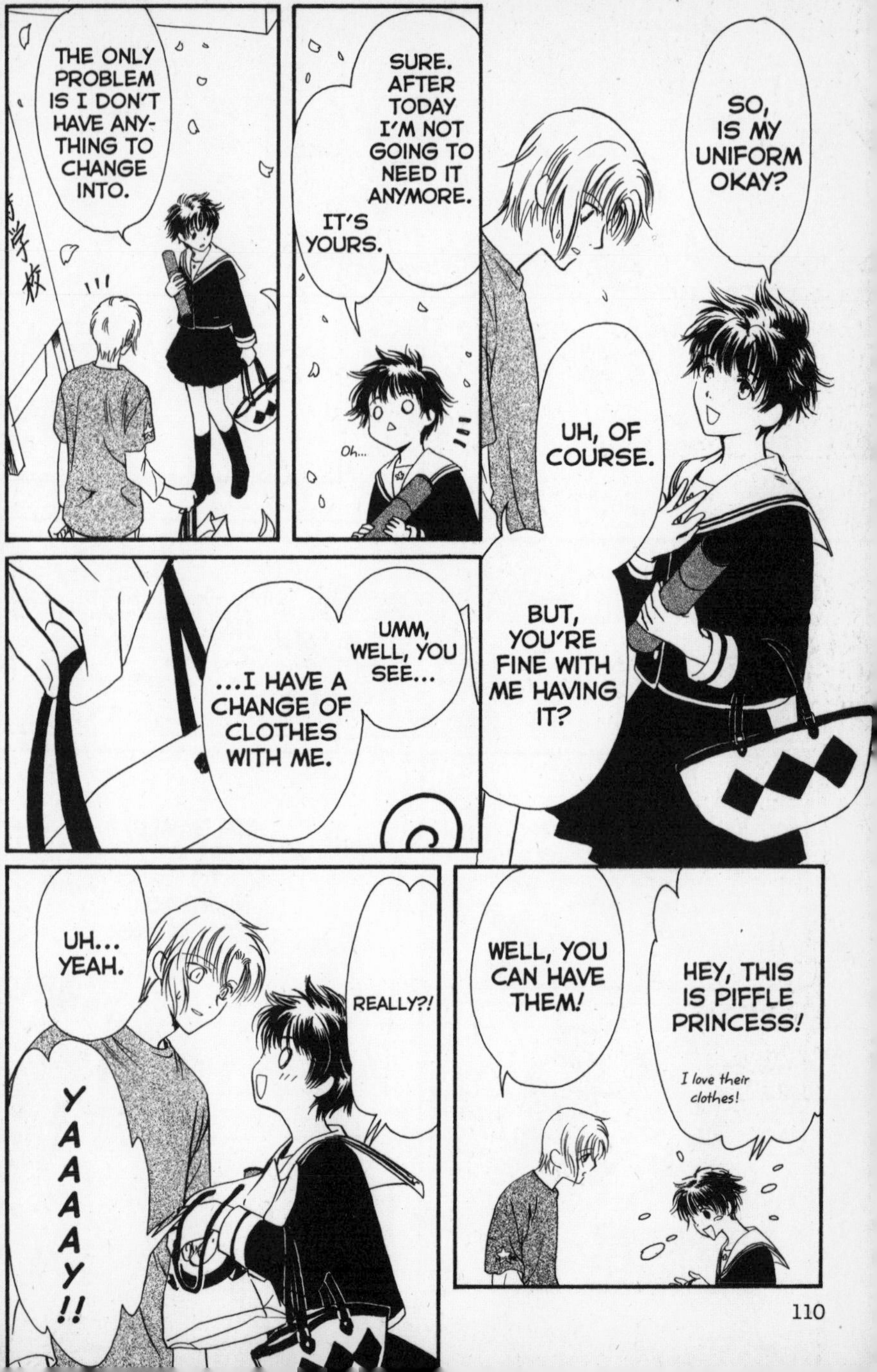
SO, IS MY UNIFORM OKAY?
UH, OF COURSE.
BUT, YOU'RE FINE WITH ME HAVING IT?
SURE. AFTER TODAY I'M NOT GOING TO NEED IT ANYMORE.
IT'S YOURS.
Oh...
THE ONLY PROBLEM IS I DON'T HAVE ANY-THING TO CHANGE INTO.
UMM, WELL, YOU SEE...
...I HAVE A CHANGE OF CLOTHES WITH ME.
HEY, THIS IS PIFFLE PRINCESS!
I love their clothes!
WELL, YOU CAN HAVE THEM!
REALLY?!
UH... YEAH.
YAAAAAY!!

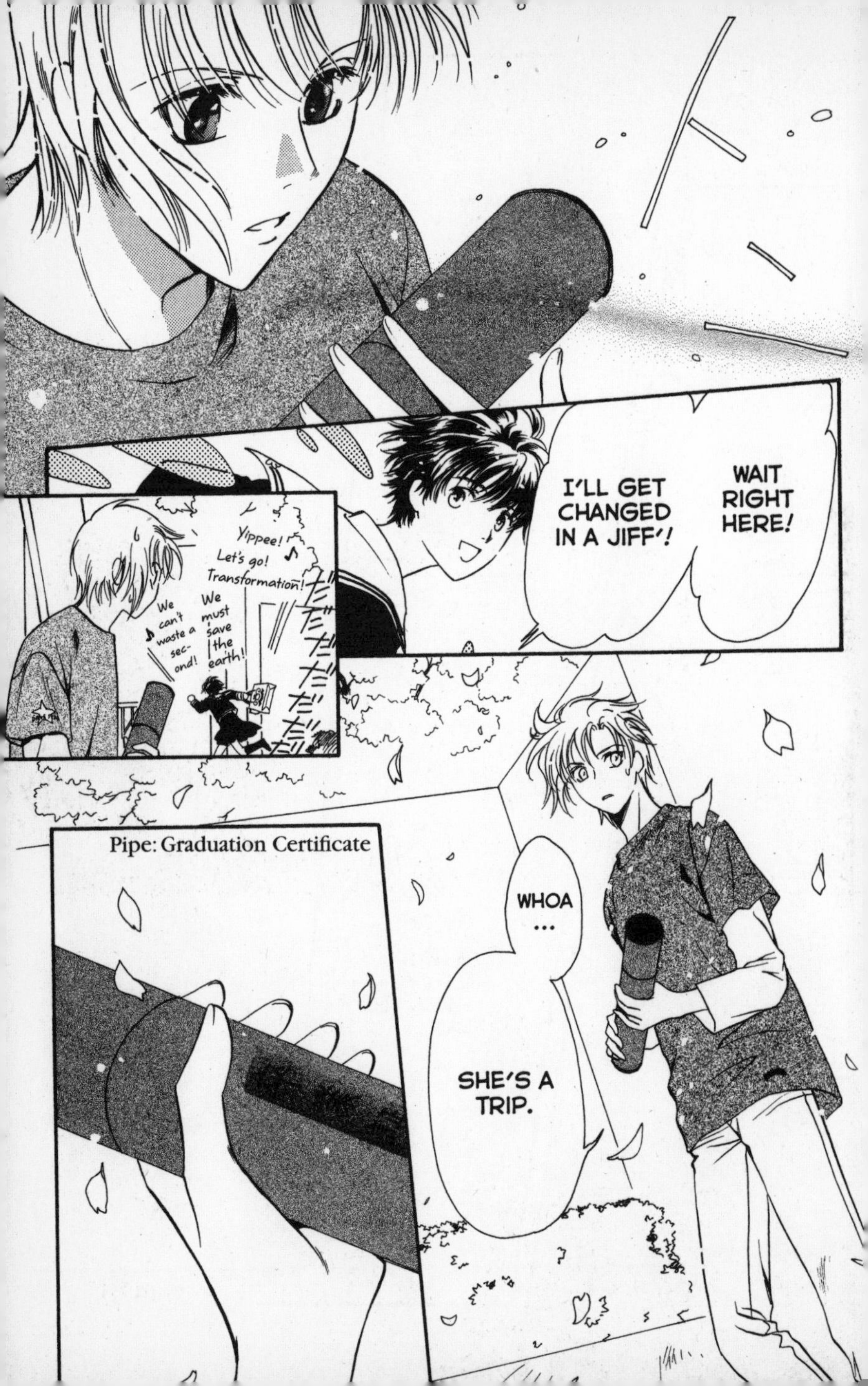
WAIT RIGHT HERE!
I'LL GET CHANGED IN A JIFF'!
Yippee! ♪
Let's go! Transformation!
We must save the earth!
We can't waste a second!
WHOA ...
SHE'S A TRIP.
Pipe: Graduation Certificate

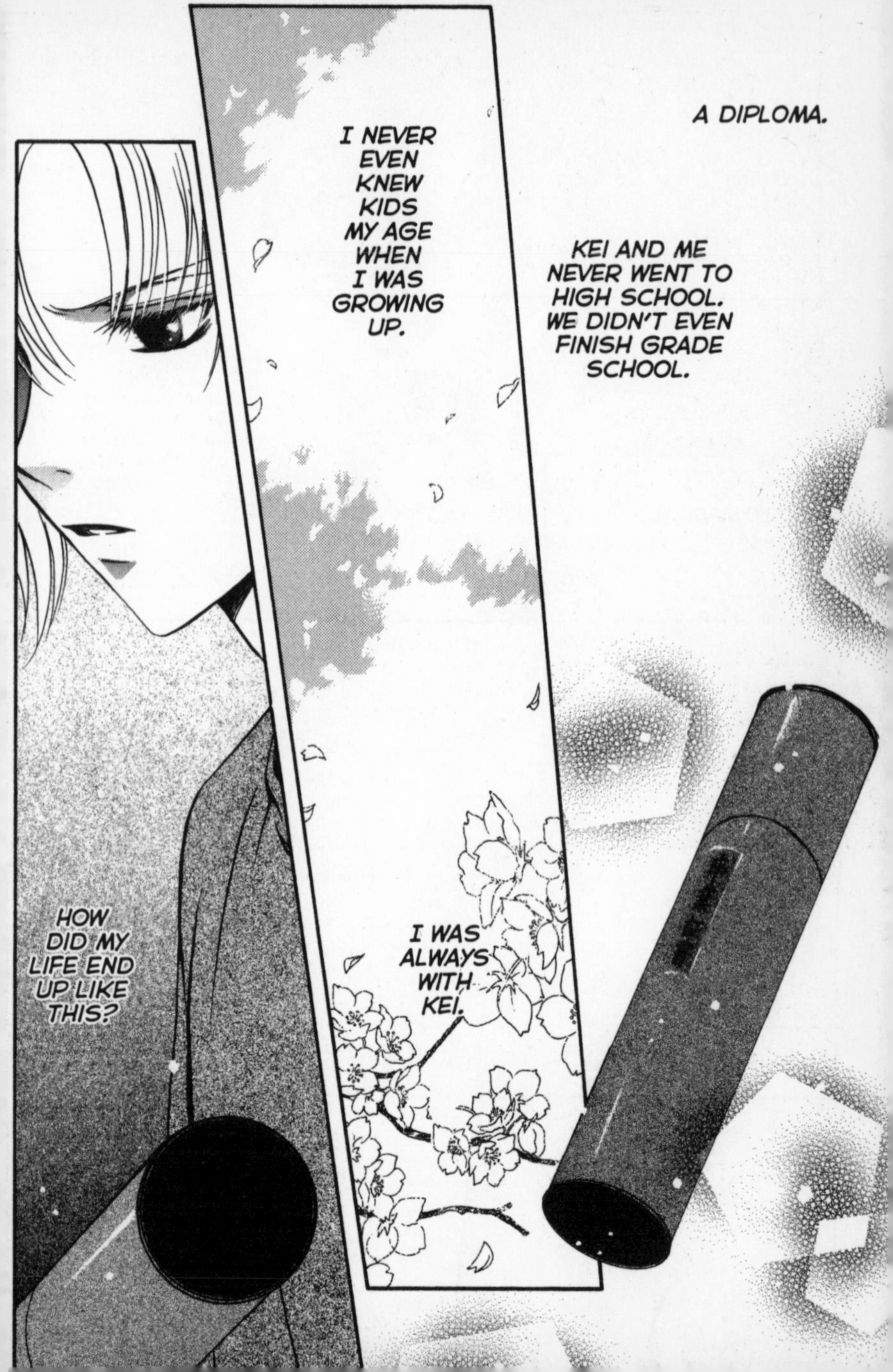
A DIPLOMA.
KEI AND ME NEVER WENT TO HIGH SCHOOL. WE DIDN'T EVEN FINISH GRADE SCHOOL.
I NEVER EVEN KNEW KIDS MY AGE WHEN I WAS GROWING UP.
I WAS ALWAYS WITH KEI.
HOW DID MY LIFE END UP LIKE THIS?

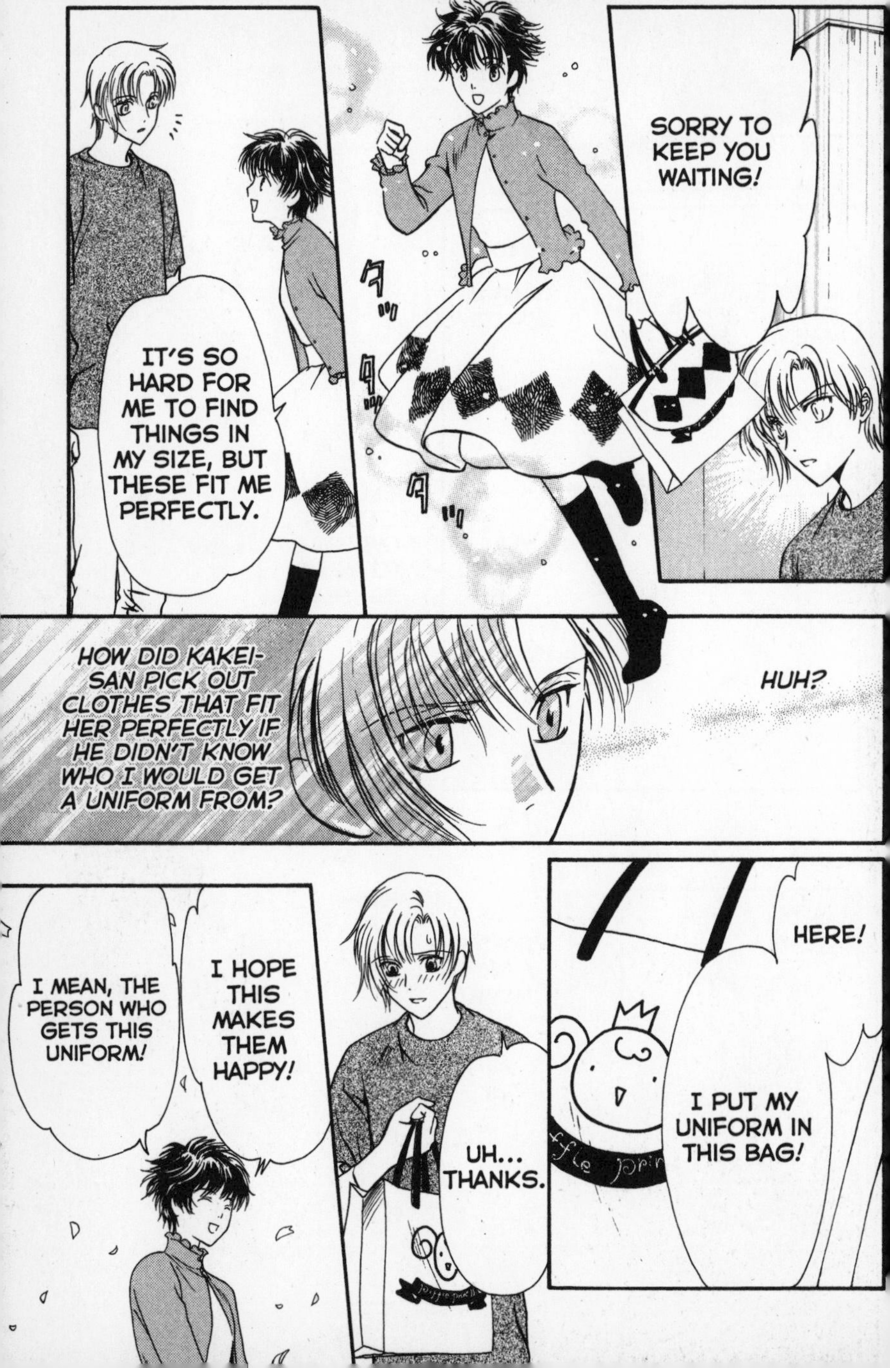
SORRY TO KEEP YOU WAITING!
IT'S SO HARD FOR ME TO FIND THINGS IN MY SIZE, BUT THESE FIT ME PERFECTLY.
HUH?
HOW DID KAKEI-SAN PICK OUT CLOTHES THAT FIT HER PERFECTLY IF HE DIDN'T KNOW WHO I WOULD GET A UNIFORM FROM?
HERE!
I PUT MY UNIFORM IN THIS BAG!
UH... THANKS.
I HOPE THIS MAKES THEM HAPPY!
I MEAN, THE PERSON WHO GETS THIS UNIFORM!

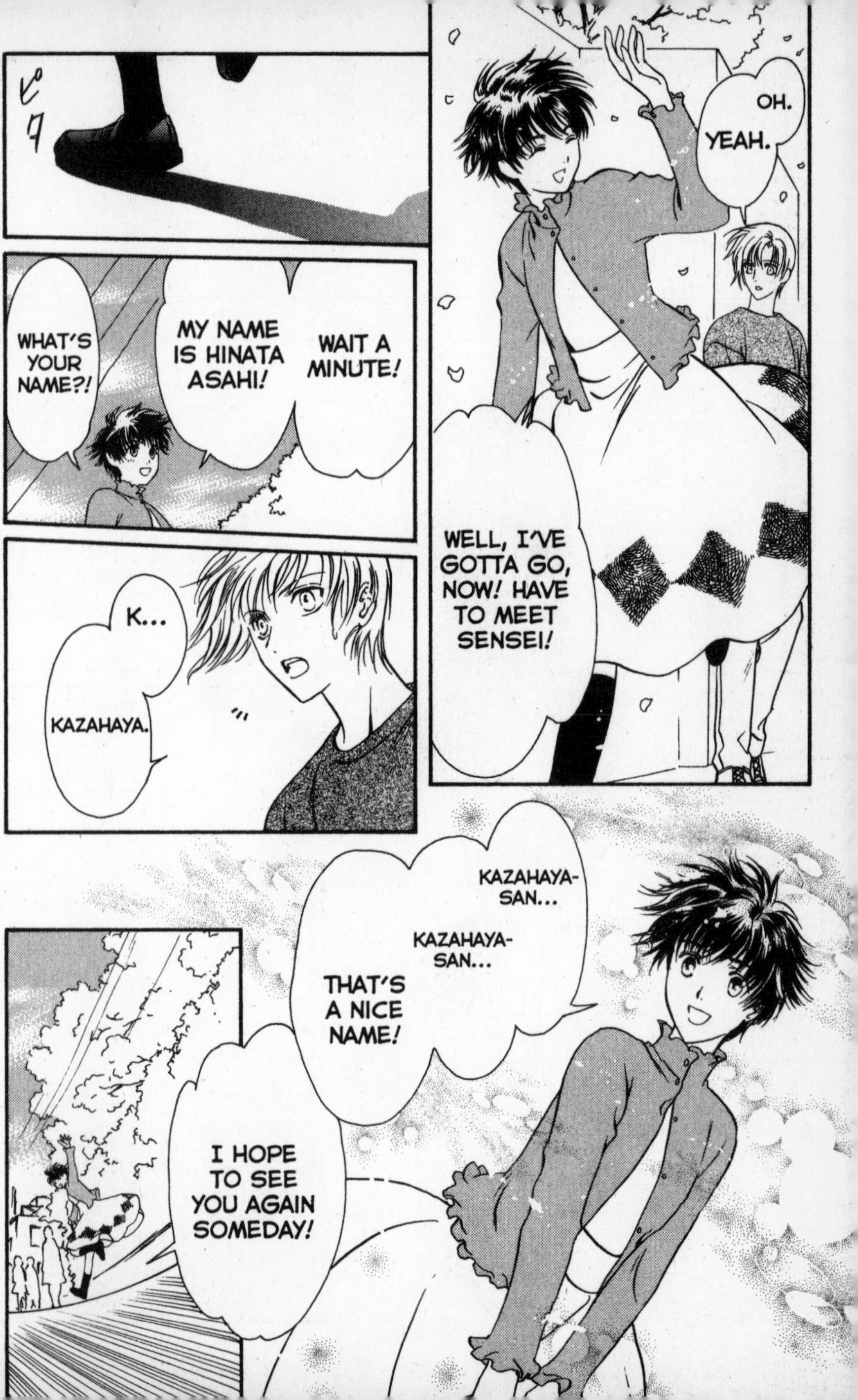
OH. YEAH.
WELL, I'VE GOTTA GO, NOW! HAVE TO MEET SENSEI!
ピク
WAIT A MINUTE!
MY NAME IS HINATA ASAHI!
WHAT'S YOUR NAME?!
K...
KAZAHAYA.
KAZAHAYA-SAN...
KAZAHAYA-SAN...
THAT'S A NICE NAME!
I HOPE TO SEE YOU AGAIN SOMEDAY!

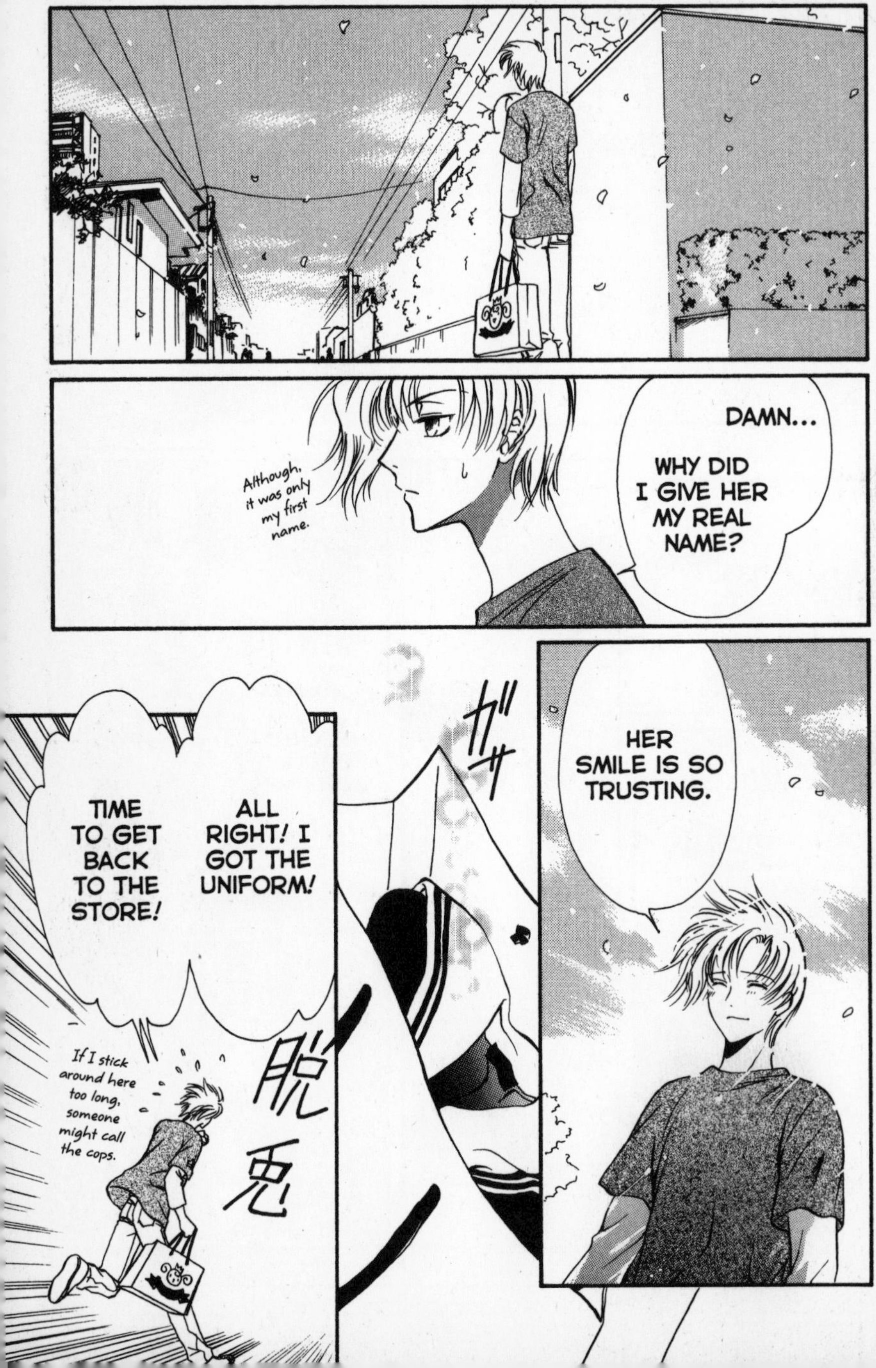
DAMN...
WHY DID I GIVE HER MY REAL NAME?
Although, it was only my first name.
HER SMILE IS SO TRUSTING.
ガサ
ALL RIGHT! I GOT THE UNIFORM!
TIME TO GET BACK TO THE STORE!
脱兎
If I stick around here too long, someone might call the cops.

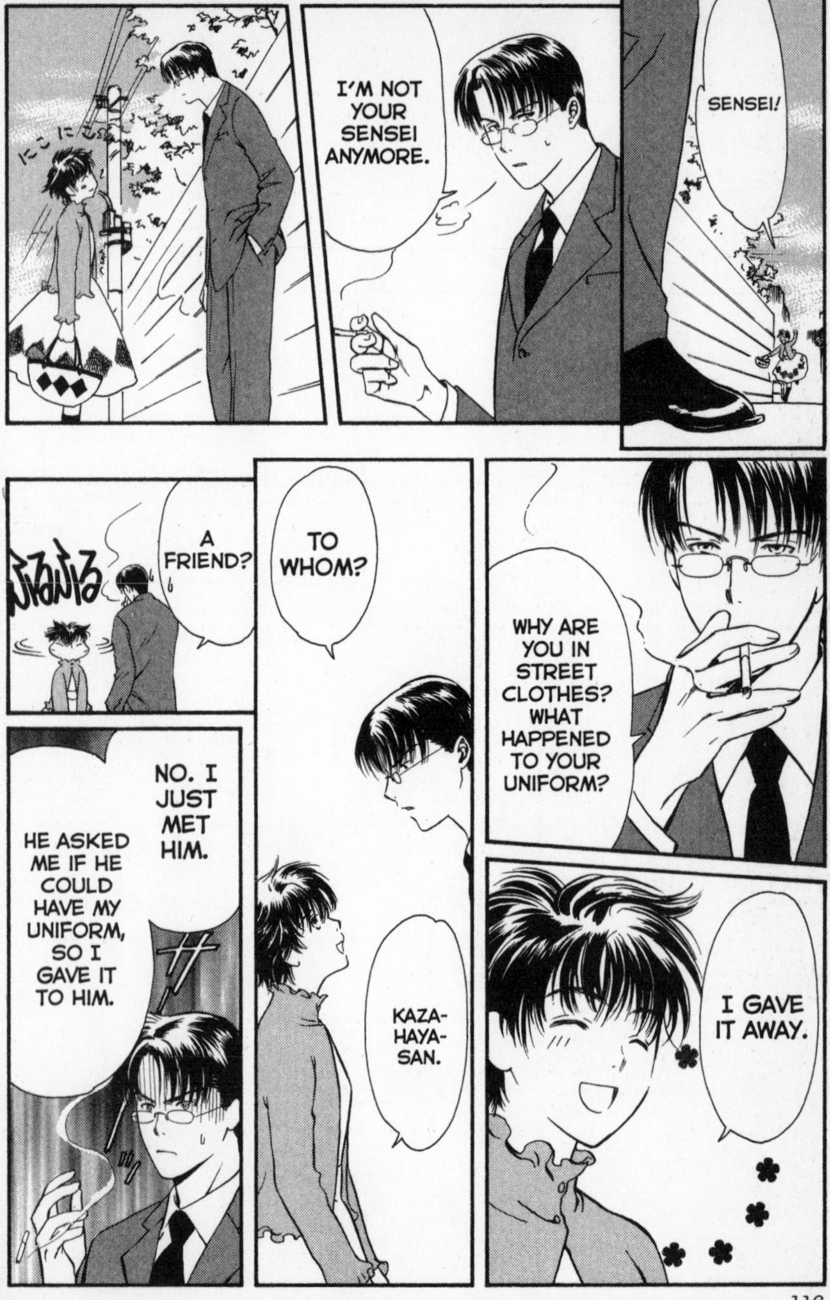
SENSEI!
I'M NOT YOUR SENSEI ANYMORE.
にこにこ
WHY ARE YOU IN STREET CLOTHES? WHAT HAPPENED TO YOUR UNIFORM?
I GAVE IT AWAY.
TO WHOM?
KAZA-HAYA-SAN.
A FRIEND?
ふるふる
NO. I JUST MET HIM.
HE ASKED ME IF HE COULD HAVE MY UNIFORM, SO I GAVE IT TO HIM.

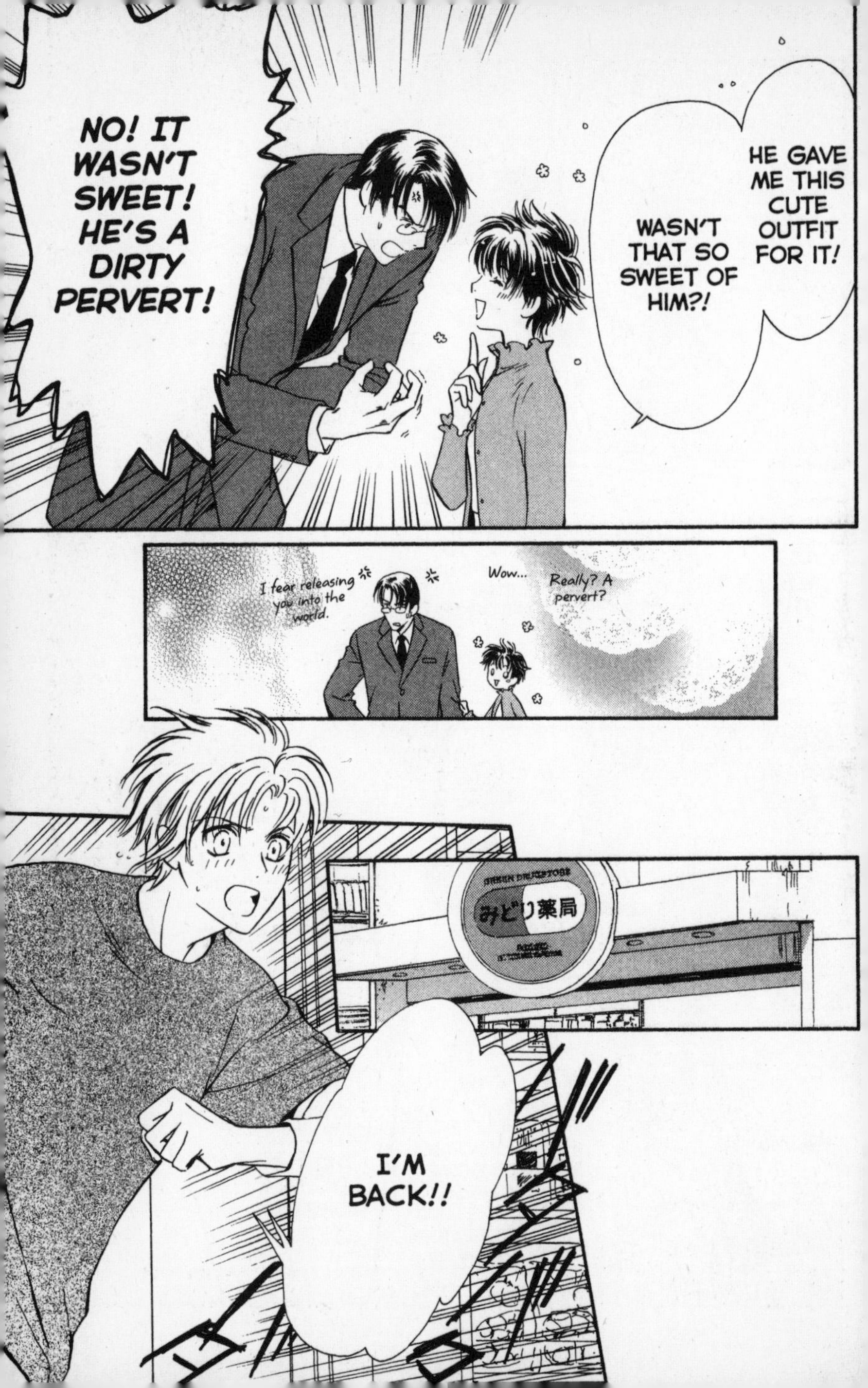
HE GAVE ME THIS CUTE OUTFIT FOR IT!
WASN'T THAT SO SWEET OF HIM?!
NO! IT WASN'T SWEET! HE'S A DIRTY PERVERT!
Really? A pervert?
Wow...
I fear releasing you into the world.
みどり薬局
I'M BACK!!

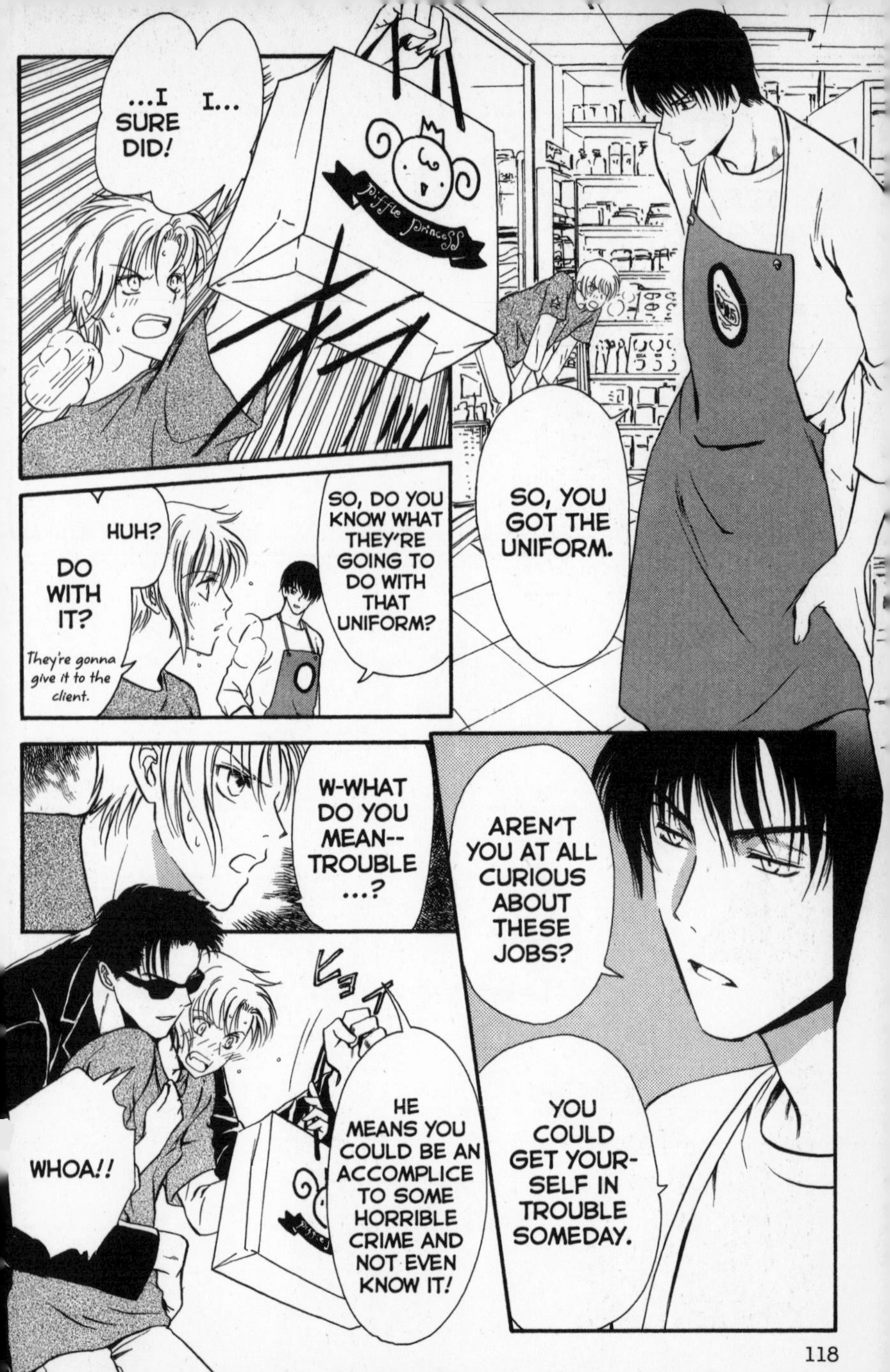
SO, YOU GOT THE UNIFORM.
I...
...I SURE DID!
Piffle Princess
SO, DO YOU KNOW WHAT THEY'RE GOING TO DO WITH THAT UNIFORM?
HUH?
DO WITH IT?
They're gonna give it to the client.
AREN'T YOU AT ALL CURIOUS ABOUT THESE JOBS?
YOU COULD GET YOURSELF IN TROUBLE SOMEDAY.
W-WHAT DO YOU MEAN--TROUBLE ...?
HE MEANS YOU COULD BE AN ACCOMPLICE TO SOME HORRIBLE CRIME AND NOT EVEN KNOW IT!
WHOA!!

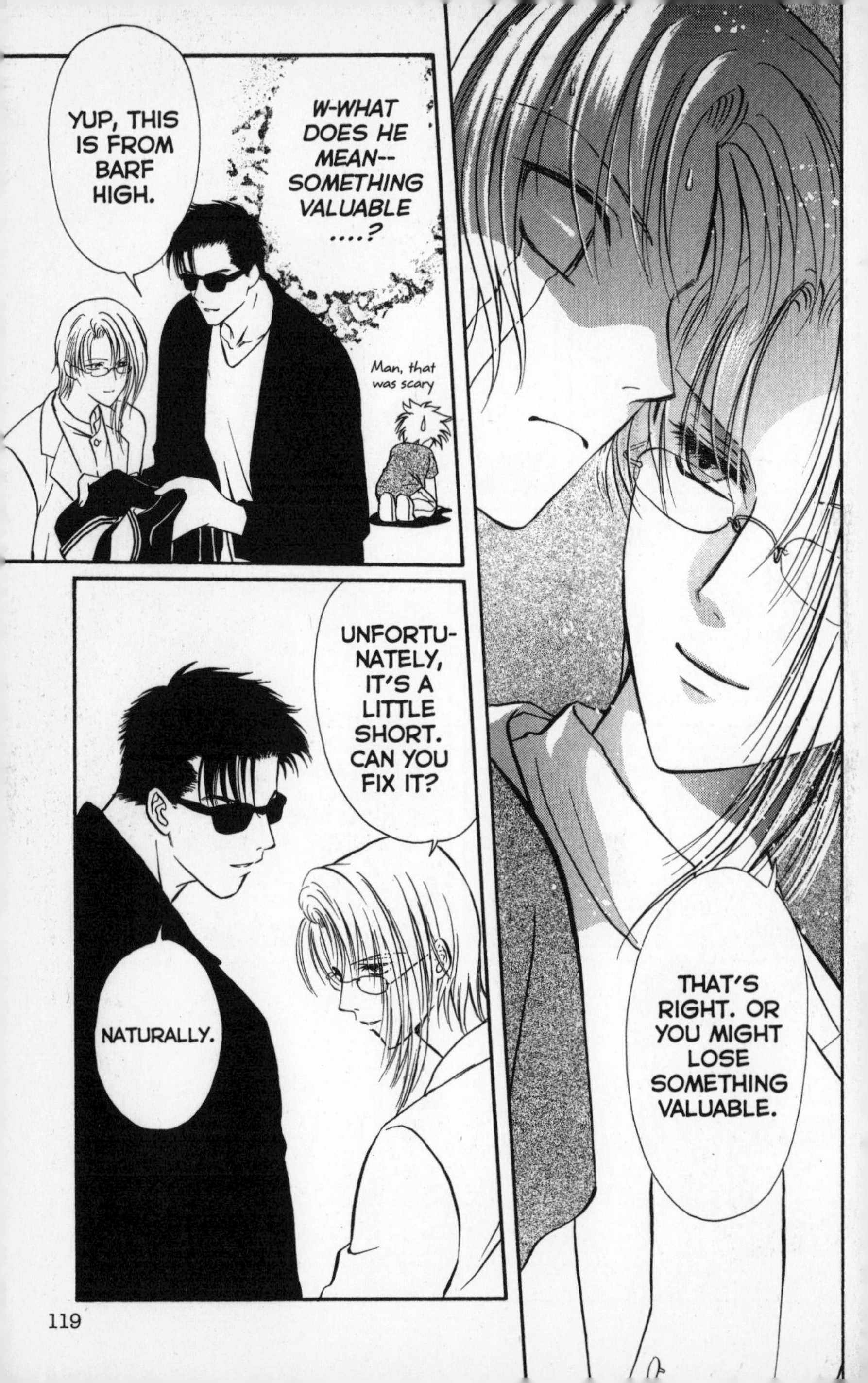
THAT'S RIGHT. OR YOU MIGHT LOSE SOMETHING VALUABLE.
YUP, THIS IS FROM BARF HIGH.
W-WHAT DOES HE MEAN--SOMETHING VALUABLE ....?
Man, that was scary
UNFORTU-NATELY, IT'S A LITTLE SHORT. CAN YOU FIX IT?
NATURALLY.

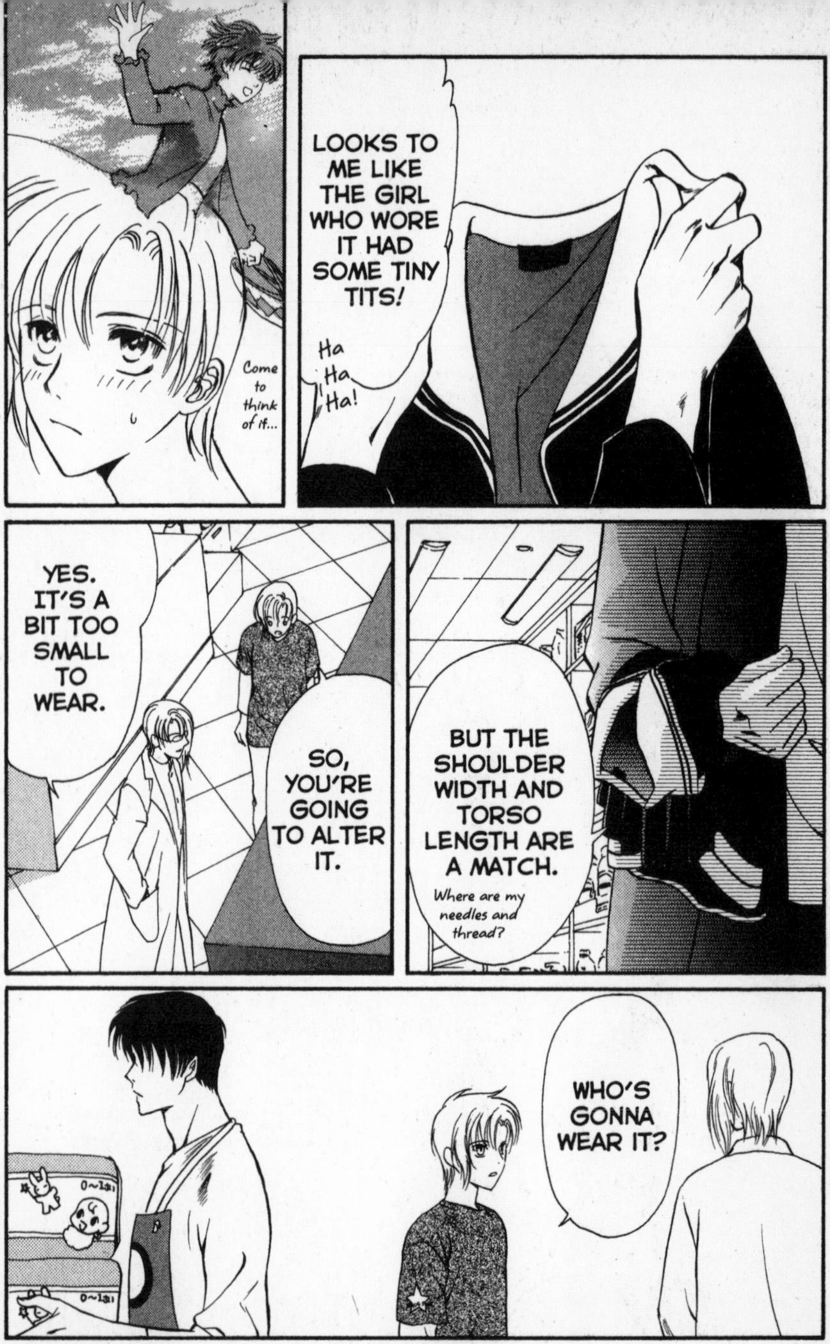
LOOKS TO ME LIKE THE GIRL WHO WORE IT HAD SOME TINY TITS!
Ha Ha Ha!
Come to think of it...
BUT THE SHOULDER WIDTH AND TORSO LENGTH ARE A MATCH.
Where are my needles and thread?
SO, YOU'RE GOING TO ALTER IT.
YES. IT'S A BIT TOO SMALL TO WEAR.
WHO'S GONNA WEAR IT?

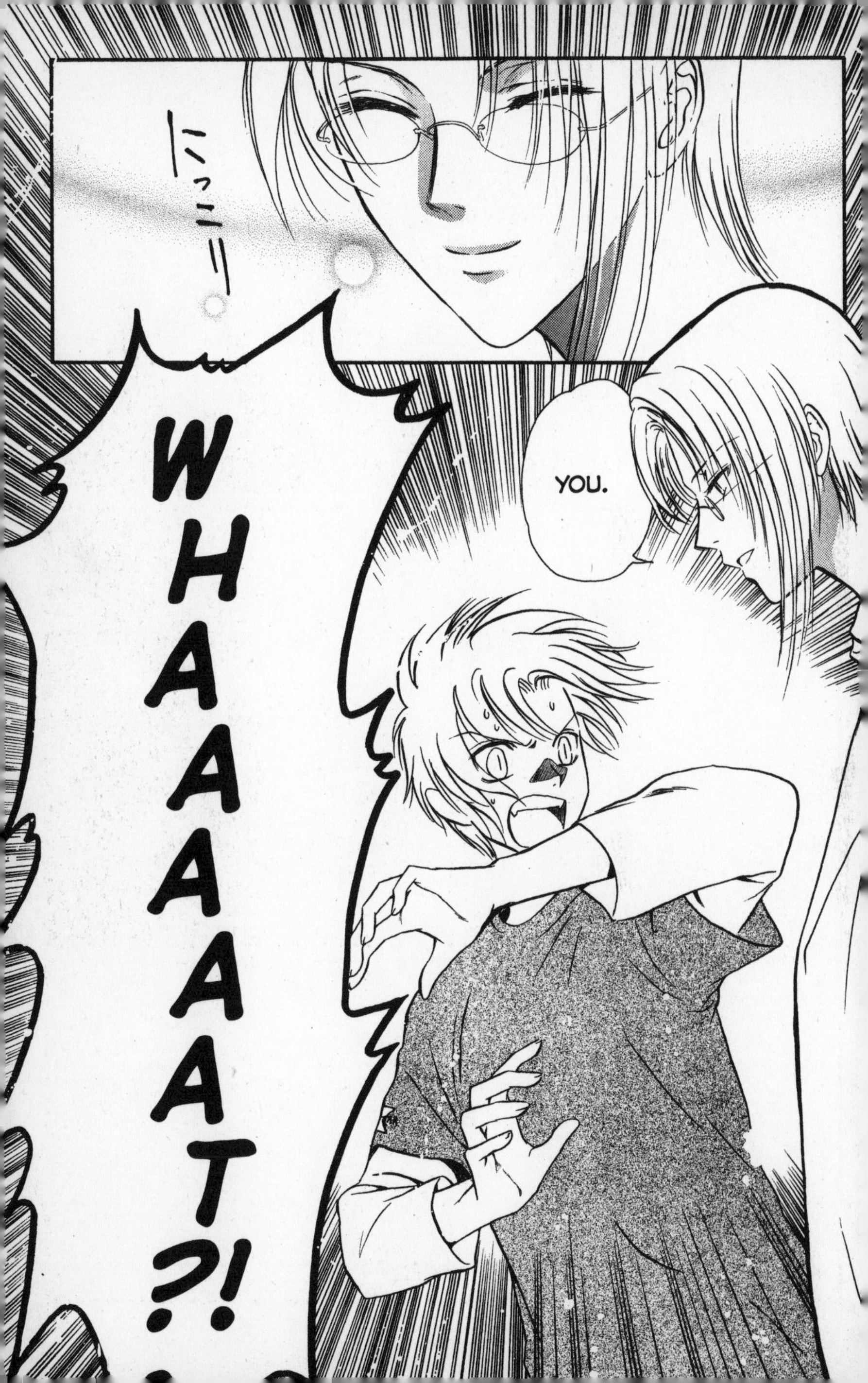
にっこり
YOU.
WHAAAAAT?!

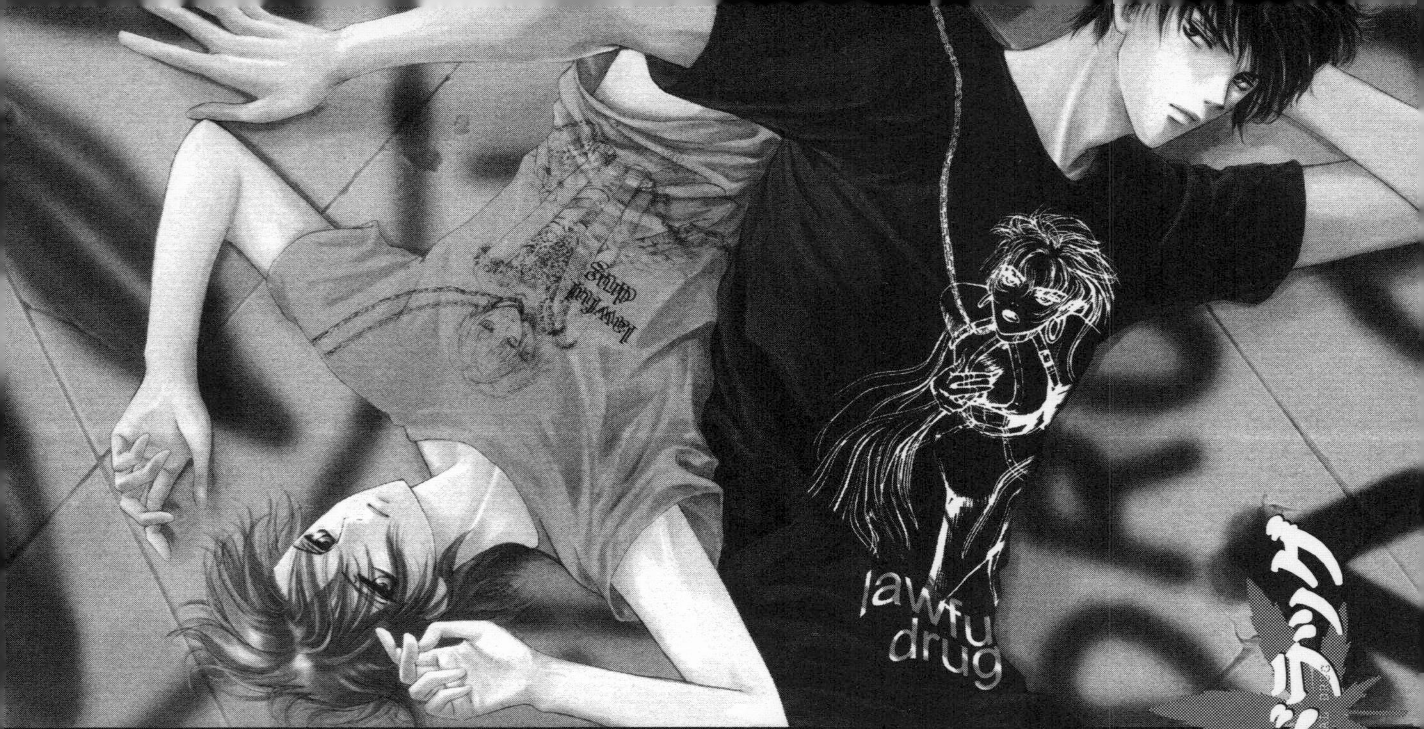
lawful
drug
lawfu
drug

合法ドラッグ

DRUG NO.10 Daily use of the drug may be hazardous.

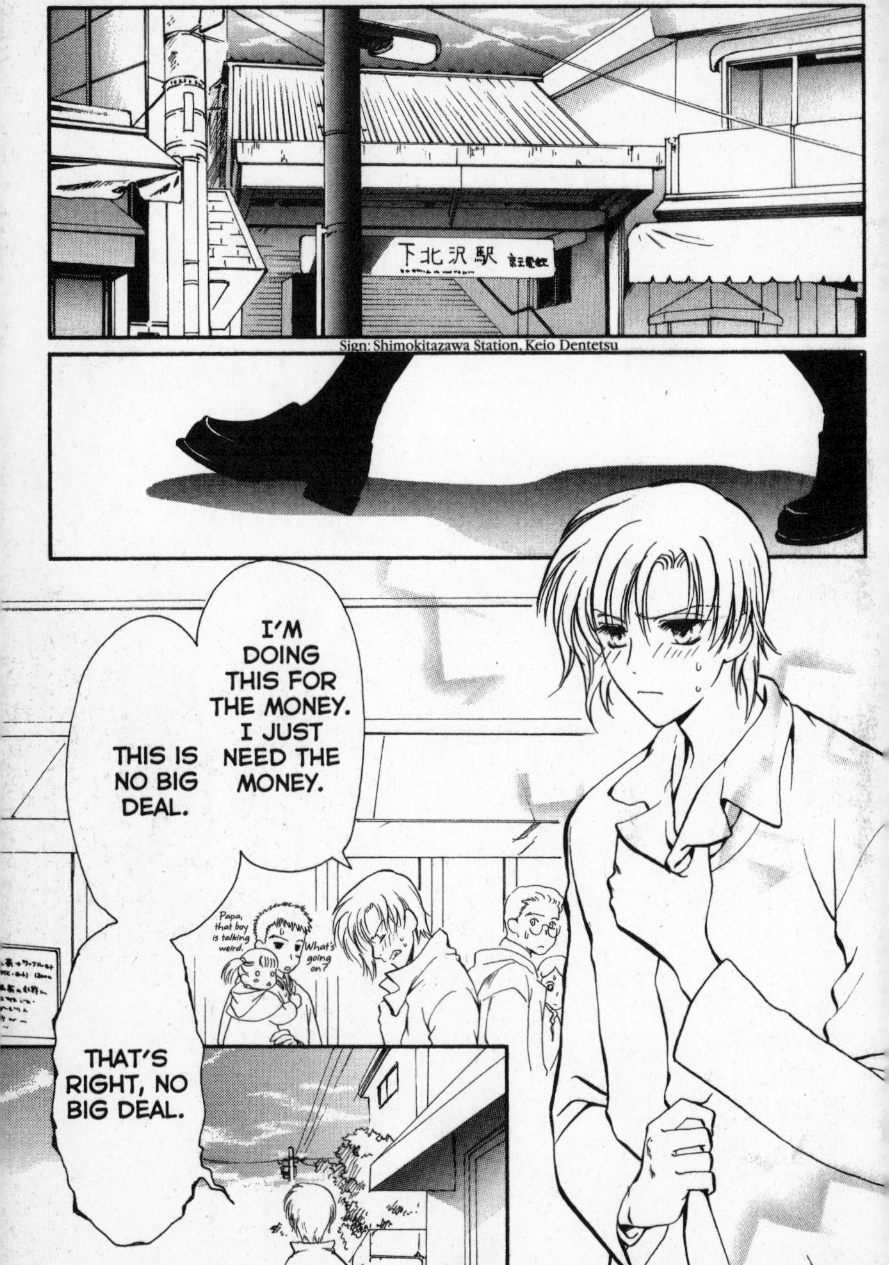
下北沢駅
Sign: Shimokitazawa Station, Keio Dentetsu
I'M DOING THIS FOR THE MONEY. I JUST NEED THE MONEY.
THIS IS NO BIG DEAL.
What's going on?
Papa, that boy is talking weird.
THAT'S RIGHT, NO BIG DEAL.

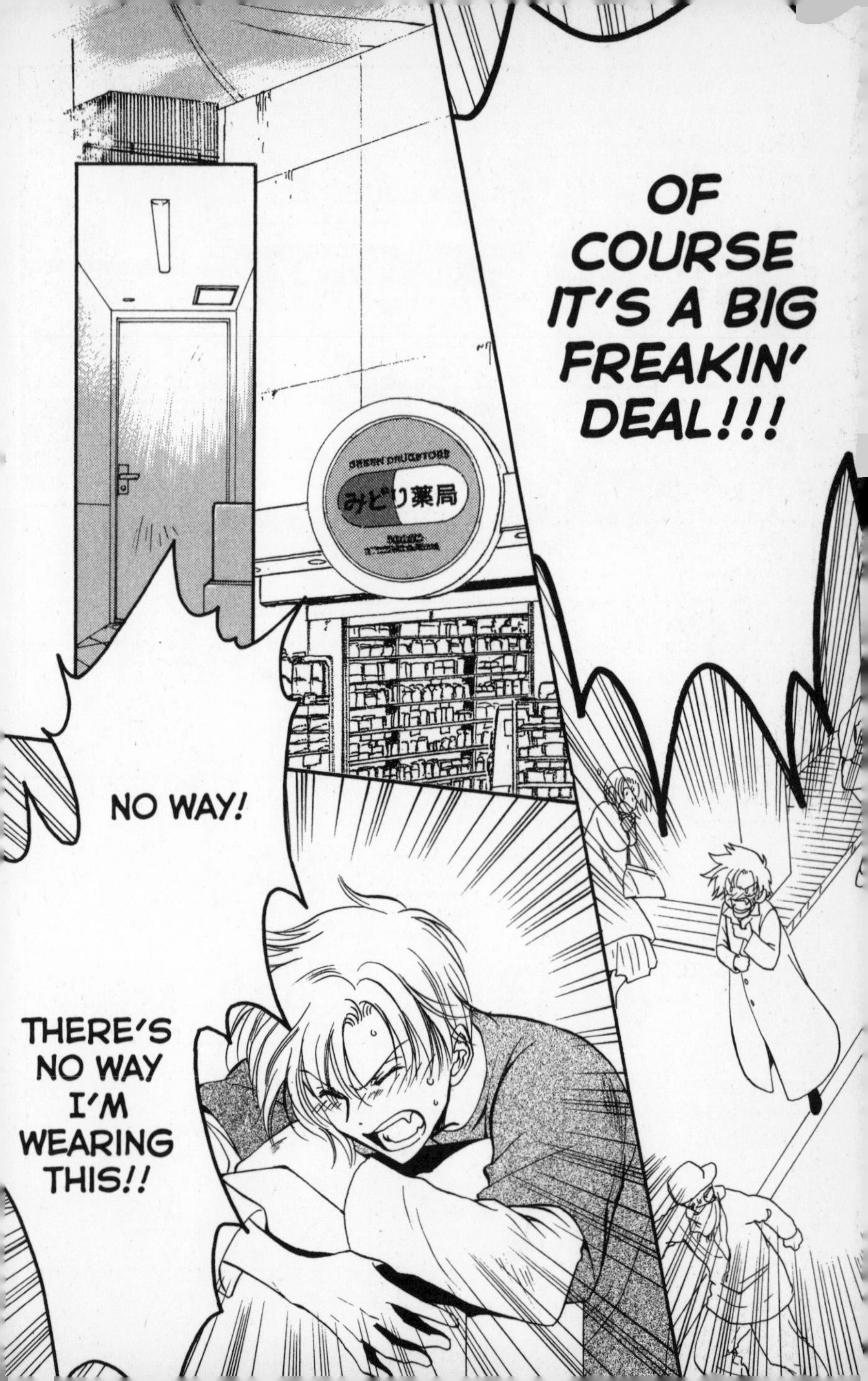
OF COURSE IT'S A BIG FREAKIN' DEAL!!!
GREEN DRUGSTORE
みどり薬局
NO WAY!
THERE'S NO WAY I'M WEARING THIS!!

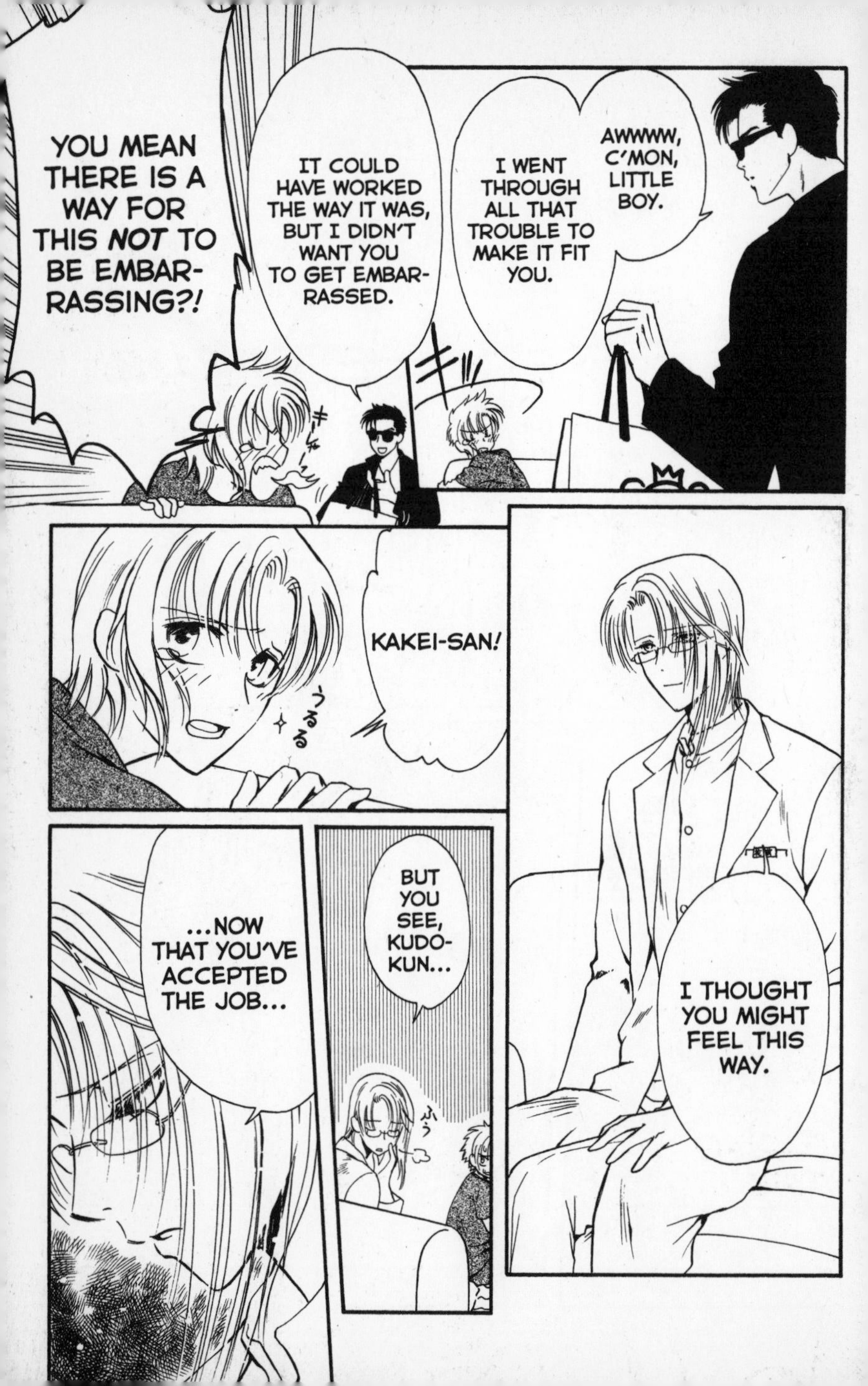
AWWWW, C'MON, LITTLE BOY.
I WENT THROUGH ALL THAT TROUBLE TO MAKE IT FIT YOU.
IT COULD HAVE WORKED THE WAY IT WAS, BUT I DIDN'T WANT YOU TO GET EMBARRASSED.
YOU MEAN THERE IS A WAY FOR THIS *NOT* TO BE EMBARRASSING?!
I THOUGHT YOU MIGHT FEEL THIS WAY.
KAKEI-SAN!
うるる
BUT YOU SEE, KUDO-KUN...
ふぅ
...NOW THAT YOU'VE ACCEPTED THE JOB...

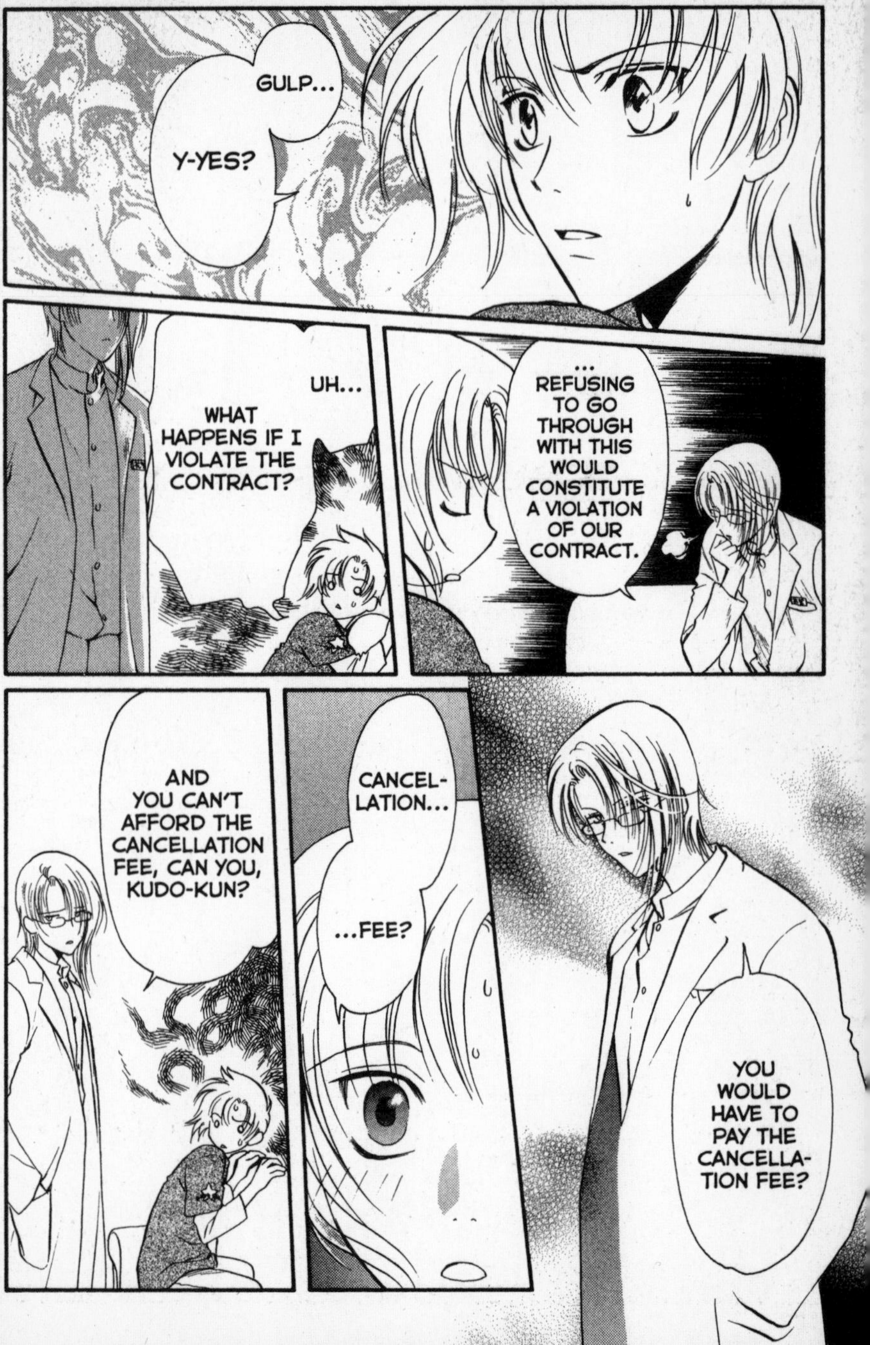
GULP...
Y-YES?
...REFUSING TO GO THROUGH WITH THIS WOULD CONSTITUTE A VIOLATION OF OUR CONTRACT.
UH...
WHAT HAPPENS IF I VIOLATE THE CONTRACT?
YOU WOULD HAVE TO PAY THE CANCELLATION FEE?
CANCELLATION...
...FEE?
AND YOU CAN'T AFFORD THE CANCELLATION FEE, CAN YOU, KUDO-KUN?

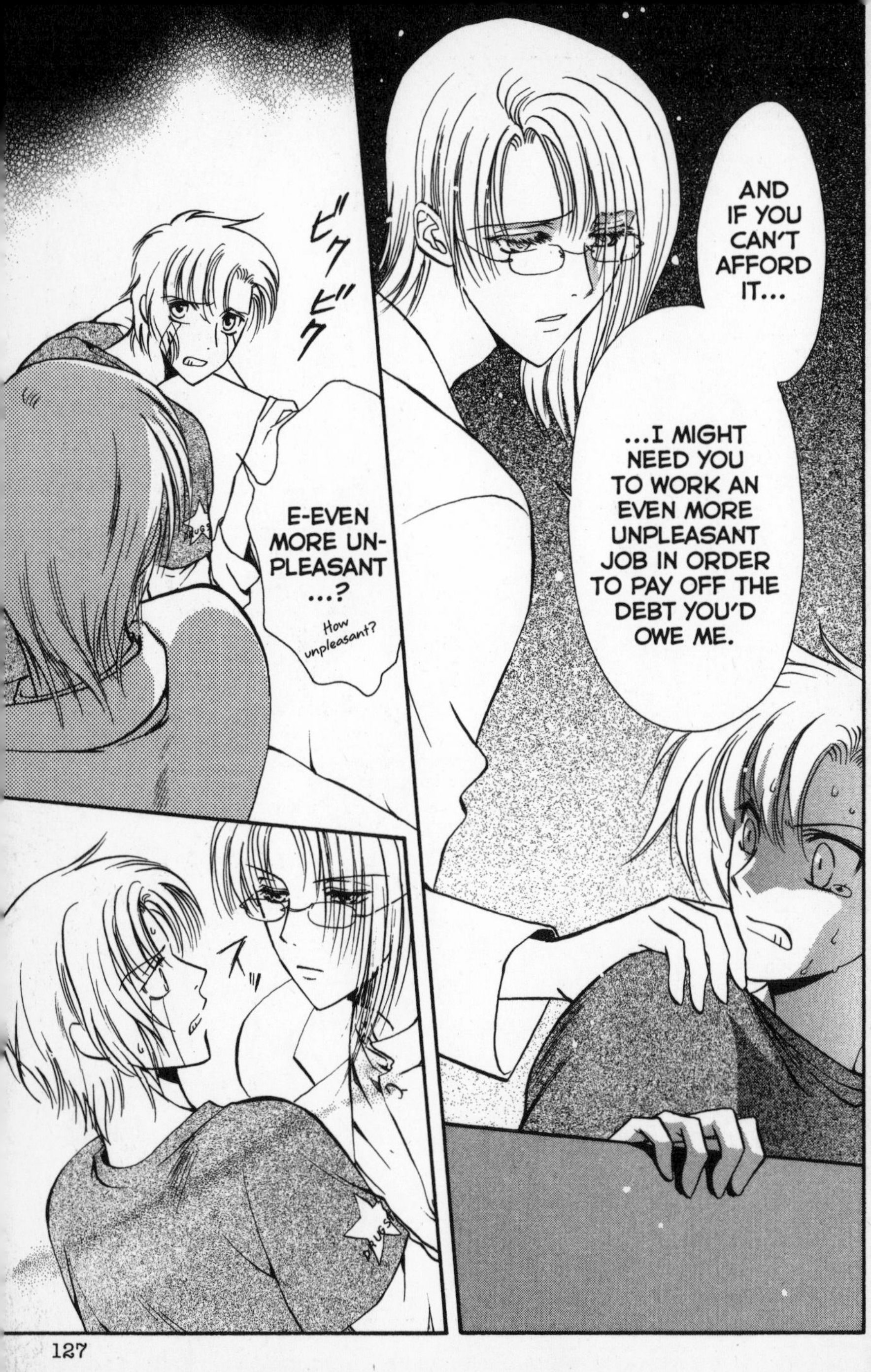
AND IF YOU CAN'T AFFORD IT...
...I MIGHT NEED YOU TO WORK AN EVEN MORE UNPLEASANT JOB IN ORDER TO PAY OFF THE DEBT YOU'D OWE ME.
ビクビク
E-EVEN MORE UN-PLEASANT ...?
How unpleasant?

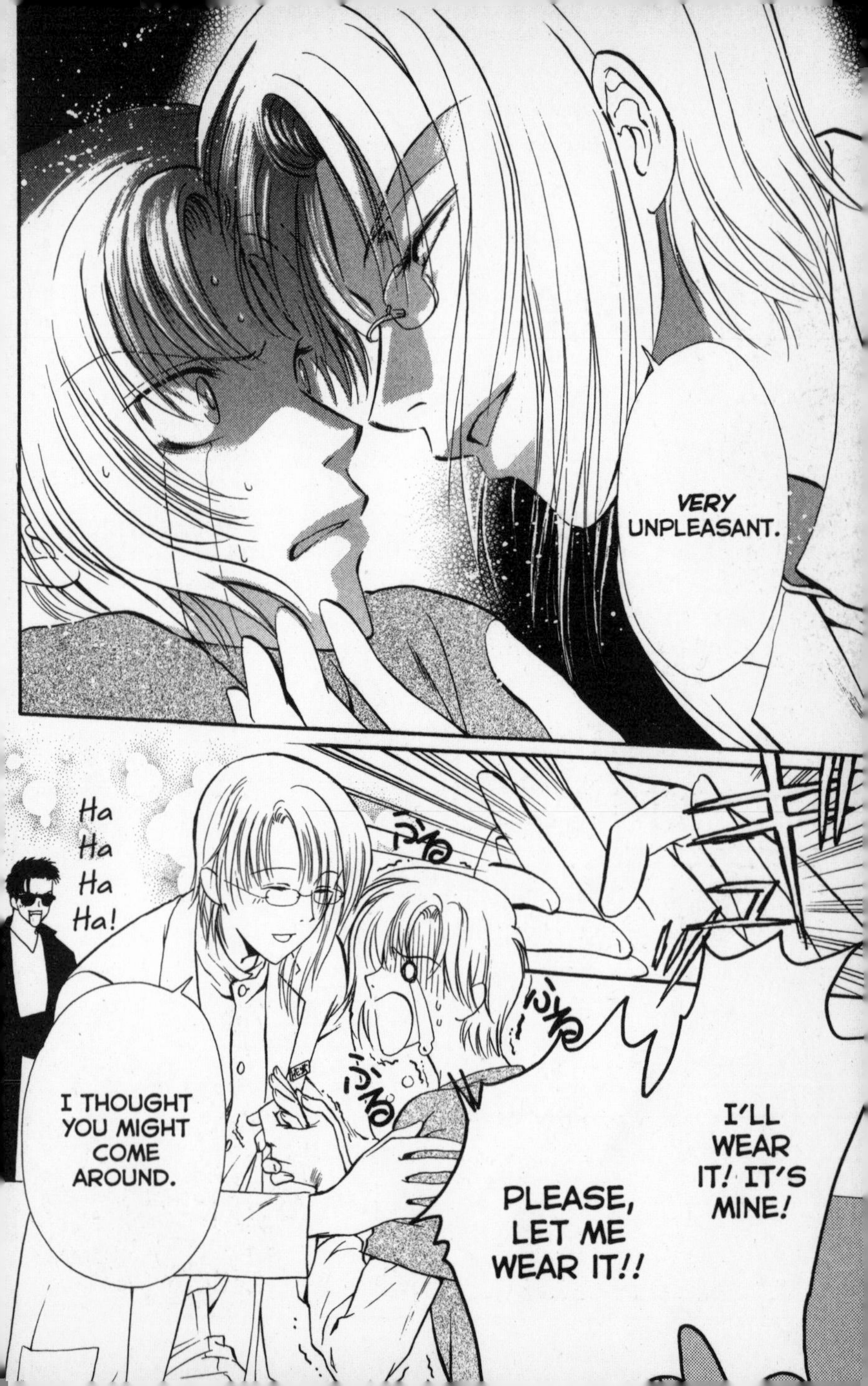
VERY UNPLEASANT.
I'LL WEAR IT! IT'S MINE!
PLEASE, LET ME WEAR IT!!
I THOUGHT YOU MIGHT COME AROUND.
Ha Ha Ha Ha!

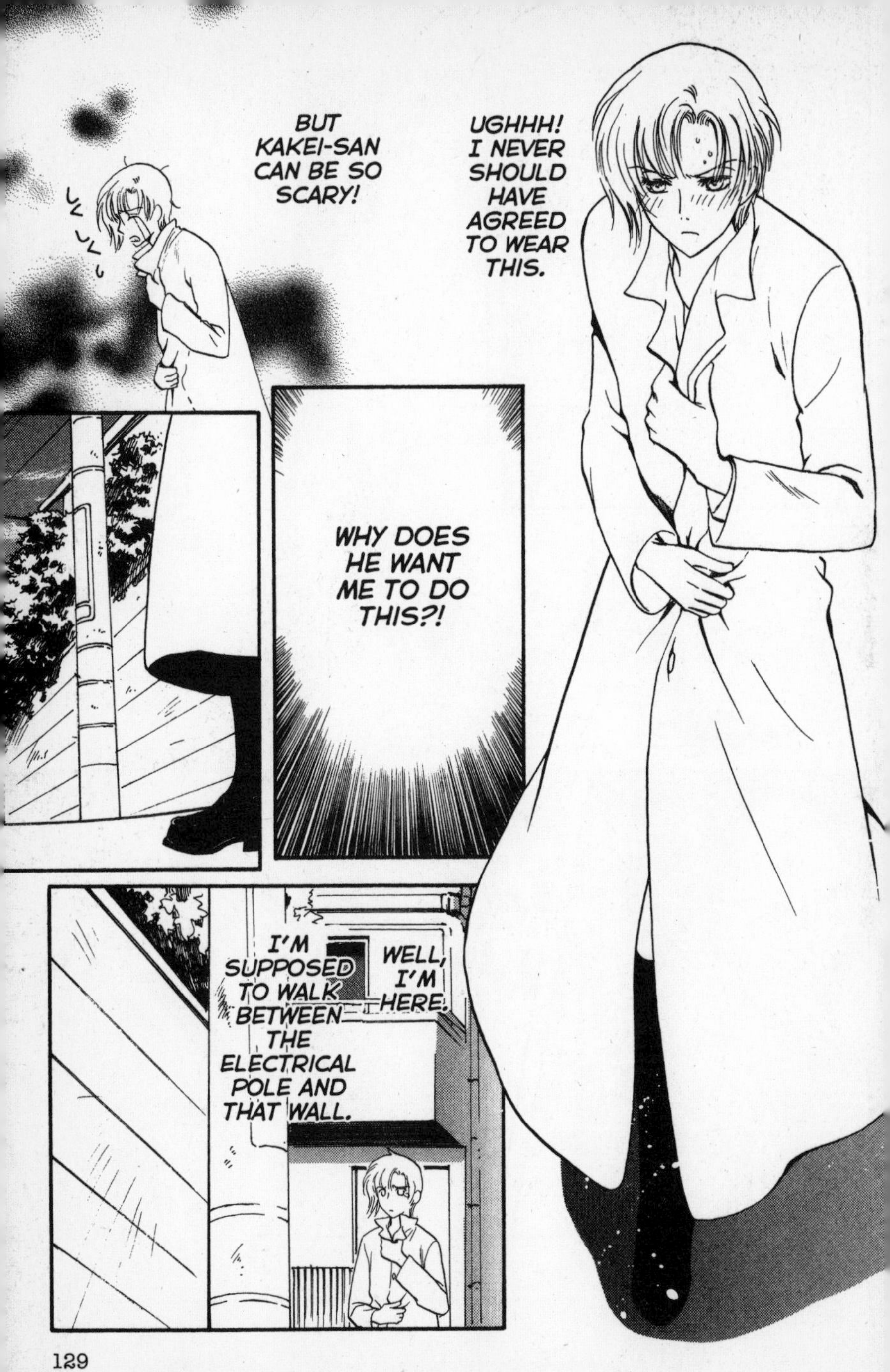
UGHHH! I NEVER SHOULD HAVE AGREED TO WEAR THIS.
BUT KAKEI-SAN CAN BE SO SCARY!
しくしく
WHY DOES HE WANT ME TO DO THIS?!
WELL, I'M HERE.
I'M SUPPOSED TO WALK BETWEEN THE ELECTRICAL POLE AND THAT WALL.

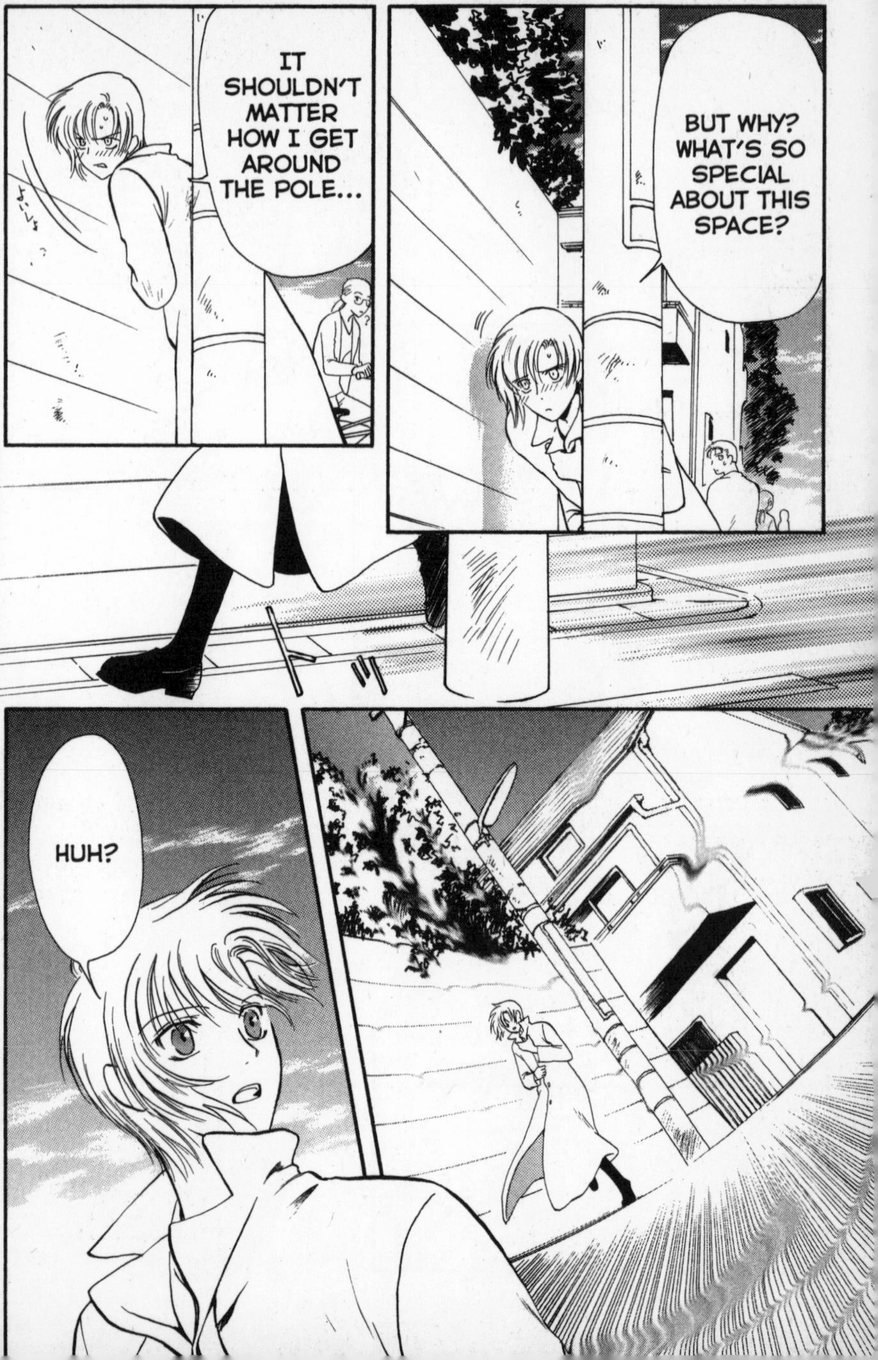
BUT WHY? WHAT'S SO SPECIAL ABOUT THIS SPACE?
IT SHOULDN'T MATTER HOW I GET AROUND THE POLE...
よいしょ
HUH?

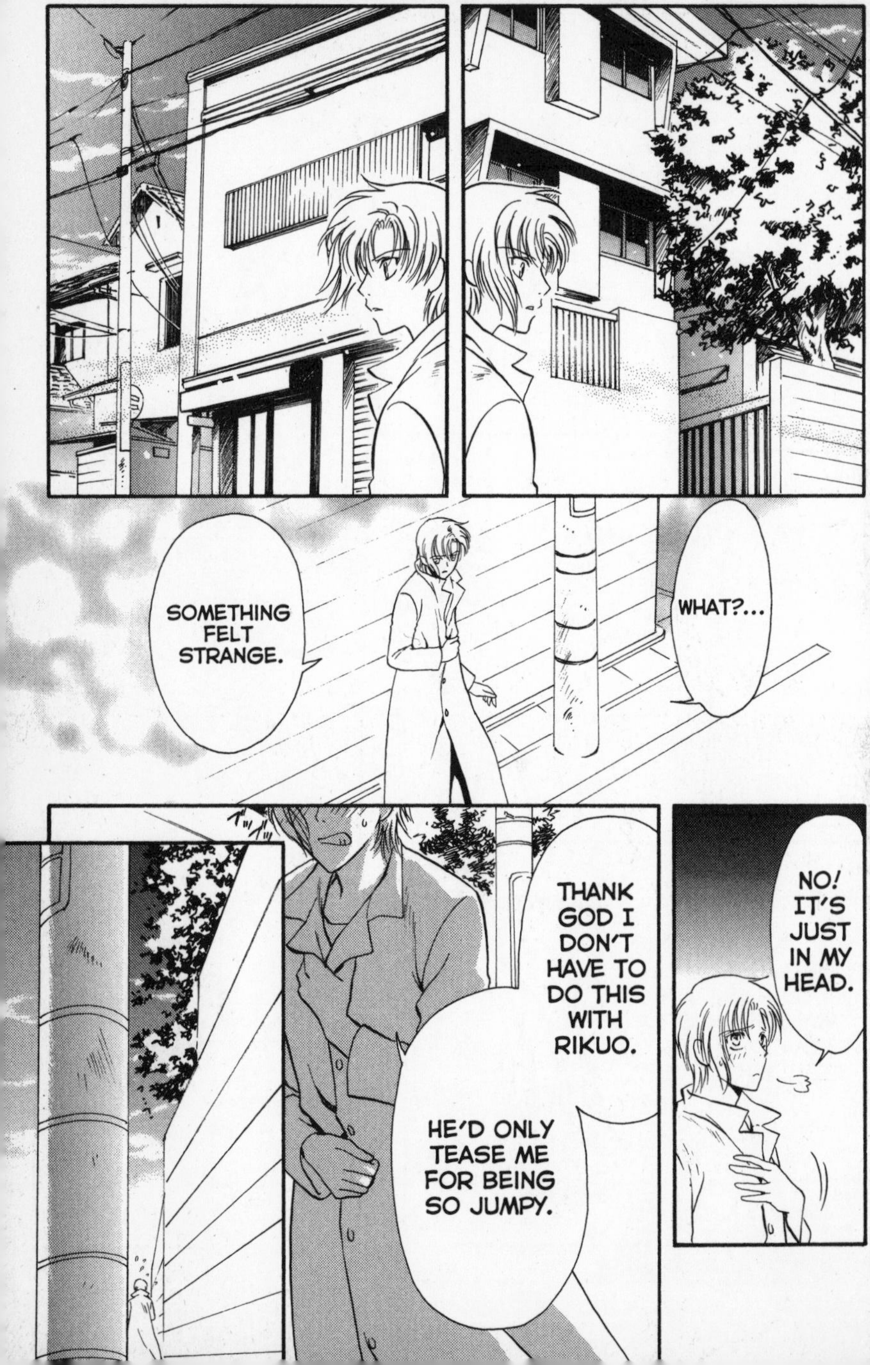
WHAT?...
SOMETHING FELT STRANGE.
NO! IT'S JUST IN MY HEAD.
THANK GOD I DON'T HAVE TO DO THIS WITH RIKUO.
HE'D ONLY TEASE ME FOR BEING SO JUMPY.

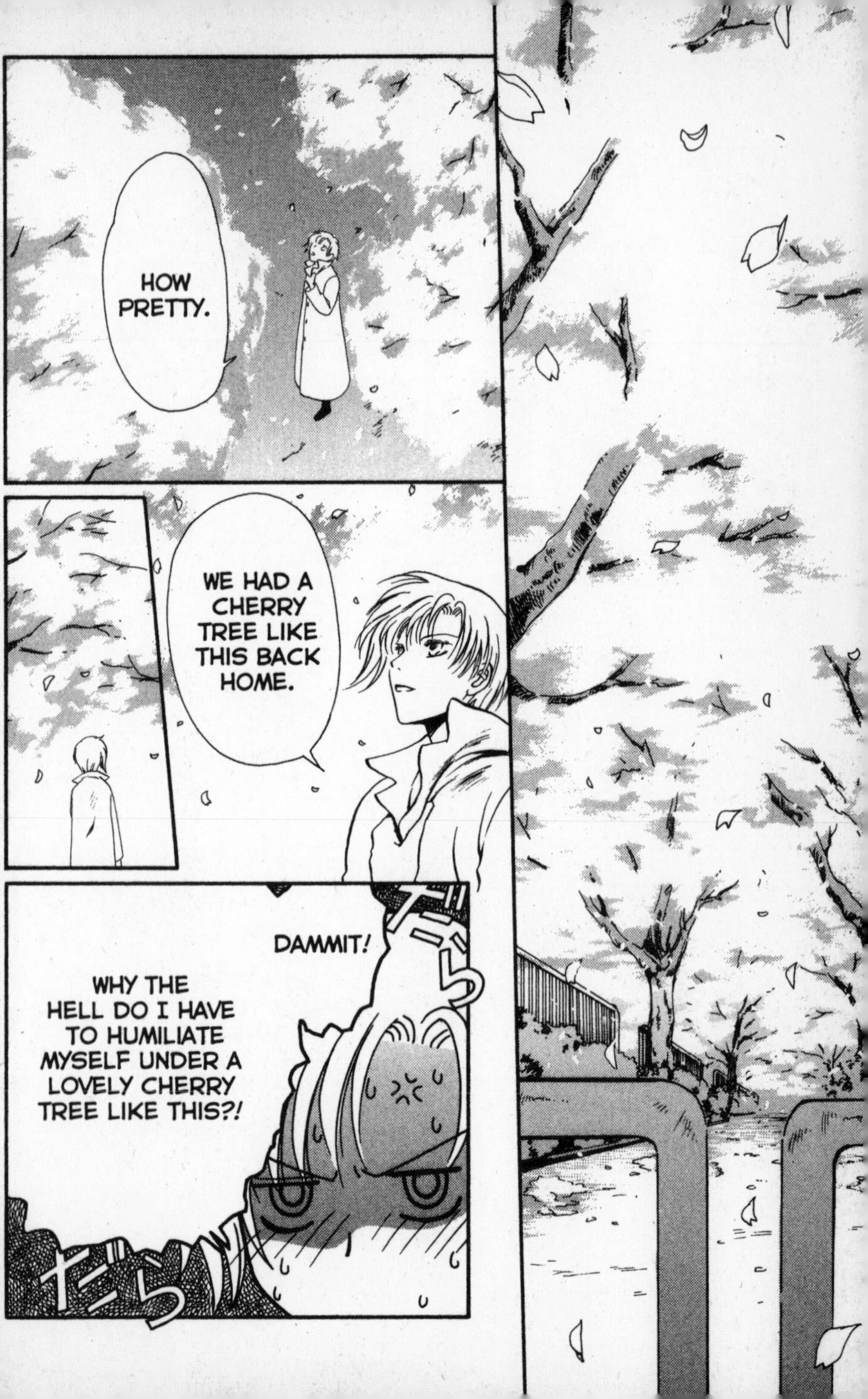
HOW PRETTY.
WE HAD A CHERRY TREE LIKE THIS BACK HOME.
DAMMIT!
WHY THE HELL DO I HAVE TO HUMILIATE MYSELF UNDER A LOVELY CHERRY TREE LIKE THIS?!

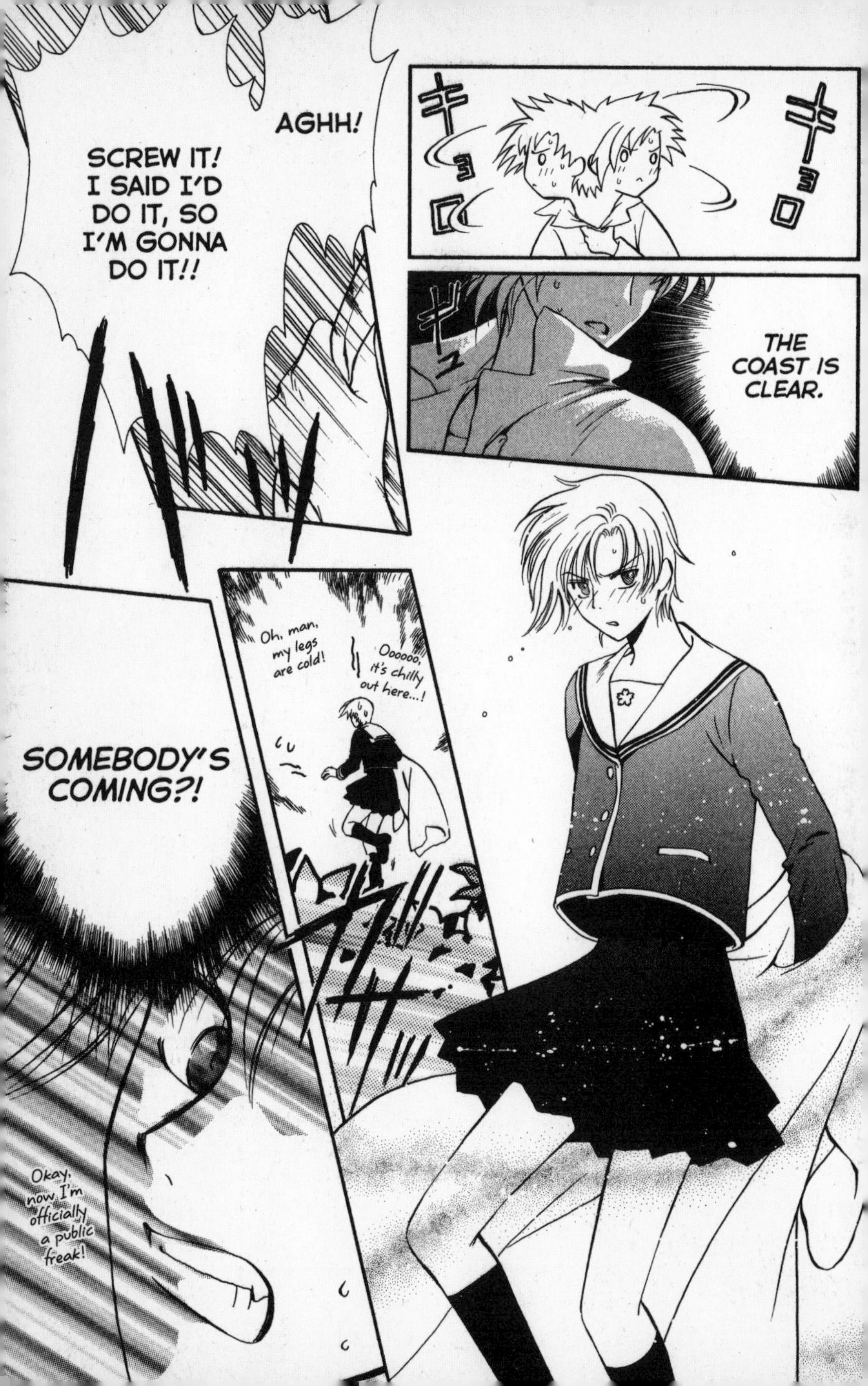

キョロ
キョロ
ギュ
THE COAST IS CLEAR.
AGHH!
SCREW IT! I SAID I'D DO IT, SO I'M GONNA DO IT!!
Ooooooo, it's chilly out here...!
Oh, man, my legs are cold!
SOMEBODY'S COMING?!
Okay, now I'm officially a public freak!

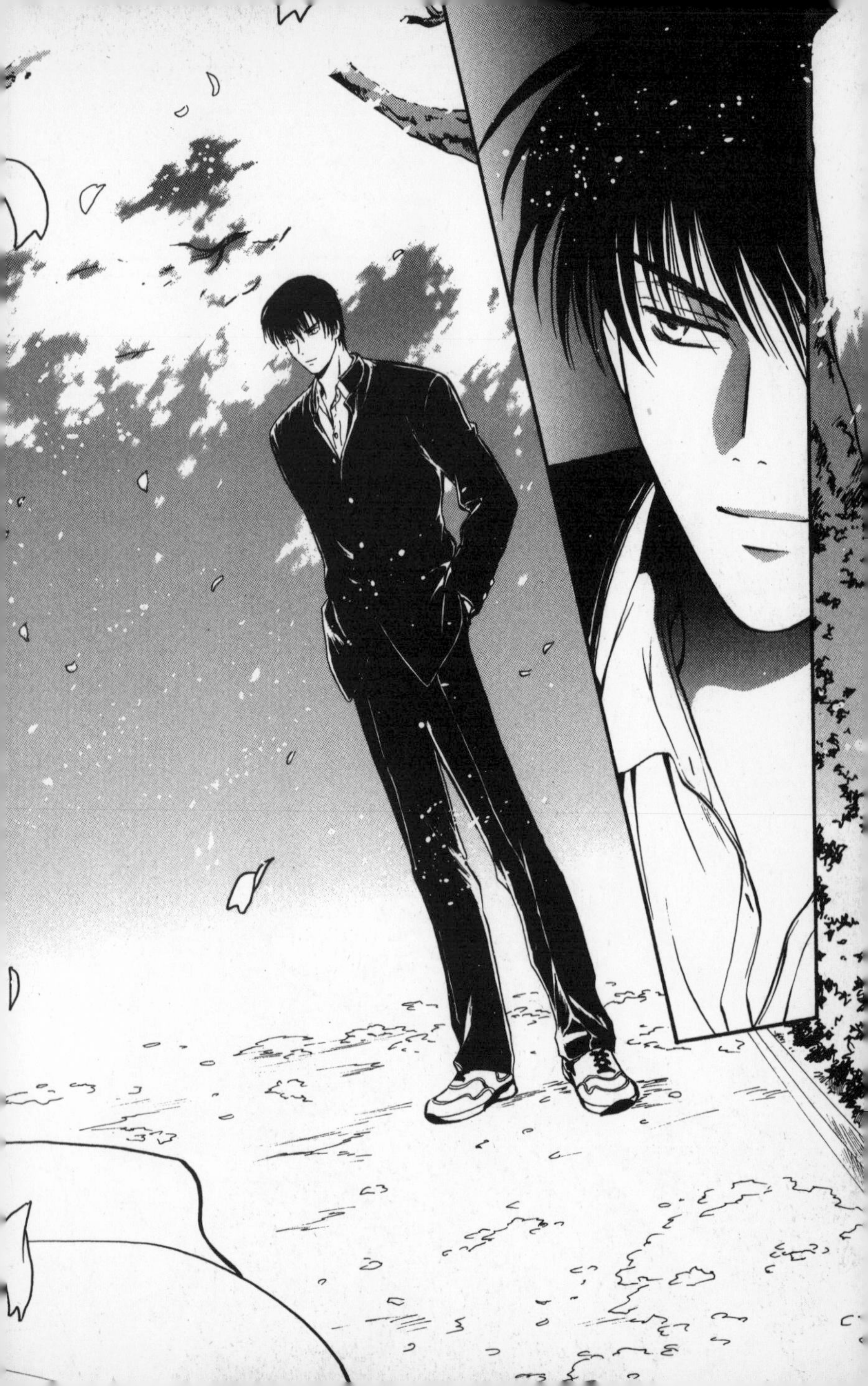

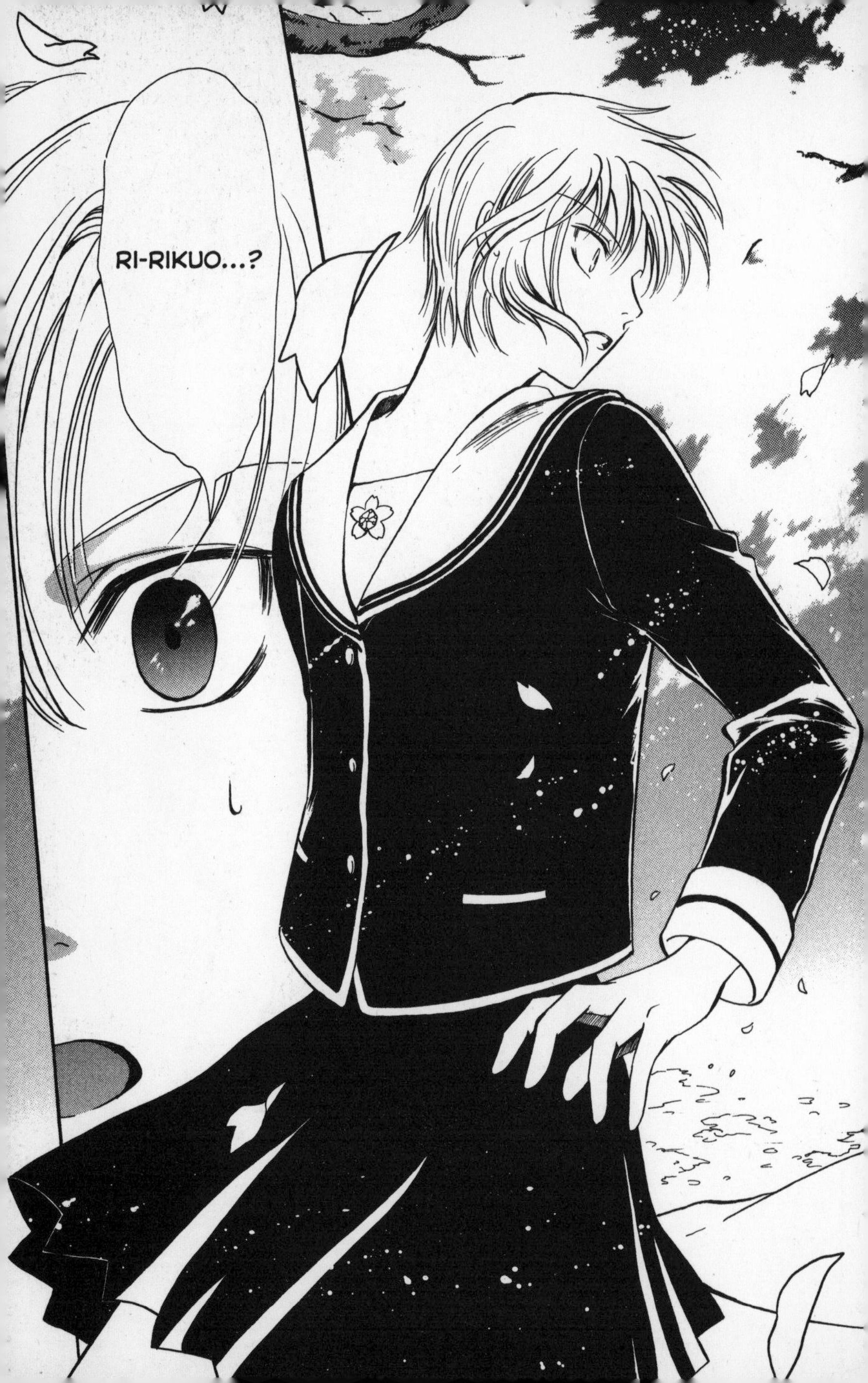
RI-RIKUO...?

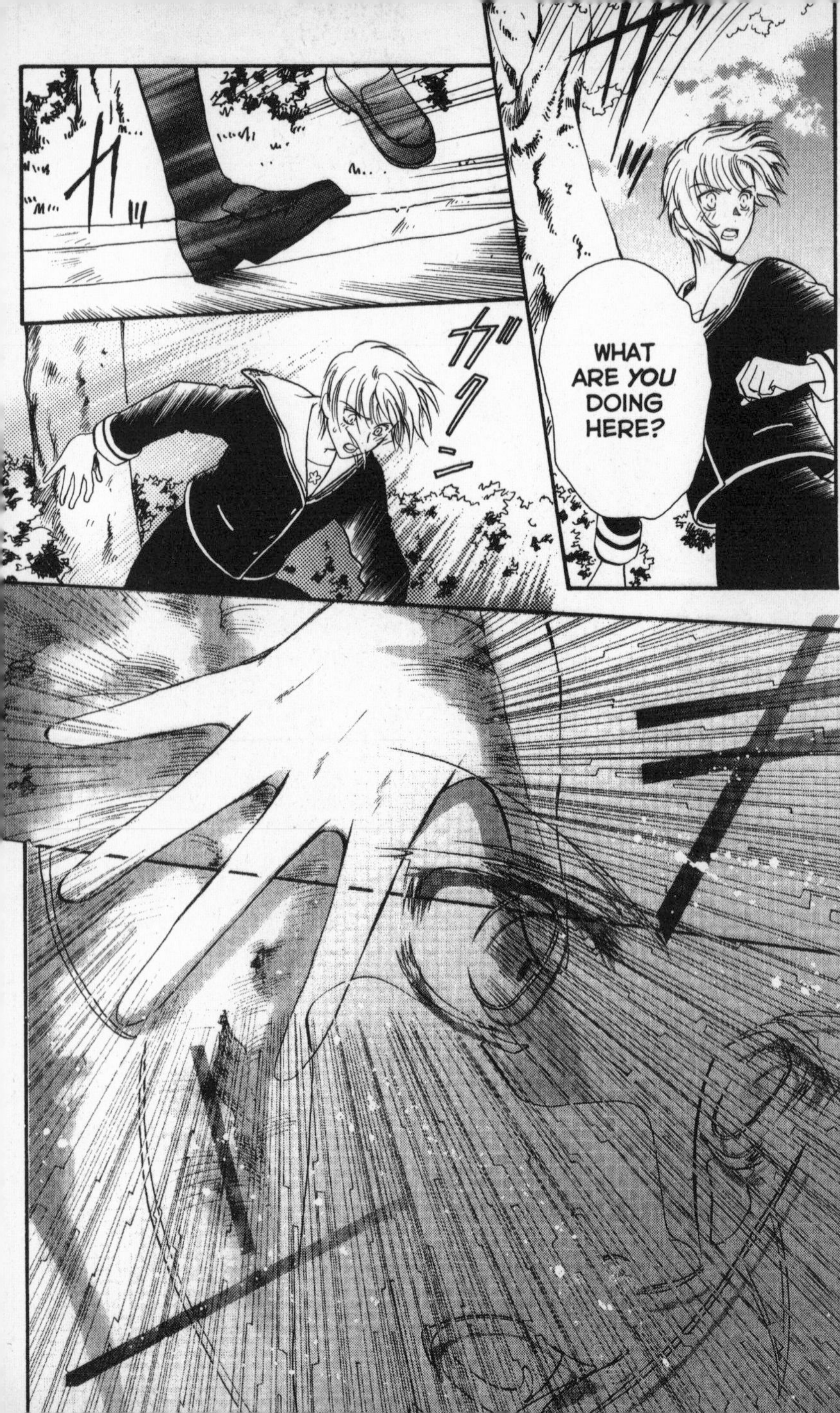
WHAT ARE *YOU* DOING HERE?

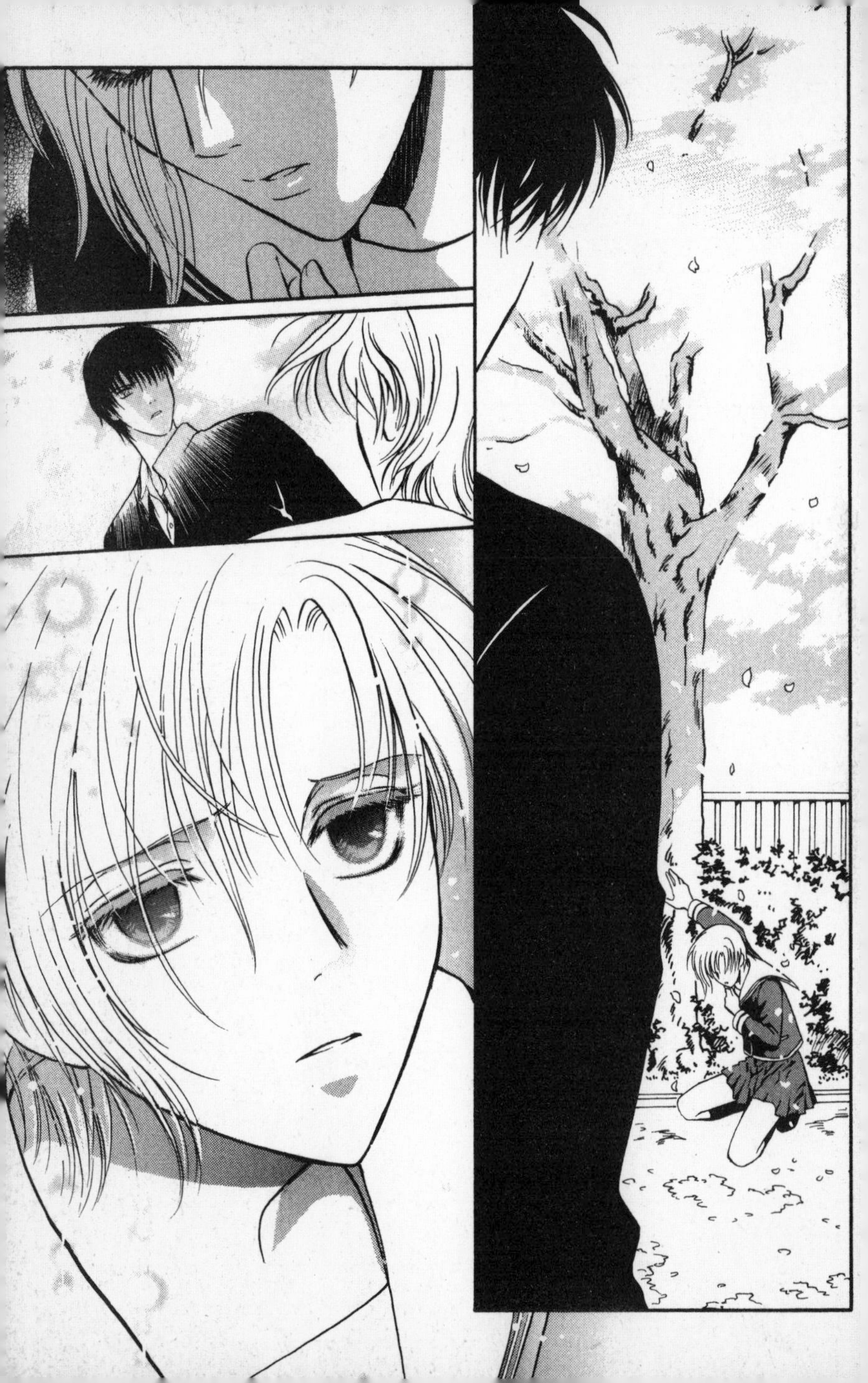

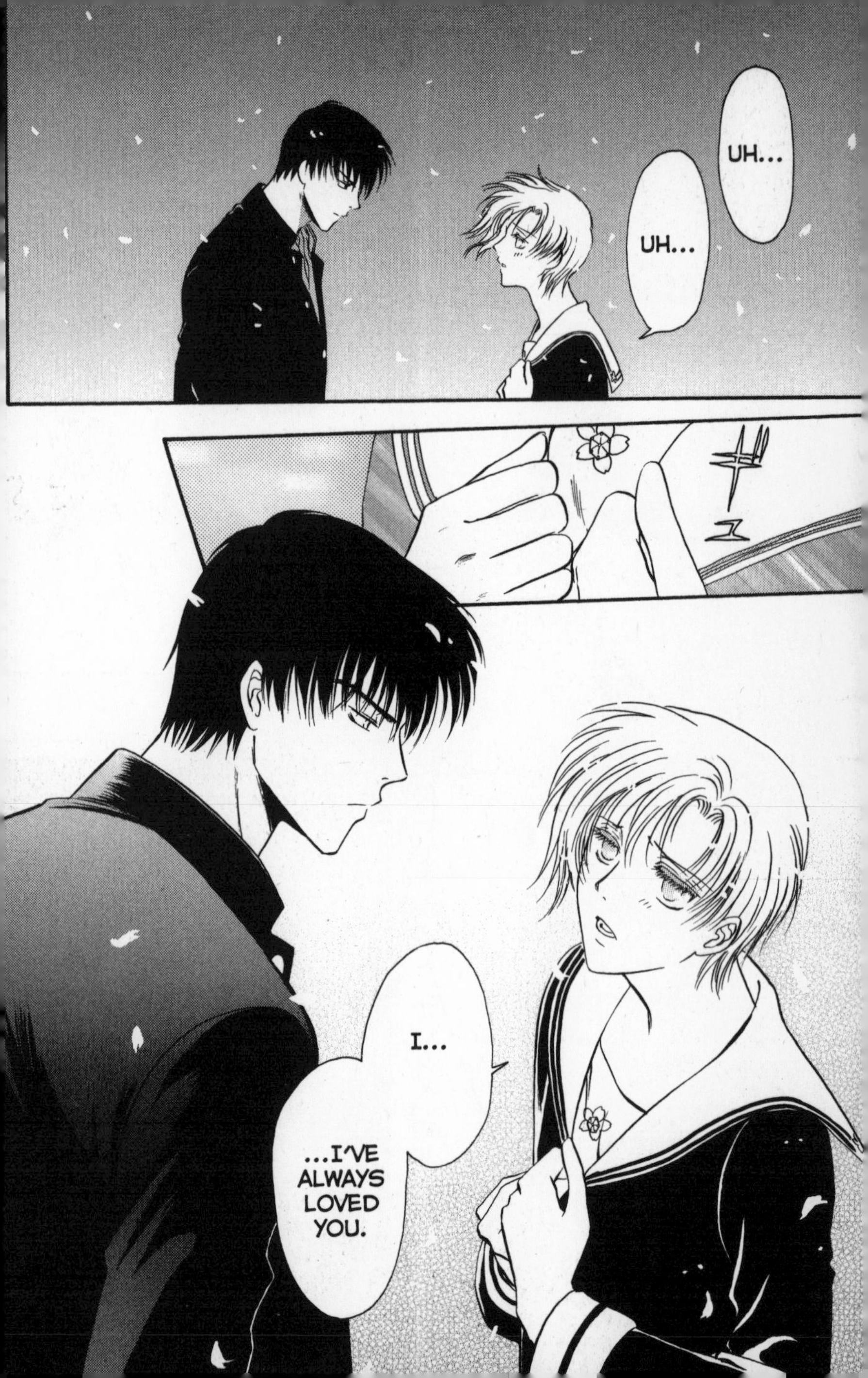
UH...
UH...
ギュ
I...
...I'VE ALWAYS LOVED YOU.

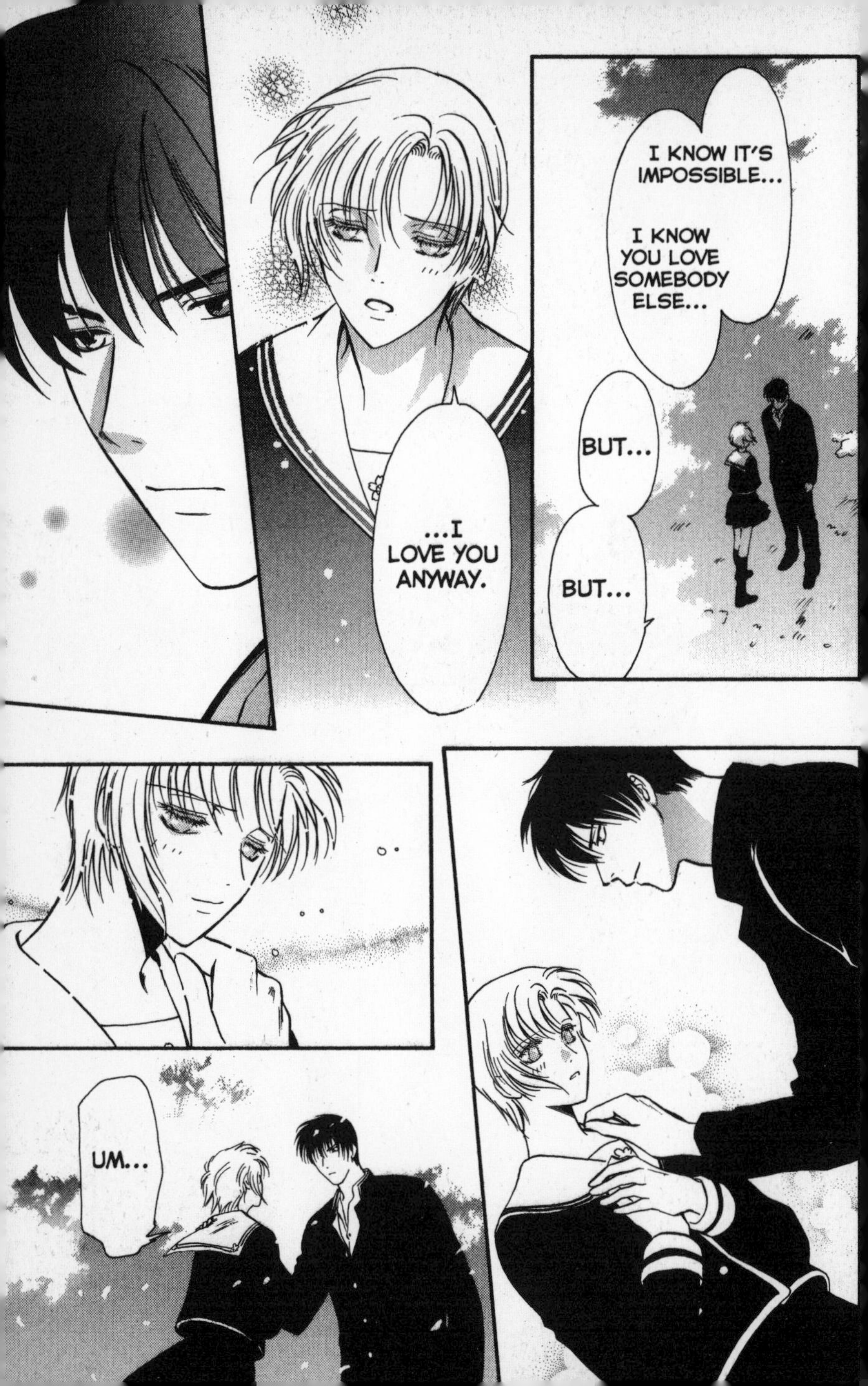
I KNOW IT'S IMPOSSIBLE...
I KNOW YOU LOVE SOMEBODY ELSE...
BUT...
BUT...
...I LOVE YOU ANYWAY.
UM...

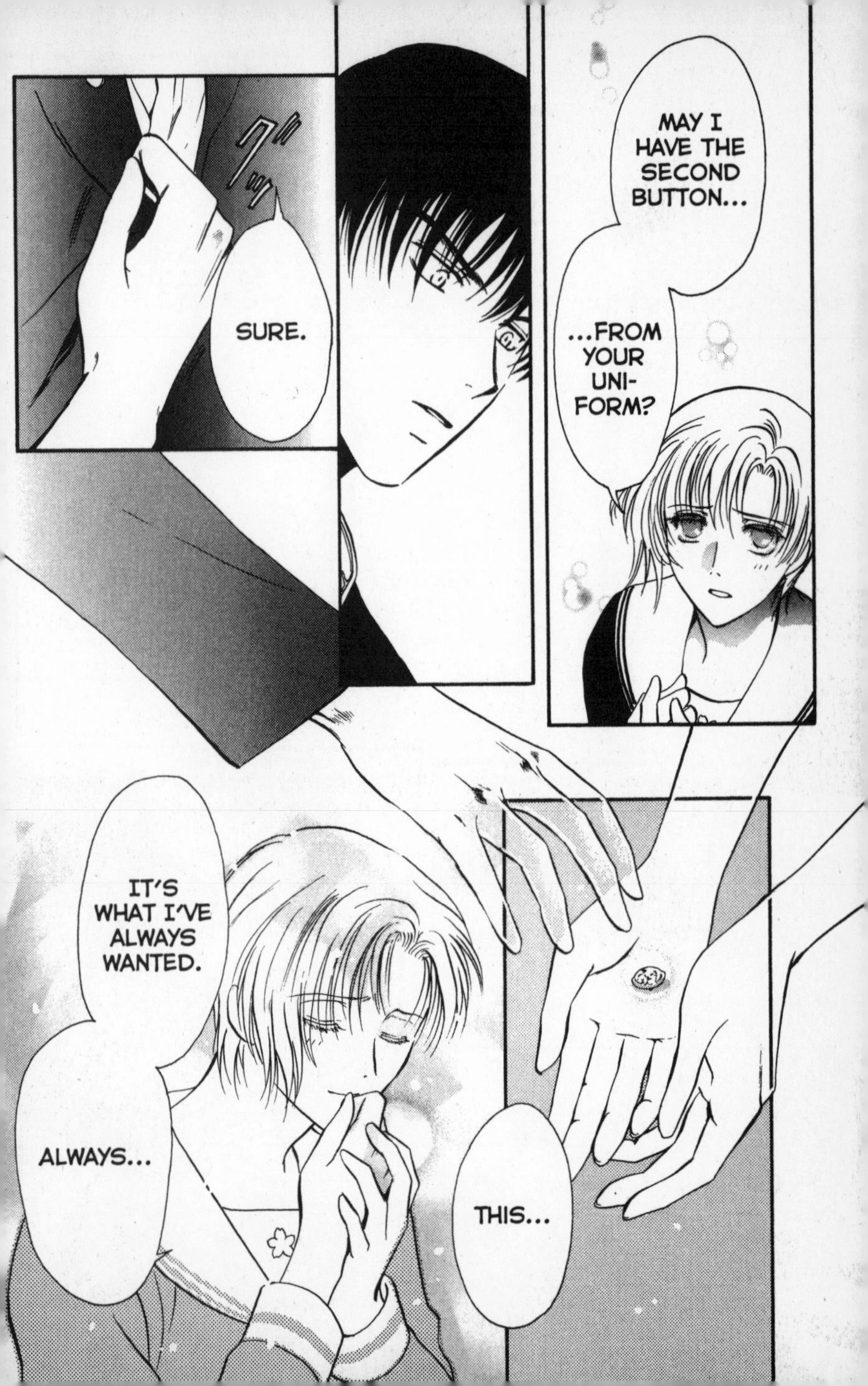
MAY I HAVE THE SECOND BUTTON...
...FROM YOUR UNI- FORM?
SURE.
THIS...
IT'S WHAT I'VE ALWAYS WANTED.
ALWAYS...

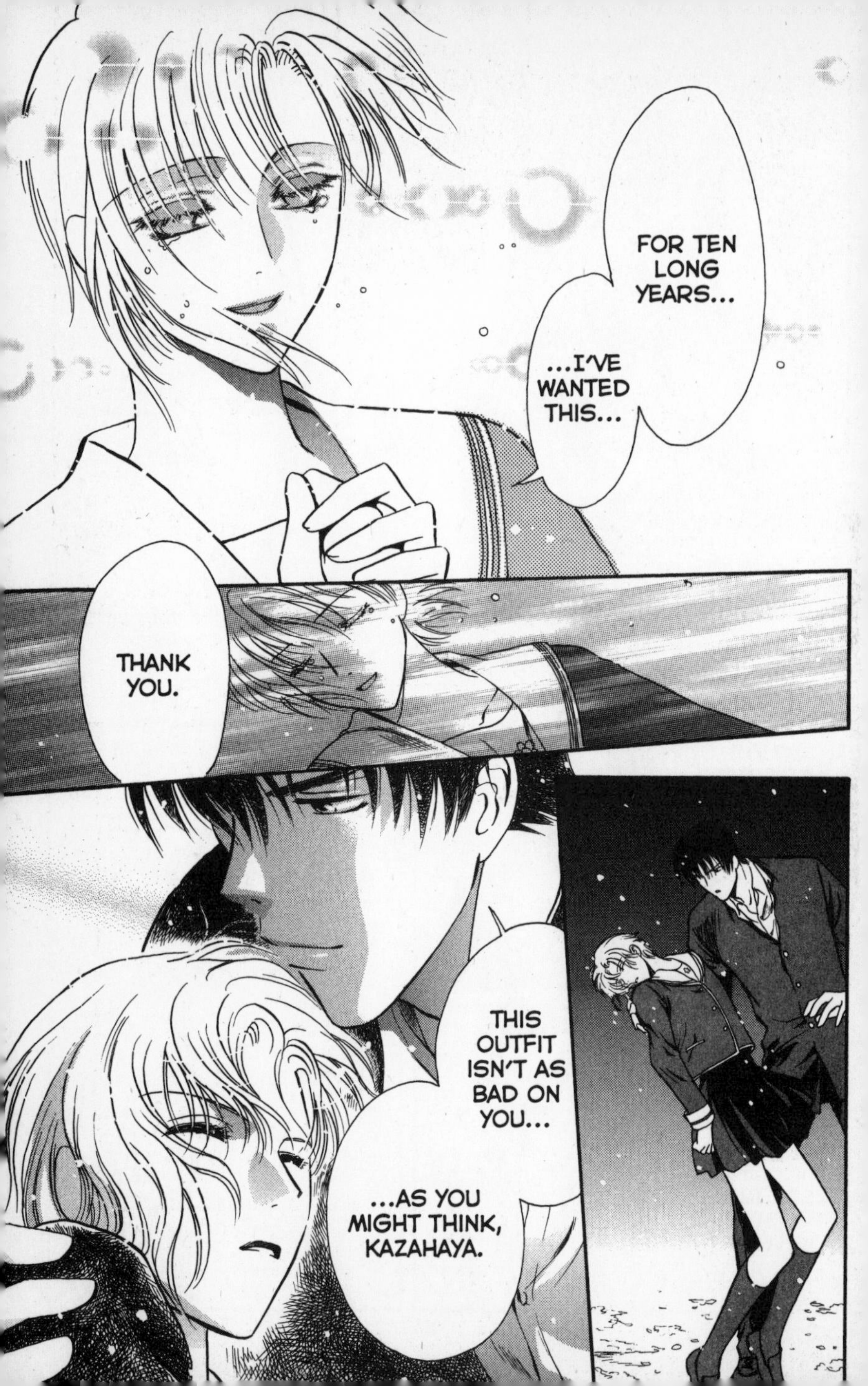
FOR TEN LONG YEARS...
...I'VE WANTED THIS...
THANK YOU.
THIS OUTFIT ISN'T AS BAD ON YOU...
...AS YOU MIGHT THINK, KAZAHAYA.

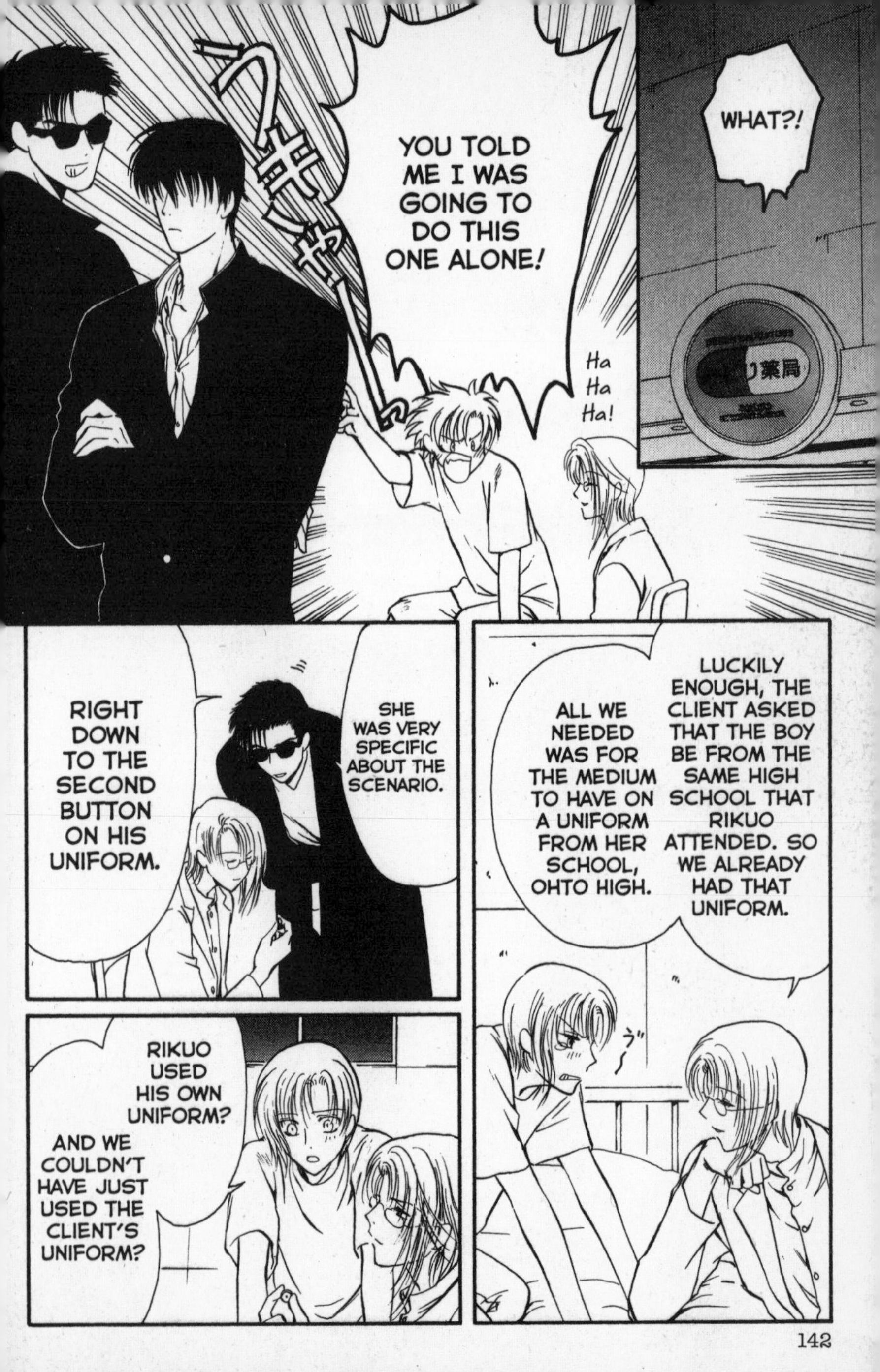
WHAT?!
YOU TOLD ME I WAS GOING TO DO THIS ONE ALONE!
Ha Ha Ha!
LUCKILY ENOUGH, THE CLIENT ASKED THAT THE BOY BE FROM THE SAME HIGH SCHOOL THAT RIKUO ATTENDED. SO WE ALREADY HAD THAT UNIFORM.
ALL WE NEEDED WAS FOR THE MEDIUM TO HAVE ON A UNIFORM FROM HER SCHOOL, OHTO HIGH.
SHE WAS VERY SPECIFIC ABOUT THE SCENARIO.
RIGHT DOWN TO THE SECOND BUTTON ON HIS UNIFORM.
RIKUO USED HIS OWN UNIFORM?
AND WE COULDN'T HAVE JUST USED THE CLIENT'S UNIFORM?

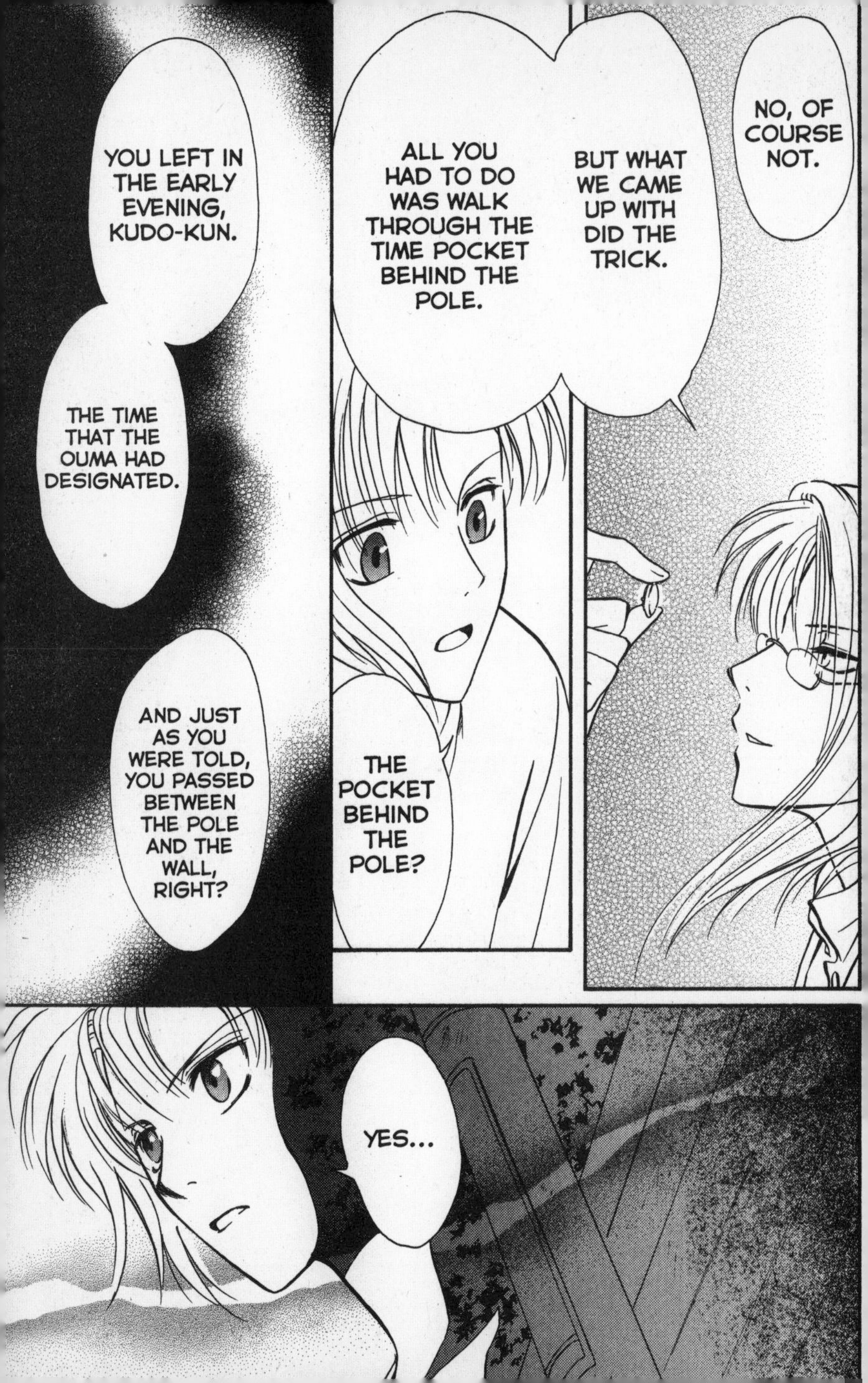
NO, OF COURSE NOT.
BUT WHAT WE CAME UP WITH DID THE TRICK.
ALL YOU HAD TO DO WAS WALK THROUGH THE TIME POCKET BEHIND THE POLE.
THE POCKET BEHIND THE POLE?
YOU LEFT IN THE EARLY EVENING, KUDO-KUN.
THE TIME THAT THE OUMA HAD DESIGNATED.
AND JUST AS YOU WERE TOLD, YOU PASSED BETWEEN THE POLE AND THE WALL, RIGHT?
YES...

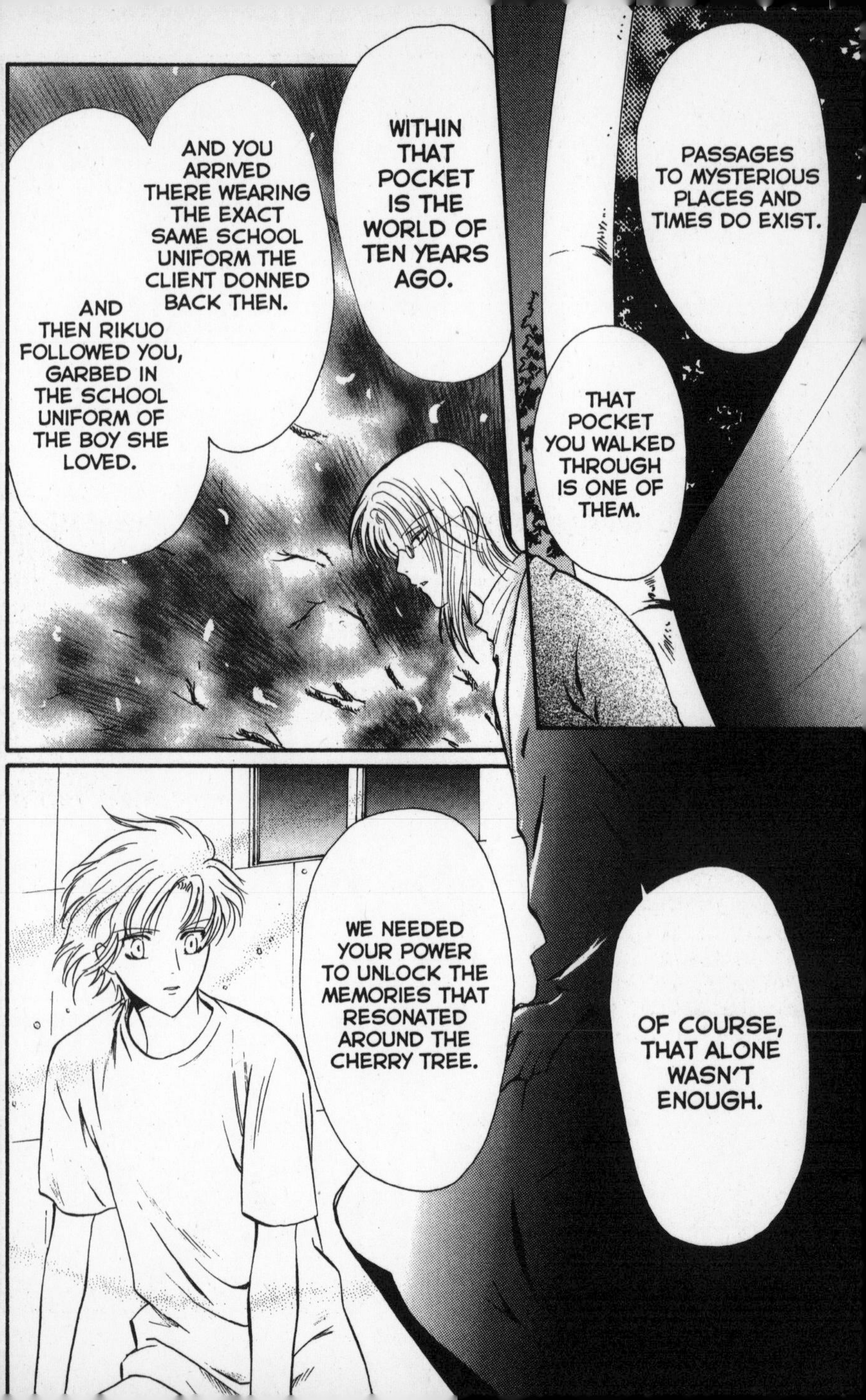
PASSAGES TO MYSTERIOUS PLACES AND TIMES DO EXIST.
THAT POCKET YOU WALKED THROUGH IS ONE OF THEM.
WITHIN THAT POCKET IS THE WORLD OF TEN YEARS AGO.
AND YOU ARRIVED THERE WEARING THE EXACT SAME SCHOOL UNIFORM THE CLIENT DONNED BACK THEN.
AND THEN RIKUO FOLLOWED YOU, GARBED IN THE SCHOOL UNIFORM OF THE BOY SHE LOVED.
WE NEEDED YOUR POWER TO UNLOCK THE MEMORIES THAT RESONATED AROUND THE CHERRY TREE.
OF COURSE, THAT ALONE WASN'T ENOUGH.

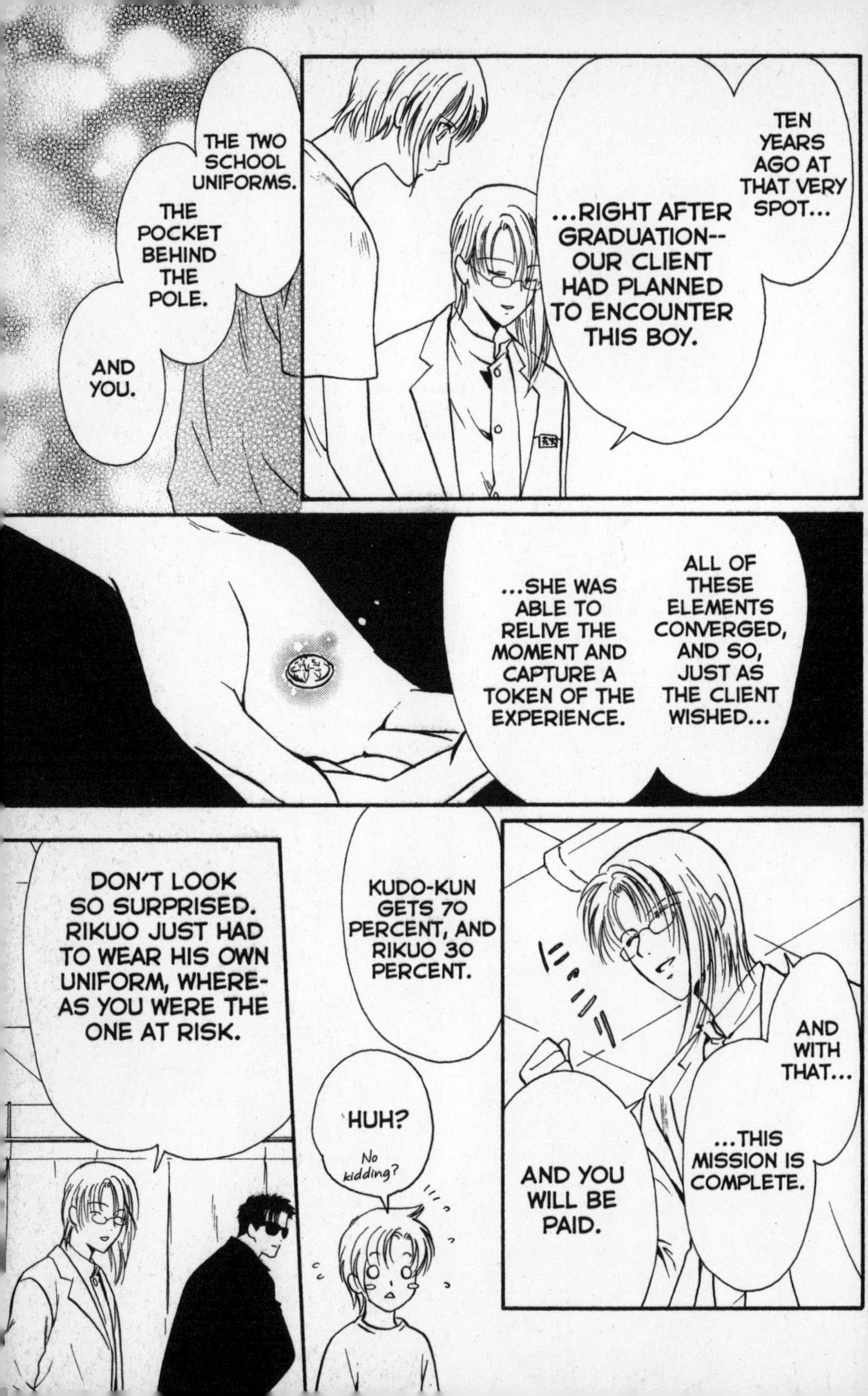
TEN YEARS AGO AT THAT VERY SPOT...
...RIGHT AFTER GRADUATION--OUR CLIENT HAD PLANNED TO ENCOUNTER THIS BOY.
THE TWO SCHOOL UNIFORMS.
THE POCKET BEHIND THE POLE.
AND YOU.
ALL OF THESE ELEMENTS CONVERGED, AND SO, JUST AS THE CLIENT WISHED...
...SHE WAS ABLE TO RELIVE THE MOMENT AND CAPTURE A TOKEN OF THE EXPERIENCE.
AND WITH THAT...
...THIS MISSION IS COMPLETE.
AND YOU WILL BE PAID.
KUDO-KUN GETS 70 PERCENT, AND RIKUO 30 PERCENT.
HUH?
No kidding?
DON'T LOOK SO SURPRISED. RIKUO JUST HAD TO WEAR HIS OWN UNIFORM, WHERE-AS YOU WERE THE ONE AT RISK.

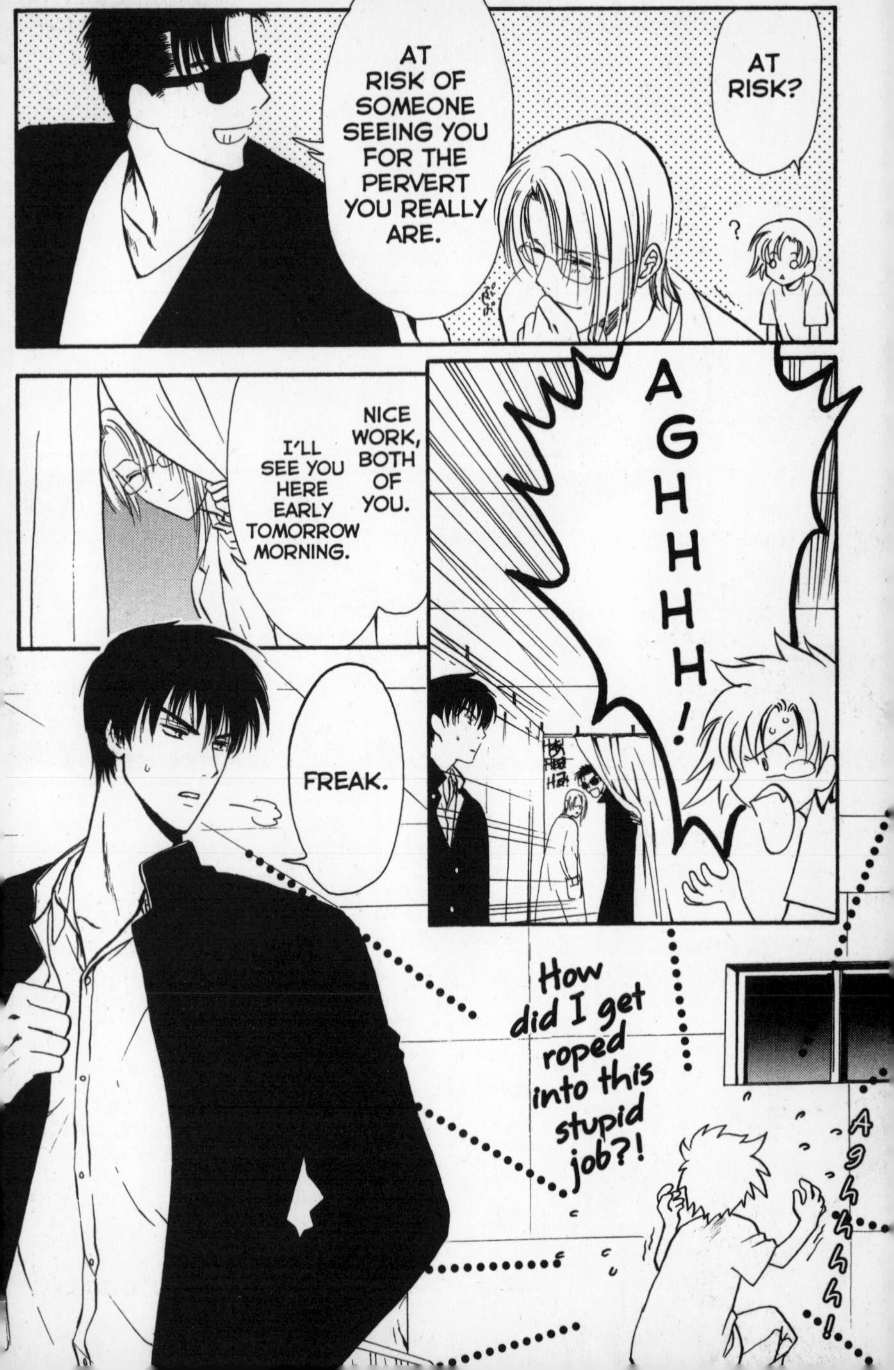

AT RISK?
AT RISK OF SOMEONE SEEING YOU FOR THE PERVERT YOU REALLY ARE.
AGHHHH!
NICE WORK, BOTH OF YOU.
I'LL SEE YOU HERE EARLY TOMORROW MORNING.
FREAK.
How did I get roped into this stupid job?!
Aghhhh!

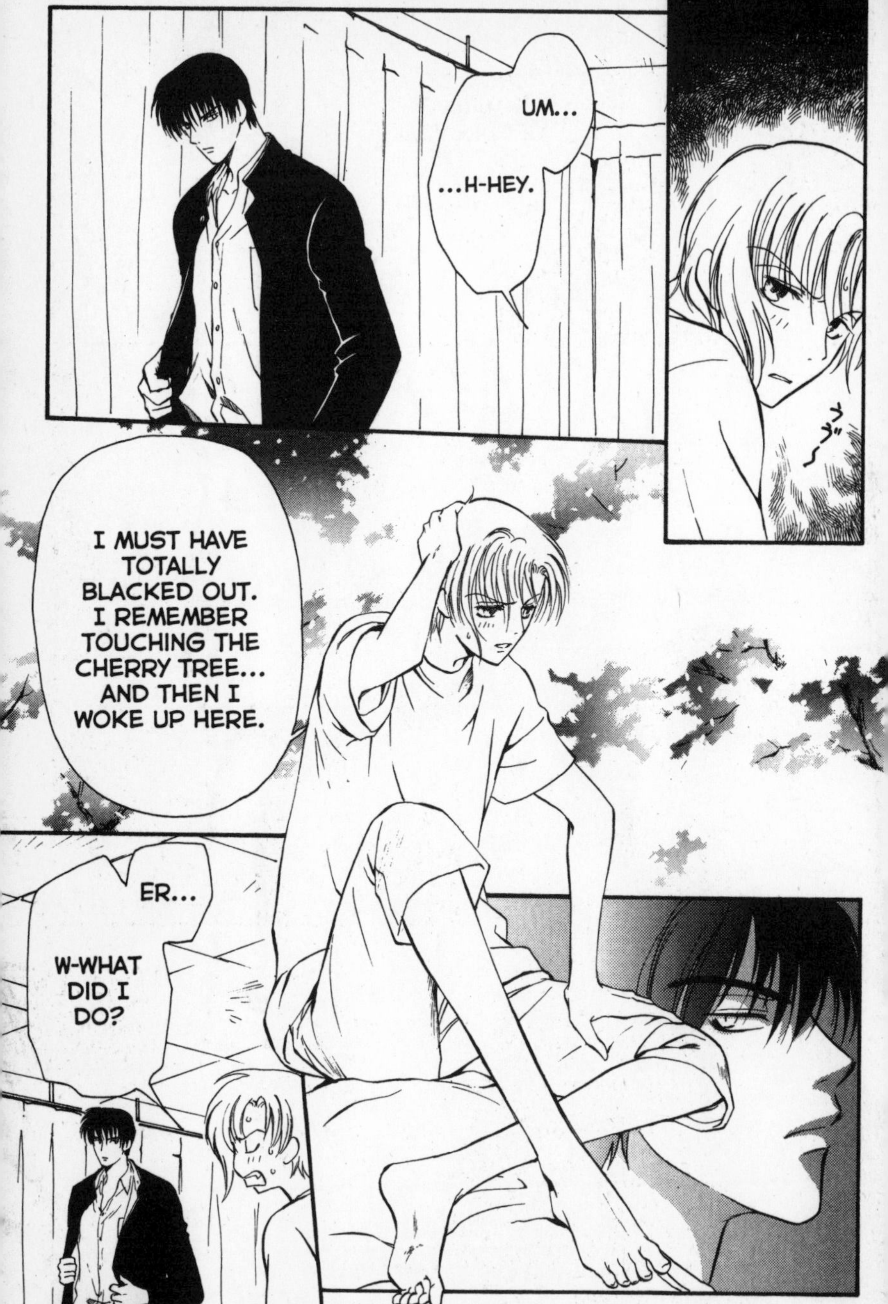
UM...
...H-HEY.
I MUST HAVE TOTALLY BLACKED OUT. I REMEMBER TOUCHING THE CHERRY TREE... AND THEN I WOKE UP HERE.
ER...
W-WHAT DID I DO?

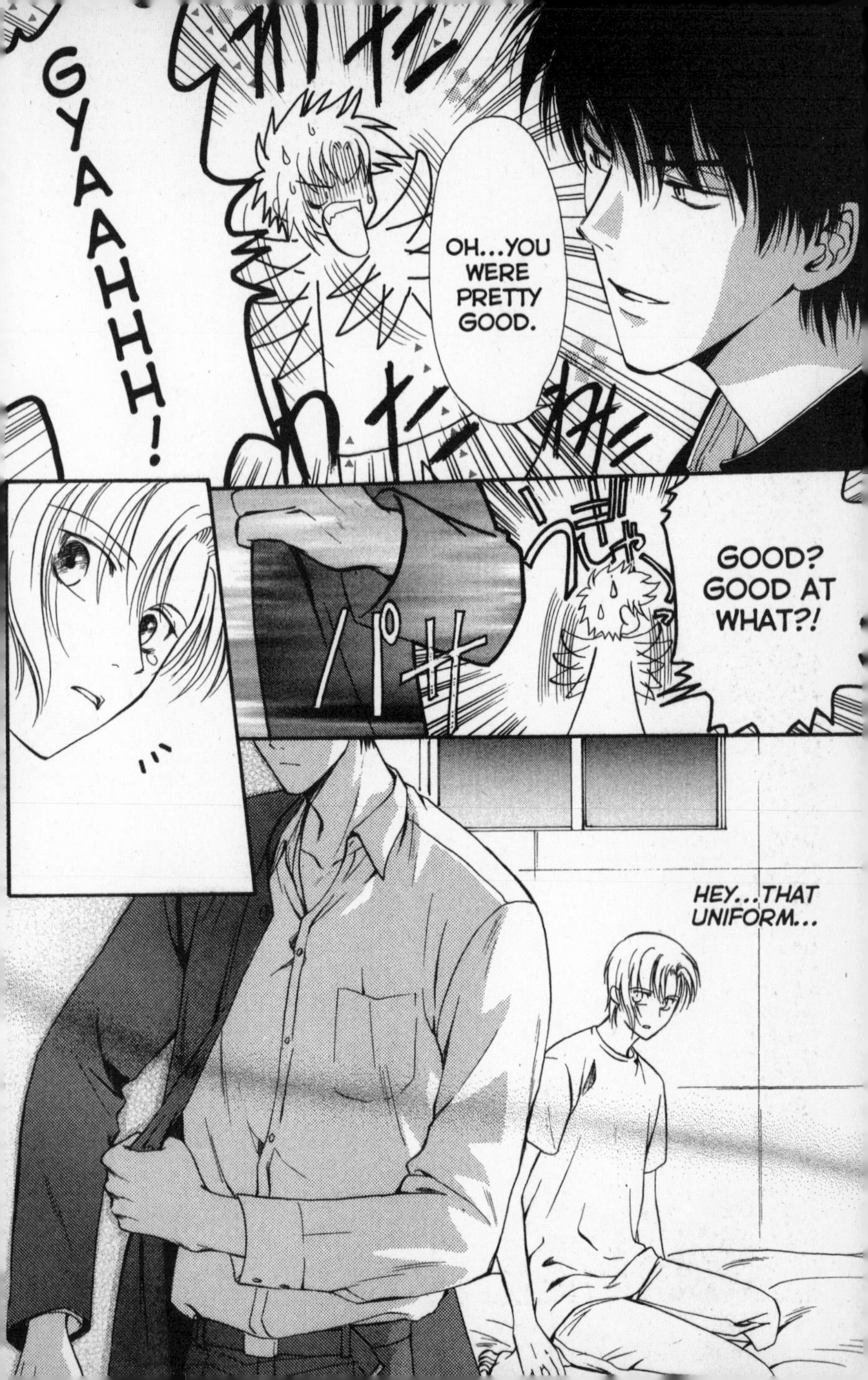
OH...YOU WERE PRETTY GOOD.
GYAAHHH!
GOOD? GOOD AT WHAT?!
HEY...THAT UNIFORM...

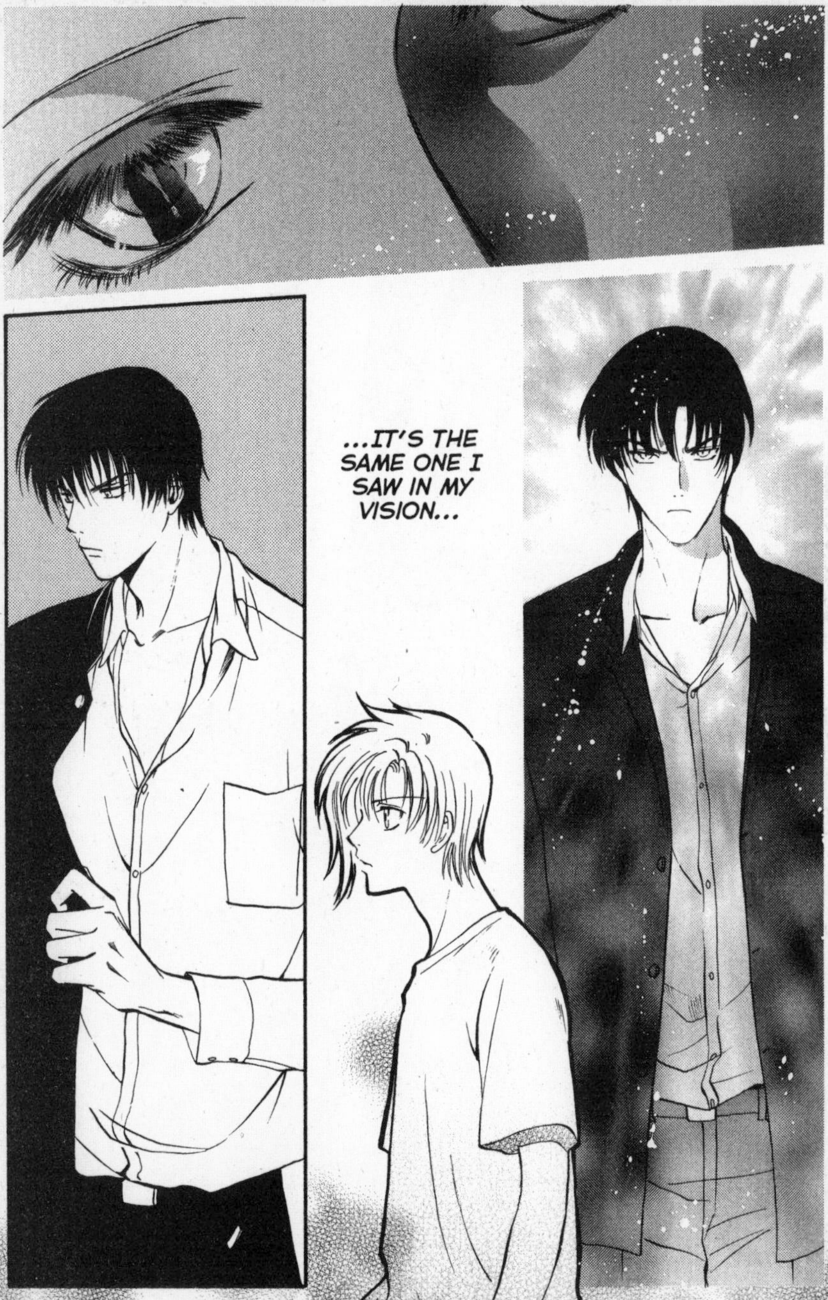
...IT'S THE SAME ONE I SAW IN MY VISION...

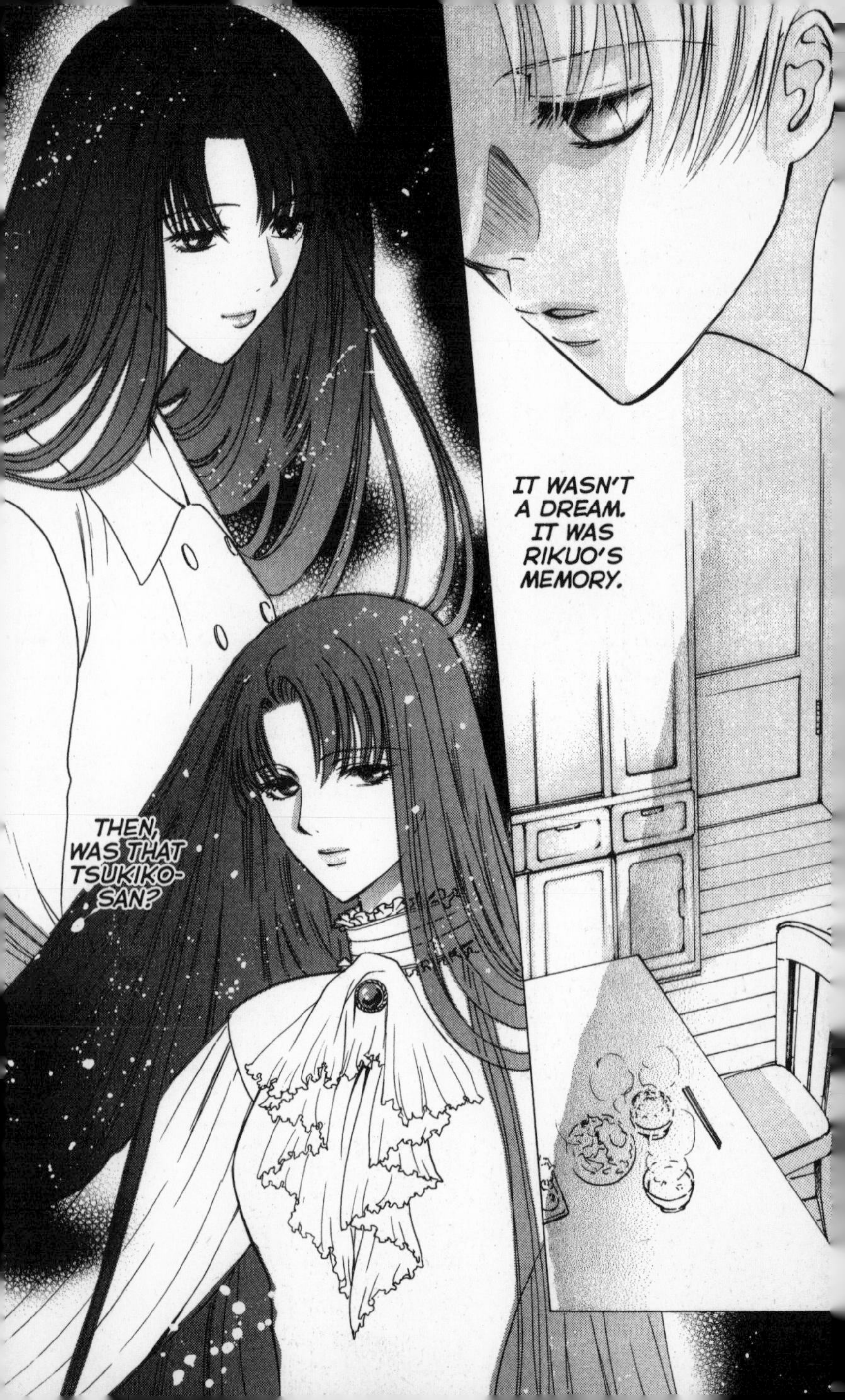
IT WASN'T A DREAM. IT WAS RIKUO'S MEMORY.
THEN, WAS THAT TSUKIKO-SAN?

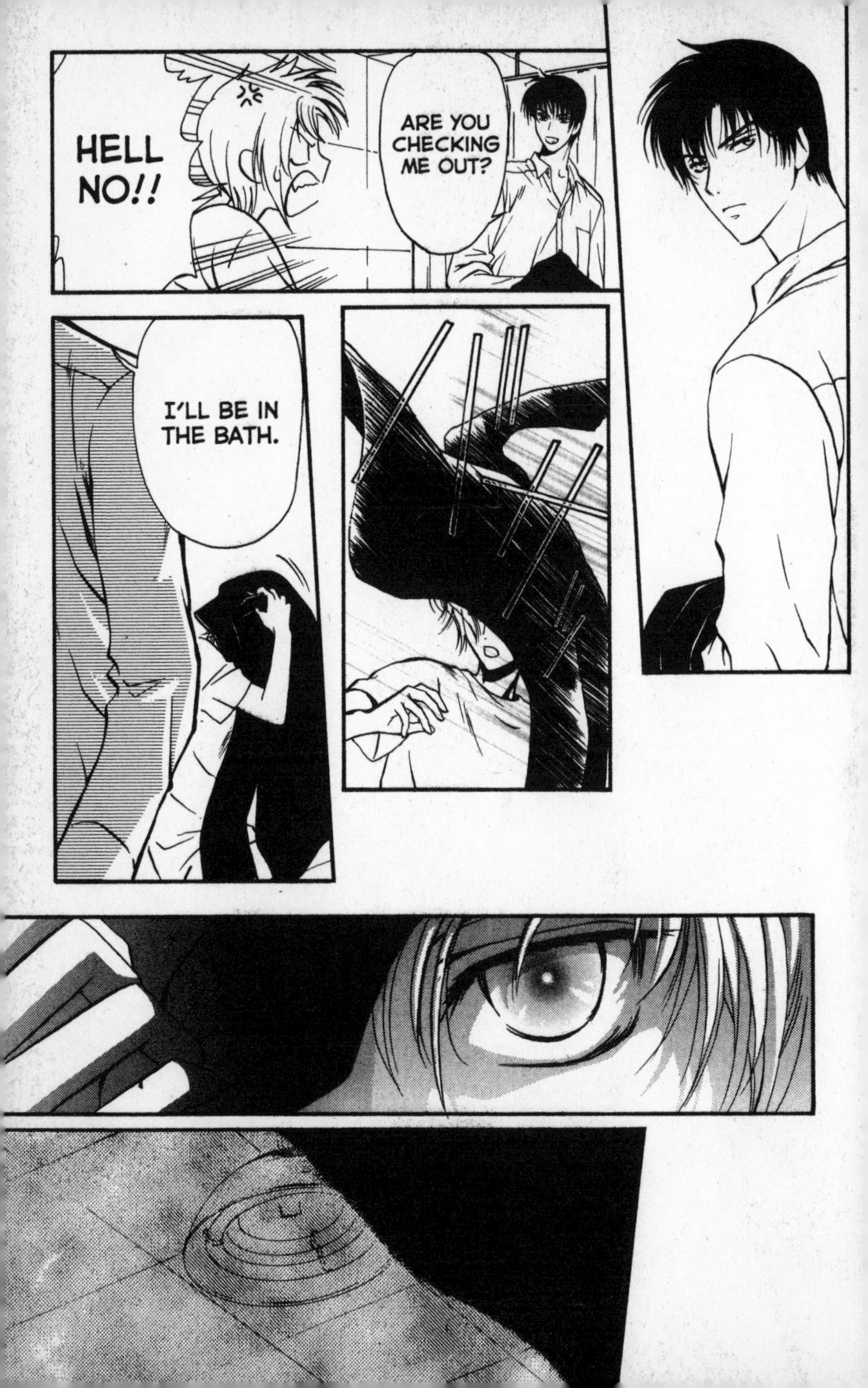
ARE YOU CHECKING ME OUT?
HELL NO!!
I'LL BE IN THE BATH.

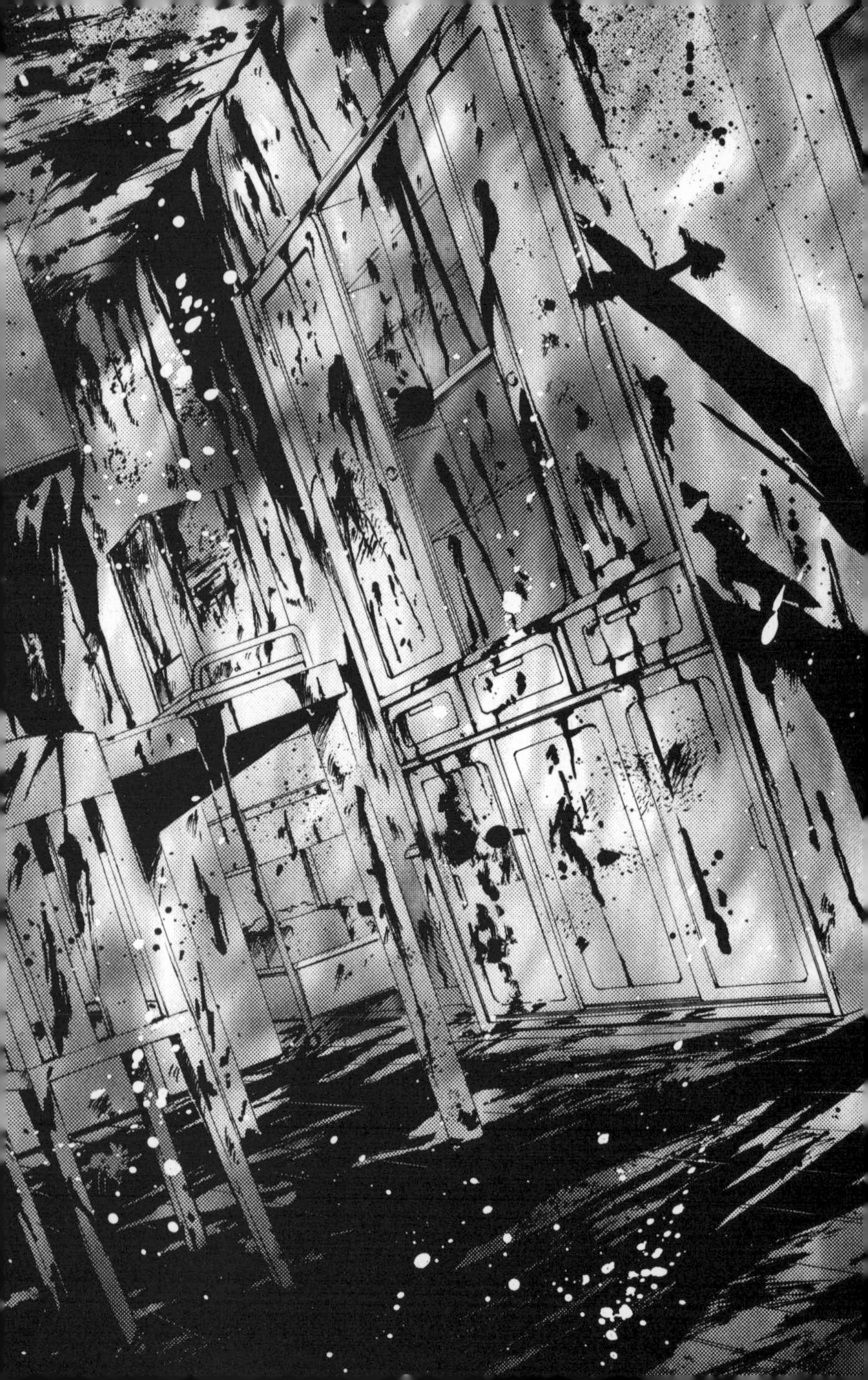

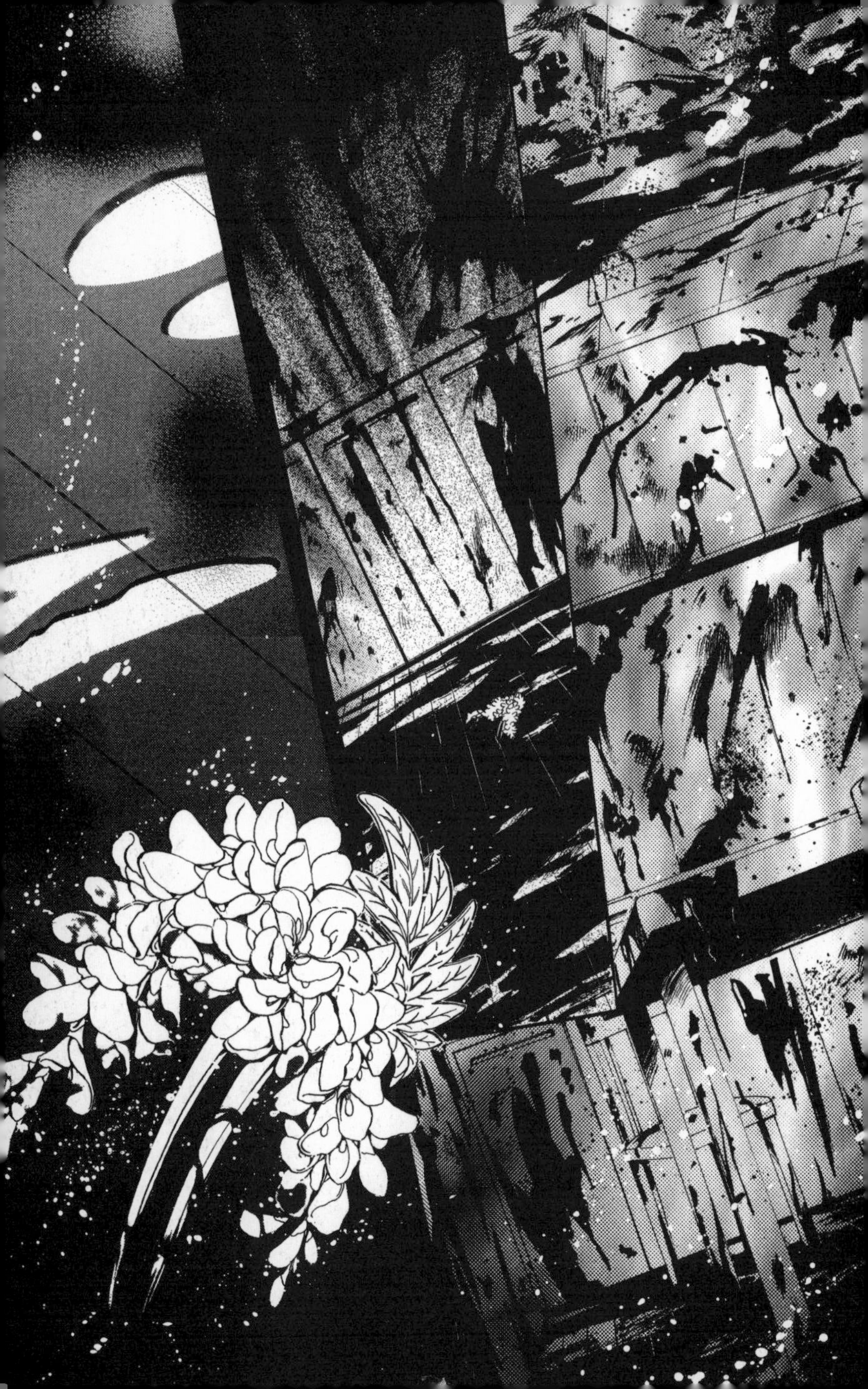

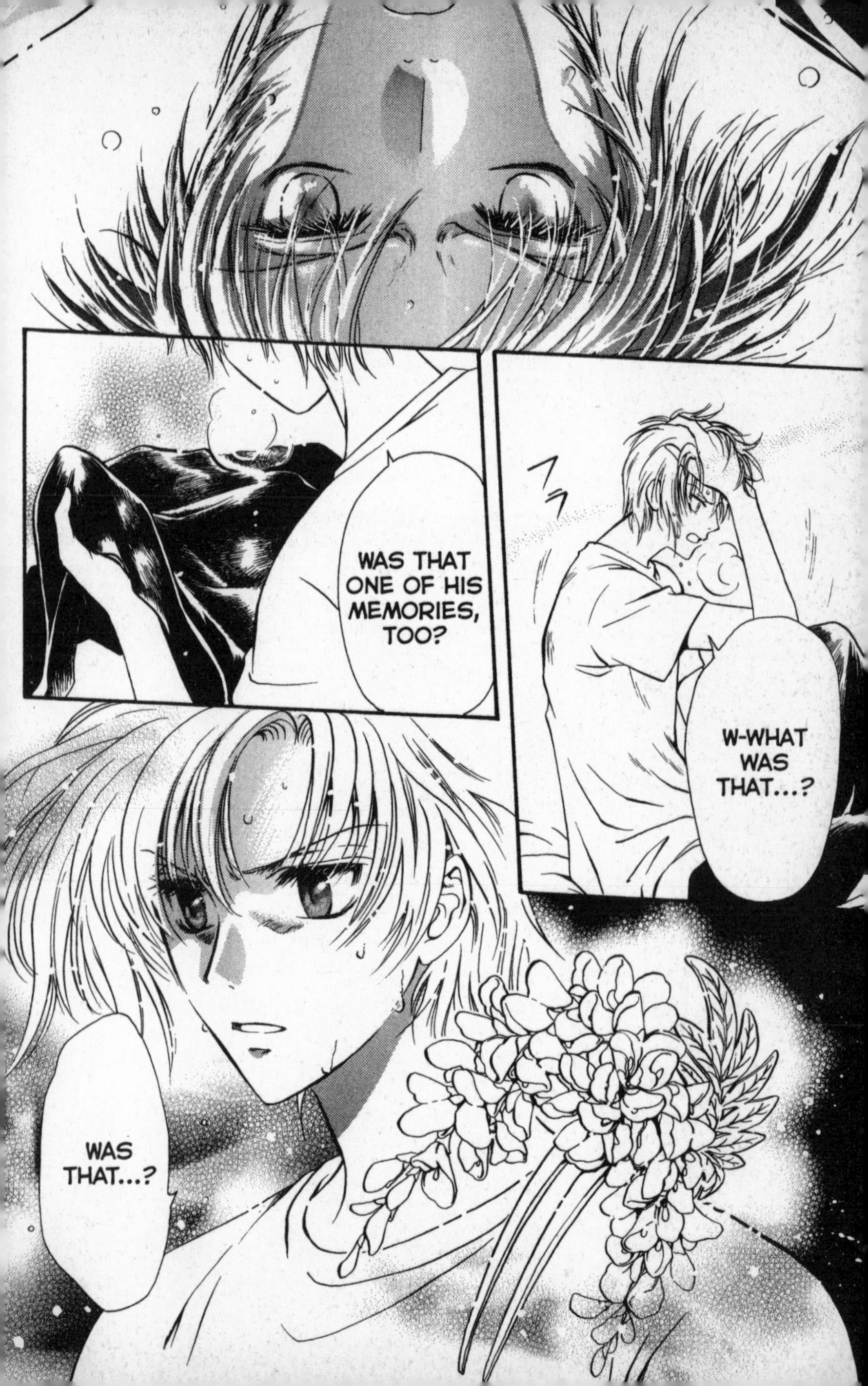
W-WHAT WAS THAT...?
WAS THAT ONE OF HIS MEMORIES, TOO?
WAS THAT...?

合法ドラッグ
LEGAL DRUG

TO BE CONTINUED

Sent by Kakei-san to enroll in a mysterious high school deep in the mountains, the boys must retrieve an equally mysterious ring. But Kudo and Himura soon discover that there is more to these hallowed halls than is out of the closet, so to speak. And their discovery may very well uncover more about each other—and hopefully more of each other—than the two boys from the Green Drugstore want to admit, face, contemplate or even casually think about. When the whole school decides to celebrate a marriage, more is set aflame than just hearts, which means that time is running out for the boys, who must hurry up and find that ring before anyone thinks that they're actually a couple. I mean, come on.

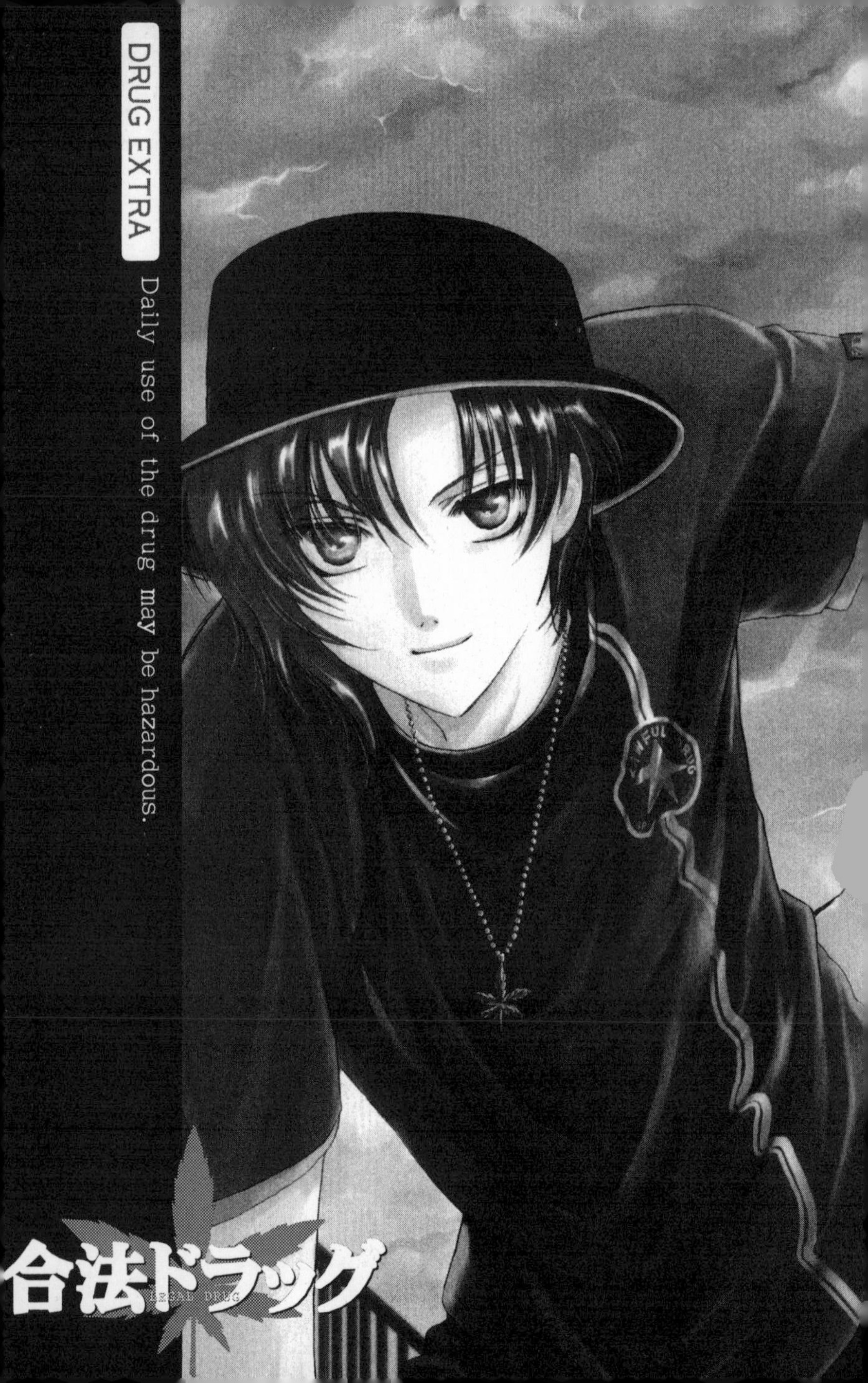
DRUG EXTRA
Daily use of the drug may be hazardous.
合法ドラッグ
LEGAL DRUG

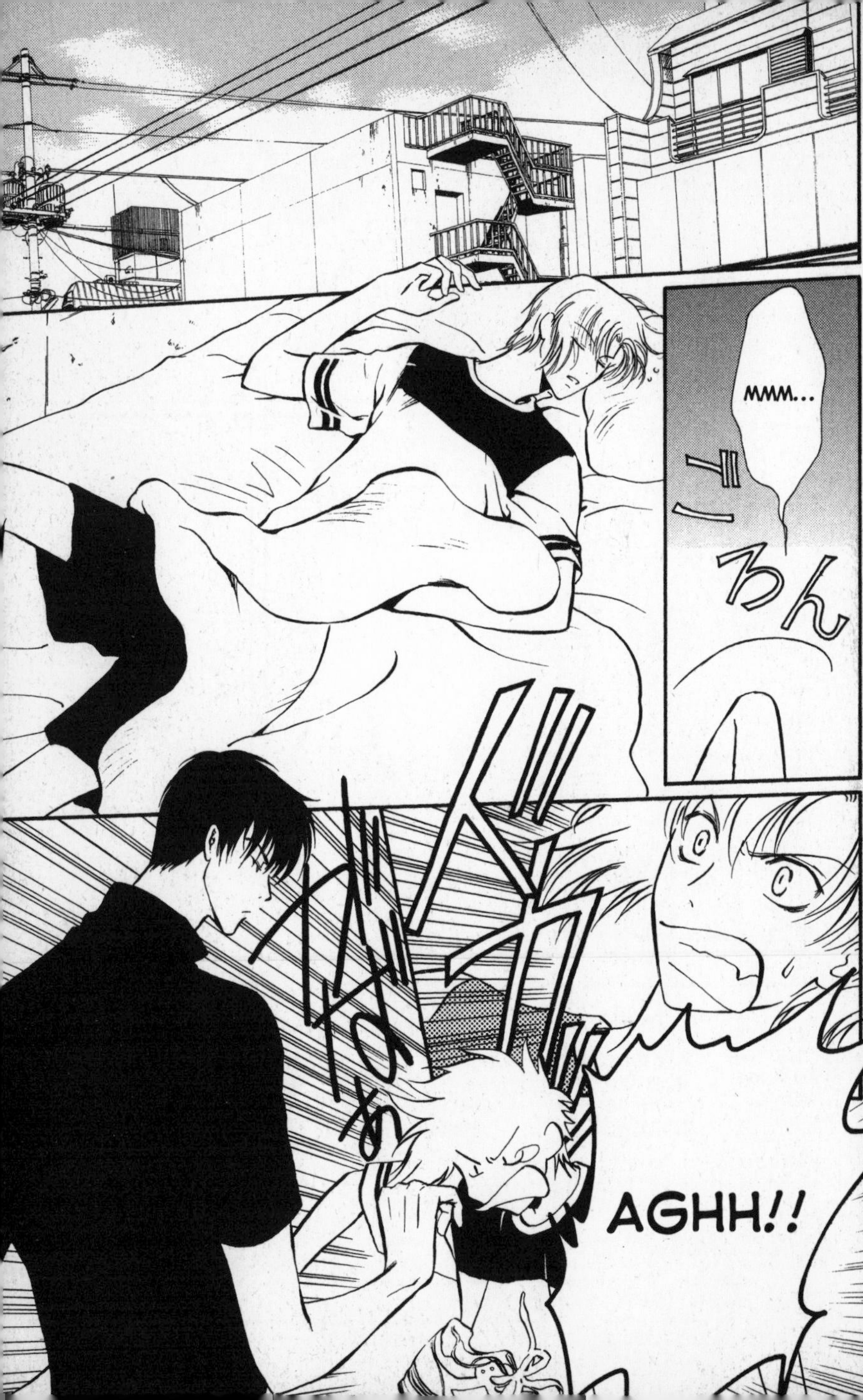
MMM...
ろん
AGHH!!

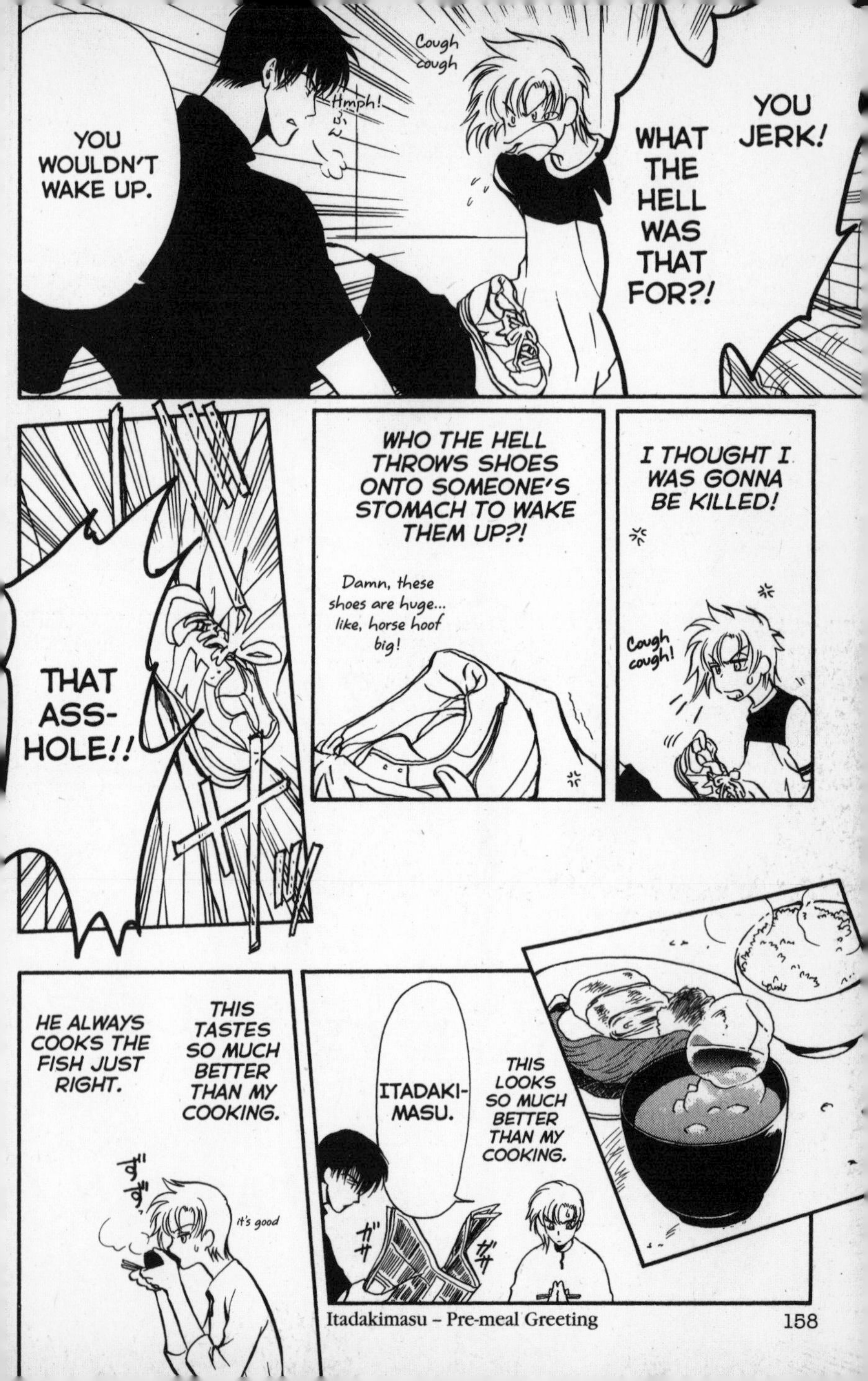
YOU JERK!
WHAT THE HELL WAS THAT FOR?!
Cough cough
Hmph!
YOU WOULDN'T WAKE UP.
I THOUGHT I WAS GONNA BE KILLED!
Cough cough!
WHO THE HELL THROWS SHOES ONTO SOMEONE'S STOMACH TO WAKE THEM UP?!
Damn, these shoes are huge... like, horse hoof big!
THAT ASS-HOLE!!
THIS LOOKS SO MUCH BETTER THAN MY COOKING.
ITADAKI-MASU.
ガサ
ガサ
THIS TASTES SO MUCH BETTER THAN MY COOKING.
HE ALWAYS COOKS THE FISH JUST RIGHT.
ずず
it's good

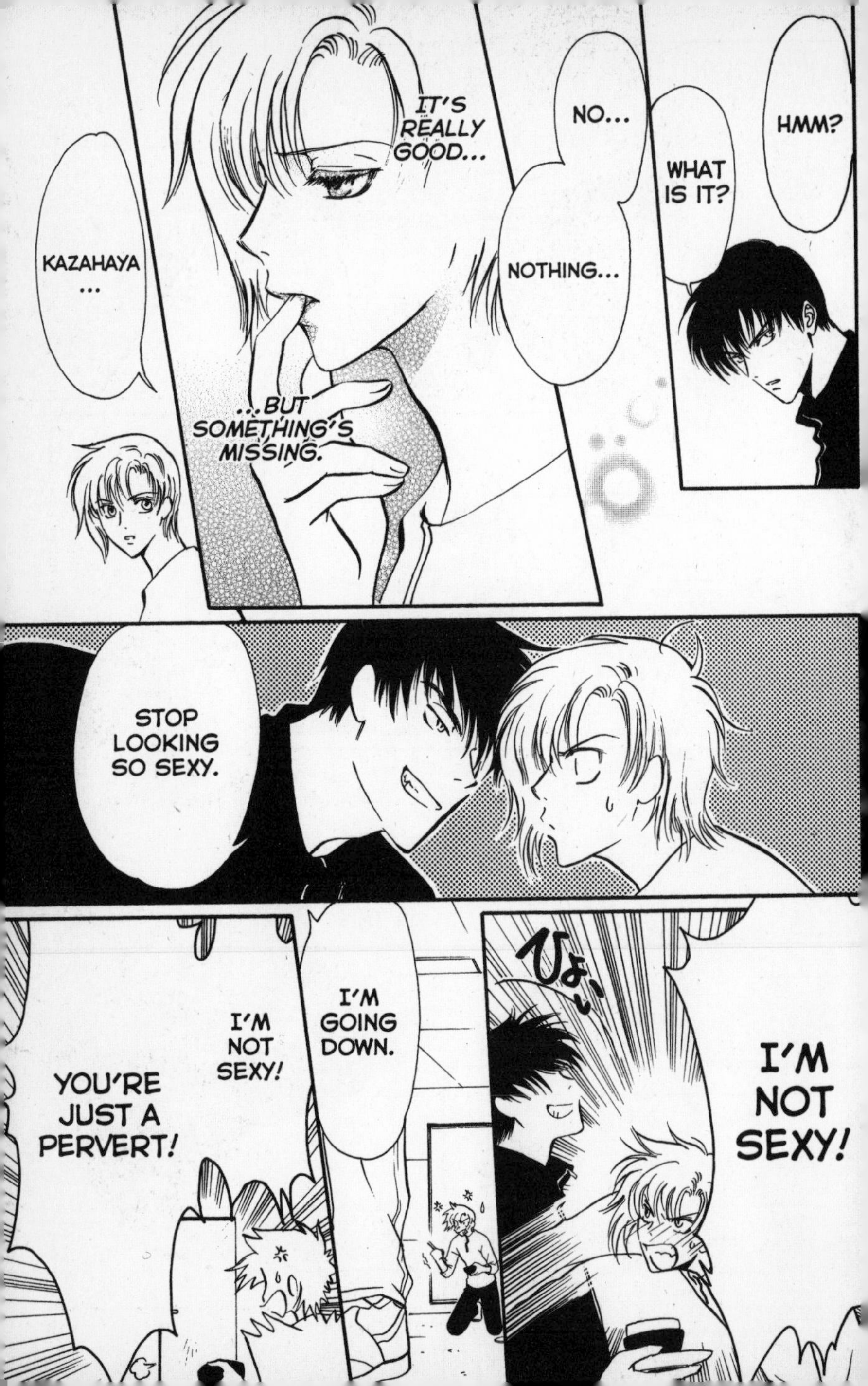
HMM?
WHAT IS IT?
NO...
NOTHING...
IT'S REALLY GOOD...
...BUT SOMETHING'S MISSING.
KAZAHAYA ...
STOP LOOKING SO SEXY.
ひょい
I'M NOT SEXY!
I'M GOING DOWN.
I'M NOT SEXY!
YOU'RE JUST A PERVERT!

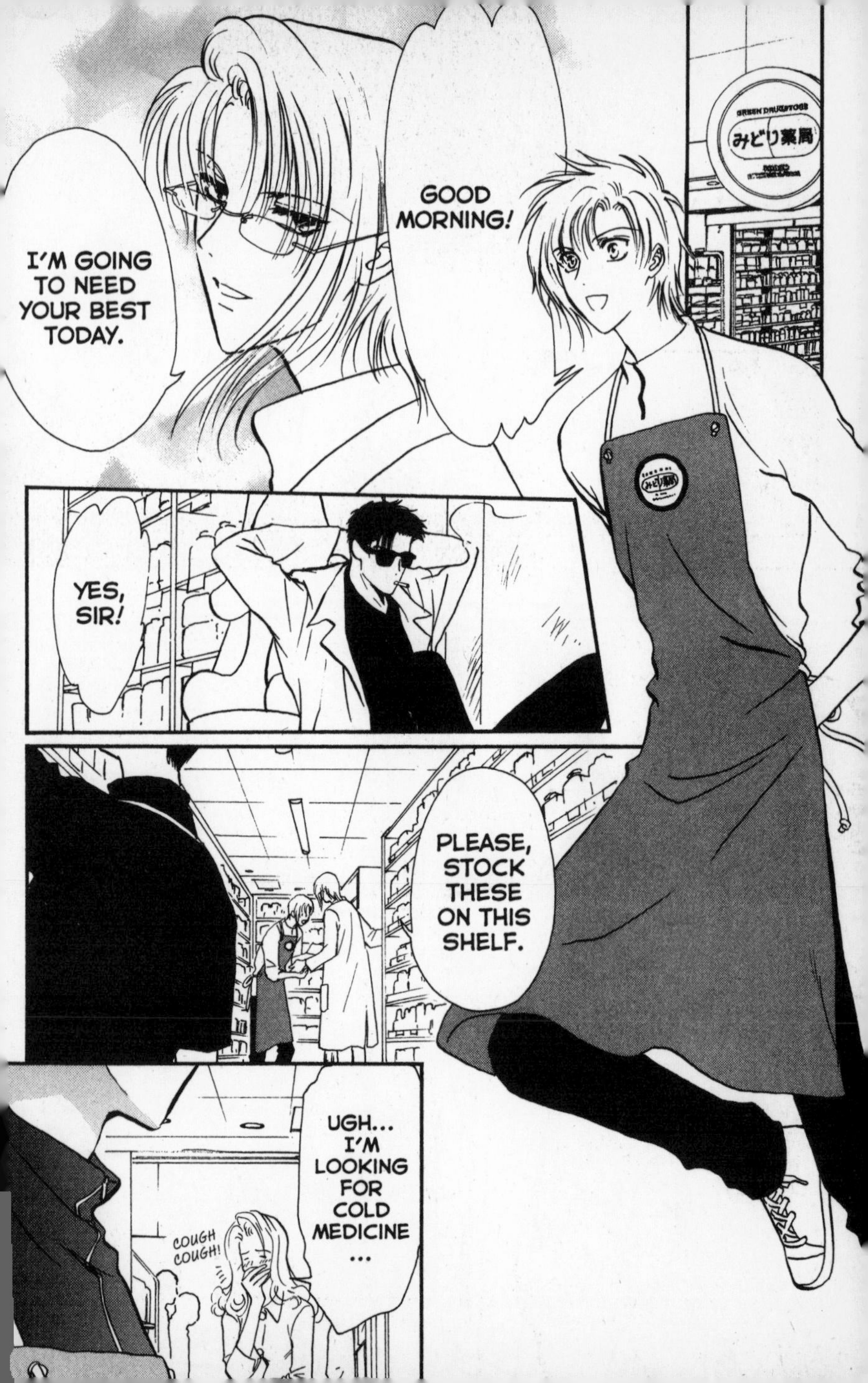
GREEN DRUGSTORE
みどり薬局
GOOD MORNING!
I'M GOING TO NEED YOUR BEST TODAY.
YES, SIR!
PLEASE, STOCK THESE ON THIS SHELF.
UGH... I'M LOOKING FOR COLD MEDICINE ...
COUGH COUGH!

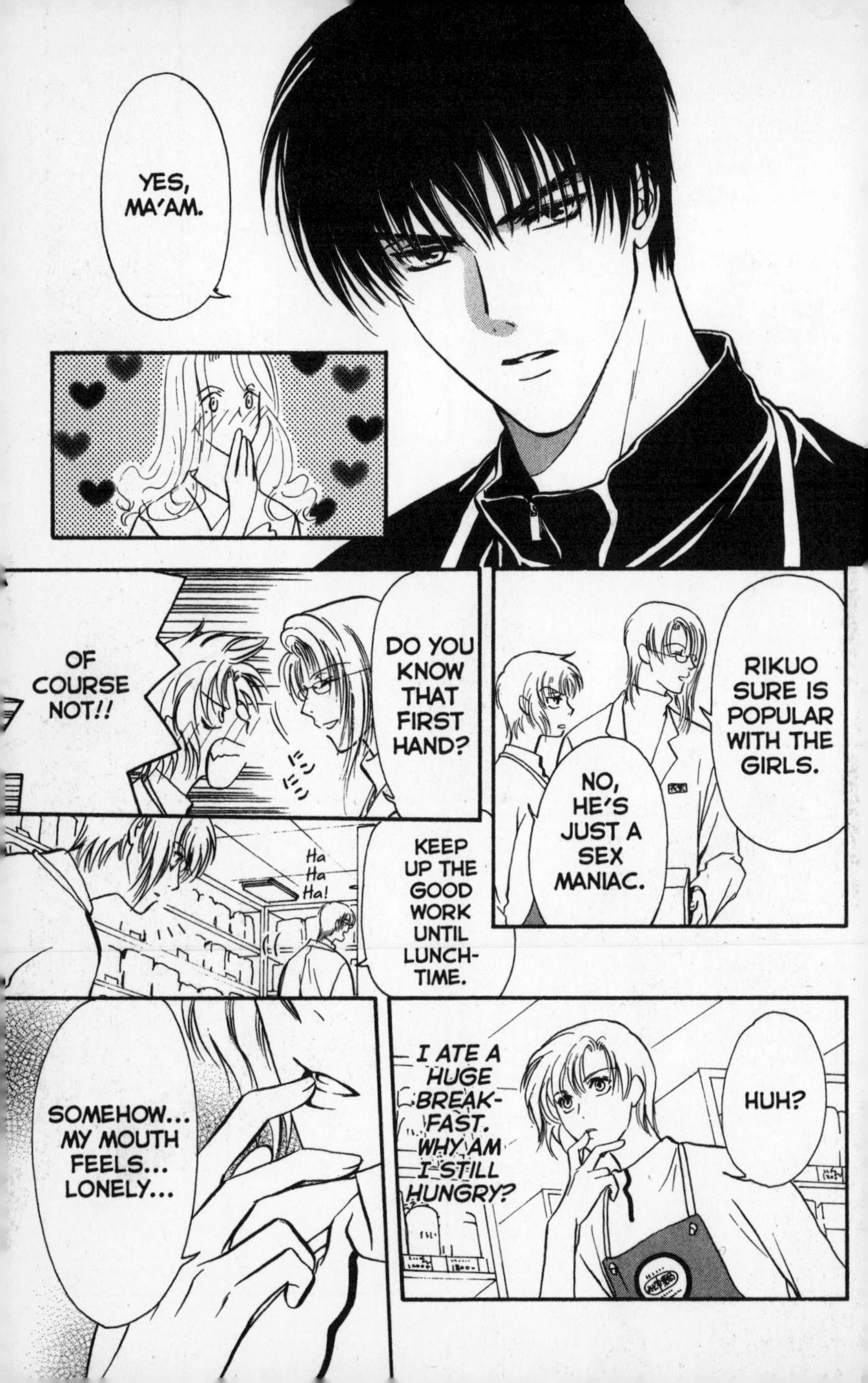
YES, MA'AM.
RIKUO SURE IS POPULAR WITH THE GIRLS.
NO, HE'S JUST A SEX MANIAC.
DO YOU KNOW THAT FIRST HAND?
OF COURSE NOT!!
KEEP UP THE GOOD WORK UNTIL LUNCH-TIME.
Ha Ha Ha!
HUH?
I ATE A HUGE BREAKFAST. WHY AM I STILL HUNGRY?
SOMEHOW... MY MOUTH FEELS... LONELY...

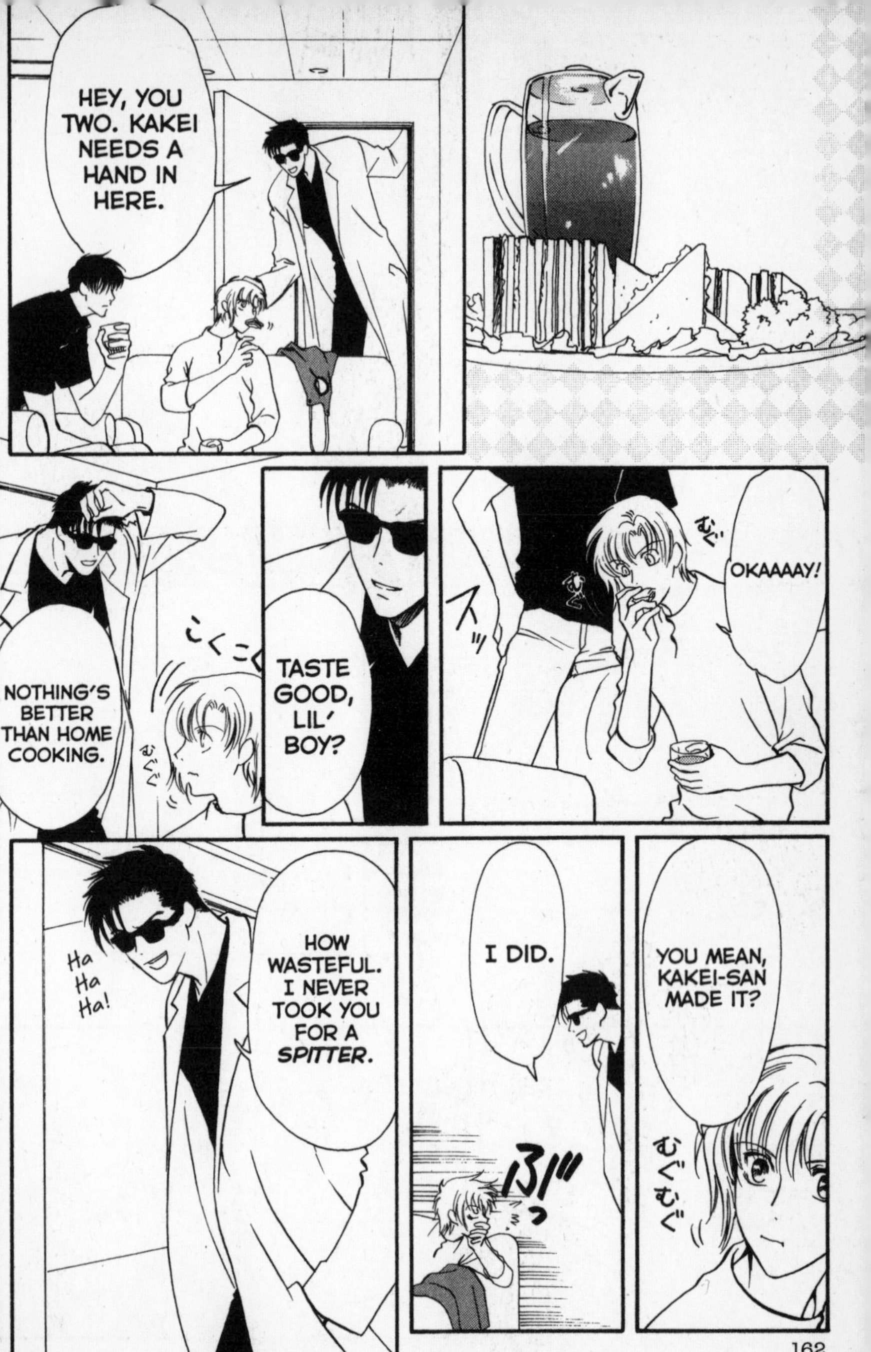
HEY, YOU TWO. KAKEI NEEDS A HAND IN HERE.
むぐ
スッ
OKAAAAY!
TASTE GOOD, LIL' BOY?
こくこく
むぐぐ
NOTHING'S BETTER THAN HOME COOKING.
YOU MEAN, KAKEI-SAN MADE IT?
むぐむぐ
I DID.
ぶっ
HOW WASTEFUL. I NEVER TOOK YOU FOR A *SPITTER*.
Ha Ha Ha!

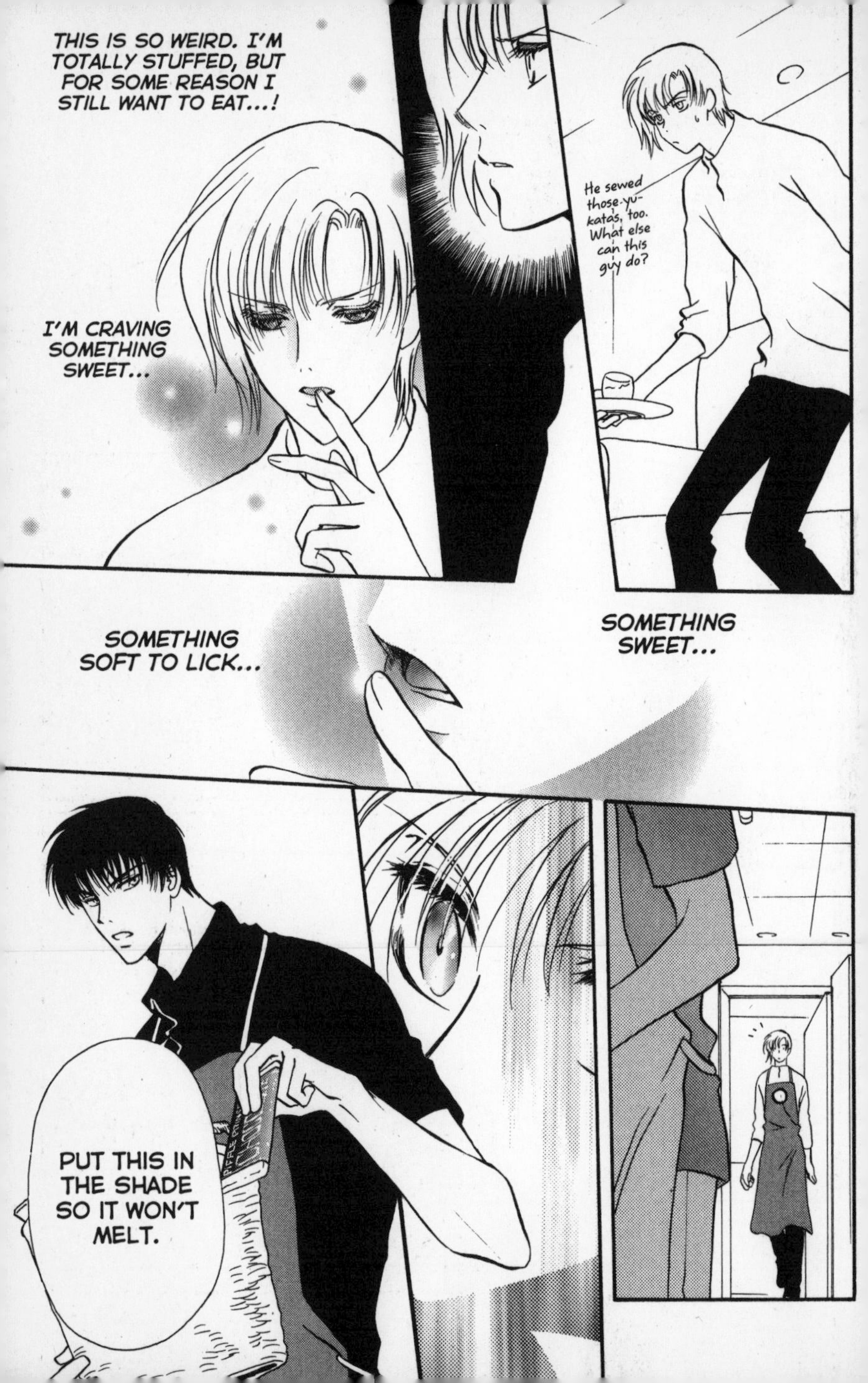
He sewed those yukatas, too. What else can this guy do?
THIS IS SO WEIRD. I'M TOTALLY STUFFED, BUT FOR SOME REASON I STILL WANT TO EAT...!
I'M CRAVING SOMETHING SWEET...
SOMETHING SWEET...
SOMETHING SOFT TO LICK...
PUT THIS IN THE SHADE SO IT WON'T MELT.

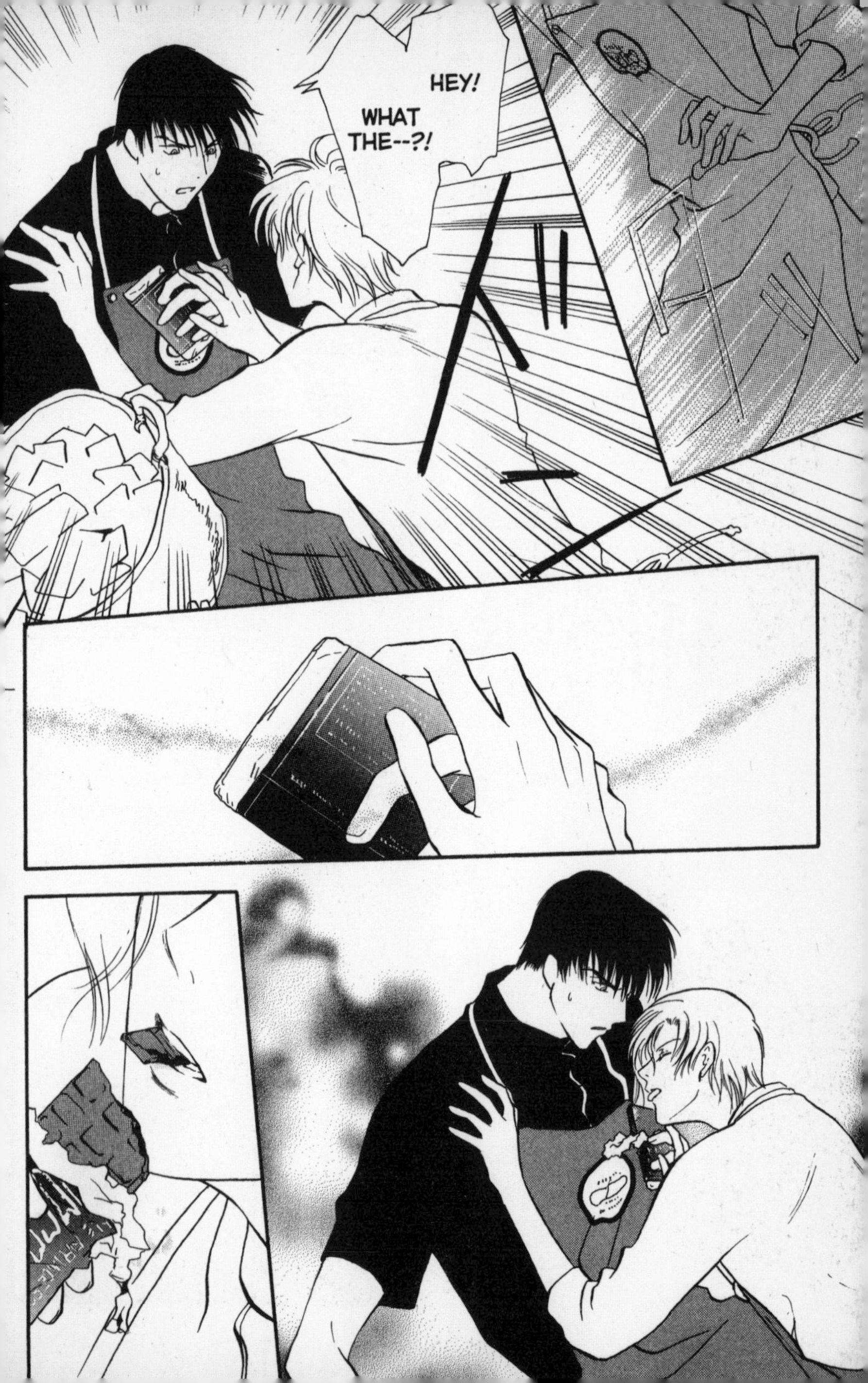
HEY!
WHAT THE--?!

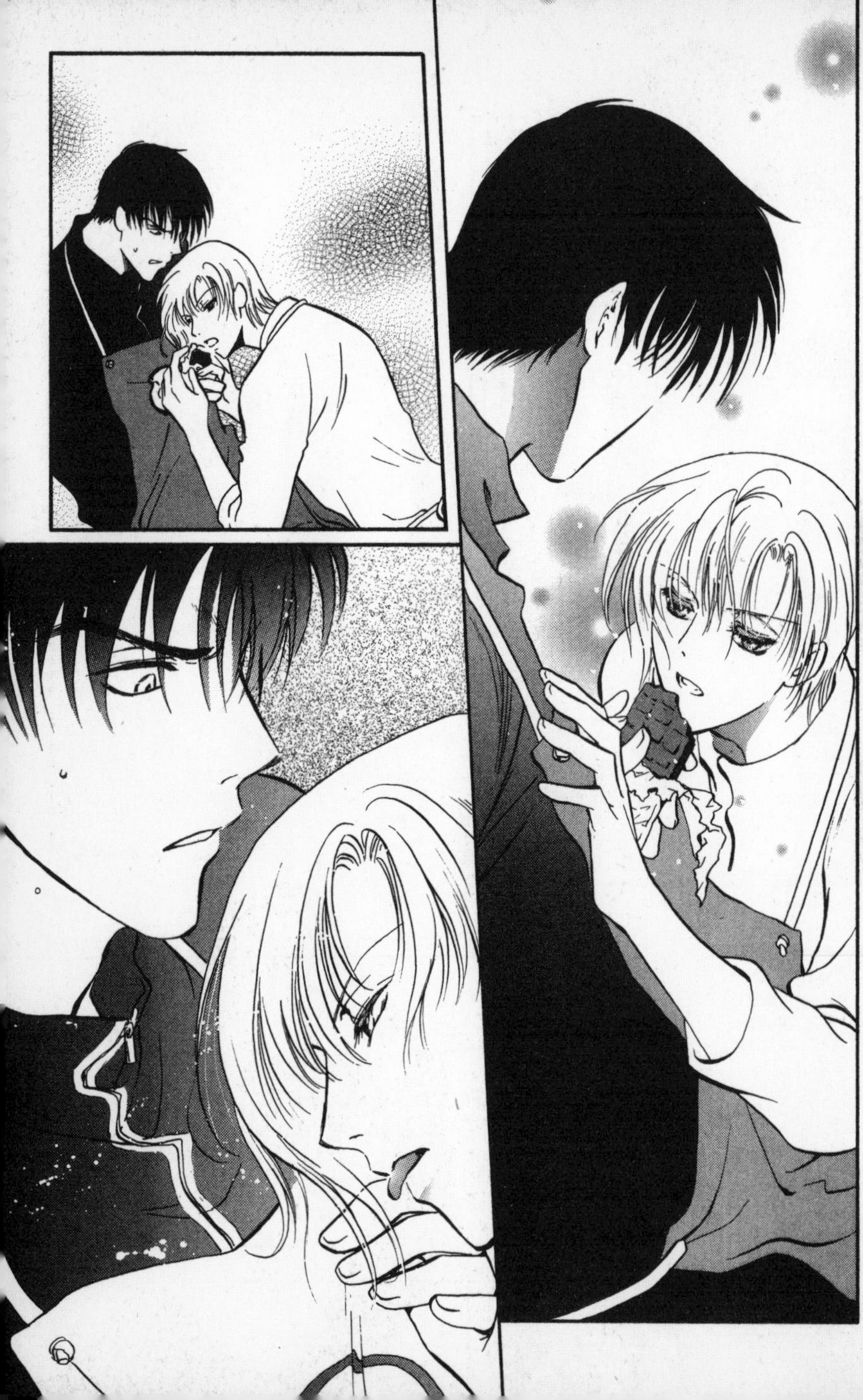

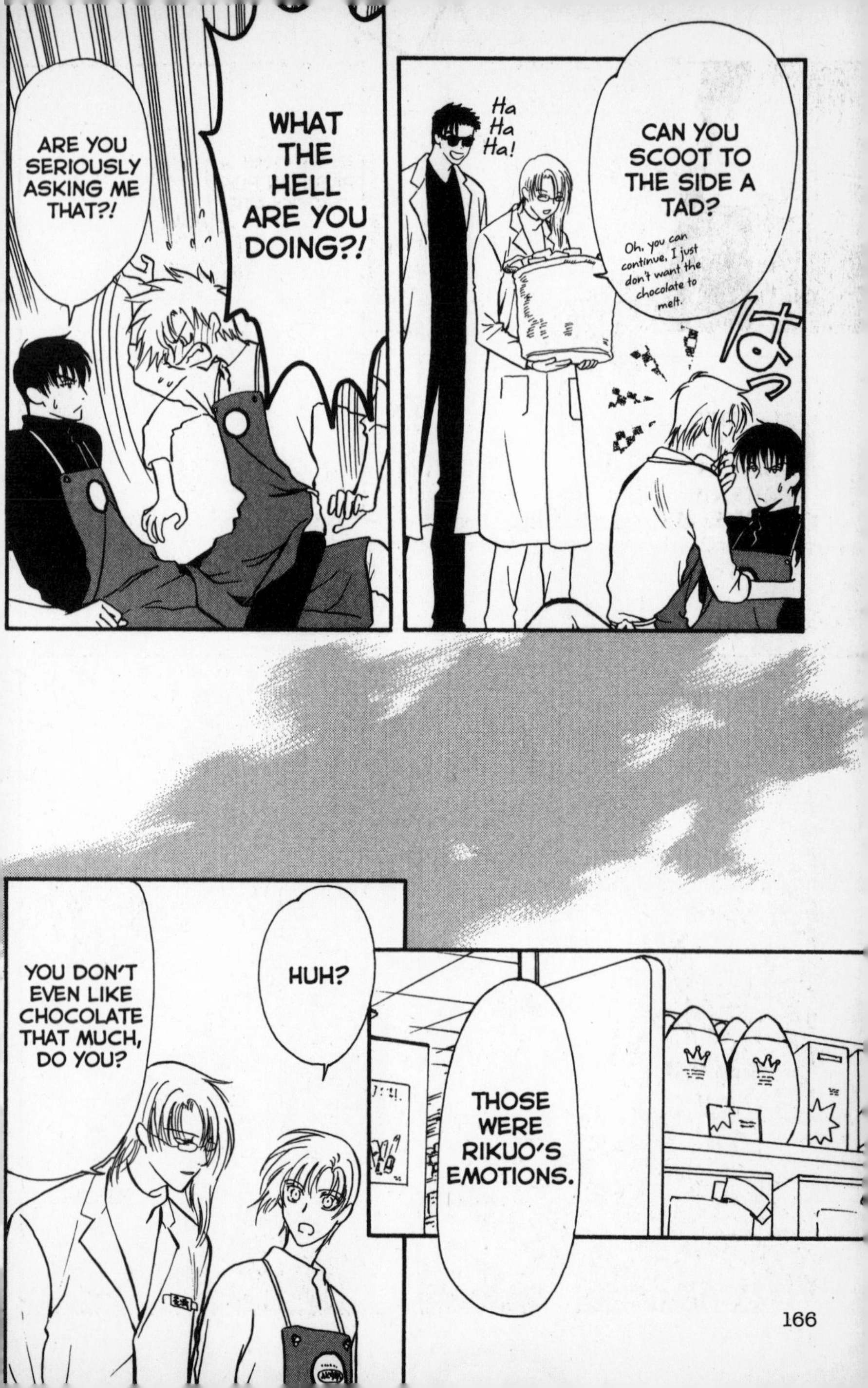
CAN YOU SCOOT TO THE SIDE A TAD?
Oh, you can continue, I just don't want the chocolate to melt.
Ha Ha Ha!
はっ
WHAT THE HELL ARE YOU DOING?!
ARE YOU SERIOUSLY ASKING ME THAT?!
THOSE WERE RIKUO'S EMOTIONS.
HUH?
YOU DON'T EVEN LIKE CHOCOLATE THAT MUCH, DO YOU?

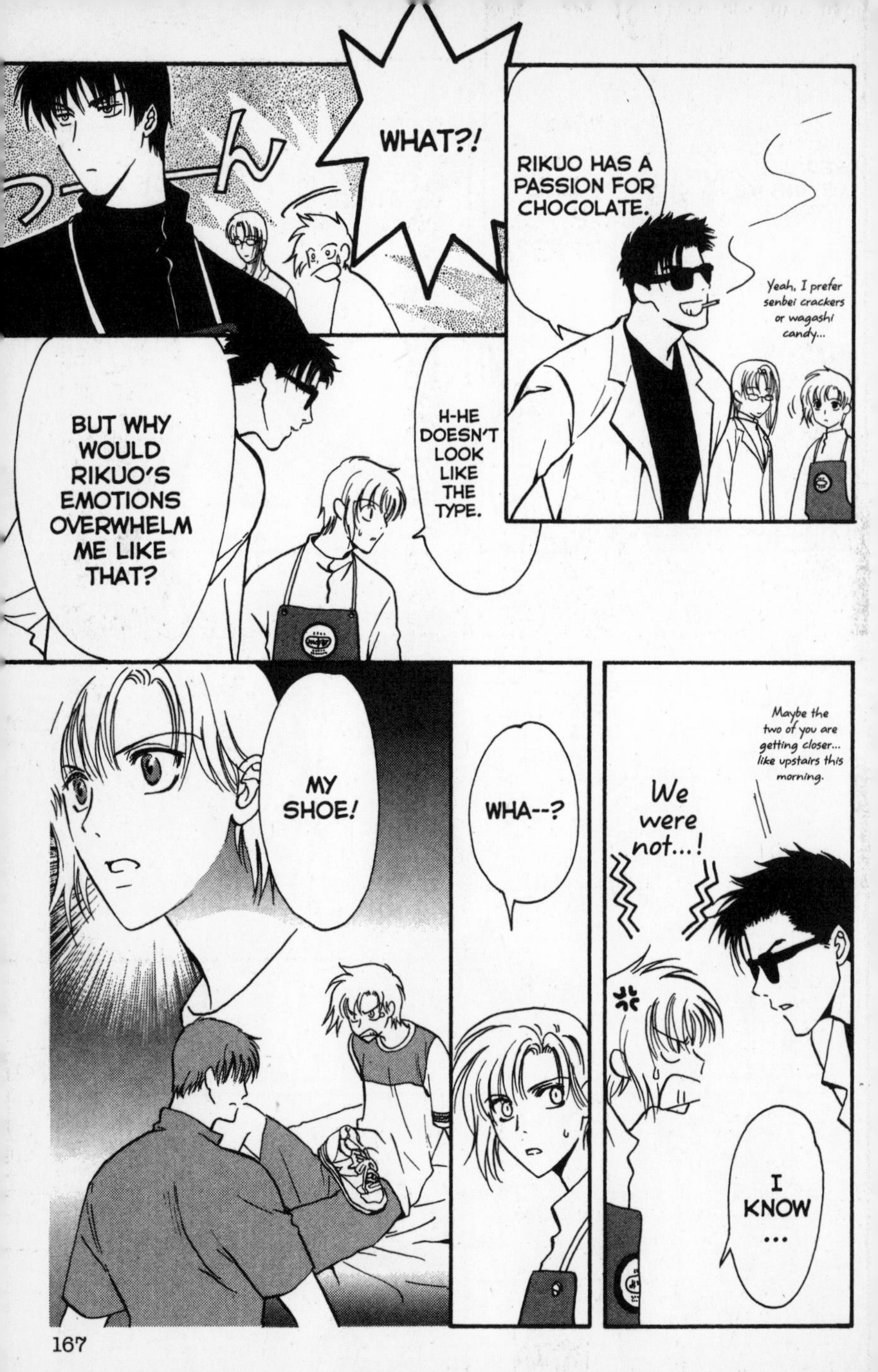
RIKUO HAS A PASSION FOR CHOCOLATE.
Yeah, I prefer senbei crackers or wagashi candy...
WHAT?!
H-HE DOESN'T LOOK LIKE THE TYPE.
BUT WHY WOULD RIKUO'S EMOTIONS OVERWHELM ME LIKE THAT?
Maybe the two of you are getting closer... like upstairs this morning.
We were not...!
I KNOW ...
WHA--?
MY SHOE!

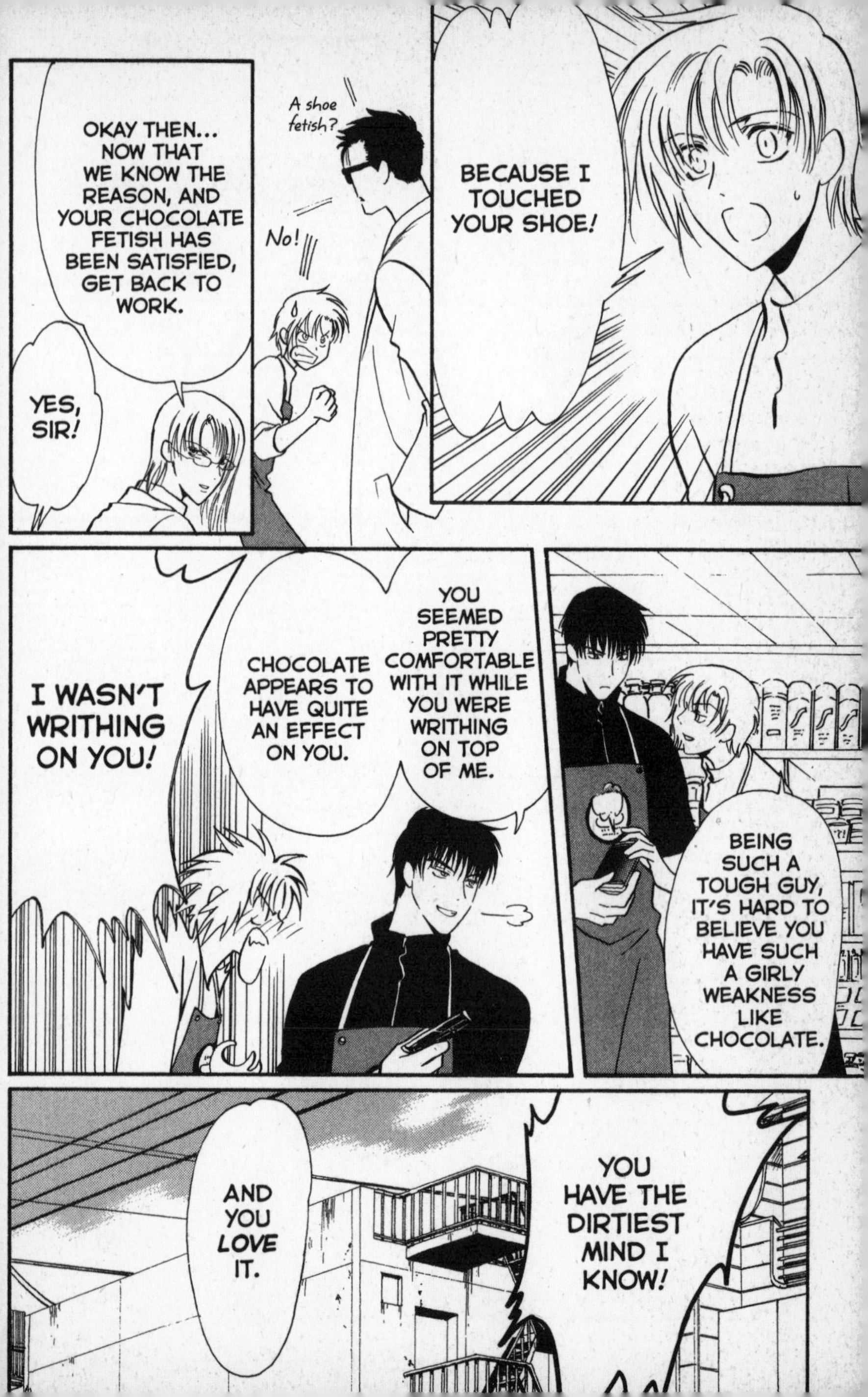
BECAUSE I TOUCHED YOUR SHOE!
A shoe fetish?
No!
OKAY THEN... NOW THAT WE KNOW THE REASON, AND YOUR CHOCOLATE FETISH HAS BEEN SATISFIED, GET BACK TO WORK.
YES, SIR!
BEING SUCH A TOUGH GUY, IT'S HARD TO BELIEVE YOU HAVE SUCH A GIRLY WEAKNESS LIKE CHOCOLATE.
YOU SEEMED PRETTY COMFORTABLE WITH IT WHILE YOU WERE WRITHING ON TOP OF ME.
CHOCOLATE APPEARS TO HAVE QUITE AN EFFECT ON YOU.
I WASN'T WRITHING ON YOU!
YOU HAVE THE DIRTIEST MIND I KNOW!
AND YOU *LOVE* IT.

STAFF DRUG

PLANNING AND PRESENTED BY
CLAMP

STORY
NANASE OHKAWA

COMIC
MICK NEKOI

ART ASSISTANT
SATSUKI IGARASHI
MOKONA APAPA

BOOK DESIGN
CLAMP

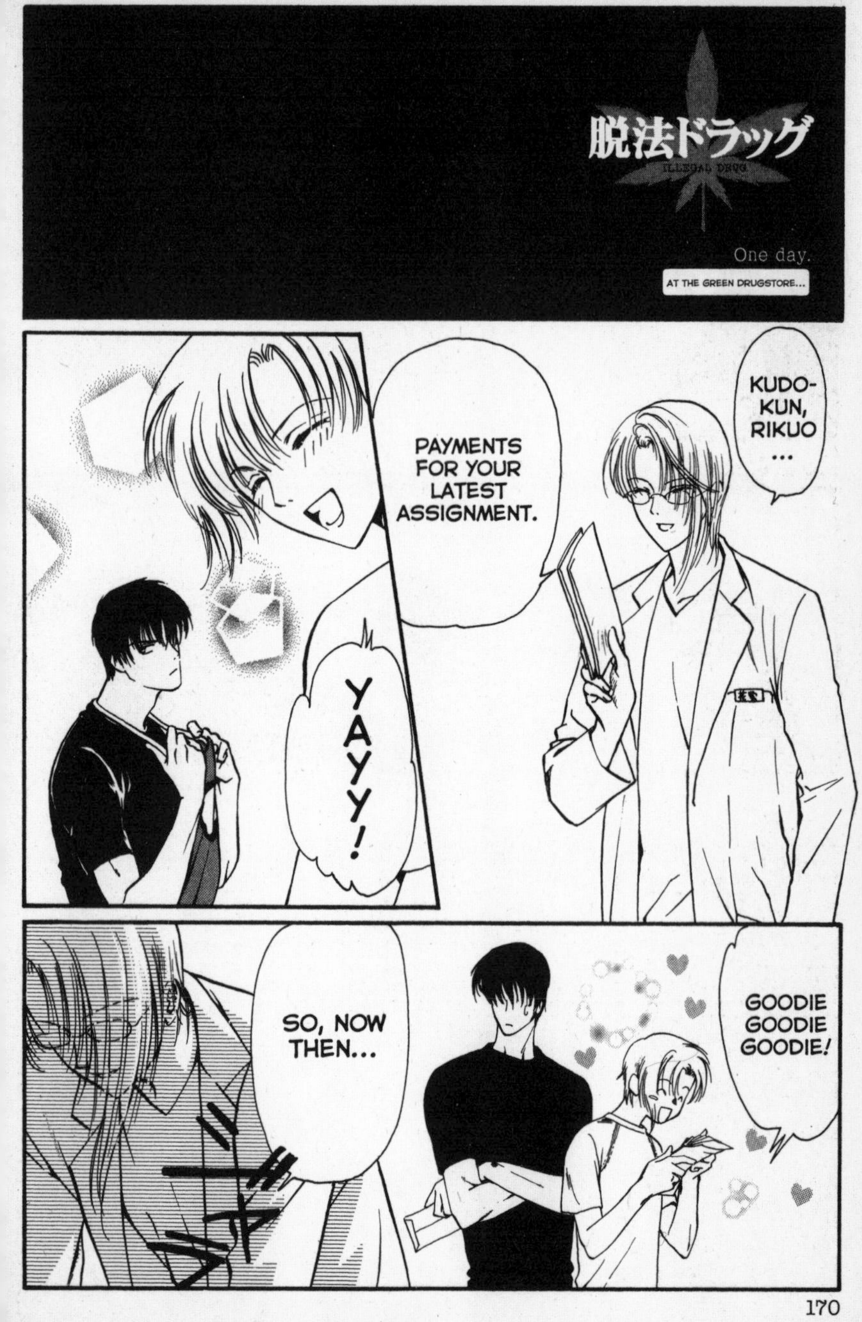
脱法ドラッグ
ILLEGAL DRUG
One day.
AT THE GREEN DRUGSTORE...
KUDO-KUN, RIKUO...
PAYMENTS FOR YOUR LATEST ASSIGNMENT.
YAYY!
GOODIE GOODIE GOODIE!
SO, NOW THEN...

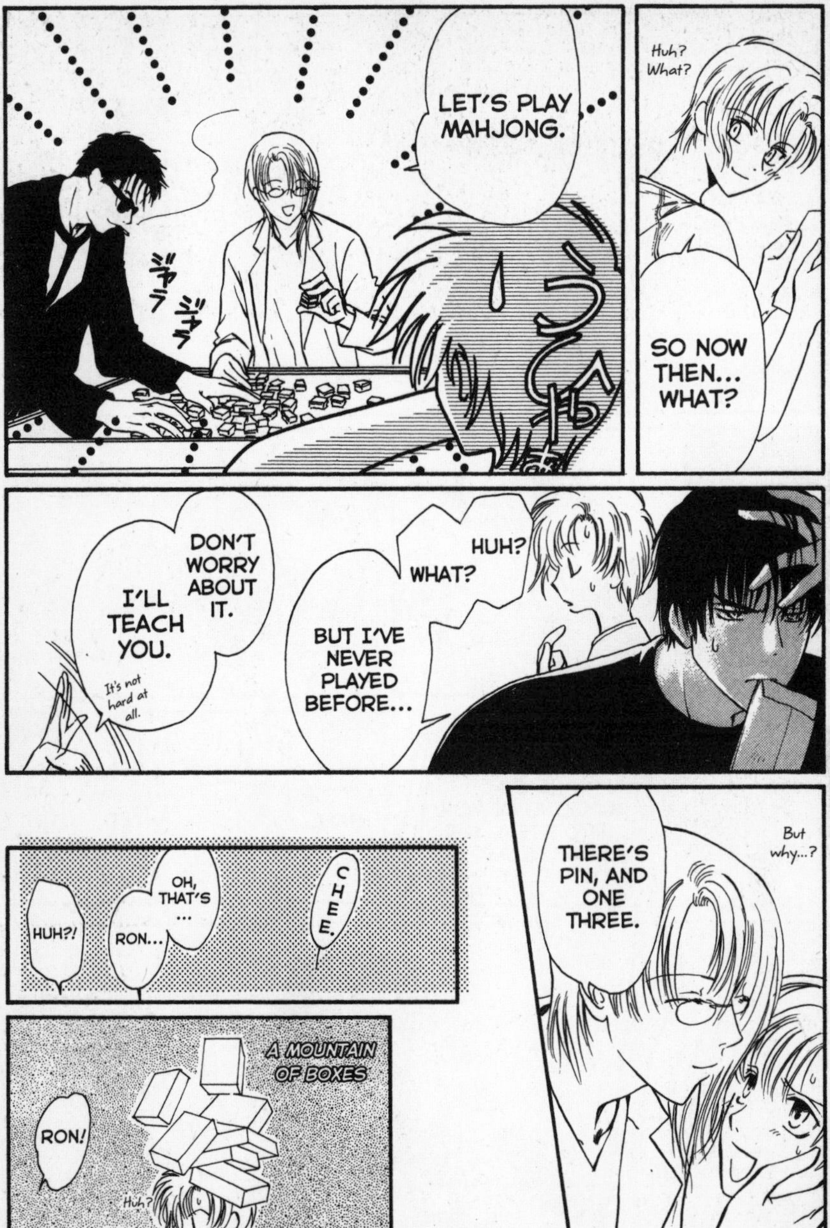
Huh? What?
SO NOW THEN... WHAT?
LET'S PLAY MAHJONG.
ジャラ
ジャラ
HUH? WHAT?
BUT I'VE NEVER PLAYED BEFORE...
DON'T WORRY ABOUT IT.
I'LL TEACH YOU.
It's not hard at all.
But why...?
THERE'S PIN, AND ONE THREE.
CHEE.
OH, THAT'S ...
RON...
HUH?!
A MOUNTAIN OF BOXES
RON!
Huh?
Huh?

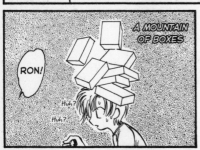

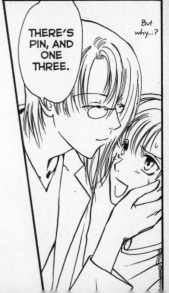

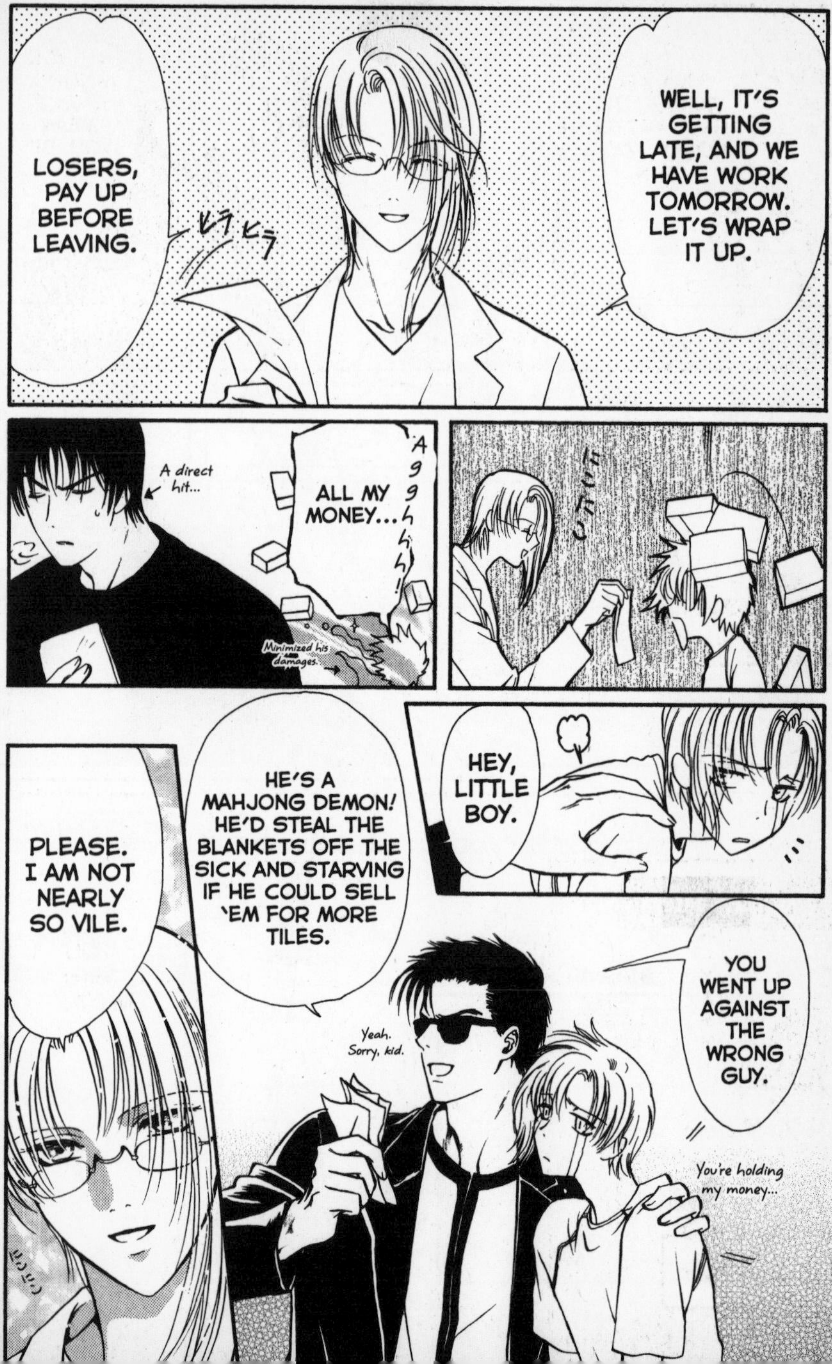
WELL, IT'S GETTING LATE, AND WE HAVE WORK TOMORROW. LET'S WRAP IT UP.
LOSERS, PAY UP BEFORE LEAVING.
ALL MY MONEY...
A direct hit...
Minimized his damages.
HEY, LITTLE BOY.
YOU WENT UP AGAINST THE WRONG GUY.
You're holding my money...
Yeah. Sorry, kid.
HE'S A MAHJONG DEMON! HE'D STEAL THE BLANKETS OFF THE SICK AND STARVING IF HE COULD SELL 'EM FOR MORE TILES.
PLEASE. I AM NOT NEARLY SO VILE.

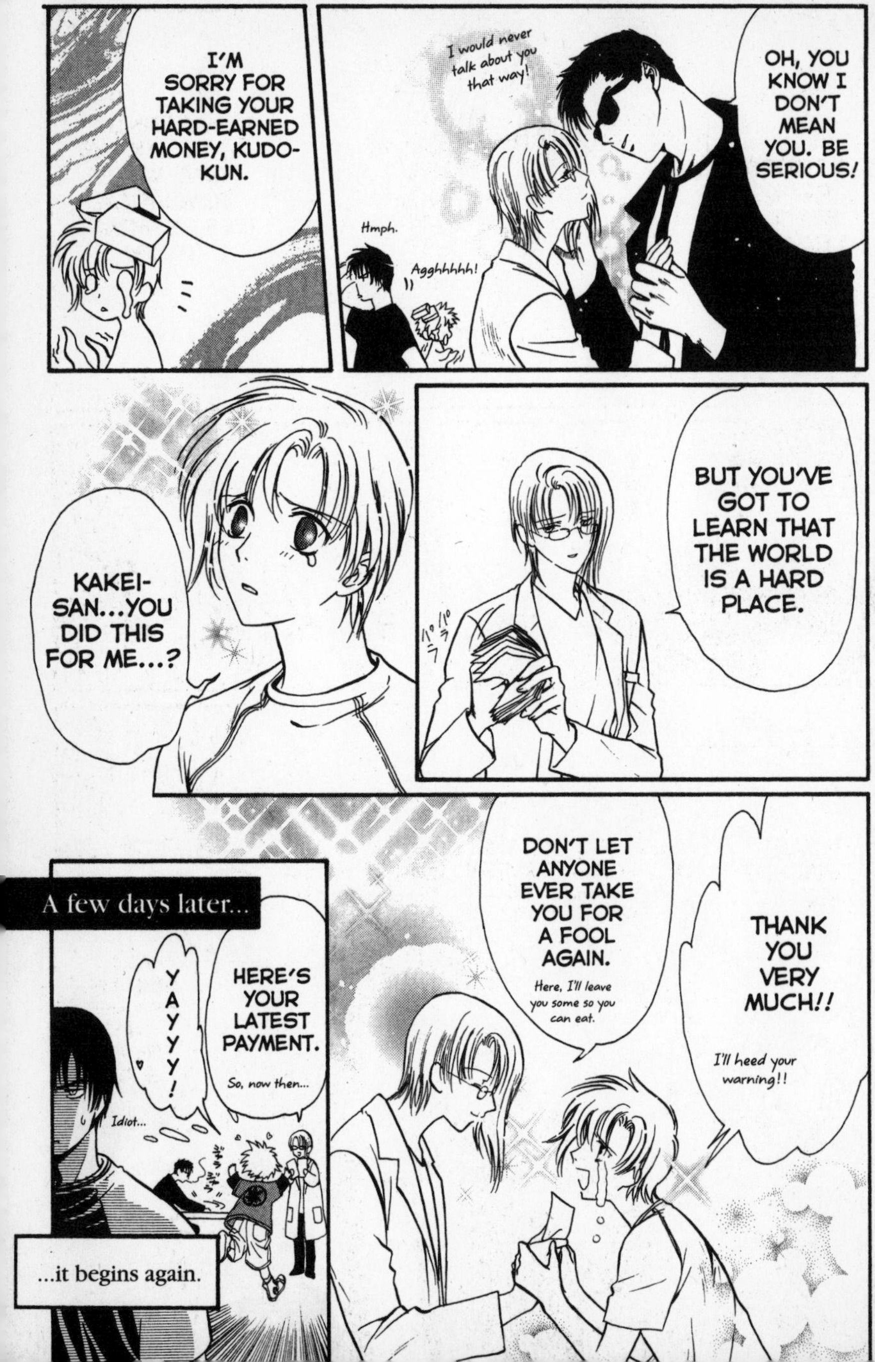
OH, YOU KNOW I DON'T MEAN YOU. BE SERIOUS!
I would never talk about you that way!
Hmph.
Agghhhhh!
I'M SORRY FOR TAKING YOUR HARD-EARNED MONEY, KUDO-KUN.
BUT YOU'VE GOT TO LEARN THAT THE WORLD IS A HARD PLACE.
KAKEI-SAN...YOU DID THIS FOR ME...?
THANK YOU VERY MUCH!!
I'll heed your warning!!
DON'T LET ANYONE EVER TAKE YOU FOR A FOOL AGAIN.
Here, I'll leave you some so you can eat.
A few days later...
HERE'S YOUR LATEST PAYMENT.
So, now then...
YAYYY!
Idiot...
...it begins again.

Legal Drug Vol. 2
Created by CLAMP

Translation - Ray Yoshimoto
English Adaptation - Jamie S. Rich
Retouch and Lettering - Vicente Rivera, Jr.
Cover Layout - Matt Alford

Editor - Luis Reyes
Digital Imaging Manager - Chris Buford
Pre-Press Manager - Antonio DePietro
Production Managers - Jennifer Miller and Mutsumi Miyazaki
Art Director - Matt Alford
Managing Editor - Jill Freshney
VP of Production - Ron Klamert
President and C.O.O. - John Parker
Publisher and C.E.O. - Stuart Levy

A **TOKYOPOP** Manga

TOKYOPOP Inc.
5900 Wilshire Blvd. Suite 2000
Los Angeles, CA 90036

E-mail: info@TOKYOPOP.com
Come visit us online at www.TOKYOPOP.com

ISBN: 1-59532-421-6

First TOKYOPOP printing: February 2005

10 9 8 7 6 5 4 3 2 1

Printed in the USA

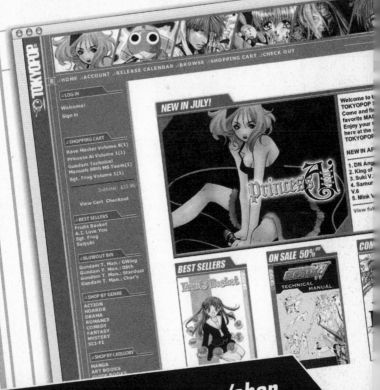

LAMENT of the LAMB

SHE CAN PROTECT HER BROTHER FROM THE WORLD.
CAN SHE PROTECT THE WORLD FROM HER BROTHER?

OT
OLDER TEEN
AGE 16+

ALSO AVAILABLE FROM TOKYOPOP®

PLANETES
PRESIDENT DAD
PRIEST
PRINCESS AI
PSYCHIC ACADEMY
QUEEN'S KNIGHT, THE
RAGNAROK
RAVE MASTER
REALITY CHECK
REBIRTH
REBOUND
REMOTE
RISING STARS OF MANGA™, THE
SABER MARIONETTE J
SAILOR MOON
SAINT TAIL
SAIYUKI
SAMURAI DEEPER KYO
SAMURAI GIRL™ REAL BOUT HIGH SCHOOL
SCRYED
SEIKAI TRILOGY, THE
SGT. FROG
SHAOLIN SISTERS
SHIRAHIME-SYO: SNOW GODDESS TALES
SHUTTERBOX
SKULL MAN, THE
SNOW DROP
SORCERER HUNTERS
SOUL TO SEOUL
STONE
SUIKODEN III
SUKI
TAROT CAFÉ, THE
THREADS OF TIME
TOKYO BABYLON
TOKYO MEW MEW
TOKYO TRIBES
TRAMPS LIKE US
UNDER THE GLASS MOON
VAMPIRE GAME
VISION OF ESCAFLOWNE, THE
WARCRAFT
WARRIORS OF TAO
WILD ACT
WISH
WORLD OF HARTZ
X-DAY
ZODIAC P.I.

NOVELS

CLAMP SCHOOL PARANORMAL INVESTIGATORS
SAILOR MOON
SLAYERS

ART BOOKS

ART OF CARDCAPTOR SAKURA
ART OF MAGIC KNIGHT RAYEARTH, THE
PEACH: MIWA UEDA ILLUSTRATIONS
CLAMP NORTH SIDE
CLAMP SOUTH SIDE

ANIME GUIDES

COWBOY BEBOP
GUNDAM TECHNICAL MANUALS
SAILOR MOON SCOUT GUIDES

TOKYOPOP KIDS

STRAY SHEEP

CINE-MANGA®

ALADDIN
CARDCAPTORS
DUEL MASTERS
FAIRLY ODDPARENTS, THE
FAMILY GUY
FINDING NEMO
G.I. JOE SPY TROOPS
GREATEST STARS OF THE NBA
JACKIE CHAN ADVENTURES
JIMMY NEUTRON: BOY GENIUS, THE ADVENTURES OF
KIM POSSIBLE
LILO & STITCH: THE SERIES
LIZZIE MCGUIRE
LIZZIE MCGUIRE MOVIE, THE
MALCOLM IN THE MIDDLE
POWER RANGERS: DINO THUNDER
POWER RANGERS: NINJA STORM
PRINCESS DIARIES 2, THE
RAVE MASTER
SHREK 2
SIMPLE LIFE, THE
SPONGEBOB SQUAREPANTS
SPY KIDS 2
SPY KIDS 3-D: GAME OVER
TEENAGE MUTANT NINJA TURTLES
THAT'S SO RAVEN
TOTALLY SPIES
TRANSFORMERS: ARMADA
TRANSFORMERS: ENERGON

You want it? We got it!
A full range of TOKYOPOP
products are available now at:
www.TOKYOPOP.com/shop

10.19.04T

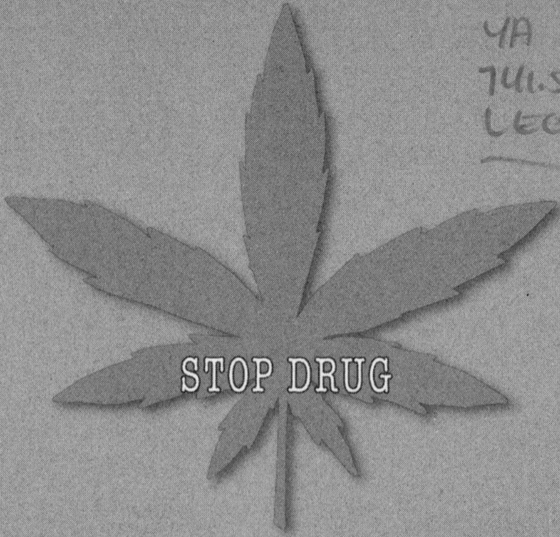
STOP DRUG

This book is printed "manga-style," in the authentic Japanese right-to-left format. Since none of the artwork has been flipped or altered, readers get to experience the story just as the creator intended. You've been asking for it, so TOKYOPOP® delivered: authentic, hot-off-the-press, and far more fun!

DIRECTIONS

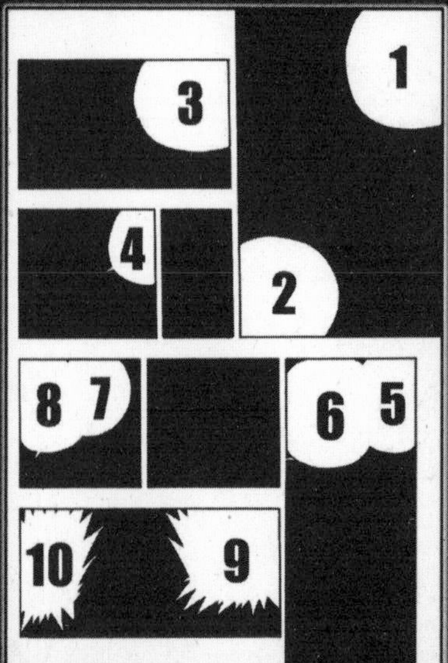
1
2
3
4
5
6
7
8
9
10

If this is your first time reading manga-style, here's a quick guide to help you understand how it works.

It's easy...just start in the top right panel and follow the numbers. Have fun, and look for more 100% authentic manga from TOKYOPOP®!